THE WHOLE DUTY OF MAN

NATURAL LAW AND
ENLIGHTENMENT CLASSICS

Knud Haakonssen
General Editor

Samuel Pufendorf

NATURAL LAW AND
ENLIGHTENMENT CLASSICS

The Whole Duty of Man,
According to
the Law of Nature

Samuel Pufendorf

Translated by Andrew Tooke, 1691

Edited and with an Introduction by
Ian Hunter and David Saunders

The Works of Samuel Pufendorf

Two Discourses and a Commentary by Jean Barbeyrac
Translated by David Saunders

LIBERTY FUND

This book is published by Liberty Fund, Inc., a foundation established to encourage study of the ideal of a society of free and responsible individuals.

The cuneiform inscription that serves as our logo and as the design motif for our endpapers is the earliest-known written appearance of the word "freedom" (*amagi*), or "liberty." It is taken from a clay document written about 2300 B.C. in the Sumerian city-state of Lagash.

© 2003 Liberty Fund, Inc.

Printed in the United States of America

Frontispiece: The portrait of Samuel Pufendorf is to be found at the Law Faculty of the University of Lund, Sweden, and is based on a photoreproduction by Leopoldo Iorizzo. Reprinted by permission.

| 21 | 22 | 23 | 24 | 25 | C | 7 | 6 | 5 | 4 | 3 |
| 21 | 22 | 23 | 24 | 25 | P | 7 | 6 | 5 | 4 | 3 |

Library of Congress Cataloging-in-Publication Data
Pufendorf, Samuel, Freiherr von, 1632–1694.
[De officio hominis et civis. English]
The whole duty of man according to the law of nature/Samuel Pufendorf;
translated by Andrew Tooke, 1691;
edited with an Introduction by Ian Hunter and David Saunders.
Two discourses and a commentary/by Jean Barbeyrac; translated by David Saunders.
p.   cm.—(Natural law and enlightenment classics)
Works by Jean Barbeyrac translated from the French.
Includes bibliographical references and index.
ISBN 0-86597-374-1 (hc: alk. paper)—ISBN 0-86597-375-X (pb: alk. paper)
1. Natural law.   2. Ethics.   3. State, The.
I. Hunter, Ian, 1949–   II. Saunders, David, 1940–
III. Barbeyrac, Jean, 1674–1744.   Two discourses and a commentary.
IV. Title: Two discourses and a commentary.   V. Title.   VI. Series.
K457.P8 D4313 2002
340′.112—dc21   2002023042

LIBERTY FUND, INC.
11301 North Meridian Street
Carmel, Indiana 46032

CONTENTS

Introduction ix

THE WHOLE DUTY OF MAN, ACCORDING
TO THE LAW OF NATURE I

Two Discourses and a Commentary
by Jean Barbeyrac 263

Note on the Translation 265

The Judgment of an Anonymous Writer on
the Original of This Abridgment 267

Discourse on What Is Permitted by the Laws 307

Discourse on the Benefits Conferred by the Laws 331

Index 361

INTRODUCTION

In 1691, eighteen years after its original publication, Samuel Pufendorf's *De officio hominis et civis* appeared in English translation in London, bearing the title *The Whole Duty of Man, According to the Law of Nature*. This translation, by Andrew Tooke (1673–1732), professor of geometry at Gresham College, passed largely unaltered through two subsequent editions, in 1698 and 1705, before significant revision and augmentation in the fourth edition of 1716. Unchanged, this text was then reissued as the fifth and final edition of 1735, which is here republished for the first time since.[1] Five editions, spanning almost half a century, bear testimony to the English appetite for Pufendorf's ideas.

There are important regards, however, in which *The Whole Duty of Man* differs from Pufendorf's *De officio*.[2] In the first place, Tooke's translation is the product and instrument of a shift in political milieu—from German absolutism to English parliamentarianism—reflected in the translator's avoidance of Pufendorf's key political terms, in particular "state" (*civitas*) and "sovereignty" (*summum imperium*). Second,

---

1. *The Whole Duty of Man, According to the Law of Nature,* by that famous civilian Samuel Pufendorf . . . now made English by Andrew Tooke. The fifth edition with the notes of Mr. Barbeyrac, and many other additions and amendments (London: R. Gosling, J. Pemberton, and B. Motte, 1735).

2. The original form of the work may be compared in the new critical edition of the first Latin and German editions. See Samuel Pufendorf, *Samuel Pufendorf: De officio,* ed. Gerald Hartung, vol. 2, *Samuel Pufendorf: Gesammelte Werke* (Berlin: Akademie Verlag, 1997). The reader should also consult the most recent and most accurate English translation: Samuel Pufendorf, *On the Duty of Man and Citizen According to Natural Law,* ed. James Tully, trans. Michael Silverthorne (Cambridge: Cambridge University Press, 1991).

the anonymous editors of the 1716/35 edition intensified Tooke's anglicization of Pufendorf through the inclusion of material—a series of important footnotes, revised translations of key passages—taken from the
first edition of Jean Barbeyrac's 1707 French translation of the *De officio*.[3] Especially in his footnotes, Barbeyrac had moderated the secular
and statist dimensions of Pufendorf's thought in order to retain some
continuity between civil duties and religious morality—enough at least
to remind citizens of a law higher than the civil law and to remind the
sovereign power of its responsibility to protect the natural rights of citizens. Those reminders, though suited to the "polite" post-Hobbesian
world of early-eighteenth-century London, had not been at all germane
to Pufendorf's original intention and text.

In the 1735 edition of *The Whole Duty of Man*, Pufendorf's thought
has thus been successively reshaped in the course of its reception into a
series of specific cultural and political milieux. To approach this text
from the right angle we must follow a similar path. We thus begin with
Pufendorf himself, and then discuss Barbeyrac's engagement with Pufendorf, before entering the English world of Andrew Tooke and the
anonymous editors who, in 1716, introduced the fruits of Barbeyrac's
engagement into Tooke's translation.

The son of a Lutheran pastor, Samuel Pufendorf was born in the
Saxon village of Dorfchemnitz in 1632, moving to the neighboring town
of Flöha the following year.[4] This was the middle of the Thirty Years'
War, whose horrors and fears Pufendorf experienced as a child, with
killings in nearby villages and the family forced to flee its home briefly

3. Jean Barbeyrac, trans., *Les devoirs de l'homme et du citoien, tels qu'ils lui sont
prescrits par la loi naturelle* (Amsterdam: H. Schelte, 1707).

4. For helpful overviews of Pufendorf's life and work, see James Tully, "Editor's
Introduction," in Tully, ed., *Man & Citizen*, xiv–xl; and Michael J. Seidler, "Samuel
Pufendorf," in the *Encyclopedia of the Enlightenment*, ed. Alan Charles Kors (New
York: Oxford University Press, 2002). There is no standard biography of Pufendorf,
but important contributions toward one can be found in Detlef Döring, *Pufendorf-
Studien. Beiträge zur Biographie Samuel von Pufendorfs und zu seiner Entwicklung als
Historiker und theologischer Schriftsteller* (Berlin: Duncker & Humblot, 1992). Also
useful is Wolfgang Hunger, *Samuel von Pufendorf: Aus dem Leben und Werk eines
deutschen Frühaufklärers* (Flöha: Druck & Design, 1991).

when he was seven. The Peace of Westphalia came about only in 1648, when Pufendorf was approaching maturity. The experience of religious civil war and the achievement of social peace remained a driving factor in Pufendorf's lifelong concern with the governance of multiconfessional societies, and hence with the critical relation between state and church.[5]

Pufendorf began to acquire the intellectual and linguistic equipment with which he would address these issues as a scholarship boy at the Prince's School (*Fürstenschule*) in Grimma (1645–50). The Saxon Prince's Schools were Protestant grammar schools in which boys, destined to become clergy and officials, learned Latin and Greek, thereby gaining access to the classical texts so crucial to the development of early modern civil philosophy. Pufendorf continued his education at the universities of Leipzig and Jena (1650–58). At Leipzig his thoughts of a clerical career soon evaporated, the result of his exposure to Lutheran orthodoxy in its uncompromising Protestant-scholastic form. Fueled by hostility to the mixing of philosophy and theology in university metaphysics, he turned to law and politics at Jena, aided by the teachings of Erhard Weigel, through whom Pufendorf encountered the "moderns"— Descartes, Grotius, and Hobbes. When Pufendorf began to formulate his moral and political philosophy, it was Grotius and Hobbes who provided his initial orientation toward a postscholastic form of natural law.

After a brief period as house-tutor to the Swedish ambassador to Denmark (1658–59)—during which he was imprisoned as a result of the war between the Scandinavian neighbors—Pufendorf spent a short interlude in Holland before gaining appointment as professor of natural and international law at the University of Heidelberg (1661–68). From there he moved to a similar professorship at the University of Lund in Sweden, where he remained from 1668 to 1676. During this time, he wrote his monumental treatise on natural law—the *De jure naturae et gentium,* or *Law of Nature and Nations* (1672)—followed a year later by

---

5. See Michael J. Seidler, "Pufendorf and the Politics of Recognition," in *Natural Law and Civil Sovereignty: Moral Right and State Authority in Early Modern Political Thought,* eds. Ian Hunter and David Saunders (Basingstoke: Palgrave, 2002).

the abridgment that he made for university students, the *De officio hominis et civis,* which in 1691 English readers would come to know as *The Whole Duty of Man.* Pufendorf completed his career with posts as court historian at the Swedish (1677–88) and then the Brandenburg courts (1688–94). In those years, he wrote major works on the European state system, on the Swedish and Brandenburg crowns, and on the place of religion in civil life.

It is Pufendorf's natural law works that concern us here. The object of natural law theory is a moral law that is natural in two senses—in being inscribed in man's nature and in being accessible via natural reason as distinct from divine revelation.[6] Furthermore, this moral law is regarded as the normative foundation and universal standard for "positive" law and politics. Building on the Aristotelian conception of man as a "rational and sociable being," Thomas Aquinas (1224–74) had grounded natural law in a reason shared with God and permitting access to a domain of transcendent values derived from the need to complete or perfect man as a moral being. In subordinating "positive" civil laws to a transcendent moral order, Thomist natural law doctrine armed the Catholic Church against the civil state. In the hands of sixteenth-century scholastics such as Francisco Suárez (1548–1627), this weapon would be used to delegitimate Protestant rulers as heretics, thereby ensuring that their positive laws would not accord with the law of nature in this its scholastic mode.[7]

In the dark shadows of the religious wars, Protestant thinkers of the sixteenth and seventeenth centuries sought a natural law that would defend the civil state against religious and moral delegitimation.[8] Hugo Grotius (1583–1645) thus viewed the laws derived from sociability as

6. For a general overview, see Ian Hunter, "Natural Law," in Kors, *Encyclopedia of Enlightenment.* For more detailed treatments, see Knud Haakonssen, *Natural Law and Moral Philosophy: From Grotius to the Scottish Enlightenment* (Cambridge: Cambridge University Press, 1996), and T. J. Hochstrasser, *Natural Law Theories in the Early Enlightenment* (Cambridge: Cambridge University Press, 2000).

7. Brian Tierney, *The Idea of Natural Rights: Studies on Natural Rights, Natural Law and Church Law, 1150–1625* (Atlanta: Scholars Press, 1997), 314–15.

8. See Richard Tuck, "The 'Modern' Theory of Natural Law," in *The Languages of Political Theory in Early-Modern Europe,* ed. Anthony Pagden (Cambridge: Cambridge University Press, 1987), 99–122; Ian Hunter, *Rival Enlightenments: Civil and*

social conventions rather than transcendent values, while the English political philosopher Thomas Hobbes (1588–1679) made social peace, not moral perfection, the goal of natural law, such that the sovereign state became the final arbiter of morality, not vice versa.[9] Following Grotius and Hobbes, Pufendorf too viewed natural law as a set of rules for cultivating the sociability needed to preserve social peace.[10] Though he differed from Hobbes by arguing that natural moral law exists in the state of nature—which Hobbes regarded as a state of moral anarchy— Pufendorf agreed with his English counterpart that only a civil government possessing supreme power could provide the security that was the goal of natural law.[11] In his *Law of Nature and Nations* and his *De officio* (*Whole Duty*), Pufendorf thus furnished the sovereign state with its own secular legitimacy as an institution created by men to achieve social peace but possessing the absolute right to determine and enforce the measures best suited to this end.

Jean Barbeyrac (1674–1744) was Pufendorf's most important publicist and commentator. Born into a family of French Calvinists (Huguenots), he too had experienced the dangers of religious civil war, his family having been driven from Catholic France by the renewed religious persecution that followed Louis XIV's revocation in 1685 of the Edict of Nantes, settling in Berlin in 1697 after some years of refuge mainly in Protestant Lausanne, Switzerland. Whereas the French state had solved the problem of governing a multiconfessional society by imposing reli-

---

Metaphysical Philosophy in Early Modern Germany (Cambridge: Cambridge University Press, 2001); and Knud Haakonssen, "The Significance of Protestant Natural Law," in *Reading Autonomy,* eds. Natalie Brender and Larry Krasnoff (Cambridge: Cambridge University Press, 2002).

9. See Conal Condren, "*Natura naturans:* Natural Law and the Sovereign in the Writings of Thomas Hobbes," in Hunter and Saunders, *Natural Law and Civil Sovereignty.*

10. For a treatment of Pufendorf as Hobbes's "disciple," see Fiammetta Palladini, *Samuel Pufendorf discepolo di Hobbes: Per una reinterpretazione del giusnaturalismo moderno* (Bologna: Il Mulino, 1990). For a different view, see Kari Saastamoinen, *The Morality of Fallen Man: Samuel Pufendorf on Natural Law* (Helsinki: Finnish Historical Society, 1995).

11. Thomas Behme, "Pufendorf's Doctrine of Sovereignty and Its Natural Law Foundations," in Hunter and Saunders, *Natural Law and Civil Sovereignty.*

gious conformity—in other words, by persecuting and expelling its Protestant population—the Calvinist rulers of Brandenburg-Prussia addressed this problem by permitting limited religious toleration. Berlin thus became a magnet for Protestant refugees, with the result that the exiled Huguenots formed a quarter of the city's population at the beginning of the eighteenth century. As if echoing Pufendorf's career, Barbeyrac turned from a clerical future to the study of natural law and moral philosophy. Appointed to a teaching position in Berlin's French Collège, Barbeyrac commenced what would become his celebrated French translations and commentaries on Pufendorf, aiming to make the latter's model of a deconfessionalized political order more widely available to a Francophone Huguenot diaspora still fearful for its survival.[12] In this context, Barbeyrac translated the *De jure* in 1706[13] and the *De officio* in 1707,[14] adding important notes—an apparatus that grew in subsequent editions into a running commentary—and later appending three of his own works to the *De officio*. These were his famous commentary on Gottfried Wilhelm Leibniz's attack on Pufendorf, the *Judgment of an Anonymous Writer,* and his twin discourses on the relation of positive and natural law—the *Discourse on What Is Permitted by the Laws* and the *Discourse on the Benefits Conferred by the Laws*—composed while he was professor of law in the Academy of Lausanne (1711–17).[15] In translating these into English for the first time, and appending them to Tooke's translation, our aim is to provide Anglophone

12. Sieglinde C. Othmer, *Berlin und die Verbreitung des Naturrechts in Europa. Kultur- und sozialgeschichtliche Studien zu Jean Barbeyracs Pufendorf-Übersetzung und eine Analyse seiner Leserschaft* (Berlin: Walter de Gruyter, 1970).

13. Jean Barbeyrac, trans., *Le droit de la nature et des gens, ou système général des principes les plus importans de la morale, de la jurisprudence, et de la politique* (Amsterdam, 1706).

14. Barbeyrac, *Les devoirs.*

15. These appendices appeared first in the fourth edition of Barbeyrac's translation: *Les devoirs de l'homme et du citoien, tels qu'ils lui sont prescrits par la loi naturelle,* quatrième édition, augmentée d'un grand nombre de notes du traducteur, de ses deux discours sur la permission et le bénéfice des loix, et du jugement de M. de Leibniz sur cet ouvrage, avec des réflexions du traducteur (Amsterdam: Pierre de Coup, 1718).

readers with a simulacrum of the most important of the early modern
Pufendorf "reception texts."

In fact Barbeyrac walks a fine line, defending Pufendorf's model of
a deconfessionalized and pacified legal-political order against its theological and metaphysical critics, yet resiling from the secular and statist
dimensions of this model.[16] Having suffered at first hand from a religiously unified state, Barbeyrac has little sympathy with a political
metaphysics that justified such unity—even a metaphysics as esoteric as
Leibniz's Platonism. Counterattacking Leibniz's political rationalism,
Barbeyrac draws on his translator's knowledge of the works to defend
Pufendorf's elevation of imposed law over transcendent reason and his
insistence that the law apply only to man's external conduct, leaving his
inner morality free—thereby opening the space of religious toleration
so crucial to the stateless Huguenots' survival. On the other hand, given
his commitment to the Reformed faith and his Huguenot fear of a religiously hostile absolute state, Barbeyrac grants individual conscience
a far greater role in his construction of political authority than does Pufendorf. While claiming to make only minor rectifications to the *De
officio,* Barbeyrac thus introduces major changes to Pufendorf's foundation of natural law in the need for civil security. In treating natural
law as an expression of the divine will to which individuals accede via
conscience, Barbeyrac undermines Pufendorf's argument that only the
civil sovereign may give efficacious interpretation to natural law. He
thus readmitted Lockean natural rights to a system from which they
had been deliberately excluded.

Little is known about the circumstances of Andrew Tooke's English
translation of the *De officio* or of the anonymous editors of 1716/35, who
borrowed footnotes from Barbeyrac's first edition and used his translation to modify Tooke's. The obscurity arises from the fact that, unlike

16. See T. J. Hochstrasser, "Conscience and Reason: The Natural Law Theory of
Jean Barbeyrac," *Historical Journal* 36 (1993): 289–308; and "The Claims of Conscience: Natural Law Theory, Obligation, and Resistance in the Huguenot Diaspora," in *New Essays on the Political Thought of the Huguenots of the Refuge,* ed. John
Christian Laursen (Leiden: E. J. Brill, 1995), 15–51.

other editions and translations of the *De officio*—for example, the edition prepared by Gershom Carmichael (1672–1729) for his students at Glasgow University[17]—Tooke's was not produced in the regulated world of academic publishing but in the altogether more freewheeling milieu of the London commercial book trade. The marks of that milieu are evident in Tooke's title, which departs significantly from Pufendorf's original in order to cash in on one of the most popular devotional manuals of the time, Richard Allestree's *The Whole Duty of Man,* published in 1658 and rapidly acquiring best-seller status.[18] Although exploiting Allestree's success by borrowing his title, Tooke's translation was nonetheless a riposte, confronting Allestree's focus on the religious duties of a Christian subject with Pufendorf's radical separation of the civil obligations of the citizen from the religious obligations of the Christian.[19] We can surmise that Tooke's 1691 translation of the *De officio* was undertaken for an audience of London Whigs—including broad-church Anglicans, moderate Puritans, and members of the Inns of Court—as a weapon against persisting high-church aspirations for an Anglican confessional state.[20] The future preservation of parliamentary rule and a Protestant peace were not yet guaranteed, nor were the relations of church and state securely settled, so soon after the revolution of 1688–89.

This context also helps explain Tooke's lexical choices for some of Pufendorf's key terms. While *civitas* and *summum imperium* were capable of several translations in the seventeenth century, depending on

17. *De officio hominis et civis, juxta legem naturalem, libri duo. Supplementis & observationibus in academicae juventutis usum auxit & illustravit Gerschomus Carmichael* (Edinburgh: 1718; 2d ed., 1724). For Carmichael's editorial material, see also *Natural Rights on the Threshold of the Scottish Enlightenment: The Writings of Gershom Carmichael,* eds. James Moore and Michael Silverthorne, trans. Michael Silverthorne (Indianapolis, Ind: Liberty Fund, 2001).

18. [Richard Allestree], *The Whole Duty of Man* (London: John Baskett, 1726 [1st ed. 1658]).

19. David Burchell, "On Office: Pre-modern Ethics and the Modern Moral Imagination," unpublished research monograph, 2001.

20. For the general context, see Mark Goldie, "Priestcraft and the Birth of Whiggism," in *Political Discourse in Early Modern Britain,* eds. Nicholas Phillipson and Quentin Skinner (Cambridge: Cambridge University Press, 1993), 209–31.

the ideological commitments of particular authors, a recent translator shows that in Pufendorf's case these are most accurately rendered as "state" and "sovereignty," respectively.[21] Indeed, it is central to Pufendorf's argument that these terms refer to the notion of a supreme political authority irreducible either to those who occupy the office of sovereign or to those over whom such authority is exercised— characteristics definitive of the modern notion of state.[22] Given that Hobbes had explicitly introduced both "commonwealth" and "state" as translations of *civitas,* it is significant that Tooke attempted to avoid both "state" and "sovereignty" as much as possible, preferring circumlocutions such as "community" and "society" for the former and "supreme authority" and "supreme governor" for the latter.[23] With his references to the exercise of sovereignty by the state routinely rendered in terms of the exercise of authority in the community, Pufendorf's absolutist statism thus undergoes a lexical and ideological softening, appearing in Tooke's English in a form better fitting the Whig view of sovereignty as shared with Parliament and embedded in society.

In borrowing certain of Barbeyrac's footnotes, and in altering Tooke's translation at certain points, the anonymous editors of 1716/35 furthered this anglicizing tendency to see sovereignty as inherent in society. At key points, Barbeyrac's notes qualify or reinterpret Pufendorf's core doctrines, arguing that it is necessary to retain some sort of continuity between natural law and divine providence, that pragmatic deductions of the rules of social peace should be supplemented with Christian conscience, that obedience to civil law and the sovereign are not enough to satisfy the demands of morality, and that natural

21. Michael J. Silverthorne, "Civil Society and State, Law and Rights: Some Latin Terms and Their Translation in the Natural Jurisprudence Tradition," in *Acta Conventus Neo-Latini Torontonensis: Proceedings of the Seventh International Congress of Neo-Latin Studies,* eds. Alexander Dalzell, Charles Fantazzi, and Richard J. Schoeck (New York: Medieval & Renaissance Texts & Studies, 1991), 677–88.

22. Quentin Skinner, "The State," in *Political Innovation and Conceptual Change,* eds. T. Ball, J. Farr, and R. L. Hanson (Cambridge: Cambridge University Press, 1989), 90–131.

23. See notes for details.

rights—including the right to punish a tyrannical sovereign—remain valid in the civil state. Perhaps in the England of 1716, with the memory of religious civil war fading, Pufendorf's Hobbesian subordination of religious morality to the needs of civil order had begun to seem less necessary, allowing the editors to readmit conscience and morality, now that they had been rendered less dangerous for the Protestant state.

Ian Hunter

David Saunders

PUFENDORF'S
WHOLE DUTY OF MAN

THE WHOLE
DUTY of MAN,
According to the
LAW
OF
NATURE.
By that famous Civilian

SAMUEL PUFENDORF,

Professor of *The Law of Nature and Nations,* in the
University of *Heidelberg,* and in the *Caroline* University,
afterwards Counsellor and Historiographer to the King of
Sweden, and to his Electoral Highness of *Brandenburgh.*
Now made ENGLISH.

The Fifth EDITION with the Notes of Mr. *Barbeyrac,* and
many other Additions and Amendments; And also an
INDEX of the Matters.

By ANDREW TOOKE, M.A. late Professor of
Geometry in *Gresham-College.*

Nunquam aliud Natura, aliud Sapientia dicit.[1]
Juv. Sat. XIV. 321.

LONDON:
Printed for R. GOSLING, at the *Mitre* and *Crown;* J. PEMBERTON,
at the *Golden Buck;* and B. MOTTE, at the *Middle-Temple-Gate,*
Fleet-Street. 1735.

1. Never does nature say one thing, and wisdom another.

To his Honoured Friend
Mr. *GEORGE WHITE,*
Of *London,* MERCHANT;

This TRACTATE
Concerning the
LAW of *NATURE,*

IS

Offered, Dedicated, Presented,
BY
His humblest
and most obliged Servant,

The Translator.

TO THE READER

The Translator having observed, in most of the Disputes wherewith the present Age is disquieted, frequent Appeals made, and that very properly, from Laws and Ordinances of a meaner Rank *to the everlasting* Law of Nature, *gave himself the Pains to turn over several Writers on that Subject. He chanced, he thinks with great Reason, to entertain an Opinion, that this Author was the clearest, the fullest, and the most unprejudiced of any he met with: And hereupon, that he might the better possess himself of his Reasonings, he attempted to render the Work into Mother-Tongue, after he had first endeavoured to set several better Hands upon the Undertaking, who all for one Reason or other declined the Toil. He thought when 'twas done, it might be as acceptable to one or other to read it, as it had been to himself to translate it.*

Concerning the Author, *'tis enough to say, that he has surely had as great Regard paid him from Personages of the highest degree, as perhaps ever was given to the most learned of Men; having been invited from his Native Country, first by the* Elector Palatine, *to be Professor of the* Law of Nature and Nations *in the University of* Heidelberg; *then by the King of* Sweden *to honour his new rais'd Academy, by accepting the same Charge therein, and afterwards being admitted of the* Council, *and made Historiographer, both to the same King, and to his Electoral Highness of* Brandenburgh, *afterwards King of* Prussia.

Concerning this his Work, it is indeed only as it were an Epitome of the Author's large Volume of The Law of Nature and Nations: *But as this Epitome was made and published by himself, the Reader cannot be under any doubt, but that he has here the Quintessence of what is there deliver'd; what is par'd off being mostly Cases in the* Civil Law, *Refutations of other*

7

Authors, and some Notions too fine and unnecessary for a Manual. How good an Opinion the learned World has of this his Performance, is very evident from the many Editions there have been of it, not only in the Original Latin, *but in the Modern Languages, publish'd in* Sweden, Holland, France, Germany, *and* England.[1]

Since[2] *the first Publication hereof in 1673, at* Lunden, *the Author revis'd his larger Work, and put out a new Edition of it, with many Additions and great Improvements; and from thence this Work also has been amended and enlarged, by extracting these additional Chapters, and inserting them as compendiously as might be into their proper Places; which was first done in a* German *Translation,*[3] *and afterwards in a* Latin *Edition, published by the Professor of* Giessen,[4] *both in the Life-time of the Author, with his Knowledge, and by his Approbation;*[5] *so that the Reader may be satisfied that these Additions, now first inserted into this Translation, are as genuine as the Rest of the Work; as he will find them as useful and necessary a Part, as any of the whole Book. Besides these, in this Impression, some other Additions and Alterations have been found necessary to be made: For whereas in some Places the Author's Opinion was delivered in so brief or obscure a Manner, that his Meaning seemed difficult to be apprehended; again in other Places the Coherence and Connection of his Discourses did not sufficiently appear; to remedy the former of these Defects, all intricate Phrases*

1. There were also Danish, Russian, and Spanish translations of the *De officio*. There were Latin editions in Sweden but none in the national tongue until 1747.

2. This and the following paragraph were added to Tooke's foreword by the anonymous editors of the 1716/35 edition, referred to hereafter as "the editors." Here they indicate the changes to Tooke's first edition of 1691, albeit none too accurately.

3. This translation, which was undertaken by Immanuel Weber, appeared in 1691 under the title *Einleitung zur Sitten- und Statslehre, oder, Kurze Vorstellung der Schuldigen Gebühr aller Menschen, und insonderbereit der Bürgerlichen Stats-Verwandten, nach Anleitung derer Natürlichen Rechte* (*Introduction to Moral and Political Philosophy, or, Short Presentation of the Bounden Duty of All Men, Especially the Civil State-Related, in Accordance with the Teachings of Natural Laws*).

4. This probably refers to the Latin edition published at Giessen in 1702, for which Weber supplied the notes.

5. In fact, these borrowings from Pufendorf's *Law of Nature and Nations* are confined to a single chapter of Weber's version of the *De officio*, Chapter V of Book I, "On the Duties of Man to Himself." See note 19, Book I, below.

and Expressions have been changed,[6] *and where even that was not sufficient to make the Author's Mind plain and clear, it is explained and illustrated by adding proper Instances and Examples;*[7] *and then to repair the latter Defect, the Order of some of the Sections hath been changed, and proper and necessary Transitions to many of them have been added;*[8] *the taking which Liberty, 'tis to be hoped, will ever appear most justifiable, since thereby the Rules of Method are better observ'd, and the Sense of the Author rendered more perspicuous than in the former Editions of this Translation.*

But farther, to make this Edition still more compleat and useful than the former, to each Section References are continually made to the large Work of The Law of Nature and Nations,[9] *and, as often as could be, to* The Rights of War and Peace;[10] *that those who read this Epitome, and have a mind to see any Point therein more fully handled and illustrated, may be readily directed, where to have recourse to the Place where it is at large discoursed of, not only by this Author himself, but also by* Grotius, *an Author of equal Reputation for his judicious and learned Writings on Subjects of the same nature. Besides these References, as some of the Author's Opinions, laid down in this Treatise, have been controverted by some Writers, and defended by the Author in some other of his Works, the Reader is directed to those Places in them where these Cavils and Exceptions are taken notice of,*

6. Which of Pufendorf's expressions the English editors found intricate or esoteric is not immediately apparent. Only Pufendorf's political vocabulary—state (*civitas*), sovereignty (*summum imperium*), citizen (*civis*)—seems to have caused problems for Tooke. This was less a matter of intricacy, however, than of the difficulties of rendering Pufendorf's "statist" lexicon in terms suited to the English setting and Whig sensibilities. This set of issues is commented on in subsequent notes.

7. The editors in fact added only a few such examples, which they indicate by square brackets.

8. With the exception of the reconstructed I.v, whose ultimate source is Weber, these reorderings derive from Barbeyrac's edition. Each is identified in the relevant notes below.

9. These added references to Pufendorf's larger work, which the editors have borrowed from Barbeyrac's first French edition of the *De officio,* occur beneath the marginal subheadings, where they are cited as L. N. N. (*Law of Nature and Nations*).

10. The references to Grotius's *Law of War and Peace,* also added by the editors of the 1716/35 edition, occur as footnotes.

and satisfactorily answered.[11] *But then, when any Exceptions can justly be made, and there is good Reason for differing from the Author's Opinion in any Point, the Reasons are given for so doing in some Notes at the Bottom of the Page;*[12] *which Notes, however, are neither many nor long, since it would be very absurd to run into Prolixity in Comments to a Work where Brevity is principally aim'd at; into which therefore nothing ought to be admitted, but what is essentially and absolutely necessary to the Subject treated of. And on this Account also it is, that whereas the same Matters have, in the former Editions, been found to occur in more than one Place, in this Edition such superfluous Repetitions have been par'd off, by putting together what has been said on the same Point in different Places, and comprehending the whole under one Head or Section.*[13] *And lastly, that nothing might be wanting to render this in all Points perfect, a* Compleat Index *is added.*

11. These references to Pufendorf's polemical defenses of his position were added by the editors and also occur as footnotes. All such footnotes—that is, those not explicitly assigned to Barbeyrac by our notes—should be regarded as additions by the editors of the 1716/35 edition.

12. These critical footnotes, marked typographically by asterisks, daggers, and similar symbols, which first appeared in the fourth edition of 1716, were taken from the first edition of Barbeyrac's French translation of the *De officio: Les Devoirs de L'Homme et du Citoien, tels qu'ils lui sont prescrits par la Loi Naturelle,* published in Amsterdam in 1707. They represent a good selection of Barbeyrac's original notes, fifty-two of a total of some eighty-nine. This seems small, however, in comparison with later editions of Barbeyrac's translation, in which the notes grew exponentially into a running commentary on Pufendorf's text. All of the footnotes borrowed from Barbeyrac are identified in square brackets after the footnote and cite Barbeyrac's note markers and page numbers from his first edition. Further, all of the important ones are discussed in terms of the manner in which Barbeyrac (and the English editors) sought to inflect Pufendorf's text for a new readership.

13. There is no evidence that this was carried out. The editors derive their reorderings of Tooke's text from Barbeyrac's unauthorized revisions to Pufendorf's original. All such changes are recorded in our numbered footnotes, including Barbeyrac's excision of certain passages for ideological reasons (see in particular notes 2 and 8, in Book II, below).

CONTENTS

BOOK I

Chap. I. *Of Human Actions*   Page 27

II. *Of the Rule of Human Actions, or of Laws in general*   42

III. *Of the Law of Nature*   52

IV. *Of the Duty of Man towards God, or concerning Natural Religion*   60

V. *Of the Duty of Man towards himself*   69

VI. *Of the Duty of one Man towards another, and first, of doing no Injury to any Man*   94

VII. *The Natural Equality of Men to be acknowledged*   100

VIII. *Of the mutual Duties of Humanity*   104

IX. *The Duty of Men in making Contracts*   108

X. *The Duty of Men in Discourse*   119

XI. *The Duty of those that take an Oath*   123

XII. *Duties to be observ'd in acquiring Possession of Things*   128

XIII. *The Duties which naturally result from Man's Property in Things*   137

XIV. *Of the Price and Value of Things* 140

XV. *Of those Contracts in which the Value of Things is presupposed, and of the Duties thence arising* 145

XVI. *The several Methods by which the Obligations arising from Contracts are dissolved* 156

XVII. *Of Meaning or Interpretation* 159

BOOK II

Chap. I. *Of the natural State of Men* 166

II. *Of the Duties of the married State* 174

III. *The Duty of Parents and Children* 179

IV. *The Duties of Masters and Servants* 184

V. *The impulsive Cause of Constituting Communities* 187

VI. *Of the Internal Frame and Constitution of any State or Government* 192

VII. *Of the several Parts of Government* 198

VIII. *Of the several Forms of Government* 203

IX. *The Qualifications of Civil Government* 208

X. *How Government, especially Monarchical, is acquired* 210

XI. *The Duty of supreme Governours* 214

XII. *Of the special Laws of a Community* 221

XIII. *Of the Power of Life and Death* 225

XIV. *Of Reputation* 232

XV. *Of the Power of Governours over the Goods of their Subjects* 236

XVI. *Of War and Peace* 238

XVII. *Of Alliances* 245

XVIII. *The Duty of Subjects* 247

THE AUTHOR'S PREFACE

Had not the *Custom* which has so generally obtain'd among Learned The Author's
Design.
Men, almost procured to it self the Force of a *Law*, it might seem altogether superfluous to premise a Word concerning the Reason of the
*present Undertaking; the Thing it self plainly declaring my whole De-
sign to be, the giving as *short*, and yet, if I mistake not, as *plain* and
perspicuous a *Compendium* of the most material Articles of the *Law of
Nature*, as was possible; and this, lest, if such as betake themselves to
this Study should enter those vast Fields of Knowledge without having
fully imbibed the Rudiments thereof, they should at first sight be ter-
rified and confounded by the Copiousness and Difficulty of the Matters occurring therein. And, at the same time, it seems plainly a very
expedient Work for the Publick, that the Minds, of Youth especially,
should be early imbu'd with that *Moral Learning*, for which they will
have such manifest Occasion, and so frequent Use, through the whole
Course of their Lives.

And altho' I have always looked upon it as a Work deserving no great
Honour, †to *Epitomize* the larger Writings of others, and more especially one's own; yet having thus done out of Submission to the commanding Authority of my Superiors, I hope no honest Man will blame
me for having endeavoured hereby to improve the Understandings of
Young Men more particularly; to whom so great Regard is to be had,
that whatsoever Work is undertaken for their sakes, tho' it may not be

---

* *Ann.* 1673, *published in* Suedish *a Year after his large Work.* [Barbeyrac's marginal
note (a), p. xix.]

† See *Julius Rondinus praef. ad Eris. Scand. in Postscripto & Comment. ad Pullum.
Ven. Lips. p.* 46, 47. [Barbeyrac's note III.1, p. xxiii (relocated).]

capable of great Acuteness or splendid Eloquence, yet it is not to be accounted unworthy of any Man's Pains. Beside, that no Man, in his Wits, will deny, that these Principles thus laid down are more conducive to the understanding of *all Laws* in general, than any Elements of the *Law Civil* can be.

And this might have sufficed for the present; but I am minded by some, that it would not be improper to lay down some few Particulars, which will conduce much to a right Understanding of the Constitution of the *Law of Nature,* and for the better ascertaining its just Bounds and Limits. And this I have been the more ready to do, that I might on this occasion obviate the Pretences of some over-nice Gentlemen, who are apt to pass their squeamish Censures on this Sort of Learning, which in many Instances, is wholly separate from their Province.

Three Sciences by which Men come to a knowledge of their Duty.[1] Now 'tis very manifest, that Men derive the Knowledge of their Duty, and what is fit to be done, or to be avoided in this Life, as it were, from *three Springs,* or Fountain-Heads; to wit, From the *Light of Nature;* From the *Laws and Constitutions of Countries;* And from the *special Revelation of Almighty God.*

From the First of these proceed all those most common and ordinary Duties of a Man; more particularly those that constitute him a *sociable Creature* with the Rest of Mankind: From the Second are derived all the Duties of a Man, as he is a *Member* of any particular *City* or *Commonwealth:*[2] From the Third result all the Duties of a *Christian* Man.

---

1. These marginal subheadings in the Author's Preface appear neither in Pufendorf's text nor in Tooke's original translation, having been borrowed from Barbeyrac by the editors of this edition.

2. Tooke's struggle with Pufendorf's political vocabulary begins here, with his choice of "City or Common-wealth" to translate *civitas,* which Pufendorf uses to signify the state. The republican terms "city," "commonwealth," and "civil society" were commonly used to translate *civitas* during the sixteenth and seventeenth centuries, even by Hobbes. Yet in the Introduction to his *Leviathan* (1651), Hobbes explicitly introduces "state" as the modern equivalent for *civitas,* and this usage was widespread in the second half of the century. Given its evident suitability for rendering Pufendorf's nonrepublican conception of political authority, we may conjecture that Tooke remained unhappy with the Hobbesian or absolutist connotations

And from hence proceed *three* distinct *Sciences:* The *first* of which is of the *Law of Nature,* common to all Nations; the *second* is of the *Civil* or *Municipal Law* peculiar to each Country, which is or may be as manifold and various as there are different States and Governments in the World; the *third* is *Moral Divinity,*[3] as it is contra-distinct to that Part of Divinity, which is conversant in explaining the Articles of our Faith.

Each of these Sciences hath a peculiar Way of proving their Maxims, according to their own Principles. The *Law of Nature* asserts, that this or that Thing ought to be done, because from *right Reason* it is concluded, that the same is necessary for the Preservation of Society amongst Men. *(The difference between the Law of Nature, Civil Law and Moral Theology.)*

The fundamental Obligation we lie under to the *Civil Law* is, that the *Legislative Power* has enacted this or that Thing.[4]

The Obligation of *Moral Divinity* lies wholly in this; because God, in the Sacred *Scripture,* has so commanded.

Now, as the *Civil Law* presupposes the *Law of Nature,* as the more general Science; so if there be any thing contained in the *Civil Law,* wherein the *Law of Nature* is altogether *silent,* we must not therefore conclude, that the one is any ways *repugnant* to the other. In like manner, if in *Moral Divinity* some Things are delivered, as from Divine Revelation, which by our Reason we are not able to comprehend, and *(The Maxims of these three Sciences in no wise opposite or contradictory to each other.)*

---

of the term. In the event, he translates *civitas* using "state" on thirty-two occasions, otherwise having recourse to a battery of circumlocutions including "community" (59), "civil society" (23), "kingdom" (21), "nation" (14), and "society" (11), in addition to "city" (3) and "commonwealth" (20).

3. Tooke's translation of Pufendorf's *theologia moralis* or "moral theology."

4. This the first sign that the editors of the 1716/35 edition were drawing on Barbeyrac's translation to make subtle ideological revisions to Tooke's. In Tooke's first edition this sentence reads: "Of *Civil Laws* and Constitutions, the supreme Reason is the *Will* of the *Law-giver,*" which is much closer to Pufendorf's original formulation in terms of what the legislator lays down (*quia legislator ita constituit*). In borrowing the phrase "legislative power" from Barbeyrac's *puissance législative,* the editors make room for a parliamentary legislator.

which on that Score are above the Reach of the *Law of Nature;* it would be very absurd from hence to set the one against the other, or to imagine that there is any real *Inconsistency* between these Sciences. On the other hand, in the Doctrine of the *Law of Nature,* if any things are to be pre-supposed, because so much may be inferred from *Reason,* they are not to be put in Opposition to those Things which the *Holy Scripture* on that Subject delivers with greater Clearness; but they are only to be taken in an abstracted Sense. Thus, for Example, from the *Law of Nature,* abstracted from the Account we receive thereof in Holy Writ, there may be formed an *Idea* of the Condition and State of the *first Man,* as he came into the World, only so far as is within the Comprehension of *Human Reason.* Now, *to set those Things in opposition to what is delivered in Sacred Writ concerning the same State, would be the greatest Folly and Madness in the World.

But as it is an easie Matter to reconcile the *Civil Law* with the *Law of Nature;* so it seems a little more difficult to set certain Bounds between the same *Law of Nature* and *Moral Divinity,* and to define in what Particulars chiefly they differ one from the other.

Upon this Subject I shall deliver my Opinion briefly, not with any Papal Authority, as if I was exempt from all Error by any peculiar Right or Priviledge, neither as one who pretends to any Enthusiastick Revelation; but only as being desirous to discharge that Province which I have undertaken, according to the best of my Ability. And, as I am willing to hear all Candid and Ingenuous Persons, who can *inform* me better; and am very ready to retract what I have said amiss; so I do not value those Pragmatical and Positive Censurers and Busie-bodies, who boldly concern themselves with Things which no ways belong to them: Of these Persons we have a very Ingenious Character given by *Phaedrus:*

---

*See *L. N. N. l.* II. *c.* I. §8. *c.* II. §2. *Dissert. Acad.* X. de statu Nat. §3. *Eris. Scand. praef. Rondini Apol. advers. Indicem Novitat.* §11, 12, 16. *p.* 20. *seq. Specim. Controv. c.* 3. §1, 3. *& p.* 20. *c.* 4. §16. *p.* 217, 258. *sequ. Spicileg. Controv. c.* 2. §1. 13, 15. *c.* 3. §1. *p.* 357, 380. *sequ. Rondin. Dissert. Epist.* §1. *p.* 396. *& Postscript. ad Seckendorff. Puf-fendorf. Epist. ad Amic. Erid. p.* 133. *Comment. super Pullo Lips. Ven. p.* 11, 16, 36, 44, 46, 52, 54.

They run about, says he, *as mightily concerned; they are very busie even when they have nothing to do; they puff and blow without any occasion; they are uneasie to themselves, and troublesome to every body else.*

Now the Chief Distinction, whereby these Sciences are separated from one another, proceeds from the different Source or Spring whence each derives its *Principles;* and of which I have already discoursed. From whence it follows, if there be some things, which we are enjoined in Holy Writ either to do or forbear, the Necessity whereof cannot be discover'd by *Reason alone,* they are to be looked upon as out of the Cognizance of the *Law of Nature,* and properly to appertain to *Moral Divinity.*

The difference between the Law of Nature and Moral Theology.

1st. They differ in the Source from whence each derives its Principles.

Moreover, in *Divinity* the Law is considered as it has the Divine Promise annexed to it, and with Relation to the Covenant between God and Man; from which Consideration the *Law of Nature* abstracts, because the other derives it self from a particular *Revelation* of God Almighty, and which *Reason* alone could not have found out.

2d. Difference in the Manner whereby the Laws of them both are proposed.

But the greatest Difference between them is this; that the main End and Design of the *Law of Nature* is included within the Compass of †this Life only, and so thereby a Man is informed how he is to live in Society with the Rest of Mankind: But *Moral Divinity* instructs a Man how to live as a Christian; who is not only obliged to live honestly and virtu-

3d. Difference in the End and Design of them both.

---

* *Est Ardelionum quaedam Romae Natio,*
Trepide concursans, occupata in otio,
Gratis anhelans, multa agendo nihil agens,
Sibi molesta & aliis odiosissima.   Phaed. Lib. II. Fab. 5.
[Barbeyrac's note III.2, p. xxv.]

† It is true that Revelation has, beyond all doubt, asserted and given full Evidence of the Immortality of the Soul, and of the Certainty of Rewards and Punishments in the World to come: It is also certain, that the fundamental and distinguishing Principle of Moral Theology, is the Hope of a blessed Eternity, promised to those who direct their Lives by Gospel Precepts. However, we must not therefore take from the *Law of Nature* all Regard to a future Life: For we may, by the meer Light of Reason, proceed so far at least, as to discover, that it's not improbable, that God

ously in this World, but is besides in earnest Expectation of the Reward of his Piety after this Life; and therefore he has his Conversation in Heaven, but is here only as a Stranger and a Pilgrim. For although the Mind of Man does with very great Ardency pursue after Immortality, and is extremely averse to its own Destruction; and thence it was, that most of the Heathens had a strong Persuasion of the separate State of the Soul from the Body, and that then Good Men should be *rewarded,* and Evil Men *punished;* yet notwithstanding such a strong Assurance of the Certainty hereof, upon which the Mind of Man can firmly and entirely depend, is to be derived only from the *Word of God.* Hence it is that the Dictates of the *Law of Nature* are adapted only to *Human Judicature,* which does not extend it self beyond this Life; and it would be absurd in many respects to apply them to the Divine *Forum,* which concerns it self only about Theology.

4th Difference in respect to the Object of each of them. From whence that also follows, that, because *Human Judicature* regards only *the external Actions of Man, but can no ways reach the Inward Thoughts of the Mind, which do not discover themselves by any outward Signs or Effects; therefore the *Law of Nature* is for the most part exercised in forming the outward Actions of Men. But *Moral Divinity* does not content it self in regulating only the *Exterior Actions;* but is

---

will punish in another World, those who have wilfully violated the *Law of Nature,* and have thereupon suffered neither Human nor Divine Punishment in this Life; nay farther, that this Opinion is much more probable than the contrary one to it. If this be so, it is agreeable to the *Laws* of Prudence and good Sense, that no Man, for the sake of a short and transient Satisfaction, should expose himself even to a Possibility of being eternally miserable: And thus far the Fear of being punished in the Life to come; may very justly be said to appertain to the Sanction of the *Law of Nature.* See *L. N. N. lib.* 2. *c.* 3. §21. [This footnote (Barbeyrac's, VI.1, p. xxvii) is the first advocating an important departure from Pufendorf's conception of natural law. By insisting that the likelihood of divine punishment is open to reason and hence forms a part of natural law, Barbeyrac seeks to evade the restriction of natural law to "this life," thereby undermining Pufendorf's attempt to reconstruct natural law as a secular civil ethics. Their inclusion of this note suggests that the English editors were also seeking to maintain some sort of continuity between natural law and moral theology, civil and religious duties.]

* *Eris. Scandic. Specim. Controvers. c.* 4. §19. *p.* 262. *Spicileg. c.* 1. §20. *p.* 355, *&c. c.* 11. §10. *p.* 371. *Epist. ad Amicos. p.* 133.

more peculiarly intent in forming the *Mind,* and its internal Motions, agreeable to the good Pleasure of the Divine Being; disallowing those very Actions, which *outwardly* look well enough, but proceed from an impure and corrupted *Mind.* And this seems to be the Reason why the Sacred Scripture doth not so frequently treat of those Actions, that are under certain Penalties by Human Laws, as it doth of those, which, as *Seneca* expresses it, *are out of the Reach of any such Constitutions. And this will manifestly appear to those, who shall carefully consider the Precepts and Virtues that are therein inculcated; altho', as even those Christian Virtues do very much dispose the Minds of Men towards the maintaining of mutual Society; so likewise *Moral Divinity* does mightily promote the Practice of all the main Duties that are enjoyn'd us in our Civil Deportment: So that, †if you should observe any one behave himself like a restless and troublesome Member in the Common-wealth, you may fairly conclude, that the Christian Religion has made but a very slight Impression on that Person, and that it has taken no Root in his Heart.

And from these Particulars, I suppose, may be easily discovered; not only the certain Bounds and Limits which distinguish the *Law of Nature,* as we have defined it, from *Moral Divinity;* but it may likewise be concluded, that the *Law of Nature* is no way repugnant to the Maxims of *sound Divinity;* but is only to be abstracted from some particular Doctrines thereof, which cannot be fathom'd by the Help of Reason alone. From whence also it necessarily follows, that in the Science of the *Law of Nature,* a Man should be now consider'd, as being deprav'd in his very Nature, and upon that Account, as a Creature, subject to many vile Inclinations: ‡For although none can be so stupid as not to discover in himself many Evil and inordinate Affections, nevertheless, unless we

In regard to the Law of Nature we are to consider Man, in the depraved State he has been, since the first Transgression.

---

* *Quam angusta innocentia est ad legem bonum esse? Quanto latiùs Officiorum patet quam Juris Regula? Quàm multa Pietas, Humanitas, Liberalitas, Justitia, Fides exigunt, quae omnia extra Publicas Tabulas sunt?* Seneca de Ira, lib. 2. cap. 27. [Barbeyrac's note 1, p. xxix.]

† *Dissert. Acad.* IV. *de Systemat Civit.* §7. & IX. *de Concord, verae polit, cum Relig. Christ.*

‡ *Specim. Controv. c.* 1. §2.

were inform'd so much by Sacred Writ, it would not appear, that this Rebellion of the Will was occasioned by the first Man's Transgression; and consequently, since the *Law of Nature* does not reach those Things which are above Reason, it would be very preposterous to derive it from the State of Man, as it was uncorrupt before the Fall; *especially since even the greatest Part of the Precepts of the *Decalogue,* as they are deliver'd in Negative Terms, do manifestly presuppose the *deprav'd State* of Man. Thus, for Example, in the First and Second Commandment, it seems to be supposed, that Mankind was naturally prone to the Belief of *Polytheism* and to *Idolatry.* For if you should consider Man in his Primitive State, wherein he had a clear and distinct Knowledge of the Deity, as it were by a peculiar Revelation; I do not see how it could ever enter into the Thoughts of such a one, to frame any Thing to himself to which he could pay Reverence, instead of, or together with, the true GOD; or to believe any Divinity to reside in that which his own Hands had form'd; therefore there was no Necessity of laying an Injunction upon him in Negative Terms, that he should not worship other Gods; but this Plain Affirmative Precept would have been sufficient; *Thou shalt love, honour, and adore GOD, whom you know to have created both your self, and the whole Universe.* And the same may be said of the Third Commandment: For why should it be forbidden, in a Negative Precept, to blaspheme God, to such a one who had at the same time a clear and perfect Understanding of his Bounty and Majesty; and who was actuated by no inordinate Affections, and whose Mind did chearfully acquiesce in that Condition, wherein he was placed by Almighty God? How could such a one be Guilty of so great Madness? But he needed only to have been admonish'd by this Affirmative Precept; *That he should glorifie the Name of GOD.* But it seems otherwise of the Fourth and Fifth Commandments; which, as they are Affirmative Precepts, neither do they necessarily presuppose the deprav'd State of Man, they

* *Praefat. p. 3. ad Jur. Nat. & Gent. Postscript. Rondini ad Seckendorf. Apol. §28. Specim. Controv. c. 4. §12, 17. Spicileg. c. 11. §1, 5, 6, 8, 14. Comment. ad Ven. Lips. p. 37.*

may be admitted, Mankind being consider'd as under *either* Condition. But the thing is very manifest in relation to the other Commandments, which concern our Neighbour; for it would suffice plainly to have enjoyn'd Man, consider'd as he was first created by GOD, that he should love his Neighbour, whereto he was beforehand inclin'd by his own Nature. But how could the same Person be commanded, that he should not *kill*, when Death had not as yet fall'n on Mankind, which enter'd into the World upon the account of Sin? But now there is very great Need of such a Negative Command, when, instead of loving one another, there are stir'd up so great Feuds and Animosities among Men, that even a great Part of them is owing purely to Envy, or an inordinate Desire of invading what belongs to another; so that they make no scruple, not only of destroying those that are innocent, but even their Friends, and such as have done them signal Favours; and all this, forsooth, they are not asham'd to disguise under the specious Pretence of Religion and Conscience. In like manner, what Need was there expressly to forbid *Adultery*, among those married Persons, whose mutual Love was so ardent and sincere? Or, what Occasion was there to forbid *Theft*, when as yet Covetousness and Poverty were not known, nor did any Man think that properly his own, which might be useful or profitable to another? Or, to what purpose was it to forbid the bearing *False Witness*, when as yet there were not any to be found, who sought after Honour and Reputation to themselves, by Slandering and Aspersing others with false and groundless Calumnies? So that not unfitly, you may here apply the Saying of *Tacitus, *Whilst no corrupt Desires deprav'd Mankind, the first Men liv'd without Sin and Wickedness, and therefore free from Restraint and Punishment; and whereas they coveted nothing but what was their due, they were barr'd from nothing by Fear.*

---

* *Vetustissimi Mortalium, nullâ adhuc pravâ libidine, sine probro, et scelere, eoque sine poena aut coercitionibus agebant; & ubi nihil contra morem cuperent, nihil per metum vetabantur.*   Tacit. Annal. Lib. III. Cap. XXVI.
[Barbeyrac's note VIII.1, p. xxxiv.]

Whether the
Law of Nature
would have
been the same
it is now, had
Man continu'd
in his State of
Innocence.

And these Things being rightly understood, may clear the way for re-moving this Doubt; *whether the Law was different, or the same, in the Primitive State of Nature, before the Fall? Where it may be briefly an-swer'd. That the most *material* Heads of the Law were the same in each State; but that many *particular* Precepts did *vary*, according to the *Di-versity* of the Condition of Mankind; or rather, that the same Summary of the Law was explain'd by *diverse*, but not *contrary* Precepts; according to the different State of Man, by whom that Law was to be observ'd. Our Saviour reduced the Substance of the Law to two Heads: *Love God, and Love thy Neighbour:* To these the whole *Law of Nature* may be re-ferr'd, as well in the Primitive, as in the Deprav'd State of Man; (unless that in the Primitive State there seems not any, or a very small Differ-ence between the *Law of Nature,* and *Moral Divinity.*) For that Mutual Society, which we laid down as a Foundation to the *Law of Nature,* may very well be resolv'd into the Love of our Neighbour. But when †we descend to particular Precepts, there is indeed a very great Difference, both in relation to the Commands and Prohibitions.

And as to what concerns the Commands, there are many which have place in this State of Mankind, which seem not to have been necessary in the Primitive State: And that partly, because they presuppose such a Condition, as, 'tis not certain, could happen to that most happy State of Mankind; partly, because there can be no Notion of them, without admitting *Misery* and *Death,* which were unknown there: As for In-stance, we are now enjoyn'd by the Precepts of the *Law of Nature,* not to deceive one another in Buying or Selling, not to make use of false Weights or Measures, to repay Money that is lent, at the appointed Time. But it is not yet evident, whether, if Mankind had continu'd without Sin, there would have been driven, any Trade and Commerce, as there is now in the World; or whether there would then have been any Occasion for the Use of Money. In like manner, if such Kind of Communities as are now adays, were not to be found in the State of Innocence, there would be then likewise no Occasion for those Laws

---

* *Eris. Scandic. Specim. Contr. l.* 4. §20. p. 263.
† *Spicileg. c.* I. §17.

which are presuppos'd as requisite for the well-ordering and Government of such Societies. We are also now commanded by the *Law of Nature, To succour those that are in Want. To relieve those that are oppressed. To take care of Widows and Orphans.* But it would be to no purpose to have inculcated these Precepts to those who were no ways subject to Misery, Poverty, and Death. The *Law of Nature* now enjoyns us, *To forgive Injuries;* and, *To use our utmost Endeavours towards the promoting of Peace amongst all Mankind.* Which would be unnecessary among those who never offended against the Laws of Mutual Society. And this too is very evident in the Prohibitory Precepts which relate to the Natural, not Positive, Law. For although every Command does virtually contain in it self a Prohibition of the opposite Vice; (as, for Instance, he that is commanded to love his Neighbour, is at the same time forbidden to do such Actions, as may any ways thwart or contradict his Duty of Love:) Yet it seems superfluous that these things should be ordain'd by express Commands, where there are no disorderly Inclinations to excite Men to the committing such Wrongs. For the Illustration of which, this may be taken notice of, that *Solon would by no Publick Law enact any Punishment for *Parricides,* because he thought that no Child could be guilty of so horrid an Impiety. In like manner we find an Account, in the †History of the *West-Indies,* concerning the People of *Nicaragua;* that in their Laws no Punishment was appointed for those who should kill the *Cacique,* by which Name they call their Princes; because, say they, there can be no Subject, who would contrive or perpetrate so base an Action. I am afraid it may savour too much of Affectation to enlarge any farther in the Proof of what is in it self so clear and evident. Yet I shall add this one Example, fitted to the meanest Capacity. Suppose there are two Children, but of different Dispositions, committed to the Care of a certain Person: One of which is Modest and Bashful, taking great delight in his Studies; the other proves Unruly, and Surly; giving

---

* *Diog. Laert. lib.* 1. §59. *Edit. Amstelod.* [Barbeyrac's marginal note (a), p. xxxviii.]

† *Franc, Lopez de Gomara, Hist. General. Ind. Occid. Cap.* 207. [Barbeyrac's marginal note (b), p. xxxviii.]

himself over more to loose Pleasures, than to Learning. Now the Duty
of both these is the same, To follow their Studies; but the particular Precepts, proper to each, are different; for it is sufficient to advise the Former to what Kind of Studies he must apply himself, at what Time, and
after what Manner they are to be follow'd: But as for the Other, he must
be enjoyn'd under severe Penalties, not to Wander abroad, not to
Game, not to sell his Books, not to get others to make his Exercises, not
to play the good Fellow, not to run after Harlots. Now if any one
should undertake, in a set Discourse, to declaim against these things to
him of the contrary Temper, the Child might very well enjoyn him Silence, and bid him inculcate them to any Body else, rather than to him,
who takes no Delight or Pleasure in such Practices. From whence I look
upon it as manifest, that the *Law of Nature* would have a quite different
Face, if we were to consider Man, as he was in his Primitive State of
Innocence.

And now since the Bounds and Limits of this Science, whereby it is
distinguish'd from Moral Divinity, are so clearly set down, it ought at
least to have the same Priviledges with other Sciences, as the Civil Law,
Physick, Natural Philosophy, and the Mathematicks; wherein if any
Unskilful Person presume to meddle, assuming to himself the Quality
of a Censor, without any Authority, he may fairly have that objected to
him, which was formerly done by *Apelles to Megabyzus,* who undertook to talk at random about the Art of Painting; *Pray,* said he, *be silent,
lest the Boys laugh at you, who pretend to talk of Matters you do not understand.*

Now, upon the whole, I am content to submit to the Judgment of
Discreet and Intelligent Persons; but as for Ignorant and Spiteful De-
tractors, 'tis better to leave 'em to themselves, to be punish'd by their
own Folly and Malice; since according to the Ancient Proverb, *The
Ethiopian cannot change his Skin.*

---

*Rather *Zeuxis, Ael. V. H.* II. 2. *Plut. de. Adulat.* [Barbeyrac's marginal note (a),
p. xl (abbreviated).]

Book I

Of Human Actions in general, the Principles of 'em, and how to be accounted for, or imputed

What we mean here by the Word DUTY, is, *That* *Action *of a Man, which is regularly order'd according to some prescrib'd Law, which he is oblig'd to obey.* To the Understanding whereof it is necessary to premise somewhat, as well touching the Nature of a *Human Action,* as concerning *Laws* in general.

By a *Human Action* we mean not *every Motion* that proceeds from the Faculties of a Man; but such only as have their Original and Direction from those Faculties which God Almighty has endow'd Mankind withal, distinct from Brutes; that is, such as are undertaken by the Light of the *Understanding,* and the Choice of the *Will.*

I. What Duty is.

II. What a Human Action.

---

*The ancient *Stoicks* call'd *Actions* by the Greek Word καθῆκον, and by the Latin OFFICIUM, and in English we use the Word *OFFICE* in the same Sense, when we say, *Friendly Offices,* &c. but then the Definition hereof given by the Philosophers, is too loose and general, since thereby they understood nothing but an *Action conformable to Reason.* As may appear from a Passage of *Cicero* (*de Fin. Bon. & Mal. L.* 3. *c.* 17.) *Quod autem ratione actum sit, id OFFICIUM appellamus.* See also *De Offic. l.* 1. *c.* 3. *& Diogenes Laertius Lib.* VII. *Sect.* 107, 108. [This slightly modified version of Barbeyrac's note I.1, p. 1 is intended to clarify Pufendorf's conception of duty (*officium*), as action commanded by a superior, by contrasting it with the philosopher's conception, as action in accordance with right reason.]

III. Human Capacity. Knowing and Chusing L. N. N. l. 1. c. 1. §2 c. 3. §1.

For it is not only put in the Power of Man to *know* the various Things which appear in the World, to *compare* them one with another, and from thence to form to himself new *Notions;* but he is able to look forwards, and to consider *what* he is to do, and to carry himself to the Performance of it, and this to do after some certain *Manner,* and to some certain *End;* and then he can collect what will be the Consequence thereof. Beside, he can make a *Judgment* upon Things already done, whether they are done agreeably to their Rule. Not that all a Man's Faculties do exert themselves continually, or after the same manner, but some of them are stir'd up in him by an internal Impulse; and when rais'd, are by the same regulated and guided. Neither beside has a Man the same Inclination to every Object; but some he Desires, and for others he has an Aversion: And often, though an Object of Action be before him, yet he *suspends* any Motion towards it; and when many Objects offer themselves, he *chuses* one and *refuses* the rest.

IV. Human Understanding. L. N. N. l. 1. c. 3.

As for that Faculty therefore of comprehending and judging of Things, which is called the *Understanding;* it must be taken for granted, first of all, *That every Man of a mature Age, and entire Sense, has so much Natural Light in him, as that, with *necessary* Care, and due Consideration, he may rightly comprehend, at least those *general Precepts* and *Principles* which are requisite in order to pass our Lives here honestly and quietly; and be able to judge that these are congruous to the Nature of Man. For if this, at least, be not admitted within the Bounds of the

---

*This is evident from the Example of the *Heathen,* and the Holy Scriptures are express in this Point; for thus they say: *For when the Gentiles, which have not the Law* (Written or Revealed, as was that of *Moses*) *do by NATURE the things contained in the Law, these having not the Law are a Law unto themselves: Which shew the Work of the Law written in their Hearts, their Conscience also bearing Witness, and their Thoughts the mean while accusing, or else excusing one another;* (that is, when they do ill, they condemn themselves in their own Conscience, and on the contrary, when they do well, they have in themselves an inward Approbation and Satisfaction: From whence it plainly appears they have Ideas of Good and Evil.) *Rom.* ii. 14, 15. [In this note (IV.1, p. 3) Barbeyrac seeks to close the gap between Pufendorf's conception of understanding (as the capacity to deduce the rules of civil tranquillity) and the Calvinist conception of conscience (as the individual's inner access to moral laws inscribed in the heart by God).]

Forum Humanum, [or Civil Judicature] Men might pretend an invincible Ignorance for all their Miscarriages; *because no Man *in foro humano* can be condemn'd for having violated a Law which it was above his Capacity to comprehend.

The *Understanding* of Man, when it is *rightly instructed* concerning that which is to be done or omitted, and this so, as that he is able to give certain and undoubted Reasons for his Opinions, is wont to be call'd CONSCIENCE RIGHTLY INFORM'D: That is, govern'd by sure Principles, and settling its Resolutions conformably to the Laws. But when a Man has indeed entertain'd the *true Opinion* about what is to be done or not to be done, the Truth whereof yet he is not able to make good by *Reasoning;* but he either drew such his Notion from his Education, way of Living, Custom, or from the Authority of Persons wiser or better than himself; and no Reason appears to him that can persuade the contrary, this uses to be call'd *Conscientia probabilis,* CONSCIENCE grounded upon PROBABILITY. And by this the greatest part of Mankind are govern'd, it being the good Fortune of few to be able to enquire into, and to know, the Causes of Things.

> V. What is meant by Conscience rightly inform'd, and what by Probable Conscience. L. N. N. l. 1. c. 3. §5.

And yet it chances often, to some Men especially in singular Cases, that Arguments may be brought on *both* sides, and they not be Masters of sufficient *Judgment* to *discern* clearly which are the strongest and most weighty. And this is call'd a †DOUBTING CONSCIENCE. In which Case this is the Rule: *As long as the Understanding is unsatisfied and in doubt,*

> VI. Conscience doubting. L. N. N. l. 1. c. 3. §8.

---

* *L. N. N. l.* 1. *c.* 3. §3. *Apol.* §21. *Eris. Scand.* p. 37.

† A *scrupulous Conscience,* proceeding mostly from Weakness and Superstition, is only to be help'd by better Information. Here our Author's Definition of *Conscience* may be noted, that it is an Act of the Mind judging of what a Man has omitted or done, according to some *Rule* to which he was rightly oblig'd. Nay, in strict Sense, to *act* against *Conscience* is no other than wittingly and willingly to do Evil. [Added by the English editors, this note expounds Pufendorf's conception of conscience rather than Barbeyrac's. In treating conscience as judgment in accordance with an imposed rule—rather than as individual insight into God's laws or intentions—Pufendorf was counteracting doctrines (some of them Calvinist) that placed conscience above civil duty.]

whether the thing to be done be good or evil, the doing of it is to be deferr'd.
For to set about doing it before the Doubt is answer'd, implies a sinful
Design, or at least a Neglect of the Law.

VII. Error, vincible and invincible.
L. N. N. l. 1. c. 3. §11.

Men also oftentimes have *wrong Apprehensions* of the matter, and take
that to be true which is false; and then they are said to be in an *Error;*
and this is called *Vincible Error,* when a Man by applying due Attention
and Diligence might have prevented his falling thereinto; and it's said
to be *Invincible Error,* when the Person, with the utmost Diligence and
Care that is consistent with the common Rules of Life, could not have
avoided it. But this sort of *Error,* at least, among those who give their
Minds to improve the Light of Reason, and to lead their Lives regularly,
happens not in the *common Rules* of living, but only in *peculiar Matters.*
For the Precepts of the Law of Nature are plain; and that Legislator who
makes positive Laws, both does and ought to take all possible Care, that
they may be understood by those who are to give Obedience to them.
So that this Sort of *Error* proceeds only from a supine *Negligence.* But
in *particular Affairs* 'tis easie for some Error to be admitted, against the
Will, and without any Fault of the Person, concerning the Object and
other *Circumstances of the Action.

VIII. Of Ignorance, and the various Kinds of it. L. N. N. l. 1. c. 3. §10.

Where Knowledge simply is wanting as to the Thing performed or
omitted, such Defect of Knowledge is call'd *Ignorance.*[1]

This *Ignorance* may be two Ways consider'd, either with respect to
its *Origin,* or with respect to its *Influence on the Action.* With reference
to this latter, *Ignorance* is of two Sorts, one being the Cause of the Thing
ignorantly done, the other not; on which account the first of these is
call'd *Efficacious Ignorance,* the other *Concomitant.*

* Such Circumstances are the *Manner,* the *Intention,* the *Instrument,* the *Quality*
of the Thing done, &c. Thus, for Example, A Man may happen to kill another without
any Thought of doing so; he may mistake him for an Enemy, may give him
Poison when he thinks what he gives him is wholsom Liquor. Tho' we may believe
Actions so circumstantiated to be innocent, yet no Man can innocently assert, that
Murder or Poisoning are lawful. [Barbeyrac's note VII.1, p. 6.]

1. This subsection is an example of the editors' attempting to improve on Tooke's
version, using Barbeyrac as their model to change the order of exposition, and then
adding their own biblical examples to clarify the different forms of morally significant ignorance. In general, Tooke's original is clearer.

EFFICACIOUS Ignorance is the Want of such Knowledge as, had it not been wanting, would have hindred the Action: Such was *Abimelech*'s Ignorance, *Gen.* xx. 4, 5. who, had he known *Sarah* to have been *Abraham*'s Wife, had never entertain'd any Thoughts of taking her to himself. *Concomitant Ignorance* is the Want of such Knowledge, as had it not been wanting, would not have hindred the Fact: As suppose a Man should kill his Enemy by a chance Blow, whom he would otherwise have kill'd, had he known him to have been in that particular Place.

Ignorance with respect to its *Origin* is either *Voluntary* or *Involuntary*. *Voluntary Ignorance* is either *contracted* by mere negligence, idleness and unattention; or else *affected,* that is, proceeding from a direct and formal Contempt of the means of informing our selves in what we were able, and what it was our Duty to come to the knowledge of. *Involuntary Ignorance* consists in the want of knowing such Things, as it was neither in our Power, nor a part of our Duty to come to the knowledge of. This likewise is of two Sorts: The former is, when in doing a Thing a Man is not able to overcome the Ignorance from which it proceeds, and yet is in Fault for falling into that Ignorance; which is the Case of Drunken Men. The latter is, when a Man is not only ignorant of such Things as could not be known before the Action, but is also *free from any Blame upon the account of his falling into that Ignorance, or his continuing in it.

The other Faculty, which does peculiarly distinguish Men from Brutes, is called the *Will;* by which, as with an internal Impulse, Man *moves himself* to Action, and *chuses* that which best pleases him; and *rejects* that which seems unfit for him. Man therefore has thus much from his *Will:* First, that he has a Power to act *willingly,* that is, he is not determin'd by any intrinsick *Necessity* to do this or that, but is himself the Author of his own Actions: Next, that he has a Power to act *freely,* that

IX. The Will, unforced and free. L. N. N. l. 1. c. 4.

---

*There is no other but this last sort of Ignorance that is really involuntary and invincible, and capable entirely to excuse Men in doing any prejudicial Acts; for it is Men's own Faults that they fall into any of the forementioned sorts of Ignorance. [Barbeyrac's note VIII.2, p. 8.]

is, upon the Proposal of one Object, he may *act* or not *act,* and either entertain or reject; or if divers Objects are propos'd, he may *chuse* one and *refuse* the rest. Now whereas among human Actions some are undertaken for their *own* Sakes, others because they are subservient to the attaining of somewhat *farther;* that is, some are as the *End,* and others as *Means:* As for the *End,* the Will is thus far concern'd, That being once known, this first *approves* it, and then moves vigorously towards the *achieving* thereof, as it were, driving at it with more or less earnestness; and this *End* once *obtain'd,* it sits down quietly and *enjoys* its Acquist with Pleasure. For the *Means,* they are first to be approv'd, then such as are most fit for the Purpose are *chosen,* and at last are *apply'd* to Use.

X. The Will spontaneous chargeable with the Action. L. N. N. l. 1. c. 4. §2.

But as Man is accounted to be the *Author* of his *own Actions,* because they are voluntarily undertaken by himself: So this is chiefly to be observ'd concerning the Will, to wit, that its *Spontaneity,* or natural Freedom, is at least to be asserted in those Actions, concerning which a Man is wont to give an Account before any human Tribunal. For *where* an absolute *Freedom* of *choice* is wholly taken away, *there* not the Man who *acts,* but he that *imposed* upon him the Necessity of so doing, is to be reputed the *Author* of that Action, to which the other unwillingly ministred with his Strength and Limbs.

XI. The Will variously affected. L. N. N. l. 1. c. 4. §4.

Farthermore, though the Will do always desire *Good* in general, and has continually an aversion for *Evil* also in general; yet a great *Variety* of *Desires* and *Actions* may be found among Men. And this arises from hence, that all Things that are Good and Evil do not appear *purely* so to Man, but *mixt* together, the good with the bad, and the bad with the good; and because different Objects do particularly affect divers Parts, as it were, of a Man; for instance, some regard that good Opinion and Respect that a Man has for himself; some affect the outward Senses; and some that Love of himself, from which he desires his own Preservation. From whence it is, that those of the first Sort appear to him as *reputable;* of the second as *pleasant;* and of the last as *profitable:* And accordingly as each of these have made a powerful Impression upon a Man, it brings upon him a peculiar Propensity towards that way; whereto may be added the particular *Inclinations* and *Aversions* that are in most Men to some certain Things. From all which it comes to pass, that upon any Action several *Sorts* of *Good* and *Evil* offer themselves, which either *are* true or *appear* so; which some have more, some less Sagacity to *distinguish* with solidity of Judgment. So that 'tis no wonder that one Man should be carried eagerly on to that which another perfectly abhors.

But neither is the Will of Man always found to stand *equally* poised with regard to every Action, that so the Inclination thereof to this or that Side should come only from an *Internal Impulse,* after a due Consideration had of all its Circumstances; but it is very often pusht on one way rather than another by *some outward Movements.* For, that we may pass by that universal Propensity to Evil, which is in all Mortals (the Original and Nature of which belong to the Examination of another **Forum;*) first, a *peculiar Disposition of Nature* puts a particular kind of *byass* upon the Will, by which some are strongly inclin'd to certain *sorts* of Actions; and this is not only to be found in single *Men,* but in whole *Nations.* This seems to proceed from the Temperature of the Air that surrounds us, and of the Soil; and from that Constitution of our Bodies which either was deriv'd to us in the Seed of our *Parents,* or was occasion'd in us by our *Age, Diet,* the want or enjoyment of *Health,* the Method of our Studies, or *way* of *Living,* and Causes of that sort; beside the various *formations* of the *Organs,* which the *Mind* makes use of in the Performance of its several Offices, and the like. And here, beside that a Man may with due Care very much *alter* the *Temperament* of his Body, and *repress* the Exorbitances of his natural *Inclination,* it is to be noted, that how much Power soever we attribute hereto, yet it is not to be understood to be of that Force as to hurry a Man into such a Violation of the *Law* of *Nature,* as shall render him obnoxious to the *Civil Judicature,* where evil *Desires* are not animadverted on, †provided they break not forth into external *Actions.* So that after all the Pains that can

XII. The Will byass'd by Natural Inclinations. L. N. N. l. 1. c. 4. §5.

---

*The Judgment of the Divines. [One of Tooke's own (rare) marginal notes from the first edition of 1691.]

† *Hugo Grotius de Jure Belli & Pacis. Lib.* ii. *c.* 20. §18.

be taken to repel Nature, if it takes its full Swinge, yet it may so far be restrain'd as not to produce *open Acts* of Wickedness; and the *Difficulty* which happens in vanquishing these Propensities is abundantly recompens'd in the *Glory* of the Conquest. But if these Impulses are so strong upon the Mind, that they cannot be contain'd from breaking forth, yet there may be found a Way, as it were to draw them off, without Sin.

XIII. By Custom or Habitude. L. N. N. l. 1. c. 4. §6.
The frequent *Repetition* of Actions of the same kind does also *incline* the Will to do certain Things; and the Propensity which proceeds from hence is called *Habit* or *Custom;* for it is by this that any Thing is undertaken readily and willingly; so that the Object being presented, the Mind seems to be forced thitherward, or if it be absent, the same is earnestly desirous of it. Concerning which this is to be observ'd, That as there appears to be no *Custom,* but what a Man may, by applying a due Care, *break* and *leave off;* so neither can any so far put a force upon the Will, but that a Man may be able at any Time to restrain himself from any *external Acts* at least, to which by that he is urged. And because it was in the Persons *own Power* to have contracted this *Habit* or not, whatsoever easiness it brings to any Action, yet if that Action be *good,* it loses nothing of its Value therefore, as neither doth an *evil* Thing abate ought of its Pravity. But as a *good Habit* brings *Praise* to a Man, so an *ill* one shews his *Shame.*

XIV. By Passion. L. N. N. l. 1. c. 4. §7.
It is also of great Consideration, whether the Mind be in a *quiet* and *placid* State, or whether it be affected with those peculiar Motions we call the *Passions.* Of these it is to be known, that how violent soever they are, a Man with the right Use of his *Reason* may yet conquer them, or at least contain them so far within Bounds, as to hinder them from producing those Actions they prompt Men to do. *But whereas of the *Passions* some are rais'd from the Appearance of *Good,* and others of *Evil;* and do urge either to the procuring of somewhat that is *acceptable,* or to the avoiding of what is *mischievous,* it is agreeable to Human Nature, that *these* should meet among Men more *favour* and *pardon,* than *those;*

* *Apolog. Sect. 22. in Eris. Scandic. p. 39.*

and that according to such degrees as the Mischief that excited them was more hurtful and intolerable. For to *want* a *Good* not altogether necessary to the Preservation of Nature is accounted more *easie,* than to *endure an Evil* which tends to Nature's Destruction.

Farthermore, as there are *certain Maladies, which take away all Use of the *Reason* either perpetually or for a time: So 'tis customary in many Countries, for Men on purpose to procure to themselves a certain kind of *Disease* which goes off in a short time, but which very much confounds the Reasoning Faculty. By this we mean *Drunkenness;* proceeding from certain kinds of Drink, and Fumes, which hurry and disturb the Blood and Spirits, thereby rendring Men very prone to *Lust, Anger, Rashness* and immoderate *Mirth;* so that many by *Drunkenness* are set as it were beside themselves, and seem to have put on *another Nature,* than that which they were of, when *sober.* But as this does not always take away the *whole* Use of *Reason;* so, as far as the Person does *willingly* put himself in this State, it is apt to procure an *Abhorrence* rather than a *favourable Interpretation* of what is done by its Impulse.

> XV. By intoxication. L. N. N. l. 1. c. 4. §8.

Now of Human Actions, as those are call'd *Voluntary,* which proceed from, and are directed by the Will; so if any thing be done *wittingly,* altogether against the Will, these are call'd *Involuntary,* taking the Word in the narrowest sense; for taking it in the largest, it comprehends even those which are done through *Ignorance.* But *Involuntary* in this place is to signifie the same as *forc'd;* that is, when by an external Power which is stronger, a Man is compell'd to use his Members in any Action, to which he yet signifies his Dissent and Aversion by Signs, and particularly by counterstriving with his Body. Less properly those Actions are also called *Involuntary,* which by the Imposition of a great Necessity are *chosen* to be done, as the lesser Evil; and for the Acting whereof the Person had the greatest Abomination, had he not been set under such Ne-

> XVI. Actions Involuntary, mixt. L. N. N. l. 1. c. 4. §11.

*The Effect of these sort of Maladies, and of *Drunkenness* is not, to speak properly, a giving to the Will a bent and inclination to this or that thing, so much as an entire destroying the Principle of Human Actions; because Men under these Circumstances know not any thing of what they do. [Barbeyrac's note XV.1, p. 14.]

cessity. These Actions therefore are call'd *Mixt*. With *Voluntary Actions* they have this in common, that in the present State of Things the Will *chuses* them as the lesser Evil. With the *Involuntary* they are after a sort the same, as to the Effect, because they render the Agent either not at all, or not *so heinously* blameable, as if they had been done spontaneously.

XVII. Voluntary Actions imputable.
L. N. N. l. 1.
c. 5. §5.

Those Human Actions then which proceed from, and are directed by the *Understanding* and the *Will,* have particularly this natural Propriety, *that they may be *imputed* to the Doer; that is, that a Man may justly be said to be the Author of them, and be oblig'd to render an *Account* of such his Doing; and the *Consequences* thereof, whether good or bad, are chargeable upon him. For there can be no truer Reason why any Action should be *imputable* to a Man, than that he did it either mediately or immediately *knowingly* and *willingly;* or that it was in his Power to have done the same or to have let it alone. Hence it obtains as the prime Axiom in Matters of Morality which are liable to the Human *Forum:* That *every Man is accountable for all such Actions, the Performance or Omission of which were in his own Choice.* Or, which is tantamount, That *every Action that lies within a Man's Power to perform or omit, is chargeable upon him who might or might not have done it.* So on the contrary, *no Man can be reputed the Author of that Action, which neither in it self nor in its cause, was in* his Power.

XVIII. Conclusions from the Premisses.

From these Premisses we shall deduce some particular *Propositions,* by which shall be ascertain'd, what every Man ought to be *accountable* for; or, in other Words, which are those Actions and Consequences of which any one is to be charged as *Author.*

The first Conclusion.
L. N. N. l. 1.
c. 5. §6.

None *of those Actions which are done by another* Man, *nor any Operation of whatsoever other* things; *neither any* Accident, *can be imputable to any Person, but so far forth as it was in* his Power, *or as he was* oblig'd *to guide such Action.* For nothing is more common in the World, than to *subject* the Doings of *one Man* to the Manage and Direction of *another.* Here then, if any thing be perpetrated by one, which had not

*L. N. N. *l.* 1. *c.* 5. §3. *Spicileg. Jur. Nat.* §12. in *Eris. Scandic. Page* 343.

been done, if the other had performed his *Duty* and exerted his *Power;* this Action shall not only be chargeable upon him who *immediately* did the Fact, but upon the other also who *neglected* to make use of his *Authority* and *Power*. And yet this is to be understood with some restriction; so as that *Possibility* may be taken *morally*, and in a *large* Sense. For no *Subjection* can be so *strict*, as to extinguish *all* manner of *Liberty* in the Person subjected; but so, that 'twill be in his Power to resist and act quite contrary to the Direction of his *Superior;* neither will the State of *Human Nature* bear, that any one should be perpetually affix'd to the side of another, so as to observe *all* his Motions. Therefore when a *Superiour* has done every thing that was requir'd by the *Rules* of his *Directorship,* and yet somewhat is acted amiss, this shall be laid only to the charge of *him* that *did* it. Thus, whereas *Man* exercises Dominion over other *Animals,* what is done by them to the detriment of another, shall be charged upon the *Owner,* as supposing him to have been wanting of due *Care* and *Circumspection*. So also all those Mischiefs which are brought upon another, may be *imputed* to that Person, who when he *could* and *ought,* yet did not take out of the way the Cause and Occasion thereof. Accordingly it being in the Power of Men to *promote* or *suspend* the Operations of many *Natural Agents,* whatsoever Advantage or Damage is wrought by these, *they* shall be accountable for, by whose *application* or *neglect* the same was occasion'd. Beside, sometimes there are extraordinary Cases, when a Man shall be charged with such Events as are above human Direction, as when *God* shall do particular *Works* with regard to some *single* Person. [So the Pestilence in *Israel* may be charg'd upon *David* for numbring the People; 2 *Sam.* xxiv. or the three Year's Drought to the Prayers of *Elijah,* 1 *Kings* xvii. and the like.] These and such Cases being excepted, *no Man is responsible but for his own Actions.*

WHATSOEVER Qualifications *a Man has or has not, which it is not in his* Power *to exert or not to exert, must not be* imputed *to him, unless so far as he is wanting in* Industry *to supply such Natural Defect, or does not rouse up his native Faculties.* So, because no man can give himself an *Acuteness* of *Judgment* and *Strength* of *Body;* therefore no one is to be

XIX. The second Conclusion. L. N. N. l. 1. c. 5. §7.

blam'd for Want of either, or *commended* for having them, except so far as he *improv'd,* or *neglected* the cultivating thereof. Thus *Clownishness* is not blameable in a Rustic, but in a *Courtier* or *Citizen.* And hence it is, that those Reproaches are to be judg'd extremely absurd, which are grounded upon Qualities, the Causes of which are not in our Power, as, *Short Stature,* a deform'd *Countenance,* and the like.

XX. The Third
Conclusion.
L. N. N. l. 1.
c. 5. §10.

Farther, *We are not chargeable for those Things, which we do thro' Invincible Ignorance.* Because we have nothing but the Light of our Understanding to direct our Actions by; and in this case it is supposed that the Agent neither had, nor *possibly* could have, this Light for his Direction at that time, and that it was not his own Fault that made it not *possible* for him then to come at proper Knowledge. When we say not *possible* for him to know, we must be understood in a Moral not a Physical Sense; that is, it was not possible to come to this Knowledge by the usual and common Means, by using his best *Care* and *Attention,* and by giving such *Diligence, Precaution,* and *Circumspection,* as in all reason may be thought sufficient for the attaining such Knowledge.

XXI. The fourth Conclusion.

Ignorance of a Man's *Duty,* or of those *Laws* from whence his *Duty* arises, or *Error* about either of them, does not excuse from blame. For whosoever imposes *Laws* and *Services,* is wont and ought to take care that the Subject have *notice* thereof. And these Laws and Rules of Duty generally are and should be order'd to the *Capacity* of such *Subject,* if they are such as he is obliged to *know* and *remember.* Hence, he who is the *Cause* of the *Ignorance* shall be bound to answer for those *Actions* which are the Effects thereof.

XXII. The fifth Conclusion.

He who, not by his own fault, wants an *Opportunity* of doing his *Duty,* shall not be accountable, because he has not done it. An *Opportunity* of doing our Duty comprehends these four requisite Conditions: 1. That an *Object* of Action be ready: 2. That a proper *Place* be had, where we may not be hindred by others, nor receive any Mischief: 3. That we have a fit *Time,* when Business of greater Necessity is not to be done, and which is equally seasonable for those Persons who are to concur with us in the Action: and 4. Lastly, That we have natural *Force suffi-cient* for the performancer. For since an Action cannot be atchiev'd without these, 'twould be absurd to blame a Man for not acting, when he had not an *Opportunity* so to do. Thus, a Physician cannot be ac-cus'd of *Sloth,* when no body is sick to employ him. Thus, no Man can be *liberal,* who wants himself. Thus he cannot be reprov'd for *burying* his Talent who having taken a due care to set himself in an useful Sta-tion, has yet miss'd of it: tho' it be said, * *To whom much is given, from him much shall be requir'd.* †Thus we cannot blow and suck all at once.

No Man is accountable *for not doing that which* exceeded *his Power, and which he had not Strength sufficient to hinder or accomplish.* Hence that Maxim, *To Impossibilities there lies no Obligation.* But this Exception must be added, Provided, that by the Person's *own Fault* he has not *im-paired,* or *lost* that Strength which was necessary to the Performance; for if so, he is to be treated after the same manner, as if he *had* all that Power which he *might* have had: Otherwise it would be easie to elude the Performance of any difficult Obligation, by weakening one's self on purpose.

XXIII. The sixth Conclu-sion. L. N. N. l. 1. c. 5. §8.

Neither can those things be *imputable,* which one acts or suffers by *Compulsion.* For it is supposed, that 'twas above his *power* to decline or avoid such doing or suffering. But we are said after a twofold manner to be *compell'd;* one way is, when another that's stronger than us *vio-lently forces* our Members to do or endure somewhat; the other, ‡when

XXIV. The seventh Con-clusion. L. N. N. l. 1. c. 5. §9.

---

* The Words of our Blessed Saviour, *Luc.* xii. 48. [Barbeyrac's note XXII.3, p. 22.]

† Our Author, who frequently makes use of *Plautus,* does without doubt in this place allude to the *Mostellaria, Act.* 3. *Sc.* 2 *v.* 104, 105.

    Simul flare sorberéque haud facile

    Est: ego hic esse & illîc simul haud potui.

[Barbeyrac's note 2, p. 22.]

‡ The Author seems here to give too great an Allowance to this second sort of *Compulsion.* It must indeed be owned, that it greatly lessens the Offence, especially in Courts of Human Judicature; but then it frees us not from Imputation intirely in the Sight of God. The Example our Author gives of the Sword or Ax reaches not the Case, for they are Instruments meerly passive: But on the other hand, a Person who

one more powerful shall *threaten* some grievous Mischief (which he is immediately able to bring upon us) unless we will, as of our *own* accord, apply our selves to the doing of this, or abstain from doing that. For in these cases unless we are *expressly obliged* to take the Mischief to our selves which was to be done to another, he that sets us under this *Necessity,* is to be reputed the *Author* of the Fact; and the same is no more chargeable upon us, than a *Murder* is upon the Sword or Ax which was the *Instrument.*

XXV. The eighth Conclusion.

The Actions of those who *want* the Use of their *Reason* are not imputable; because they cannot distinguish clearly what they do, and bring it to the Rule. Hitherto appertain the Actions of *Children,* before their reasoning Faculties begin to exert themselves. For though they are now and then chid or whipt for what they do; yet it is not from hence to be concluded, that their Actions are really Crimes, or that in strictness they

---

is no other ways forced but by the Menaces of some great Mischief, without any physical or irresistible Violence, acts with some degree of Willingness, and gives a sort of a Concurrence to an Action which he plainly knows to be ill, when he is thus constrained to do it. There is but one Case wherein, with a safe Conscience, we may obey the injurious Orders of a Superior, in order to avoid the Mischiefs he menaces us with in case of a Refusal; and that is, when the Person, on whom the Mischief is to fall by our Compliance with the injurious Orders of a Superior, does himself consent that we should avoid the Mischief threatned to us, by doing the Action commanded, altho' it be injurious to him, and rather contents himself to suffer such Injury, than to expose us to the Violence of the Person menacing: But this also must be understood only of such Cases as the Person has it in his Power to give Consent, namely, when the Injury he consents to suffer is the Violation only of such a Right as is in the power of the suffering Person to quit; otherwise this Case holds not good; for should any one, for example, consent that I should act the Command of another to kill him, such consent would not acquit me of the Guilt of Murder, should I by the Menaces of any one be constrained to take away his Life. *See L. N. N. lib.* I. *cap.* V. §9. *& lib.* VIII. *cap.* I. §6. [This note (Barbeyrac's XXIV.1, p. 23) continues his attempt to blur Pufendorf's strict separation of the civil and religious judgment. By insisting against Pufendorf that someone who commits an evil act under coercive threats may still be blameworthy in the sight of God, Barbeyrac refuses to allow civil obligation to cancel out the individual's conscience and moral responsibility.]

deserve this punishment for them; which they receive not as from Justice, but in Prudence to prevent their growing troublesome to others, and lest they contract ill Habits in themselves when they are little, and so keep them when they are grown up. So also the Doings of *Franticks, Crackbrains,* and *Dotards* are not accounted *Human Actions,* nor *imputable* to those who contracted such incapacitating Disease, without any *fault* of their *own.*

Lastly, A Man is not chargeable with what he seems to do in his *Dreams;* unless by *indulging himself* in the *Day-time* with idle Thoughts, he has deeply impressed the *Ideas* of such Things in his Mind; (tho' Matters of this Sort can rarely be within the Cognizance of the Human *Forum.*) For indeed the Fansie in Sleep is like a Boat adrift without a Guide; so that 'tis impossible for any Man to order what Ideas it shall form. XXVI. The ninth Conclusion. L. N. N. l. 1. c. 5 §11.

But concerning the *Imputation of another* Man's Actions, it is somewhat more distinctly to be observ'd, that sometimes it may so happen, that an Action ought not at all to be charged upon him that *immediately* did it, but upon another who made use of this only as an *Instrument.* But it is more frequent, that it should be imputed *both* to *him* who perpetrated the thing, and to the *other,* who by doing or omitting something, shew'd his *concurrence* to the Action. And this is chiefly done after a threefold manner; either, 1. As the other was the *principal* Cause of the Action, and this *less principal.* Or, 2. As they were both *equally* concern'd. Or, 3. As the other was *less principal,* and he that did the Act was *principal.* To the first Sort belong those who shall *instigate* another to any thing by their Authority; those who shall give their necessary *Approbation,* without which the other could not have acted; those who *could* and *ought* to have hindred it, but did not. To the second Class appertain, those who *order* such a thing to be done, or *hire* a Man to do it; those who *assist;* those who afford *harbour* and *protection;* those who had it in their *Power,* and whose *Duty* it was to have succour'd the XXVII. Imputation of another's Actions. L. N. N. l. 1. c. 5. §14.

L. N. N. l. 1.   wronged Person, but refus'd it. To the third Sort are refer'd such as are
c. 5. §14.   of *counsel* to the Design; †those that *encourage* and *commend* the Fact
before it be done; and such as *incite* Men to sinning by their *Example,*
and the like.

❦✠❦   C H A P T E R   I I   ❦✠❦

Of the Rule of Human Actions, or of Laws in general; and the different Qualifications of those Actions

I. The Neces-   Because all *Human Actions* depending upon the *Will,* have their Esti-
sity of a Rule.   mate according to the concurrence thereof; but the *Will* of every Person
not only differs in many respects from that of all others, but also alters
and changes it self, becoming different in the same Person at one time
from what it was before at another; therefore to preserve Decency and
L. N. N. l. 2.   Order among Mankind, it was necessary there should be some *Rule,* by
c. 1.   which they should be regulated. For otherwise, if, where there is so
great a *Liberty* of the *Will,* and such *Variety* of *Inclinations* and *Desires,*
any Man might do whatsoever he had a mind to, without any regard to
some *stated Rule,* it could not but give occasion to vast *Confusions*
among Mankind.

---

* That is, when, for example, a Man advises another to steal this or that thing,
shewing him at the same time the properest Manner to take it without discovery, the
favourablest Time of conveying himself into the House where it is, the Place where
the thing is reposited, the best Way of getting off with it, and the like Particulars;
but this is not meant of simply advising any one in general terms to steal for his
Support rather than starve. *L. N. N. lib.* I. *cap.* V. §14. [Barbeyrac's XXVII.1, p. 26.]

† That is, provided this Advice, these Encouragements and Commendations contribute to make him do the criminal Act; for in such case only the Imputation lies;
otherwise the Person thus counselling and encouraging is only guilty of the ill Intention which he had. *Lib.* III. *cap.* I. §4. [Barbeyrac's XXVII.2, p. 27.]

This *Rule* is call'd Law; which is, **A Decree by which the Superior obliges one that is subject to him, to accommodate his Actions to the Directions prescrib'd therein.*[2]

II. Law, defined. L. N. N. l. 1. c. 6. §4.

That this Definition may the better be understood, it must first be enquired, What is an *Obligation; whence* is its Original; *who* is capable of *lying under* an Obligation; and *who* it is that can *impose* it. By *Obligation* then is usually meant, *A moral Bond, whereby we are ty'd down to do this or that, or to abstain from doing them.*[3] That is, hereby a kind of a Moral Bridle is put upon our *Liberty;* so that though the *Will* does actually drive *another* way, yet we find our selves hereby struck as it were with an *internal* Sense, that if our Action be not perform'd according to the *prescript Rule,* we cannot but confess we have not done *right;* and if any Mischief happen to us upon that Account, we may fairly charge *our selves* with the same; because it might have been avoided, if the *Rule* had been follow'd as it ought.

III. Obligation. L. N. N. l. 1. c. 6. §5.

And there are two Reasons why *Man* should be subject to an *Obligation;* one is, because he is endow'd with a *Will,* which may be divers ways *directed,* and so be *conform'd* to a Rule: the other, because *Man* is not exempt from the Power of a *Superior.* For where the *Faculties* of any Agent are by *Nature* form'd only for *one Way* of acting, there 'tis to no purpose to expect any thing to be done of *choice:* and to such a Creature 'tis *in vain* to prescribe any *Rule;* because 'tis uncapable of *understanding* the same, or *conforming* its Actions thereto. Again, if there be any one who has no *Superior,* then there is no *Power* that can of right impose a Necessity upon him; and if he perpetually observes a certain Rule in what he does, and constantly abstains from doing many things, he is

IV. Man capable of being obliged. L. N. N. l. 1. c. 6. §6.

---

*On this Head consult *H. Grotius de Jure Belli & Pacis,* l. 1. c. 1. §9.

2. Pufendorf's construction of law in terms of the commands of a superior is aimed squarely at the Thomistic-scholastic conception of law as the rule of an (independently) moral action or nature.

3. The phrases "moral Bond" and "Moral Bridle" are innovations by the English editors. Pufendorf's original phrase is *vinculum juris,* which Tooke translated correctly as "rightful Bond" and Barbeyrac as *lien de Droit.* Here the editors seek to add a moral-philosophical inflection to Pufendorf's juristic construction of obligation.

not to be understood to act thus from any *Obligation* that lies upon *him,* but from his own *good pleasure.* It will follow then, for any one to be capable of lying under Obligation, it is necessary, that on the one hand he have a *Superior,* and on the other, that he be both capable of understanding the Rule prescrib'd him by his Superior, and also endu'd with a *Will* which may be *directed* several ways; and yet which (when the Law is promulged by his Superior) knows he cannot rightly depart therefrom. And with all these *Faculties,* 'tis plain, Mankind is furnish'd.

V. Who can oblige. L. N. N. l. 1. c. 6. §9.

An *Obligation* is superinduced upon the Will of Men properly by a *Superior;* that is, not only by such a one as being *greater* or *stronger,* can punish Gainsayers: but by him who has *just Reasons* to have a Power to restrain the Liberty of our Will at his own Pleasure.[4] Now when any man has either of these, as soon as he has signify'd what he would have, it necessarily stirs up, in the Mind of the party concern'd, *Fear* mixt with *Reverence;* the first arises from the consideration of his Power, the[5] other proceeds from those Reasons on which the Authority of our Superior is founded; by which we are convinced, that had we nothing to fear from him, yet we ought to conform our Actions to his Will. For he that can give me no *other Reason* for putting me under an Obligation

---

4. Pufendorf's construction of the superior—hence of obligation—in terms of the *combination* of coercive power and just reasons is one of the most crucial and controversial passages in the *Whole Duty.* This is largely because moral theologians and moral philosophers, including Barbeyrac, require their *separation,* insisting on the priority of the just reasons, understood as moral justifications for the exercise of political authority. Pufendorf, however, treats the power of the superior and the rationale ("just reasons") for accepting one as conjoint conditions for the creation of obligation. (See note 6 on p. 45). This is one of the central points at issue in Barbeyrac's commentary on Leibniz's attack on Pufendorf. See Barbeyrac's *Judgment of an Anonymous Writer* in the appendix to this volume.

5. The following formulation—"the other proceeds . . . is founded"—in which the reasons for complying with the superior's will are characterized as founding his authority, is not Pufendorf's, having been borrowed from Barbeyrac by the editors. Tooke's original rendering—"for the sake of those other Reasons, which even without Fear, ought to allure any man to compliance with his [the superior's] Will"—is accurate. Barbeyrac's modification is an attempt to insert the notion of a rational moral grounding of political authority into a text from which it has been deliberately excluded.

against my *Will*, beside this, that he's too *strong* for me, he truly may so terrifie me, that I may think it better to *obey* him for a while than suffer a *greater Evil:* but when this *Fear* is over, nothing any longer hinders, but that I may act after my *own Choice* and *not his.* On the contrary, he that has nothing but *Arguments* to prove that I should obey him, but wants *Power* to do me any Mischief, if I deny: I may with Impunity slight his Commands, except one more potent take upon him to make good his despis'd Authority. Now the *Reasons* upon which one Man may *justly* exact *Subjection* from another, are two: [6] First, if he have been to the other the *Original* of some extraordinary *Good;* and if it be plain, that he designs the others *Welfare,* and is *able* to provide better for him than 'tis possible for *himself* to do; and on the same Account does actually lay *claim* to the Government of him: Secondly, if any one does *voluntarily* surrender his Liberty to another, and subject *himself* to his Direction.

Farthermore, that a Law may exert its Force in the Minds of those to whom it is promulged, it is requir'd, that both the *Legislator and the Law also be known.* For no Man can pay Obedience, if he know not *whom* he is to *obey,* and *what* he is to *perform.* Now the Knowledge of the *Legislator* is very easy; because from the Light of Reason 'tis certain the *same* must be the *Author* of all the *Laws* of *Nature,* who was the *Creator* of the *Universe:* Nor can any Man in *Civil Society* be ignorant *who* it is that has Power over him.[7] Then for the *Laws* of *Nature,* it shall

VI. The Legislator and the true meaning of the Law to be known. L. N. N. l. 1. c. 6. §14.

6. This division of the "just reasons" for political subjection into two groups—the first concerning the relations of vulnerability and protection linking subject and superior, the second with the subject's voluntary consent to subjection—is another of Barbeyrac's innovations carried across by the editors of the 1716/35 edition. Absent this division, Pufendorf's original (and Tooke's translation) treats consent not as a separate condition for legitimate subjection but simply as the subject's agreement to exchange obedience for security. The exchange of obedience for security *constitutes* the "just reasons" for legitimate political authority.

7. This and the sentences immediately following contain characteristic instances of the manner in which Tooke adapts Pufendorf's political lexicon to its English dissemination. Tooke's "Man in Civil Society" translates Pufendorf's *civis,* or citizen, translated by Barbeyrac as *citoien* and by Weber as *Bürger.* Similarly, in the next sen-

be hereafter declar'd how we come to the Knowledge of them. And as to the *Laws* of a Man's *Country* or *City,* the Subject has notice given of them by a *Publication* plainly and openly made. In which these two Things ought to be ascertain'd, that the *Author* of the Law is he, who hath the *Supreme Authority* in the Community; and that *this* or *that* is the true Meaning of the *Law.* The *First* of these is known, if he shall promulge the Law with his *own Mouth,* or deliver it under his *own Hand;* or else if the same be done by such as are *delegated* to that purpose by him, whose Authority there is no Reason to call in question, if it be manifest, that such their acting belongs to that *Office* they bear in the Publick, and that they are *regularly placed* in the Administration thereof; if these Laws are brought in use at judicial Proceedings, and if they contain nothing *derogatory* to the *Sovereign's Power.* That the *Latter,* that is, the true *Sense* of the *Law* may be known, it is the Duty of those who promulge it, in so doing to use the greatest *Perspicuity* and *Plainness;* and if any thing *obscure* do occur therein, an *Explanation* is to be sought of the *Legislator,* or of those who are *publickly constituted* to give judgment according to the Laws.

VII. Two parts of a perfect Law. L. N. N. l. 1. c. 6. §14. Of every *perfect Law* there are two Parts: One, [Precept] whereby it is directed *what* is to be *done* or *omitted:* the other, [the Sanction] wherein is declared what *Punishment* he shall incur, who *neglects* to do what is commanded, or *attempts* that which is prohibited. For as through the Pravity of Human Nature ever inclining to things forbidden, it is to no purpose to say, *Do this,* if no Punishment shall be undergone by him who disobeys; so it were *absurd* to say, *You shall be punish'd,* except some Cause preceeded, by which a Punishment was deserv'd. Thus

---

tence but one, Tooke's "Laws of a Man's Country or City" represents his domestication of Pufendorf's *leges civiles,* or civil laws. Finally, in the next sentence, Tooke's characterization of the author of the law as "he, who hath the Supreme Authority in the Community" is his rendering of Pufendorf's *quem summum in civitate est imperium,* "he who holds sovereignty in the state." These and similar circumlocutions, which are used throughout Tooke's translation, represent his transposition of Pufendorf's statist political vocabulary—derived from Roman law and German political jurisprudence (*Staatsrecht*)—into a cultural register dominated by English common law and sovereignty conceived of as the "king in parliament."

then all the force of a Law consists in signifying what the *Superior requires* or *forbids* to be done, and what *Punishment* shall be inflicted upon the Violators. But the Power of *obliging*, that is, of imposing an intrinsick Necessity; and the Power of *forcing*, or, by the proposal of Punishments *compelling* the Observation of Laws, is properly in the Legislator, and in him to whom the Guardianship and Execution of the Laws is committed.

Whatsoever is enjoyn'd by any Law, ought not only to be in the *Power* of him to perform on whom the Injunction is laid, but it ought to contain somewhat *advantagious* either to him or others. For as it would be *absurd* and *cruel* to exact the doing of any thing from another, under a Penalty, which it is and always was beyond his *Power* to perform; so it would be silly and to *no purpose* to put a Restraint upon the natural Liberty of the Will of any man, if no one shall receive any Benefit therefrom.

VIII. It ought to command things possible and beneficial.

But though a Law does strictly include *all* the *Subjects* of the Legislator who are *concern'd* in the Matter of the same, and whom the same Legislator at first *intended* not to be exempted: yet sometimes it happens that particular persons may be clear'd of any obligation to such Law: and this is call'd *Dispensing.* But as he *only* may dispense, in whose Power it is to *make* and *abrogate* the Law; *so great Care is to be taken, lest by too frequent Dispensations, and such as are granted without very weighty Reasons, the Authority of the Law be shaken, and occasion be given of Envy and Animosities among Subjects.

IX. Power of Dispensing.
L. N. N. l. 1.
c. 6 §17.

Yet there is a great Difference between *Equity* and *Dispensing: Equity* being a *Correction of that in which the Law, by reason of its General Comprehension, was deficient:* or an *apt Interpretation* of the Law, by which it is demonstrated, that there may be some *peculiar* Case which is not compriz'd in the *Universal Law,* because if it were, some Absurdity would follow. For it being impossible that *all Cases,* by Reason of their

X. Equity.
L. N. N. l. 5.
c. 2. §21.

---

* See *Grotius de Jure Belli & Pacis, L.* 2. c. 20. Sect. 21. &*c.*

infinite *Variety,* should be either foreseen or explicitly provided for; therefore the *Judges,* whose Office it is to apply the *general* Rules of the Laws to *special* Cases, ought to except such from the Influence of them, *as the *Lawgiver himself* would have excepted if he were *present,* or had *foreseen* such Cases.

XI. Actions al-
lowable, good
and bad.
L. N. N. l. 1.
c. 7. §1.

Now the Actions of Men obtain certain Qualities and Denominations from their relation to and agreement with the Law of Morality. And all those Actions, concerning which the Law has determin'd nothing on either side, are call'd *allowable,* [indifferent] or *permitted.* Here we may observe, that in Civil Life, where it is impossible to come to perfect Exactness in all points, even †those things are said to be *allowable,* upon which the Law has not assign'd some *Punishment,* though they are in themselves repugnant to *Natural Honesty.* We call those Actions which are *consonant* to the Law *good,* and those that are *contrary* to it *bad:* But that any Action should be *good,* 'tis requisite, that it be exactly agreeable in every ‡point to the Law; whereas it may be *evil* if it be deficient in one Point only.

---

* See *Grotius de Jure Belli & Pacis, L.* 2. c. 20. *Sect.* 26, 27.

† See *Grotius de Jure Belli & Pacis, Lib. 3. cap. 4.* §2.

‡ The Points here spoken of mean the *Quality,* or the *Intention of the Agent; the Object, the End* pursued thereby, and other like Circumstances of the Action. Thus, though an Action may in every respect answer the Direction of the Law, it may be nevertheless charged on the Doer as a bad Action, especially in the Sight of God, not only when it was done upon an ill Principle with a vitious Intention, but also when it was done through Ignorance, or on some other Motive different from what the Law prescribes. I say it may be accounted a bad Action *in the Sight of God;* for the outward Obedience of the Laws sufficiently answering the Ends of Civil Society, which is the Aim only of Politick Legislators, they never concern themselves with the Intention of the Agent, whether it be just or unjust, provided the External Act has nothing in it but what is conformable to the Law. *See L. N. N. L.* I. *Cap.* VII. §3, 4 *and Lib.* I. *Cap.* VIII. §2, 3. [In borrowing Barbeyrac's note (XI.2, p. 36) the editors again make use of his softening of Pufendorf's strict separation of the civil and theological domains. In observing that not all natural law will be enacted as civil law, Pufendorf accepts that the civil law will permit actions contrary to morality. In keeping with his desire to maintain some continuity between civil and religious morality, however, Barbeyrac treats this state of affairs as lamentable, insisting that the perpetrators of such actions remain guilty in the sight of God. This is a central

As for *Justice,* it is sometimes the Attribute of *Actions,* sometimes of *Persons.* When it is attributed to *Persons,* 'tis usually defin'd to be, A constant and perpetual *Desire* of giving every one their own.[8] For he is called a *just* Man, who is delighted in doing righteous Things, who studies Justice, and in all his Actions endeavours to do that which is right. On the other side, the *unjust* Man is he that neglects the giving every Man his own, or, if he does, 'tis not because 'tis due, but from expectation of Advantage to himself. So that a *just Man* may sometimes do unjust Things, and an *unjust Man* that which is just. But the *Just* does that which is right, because he is so *commanded* by the Law; and never commits any unjust Acts but only through *Infirmity;* whereas the *wicked Man* does a just Thing for fear of the *Punishment* which is the Sanction of the Command, but such unjust Acts as he commits proceed from the *Naughtiness* of his *Heart.*

XII. Justice of Persons. L. N. N. l. 1. c. 7. §6.

But the *Justice of Actions* not only consists in their due Conformity to Law, but it includes in it likewise a right Application of them to those Persons to whom the Action is perform'd: So that we apprehend that *Action* to be *just,* which, with full Design and Intention, is apply'd to the Person to whom it is due. Herein therefore, the *Justice* of Actions differs from their *Goodness* chiefly, that the latter simply denotes an Agreement with the Law; whereas *Justice* also includes the Regard they have to those *Persons upon whom they are exercised. Upon which Account Justice is call'd a *Relative Virtue.*

XIII. Of Actions. L. N. N. l. 1. c. 7. §7.

---

theme of Barbeyrac's two discourses—the *Discourse on What Is Permitted by the Laws* and the *Discourse on the Benefits Conferred by the Laws*—which are reproduced in the appendix to this volume.]

8. Here Pufendorf invokes the standard Roman law formula, from the *Institutes of Justinian,* that *Justitia est constans et perpetua voluntas jus suum cuique tribuere.* Like Hobbes, Pufendorf restricts this concept to the civil state, for only under civil authority are men capable of adhering to contracts.

*Good Actions might have been more properly distinguished with respect to the three Objects they may have; which are, *G O D, our Neighbour,* and *our selves.* (see §13. of the following Chapter.) Such good Actions, as have G O D for their Object, are comprehended under the general Name of *P I E T Y.* Such good Actions as have for their Object *other Men,* are signify'd by the Name of *J U S T I C E.* And those

XIV. Division of Justice. L. N. N. l. 1. c. 7. §8.

Men do not generally agree about the Division of *Justice.* The most re-ceiv'd Distinction is, into *Universal* and *Particular.* The first is, when *every Duty* is practised and *all right* done to others, *even that which could not have been extorted by Force, or by the Rigor of Law. The latter is, when *that Justice* only is done a Man, which in his own right he could have *demanded;* and this is wont to be again divided into † *Dis-*

---

good Actions which have only a direct respect to *our selves,* may be contain'd in the Term *Moderation,* or *T E M P E R A N C E.* This Division of good Actions being the most Simple and Natural one, is also the most Ancient one. *See L. N. N. Lib.* II. *Cap.* III. §24. [Barbeyrac's note (XIII.1, p. 38) is a response to Pufendorf's discussion of justice as a relational virtue, which derives from Aristotle's *Nichomachean Ethics* (V. 4–5). Having already refused to accept that goodness can be equated with con-formity to the law, Barbeyrac now provides it with an independent foundation, in the relations to God, others, and myself. He thus seeks to outflank Pufendorf's civil ethics, where these relations are subordinated to natural law understood as the rules of sociability. For more on this, see Barbeyrac's two discourses in the appendix.]

*The Duties here meant, by *such as could not have been extorted by Force or Law,* are such as are not absolutely necessary for the Preservation of Mankind, and for the Support of Human Society in general, although they serve to embellish it, and ren-der it more commodious. Such are the Duties of *Compassion, Liberality, Beneficence, Gratitude, Hospitality,* and in one word all that is contain'd under that comprehen-sive Name of *Charity,* or *Humanity,* as it is oppos'd to rigorous *Justice* properly so call'd, the Duties of which, generally speaking, have their Foundation in Agreement. I say *generally speaking;* for tho' there be no Agreement made, we lie under an indis-pensible Obligation to do wrong to no one, to make good the Damage any one has sustain'd by us, to look upon each other as Equals by Nature, &c. But here we ought to observe, that in case of extream Necessity, the *Imperfect Right* that others have to these Duties of Charity from us, becomes a *Perfect Right;* so that Men may by force be obliged to the performance of these Duties at such a time, tho' on all other Oc-casions the Performance of them must be left to every Man's Conscience and Hon-our. *See L. N. N. lib.* 1. *cap.* 7. §7. *lib.* 3. *cap.* 4. §6. [In this note (XIV.1, p. 38), Barbeyrac seeks to soften Pufendorf's distinction between imperfect duties (duties of conscience incapable of being compelled as strict right) and perfect duties (com-pellable duties grounded in contract and positive law). He argues that some moral duties are also compellable, while others may become so under conditions of ex-tremity.]

† This Division is not compleat, because it comprehends no other Duties but what Men are oblig'd to the performance of towards others, by virtue of an Engage-ment enter'd into to that purpose; but there are Duties that our Neighbour may in strict justice demand at our hands, independently of all such Engagement or Agree-ment. *See the preceeding Note.* I should rather approve of Mr. *Buddeus's* Division of this *Particular,* or *Strict Justice* (*Elem. Pract. Phil. par.* II. *Cap.* II. §46) into Justice as

tributive and *Commutative.* The *Distributive* takes place in Contracts made between Partners in Fellowship, concerning fair Partition of Loss and Gain according to a rate. *The *Commutative* is mostly in Bargains made upon even hand about Things and Doings relating to Traffick and Dealing.

Knowing thus, what *Justice* is, 'tis easie to collect what is *Injustice.* Where it is to be observ'd, that such an unjust Action is call'd *Wrong-doing,* which is premeditately undertaken, and by which a Violence is done upon somewhat which of absolute Right was another Man's due, or, which by like Right he one way or other stood possess'd of. And this Wrong may be done after a threefold Manner: 1. If that be deny'd to another which in his own right he might demand (not accounting that which from Courtesie or the like Virtue may be another's due): Or, 2. If that be taken away from another, of which by the same right, then valid against the Invader, he was in full possession: Or, 3. If any Damage be done to another, which we had not Authority to do to him. Beside which, that a Man may be charged with *Injustice,* it is requisite that there be a naughty *Mind* and an evil *Design* in him that acts it. For if there be nothing of these in it, then 'tis only call'd *Misfortune,* or an *Error;* and that is so much slighter or more grievous, as the Sloth and Negligence which occasion'd it was greater or less.

XV. Injustice what. L. N. N. l. 1. c. 7. §14.

---

it is exercised between *Equals and Equals,* and as it is exercised between *Superiors and Inferiors.* The Former of these is subdivided into as many different Sorts as there are Duties, which one Man may demand in strictness the performance of from every other Man, consider'd as such, and one Citizen from every other Member of the same Body. The Latter of these comprehends as many different Sorts as there are kinds of Societies wherein some command and others obey. [As in the preceding note, in this one (XIV.2, p. 39) Barbeyrac attempts to forestall the clear tendency of Pufendorf's discussion, namely, the identification of strict or particular justice with positive law. As always, Barbeyrac wishes to subordinate the positive institutions of law and state to the higher moral necessities of conscience and universal justice, arguing that some moral rights might be claimed as a matter of justice.]

* See *Grotius de Jure Belli & Pacis, l.* 1. *c.* 1. §8.

XVI. Laws dis-
tinguisht. Nat-
ural and Posi-
tive L. N. N.
l. 1. c. 6. §18.
Laws, with respect to their Authors, are distinguished into *Divine* and *Humane; that* proceeds from *God,* and *this* from *Men.* But if Laws be considered, as they have a necessary and universal Congruity with Mankind, they are then distinguisht into *Natural* and *Positive.* *Natural Law is that which is so agreeable with the* rational *and* sociable *Nature of Man, that* honest *and* peaceable Society *could not be kept up amongst Mankind without it,* Hence it is, that *this* may be sought out, and the knowledge of it acquired by the light of that *Reason,* which is born with every Man, and by a consideration of *Human Nature* in general. *Positive Law* is *that which takes not its rise from the common condition of* Human Nature, *but only from the good pleasure of the* Legislator: This likewise ought to have its Foundation in *Reason,* and its End ought to be some *Advantage* to those Men, or that Society, for which it is designed. Now the Law *Divine,* is either *Natural* or *Positive;* but all *Human Laws,* strictly taken, are *Positive.*

⟡ CHAPTER III ⟡

Of the Law of Nature in general

I. Law Natural
obvious.
L. N. N. l. 2.
c. 3.
That Man, who has thoroughly examined the *Nature* and *Disposition* of Mankind, may plainly understand what the *Law Natural* is, the *Necessity* thereof, and which are the *Precepts* it proposes and enjoyns to Mankind. For, as it much conduces to him who would know exactly the *Polity* of any *Community,* that he first well understand the *Condition* thereof, and the *Manners* and *Humours* of the Members who constitute it: So to him who has well studied the common *Nature* and *Condition* of *Man,* it will be easie to discover those *Laws* which are necessary for the Safety and common Benefit of Mankind.

---

*See *Grotius de Jure Belli & Pacis, Lib.* I. *Cap.* i. §10.

This then Man has in common with all the *Animals,* who have a Sense of their own Beings; that he accounts nothing dearer than *Himself;* that he studies all manner of ways *his own Preservation;* and that he endeavours to *procure* to himself such things as seem *good* for him, and to *avoid* and *keep off* those that are *mischievous.* And this Desire of *Self-Preservation* regularly is so strong, that all our other *Appetites and Passions* give way to it. So that whensoever an *Attempt* is made upon the Life of any man, though he escape the danger threatned, yet he usually resents it so, as to retain a *Hatred* still, and a desire of *Revenge* on the Aggressor.

(margin: II. Self Preservation.)

But in one particular, *Man* seems to be set in a *worse* condition than that of *Brutes,* that hardly any other Animal comes into the world in so great *weakness;* so that 'twould be a kind of Miracle, if any man should arrive at a mature Age, without the *aid* of some body *else.* For even now, after so many helps found out for the *Necessities* of *Human Life;* yet a many Years *careful Study* is required before a Man shall be able of himself to get *Food* and *Raiment.* *Let us suppose a Man come to his full Strength without any *oversight* or *instruction* from *other* Men; suppose him to have no manner of *Knowledge* but what springs of it self from his *own natural Wit;* and thus to be placed in some *Solitude,* destitute of any *Help* or *Society* of all Mankind beside. Certainly a more miserable Creature cannot be imagined. He is no better than *dumb, naked,* and has nothing left him but *Herbs* and *Roots* to pluck, and the *wild Fruits* to gather; to quench his thirst at the next *Spring, River,* or *Ditch;* and to shelter himself from the Injuries of the Weather, by creeping into some *Cave,* or covering himself after any sort with *Moss* or *Grass;* to pass away his tedious life in *Idleness;* to start at every Noise, and be afraid at the sight of any *other* Animal; in a Word, at last to perish either by *Hunger,* or *Cold,* or some wild *Beast.* It must then follow, that whatsoever Ad-

(margin: III. Society absolutely necessary. L. N. N. l. 2. c. 1. §8.)

---

* *L. N. N. l.* II. *c.* 1. §8. *c.* 2. §2. *Dissert. Acad. ult. p.* 458. *Eris. Scandic. in Apol. p.* 20. *seq Specim. Controv. c.* 3. *p.* 217. *c.* 4. §161. *p.* 258. *Spicileg. Controv. c.* 3. §1. *p.* 379. *Jul. Rondin. Dissert. Epist.* §1. *seq. p.* 396, *Comment. super invenusto Ven. Lipsiens. pull. p.* 11, 16, 36, 44, 46, 52, 54.

vantages accompany Human Life, are all owing to that *mutual Help* Men afford one another. So that, next to *Divine Providence,* there is nothing in the world more *beneficial* to Mankind than *Men themselves.*

IV. Men to
Men inclinable
to do hurt.
L. N. N. l. 2.
c. 1. §6. l. 7.
c. 1. §4. And yet, as *useful* as this Creature is, or may be, to others of its kind, it has many Faults, and is capable of being *equally noxious;* which renders mutual Society between Man and Man not a little dangerous, and makes *great Caution* necessary to be used therein, lest *Mischief* accrue from it instead of *Good.* In the first place, a stronger *Proclivity* to injure another is observ'd to be generally in *Man,* than in any of the *Brutes;* for they seldom grow outragious, but through *Hunger* or *Lust,* both which Appetites are satisfi'd without much Pains; and that done, they are not apt to grow furious, or to hurt their Fellow-Creatures, without some *Provocation.* Whereas Man is an Animal always *prone* to *Lust,* by which he is much more frequently instigated, than seems to be necessary to the Conservation of his Kind. His *Stomach* also is not only to be *satisfied,* but to be *pleased;* and it often desires more than Nature can well digest. As for *Raiment,* Nature has taken Care of the *rest* of the Creatures that they don't *want* any: But *Men* require not only such as will answer their *Necessity,* but their *Pride* and *Ostentation.* Beside these, there are many *Passions* and *Appetites* unknown to the *Brutes,* which are yet to be found in *Mankind;* as, an unreasonable *Desire* of possessing much *more* than is *necessary,* an earnest pursuit after *Glory* and *Pre-eminence; Envy, Emulation,* and *Outvyings* of Wit. A Proof hereof is, that most of the Wars with which *Mankind* is harrass'd, are rais'd for Causes altogether unknown to the *Brutes.* Now all these are able to provoke *Men* to hurt one another, and they frequently do so. Hereto may be added the great *Arrogance* that is in many Men, and *Desire* of *insulting* over others, which cannot but exasperate even those who are naturally meek enough; and from a Care of preserving themselves and their Liberty, excite them to make Resistance. Sometimes also *Want* sets Men together by the Ears,[9] or because that Store of Necessaries which they have at *present* seems not *sufficient* for their *Needs* or *Appetites.*

9. I.e., sets them to harm each other.

Moreover, Men are more *able* to do one another Harm than *Brutes* are. For tho' they don't look formidable with *Teeth, Claws,* or *Horns,* as many of *them* do; yet the *Activity* of their *Hands* renders them very effectual Instruments of Mischief; and then the Quickness of their *Wit* gives them *Craft,* and a Capacity of attempting that by Treachery which cannot be done by open Force. So that 'tis very *easie* for one Man to bring upon another the *greatest* of all *Natural Evils,* to wit, *Death* itself.

V. And very capable of it.

Beside all this, it is to be consider'd, that among *Men* there is a vast *Diversity* of *Dispositions,* which is not to be found among *Brutes;* for among Brutes, all of the same Kind have the *like Inclinations,* and are led by the *same* inward *Motions* and *Appetites:* Whereas among *Men,* there are so many *Minds* as there are *Heads,* and every one has his *singular* Opinion; nor are they all acted with *simple* and *uniform* Desires, but with such as are *manifold* and *variously mixt* together. Nay, *one* and the *same* Man shall be often seen to *differ* from *himself,* and to *desire* that at *one* Time which at *another* he extremely *abhorred.* Nor is the Variety less discernable, which is now to be found in the almost *infinite Ways* of living, of directing our Studies, or Course of Life, and our Methods of making use of our Wits. Now, that by Occasion hereof Men may not dash against one another, there is need of wise *Limitations* and careful *Management.*

VI. And likely so to do. L. N. N. l. 2. c. 1. §7.

So then Man is an Animal very desirous of his own *Preservation;* of *himself* liable to many *Wants; unable* to Support himself without the Help of *other* of his Kind; and yet wonderfully fit in *Society* to promote a *common Good:* But then he is *malicious, insolent,* and easily *provok'd,* and not less *prone* to do Mischief to his Fellow than he is *capable* of effecting it. Whence this must be inferr'd, that in order to his Preservation, 'tis absolutely necessary, that he be *sociable,*[10] that is, that he *join* with those

VII. The Sum of the foregoing Paragraphs.

10. In treating it not as man's natural condition or destiny, but as something for which he must strive against his own propensity for mutual harm, Pufendorf's conception of sociability differs from the Aristotelian-scholastic conception, and also from Grotius's. Natural law for Pufendorf is thus not the law realizing man's essentially sociable nature, or *telos,* but consists of the rules through which man imposes sociability on himself, as the comportment needed for security.

of his Kind, and that he so *behave* himself towards them, that they may have no justifiable Cause to do him *Harm,* but rather to *promote* and *secure* to him all his Interests.

VIII. Law Nat-
ural defin'd.

The Rules then of this Fellowship, which are the Laws of *Human Society,* whereby Men are directed how to render themselves useful Members thereof, and without which it falls to pieces, are called the *Laws of Nature.*

IX. The Means
design'd where
the End is so.
L. N. N. l. 2.
c. 3. §15.

From What has been said, it appears, that this is a[11] *fundamental Law of Nature,* That EVERY MAN OUGHT, AS MUCH AS IN HIM LIES, TO PRESERVE AND PROMOTE SOCIETY: That is, the *Welfare of Mankind.* *And since he that designs the *End,* cannot but be supposed to design those *Means* without which the *End* cannot be obtain'd, it follows that all such Actions as tend generally and are absolutely necessary to the Preservation of this *Society,* are *commanded* by the *Law of Nature;* as, on the contrary, those that disturb and dissolve it are forbidden by the same. All other Precepts are to be accounted only *Subsumptions,* or *Consequences* upon this Universal Law, the Evidence whereof is made out by that Natural Light which is engrafted in Mankind.

X. A God and
Providence.
L. N. N. l. 2.
c. 3. §19.

Now though these *Rules* do plainly contain in themselves that which is for the general *Good;* yet that the same may obtain the Force of *Laws,* it must necessarily be presuppos'd, that there is a GOD, who governs all Things by his Providence, and that He has enjoyn'd us Mortals, to observe these *Dictates* of our Reason as *Laws,* promulged by him to us by the powerful Mediation of that Light which is born with us. Otherwise we might perhaps pay some obedience to them in contemplation of their *Utility,* so as we observe the Directions of Physicians in regard to

---

11. Should be "the" fundamental law of nature.

* See *Grotius de Jure Belli & Pacis in Prolegomenis passim. L. N. N. l. 2. c. 3. §14. seq. Element. Jurispr. universal. l. 2. observ 14. Eris. Scandic. Apol. p. 46, 75. Specim. Controvers. c. 4. p. 231. sequ. Spicileg. Jur. Nat. c. 1. §14. p. 348. seq. c. 2. §8. p. 366. c. 3. §13. p. 389. seq. Venet. Lipsiens. pull. p. 11. & passim.*

our Health, *but not as *Laws,* to the Constitution of which a *Superior* is necessary to be supposed, and *that* such a one as has actually undertaken the Government of the other.[12]

But, that God is the Author of the *Law of Nature,* is thus demonstrated[13] (considering Mankind only in its *present* State, without enquiring whether the *first* Condition of us Mortals was *different* from this, nor *how* the Change was wrought.) Whereas our Nature is so framed, that Mankind cannot be preserv'd without a *sociable Life,* and whereas it is plain that the *Mind of Man* is capable of all those Notions which are *subservient* to this purpose; and it is also manifest, that Men not only, like the other Creatures, owe their *Original* to God, but that He *governs* them, (let their Condition be as it will) by the Wisdom of his *Providence.* Hence it follows, that it must be supposed to be the *Will of God,* that Man should make use of those Faculties with which he is peculiarly endow'd beyond the Brutes, to the *Preservation* of his own Nature: and consequently, that the Life of Man should be different from the lawless Life of the *Irrational Creatures.* And since this cannot otherwise be atchiev'd, but by an Observance of the *Law Natural,* it must be understood, that there is from God an obligation laid upon Man to pay Obedience hereto, as a Means not *invented* by the Wit, or *imposed* by the Will of Men, nor capable of being *changed* by their Humours and Inclinations; but *expressly* ordain'd by God himself in order to the *accomplishing* this End. For he that obliges us to pursue such an *End,* must be thought to oblige us to make use of those *Means* which

XI. God the Author of the Law of Nature. L. N. N. l. 2. c. 3. §20.

---

* *Grotius de Jure Belli & Pacis, Lib.* i. *Cap.* i. §io.

12. Pufendorf thus invokes God after the fact, in order to provide the rules of sociability with the obligatory force of law. Yet he simultaneously denies that God directly enforces natural law commands, thereby calling their obligatoriness into question. This is the gap that will be filled by the civil sovereign, whose role is to transform natural law into enforceable civil law.

13. The ensuing treatment of God as the author of natural law is limited and indirect in comparison with scholastic accounts. For Pufendorf, man comes to understand natural law as commanded by God not by recovering a transcendent reason he shares with God, but by observing what it takes to preserve a creature whose existence must be regarded as willed by its creator.

are necessary to the attainment thereof. And that the *Social Life* is positively enjoyn'd by God upon *Men,* this is a Proof, that in no other *Animal* is to be found any Sense of *Religion* or Fear of a *Deity,* which seems not so much as to fall within the Understanding of the ungovernable Brute; and yet it has the power to excite in the minds of *Men,* not altogether profligate, the tenderest Sense; by which they are convinced, that by sinning against this *Law Natural,* they offend him who is Lord of the Soul of Man, and who is to be fear'd, even where we are secure of any Punishment from our Fellow-Creatures.

XII. This Law how written in Man's Heart. Though it be usually said, that we have the Knowledge of this Law from *Nature* it self, yet this is not so to be taken, as if there were implanted in the Minds of Men just *new born,* plain and distinct Notions concerning what is to be *done* or *avoided.* But Nature is said thus to teach us, *partly because the Knowledge of this Law may be attain'd by the help of the *Light* of *Reason;* and partly because the general and most useful Points thereof are so *plain* and *clear,* that they at first sight force the Assent, and get such root in the minds of Men, that nothing can eradicate them afterwards; let wicked Men take never so much pains to blunt the edge and stupifie themselves against the Stings of their *Consciences.* And in this Sense we find in Holy Scripture, that this Law is **Rom. ii. 15.** said to be *written in the hearts of Men.* So that having from our Childhood had a Sense hereof instill'd into us, together with other Learning in the usual Methods of Education, and yet not being able to remember the *punctual time* when first they took hold of our Understanding and possess'd our Minds; we can have no other opinion of our knowledge of this Law; but that it was *connate* to our Beings, or born *together* and at the *same time* with our selves. The Case being the same with every Man in learning his *Mother Tongue.*

* *L. N. N. lib* 2. *c.* 3. §13. *seq. Eris. Scandic. Apol.* §24 *p.* 40. *Epist. ad Amicos.*

Those *Duties,* which from the Law of Nature are incumbent upon Man, seem most aptly to be *divided* according to the *Objects* about which they are conversant. With regard to which they are ranged under three principal Heads; the *first* of which gives us Directions how by the single Dictates of right Reason Man ought to behave himself towards *God;* the *second* contains our Duty towards *our selves;* and the *third* that towards *other Men.* But though those Precepts of the Law Natural, which have a relation to *other Men,* may primarily and directly be derived from that *Sociality,* which we have laid down as a Foundation; yet even the Duties also of Man towards *God* may be *indirectly deduc'd from thence, upon this Account, that the strongest Obligation to mutual Duties between Man and Man arises from *Religion* and a Fear of the *Deity;* so as that Man could not become a *sociable* Creature if he were not imbu'd with *Religion;* and because *Reason* alone can go no farther in *Religion* than as it is useful to promote the common Tranquillity and Sociality or reciprocal Union in this Life: For so far forth as Reli-

*But these Duties, as well as those which regard our selves, have another more immediate and direct Foundation, which makes part of the general Principles of the Law of Nature. For it is not necessary that all those Duties, the Necessity and Reasonableness of which may be collected from the Light of Reason only, should be deduced from this one Fundamental Maxim. It may more justly be said, that there are three grand Principles of Natural Right, that is, *RELIGION,* which comprehends all the Duties of Man towards God; the *LOVE OF OUR SELVES,* which contains all those Duties which we are bound to do, with respect only and directly to our selves; and *SOCIABILITY,* from whence results all that is due from us to our Neighbour. These are fruitful Principles, which, tho' they have a great Affinity and Respect to each other, are yet very different at the bottom, and ought wisely to be considered and regarded, so that an equal and just Balance may, as much as possible, be preserv'd between them. See *L. N. N. lib. 2. cap. 3. §15.* [In selecting this note (Barbeyrac's XIII.1, p. 53) the editors import one of Barbeyrac's central disagreements with Pufendorf. Pufendorf conceives of natural religion—that is, of the duties to God known through reason alone—as a subordinate part of natural law. He thus derives its duties from the requirements of sociability and denies it any role in salvation, which is to be pursued through faith in revealed religion. Barbeyrac rejects this civil subordination of natural religion, insisting that duties to God (and to one's neighbor and oneself) should be treated as an independent principle of natural law alongside the principle of sociability. Once again, the editors use Barbeyrac to soften or evade Pufendorf's secularization of civil ethics.]

gion procures the Salvation of Souls, it proceeds from peculiar Divine
Revelation. But the Duties a man owes to *Himself* arise jointly from
Religion, and from the Necessity of *Society.* So that no Man is so Lord
of himself, but that there are many things relating to *himself,* which are
not to be disposed altogether according to his Will; partly because of
the Obligation he lies under of being a religious Adorer of the *Deity,*
and partly that he may keep himself an useful and beneficial Member
of *Society.*

ʊʊ C H A P T E R I V ʊʊ

Of the Duty of Man towards God,
or, concerning Natural Religion

I. Natural Re-
ligion, its
Parts.

The Duty of Man towards GOD, so far as can be discover'd by Natural
Reason, is comprehended in these two; that we have *true* Notions concerning him, or *know* him aright; and then that we conform all our Actions to his Will, or *obey* him as we ought. And hence Natural Religion
consists of two sorts of Propositions, to wit, * *Theoretical* or Speculative,
and *Practical* or Active.

II. That God
is. L. N. N.
l. 2. c. 4. §3.

Amongst those *Notions* that every Man ought to have of GOD, the *first*
of all is, that he firmly believe his *Existence,* that is, that there *is* indeed
some *supreme* and *first Being,* upon whom this Universe depends. And
this has been most plainly demonstrated by learned and wise Men from
the *Subordination* of *Causes* to one another, which must at last be found
to have their Original in somewhat that was before them all; from the

---

* See Mons. *Le Clerc's Pneumatologia,* §3. and Mons. *Budaeus's* Discourse, *de Pie-
tate Philosophica,* being the fourth Discourse in his *Selecta Jura Naturae & Gentium.*
[Barbeyrac's note (I.1, p. 54), where he indicates that these texts should be consulted
for "all of this."]

necessity of having a *first Mover;* from the Consideration of this great *Machin,* the World, and from the like Arguments.[14] Which if any Man denies himself to be able to *comprehend,* he is not therefore to be excus'd for his Atheism. For all Mankind having been perpetually, as it were, possest of this Persuasion, that Man who undertakes to oppose it, ought not only solidly to *confute* all those Arguments that are brought to *prove* a God, but should advance *Reasons* for his own Assertion, which may be *more plausible* than those. And since by this Belief of the *Deity* the Weal of Mankind may be supposed to have been *hitherto* preserv'd, he ought to shew that Atheism would *better* answer that End than sober Religion and the Worship of God. Now seeing this can by no means be done, the Wickedness of those Men who attempt any way to eradicate this Persuasion out of the Minds of Men, is to be above all things abominated, and restrain'd by the severest Punishments.

The Second is, that *God is the Creator of this Universe.* For it being manifest from Reason, that none of these Things could exist of *themselves,* it is absolutely necessary that they should have some supreme *Cause;* which *Cause* is the very same that we call GOD,

III. God the Creator of the World.
L. N. N. l. 3. c. 4. §4.

And hence it follows, that those Men are cheated, who every now and then are putting upon us **Nature,** forsooth, as the original Cause of all Things and Effects. For, if by that Word they mean that *Energy* and *Power of Acting* which we find in every Thing, this is so far from being of any force to prove there is *no God,* that it proves him to be the *Author* of *Nature it self.* But if by *Nature* they would have us understand the *Supreme Cause* of all Things, this is only out of a profane Nicety to avoid the receiv'd and plain Appellation of GOD.

Those also are in a great Error, who believe that any thing can be GOD, which is the Object of our *Senses,* and particularly the *Stars,*

14. The prime-mover argument—that, considering the whole chain of causes and effects, there must be a first cause—was a standard nonrevealed demonstration of God's existence, hence compatible with a natural law known through the light of reason alone.

among the rest. For the *Substance* of these argues them all to derive their Beings from somewhat else, and not to be the *first* Things in Nature.

Nor do they think less unworthily of *God,* who call him the **Soul of the World.* For the Soul of the World, let them conceive of it as they please, must signifie a *Part* of the World; and how can a *Part* of a Thing be the *Cause* of it, that is, be something *before* it self? But if by the *Soul* of the World, they mean that *first* and *invisible Being,* from which all Things receive their Vigour, Life, and Motion, they only obtrude upon us an *obscure* and *figurative* Expression for one that is *plain* and *obvious.* From hence also it appears, that the *World* did not exist from *all Eternity;* this being contrary to the Nature of that which has a *Cause.* And he that asserts, that the *World is Eternal,* denies that it had any *Cause* of its being, and consequently denies *God* himself.

IV. God governs the World.

The Third is, that GOD *governs the whole World,* and particularly *Mankind;* which plainly appears from the admirable and constant *Order* which is to be seen in this Universe; and 'tis to the same *moral* Purpose whether a Man deny that GOD *is,* or that he *rules* and *regards the Affairs of Men;* since either of them destroy all Manner of Religion. For let him be never so *excellent* in himself, 'tis in vain to fear or worship him, if he be altogether regardless of us, and neither *will* nor *can* do us either Good or Hurt.

V. God infinitely perfect.

The Fourth is, that *no Attribute can belong to God, which implies any manner of Imperfection.* For it would be absurd, (He being the *Cause* and *Source* of all Things) for any Creature of his to think it self able to form a notion of any *Perfection,* of which he is not fully possest. Nay, His *Perfection* infinitely surmounting the Capacity of so mean a Creature, it is most reasonable to express the same in *negative* rather than in *positive* Terms. Hence nothing is to be attributed to God that is *finite*

---

*See the Continuation of *various Thoughts about Comets, &c.* by Mr. *Bayle.* [(Barbeyrac's note III.1, p. 57.) Like Bayle, Pufendorf was opposed to Stoic and Deistic treatments of God, in the pantheistic manner, as the world's animating principle. This formed part of Pufendorf's rejection of natural theologies purporting to offer metaphysical insight into God's nature.]

or *determinate;* because what is *finite* has always somewhat that is *greater* than it self: And whatsoever is *determinate,* or subject to *Figure* and *Form,* must suppose *Bounds* and *Circumscription:* Neither can He be said to be *distinctly* and *fully comprehended* or conceiv'd in our Imagination, or by any Faculty of our Souls; because whatsoever we can comprehend fully and distinctly in our Minds, must be *Finite.* And yet, when we pronounce God to be *Infinite,* we are not to think we have a full *Notion* of Him; for by the word *Infinite* we denote nothing in the Thing it self; but only declare the Impotence of our Understandings, and we do, as it were, say, that we are not able to comprehend the Greatness of his Essence. Hence also it is, that we cannot rightly say of God that he has any *Parts,* as neither that *He* is *All* any thing; for these are Attributes of things *finite;* nor that he is contain'd in any *Place,* for that denotes Limits and Bounds; nor that He *moves* or *rests,* for both those suppose Him to be in a place: So neither can any thing be properly attributed to God which intimates *Grief,* or any *Passion,* such as *Anger, Repentance, Mercy.* I say *properly;* because when the inspir'd Writers sometimes use such Expressions, speaking of the Almighty, they are not to be understood in a proper Sense, but as accommodating their Language to the common Apprehensions and Capacities of Men; so that we are not to understand hereby that GOD receives the same Impressions from external Objects that Man receives, but only by way of similitude, as to the *Event* or *Effect;* thus God is said to be angry with, and to be offended at Sinners, not that such Passions or Affections can possibly be in the Divine Nature, but because he will not suffer those who break his Laws to go unpunish'd. Nor may we say of Him ought that denotes the *Want* or Absence of any Good, as *Appetite, Hope, Concupiscence, Desire* of any thing; for these imply *Indigence* and consequently *Imperfection;* it not being supposable that one should desire, hope, or crave any thing of which he does not stand in some need. And so when *Understanding, Will, Knowledge,* and acts of the Senses, *Seeing, Hearing, &c.* are attributed to God, they are to be taken in a much more sublime Sense, than we conceive them in our selves. For the Will in us is a *rational Desire;* but *Desire,* as it is said afore, presupposes the *Want* or *Absence* of something that is agreeable and necessary. And *Under-*

standing and *Sense* imply some Operation upon the Faculties of Man, wrought by exterior Objects upon the Organs of his Body and the Powers of his Soul; which being Signs of a Power *depending* upon some other Thing, demonstrate it not to be *most perfect.*

God but One. Lastly, it is utterly repugnant to the Divine Perfection to say there are *more Gods* than *one;* for, beside that the admirable Harmony of the World argues it to have but *one* Governour, GOD would not be *infinite,* if there were more Gods of equal Power with himself, and not depending upon Him; for it involves a Contradiction to say, There are *many Infinites.* Upon the whole then, 'tis most agreeable to Reason, when we attempt to express the *Attributes* of God, either to make use of Words of a *Negative* signification, as Infinite, Incomprehensible, Immense, Eternal, *i.e.* which had no Beginning nor shall have End; or *Superlative,* as most Excellent, most Powerful, most Mighty, most Wise, &c. or *Indefinite,* as Good, Just, Creator, King, Lord, &c. and this in such a Sense as we would not think our selves to express *What* he is, but only in some sort to declare our *Admiration* of Him, and profess our *Obedience* to Him; which is a token of an humble Soul, and of a Mind paying all the Veneration it is capable of.[15]

VI. Internal Worship of God. The Propositions of *Practical* Natural Religion are partly such as concern the *Internal,* and partly the *External Worship of God.* The *Internal* Worship of God consists in *honouring* Him. Now *Honour* is a high Opinion of another's *Power* conjoyn'd with *Goodness:* And the Mind of Man is obliged, from a Consideration of this his Power and Goodness, to fill it self with all that Reverence towards him, of which its Nature is susceptible. Hence it is, that it is our Duty to *love* him, as the Author and Bestower of all Manner of Good; to *hope* in him, as from whom only all our Happiness for the future does depend; to *acquiesce* in his

---

15. This sentence summarizes Pufendorf's almost entirely negative view of metaphysics and speculative (natural) theology. God is not an object of knowledge and understanding but of faith and will. Leibniz's metaphysical counterattack is presented, and criticized in turn, in Barbeyrac's *Judgment of an Anonymous Writer* in the appendix.

Will, he doing all things for the best, and giving us what is most expedient for us; to *fear* him, as being most powerful, and the offending whom renders us liable to the greatest Evil; Lastly, in all things most humbly to *obey* him, as our Creator, our Lord, and our best and greatest Ruler.

The *External Worship* of God is chiefly shewn in these Instances:

VII. External Worship of God.

1. WE must *render Thanks to God for all* those manifold *Blessings* he has so bountifully bestow'd upon us.

2. WE must conform, as far as we possibly can, all our Actions to his Will; that is, we must *obey all his Commands.*

3. WE must *Admire and Adore his infinite Greatness.*

4. WE must *Offer up to him our Prayers and Supplications,* to obtain from him those Benefits we stand in need of, and to be delivered from those Evils we are in fear of. Indeed our Prayers are Proofs of our *Trust* and *Hope* in Him, and our Hope is a plain Acknowledgment of the Power and Goodness of him in whom it is placed.

5. WHEN we find it necessary to take an Oath, we must *swear by no other Name than the Name of God;* and then we must *most religiously observe what we have engaged our selves to in calling GOD to witness;* and this we are indispensably obliged to, from the Consideration of God's infinite Knowledge and his Almighty Power.

6. WE must *never speak of GOD but with the highest Respect and utmost Reverence.* Such a Behaviour is a Proof of our Fear of GOD; and Fear is an Acknowledgment of his Power over us, whom we dread. Hence then it follows, that *the Holy Name of GOD is not to be mention'd in our Discourse upon unnecessary and trifling Occasions,* since this would be great Disrespect; That *we ought not to swear at all but upon great and solemn Occasions;* for calling GOD to witness upon Matters of small Weight and Moment, is a great Abuse of his Holy Name. That *we engage not our selves in overnice and curious Enquiries and Disputes about the Nature of GOD, and the Methods of his Providence:* This would be to magnify and exalt our own Capacities, and vainly to imagine, that the unsearchable Nature and Providence of GOD could be comprehended within the narrow Limits of our shallow Reason.

7. *Whatsoever is done for the Sake of GOD, or in Obedience to his Will,*

ought to be the most excellent in its Kind, and done after such a Manner, and with such Circumstances, as are most proper to express the profound Honour and Veneration we have for Him.

8. WE must *serve and worship him, not only in private, but also in publick, in the sight of Men;* for to do any thing in secret only, seems to hint as if we were ashamed to act it openly; but Worship *publickly* paid, not only gives Testimony of our own Devotion, but excites others by our Example to do the like.

9. AND Lastly, We are to use our utmost Endeavour to *observe the Laws of Nature;* for as it is the greatest Affront to slight the Commands of God, so, on the contrary, Obedience to his Laws is more acceptable than any Sacrifice; and we have proved, that the *Law of Nature* is the *Law of God.*

VIII. Eternal Salvation not acquired by Natural Religion alone.[16]

And yet, after all, it must be confest, that the Effects of this *Natural Religion,* nicely consider'd, and with regard to the *present State of Mankind,* are concluded within the Prospect of *this* Life; but that it is of no Avail towards procuring *eternal Salvation.*[17] For *Human Reason,* left alone to it self, knows not that the *Pravity,* which is so discernable in our Faculties and Inclinations, proceeded from Man's *own Fault,* and that, hereby he becomes obnoxious to the *Wrath* of God, and to *eternal Damnation:* So that with the Guidance of *this* only, we are altogether ignorant of the Necessity of a *Saviour,* and of his *Office* and *Merit;* as well as of the *Promises* made by God to Mankind, and of the several *other* Matters thereupon depending, by which alone, it is plain from the holy Scriptures, that everlasting Salvation is procured to mortal Men.

16. Tooke's subheading is quite contrary to the spirit of this section, in which Pufendorf states that eternal salvation is not acquired by natural religion *at all.*

17. Pufendorf's denial that natural religion has any role to play in salvation—his insistence that the whole soteriological drama of sin, justification, and redemption is inaccessible to natural reason—demonstrates the non-transcendental, wholly civil character of his natural religion.

It may be worth the while, yet a little more distinctly to consider the Benefits which through *Religion* accrue to Mankind; from whence it may appear, that **It is in truth the utmost and firmest Bond of Human Society.*[18] For in the Natural Liberty, if you take away the *Fear* of a *Divine Power,* any Man who shall have confidence in his own *Strength,* may do what Violences he pleases to others who are weaker than himself, and will account *Honesty, Modesty,* and *Truth* but as empty Words; nor will he be persuaded to do that which is right by any Arguments, but from a Sense of his own *Inability* to act the contrary. Moreover, lay aside *Religion,* and the *Internal Bonds* of Communities will be always slack and feeble; the Fear of a temporal *Punishment,* the *Allegiance* sworn to Superiours, and the *Honour* of observing the same, together with a *grateful Consideration* that by the Favour of the supreme Government they are defended from the Miseries attending a *State of Nature;* all these, I say, will be utterly insufficient to contain unruly Men within the Bounds of their Duty. For in this case that Saying would indeed have place, † *He that values not Death, can never be compell'd;* because to those who fear not *God* nothing can be more formidable than *Death.* He that can once bring himself to despise *this,* may attempt what he pleases upon those that are set over him; and to tempt him so to do, he can hardly want some *Cause* or *Pretence;* as, either to free himself of the Uneasiness he seems to lie under by being subject to another's Command, or that himself may enjoy those Advantages which

IX. Religion the firmest Bond of Society.

---

* *L. N. N. lib.* 7. *cap.* 4. §8. *Eris. Scand* §6. *p.* 7. *Epist. ad Schetzer, p.* 84. *Append. p.* 108. *seq. Spicileg. Controv.* §16. *p.* 350. *Exam. Doctrin.* §2. *quaest.* 316. *Discuss. Calumn. Beckmann. p.* 169.

18. The theme of religion as the cement of society (*societatis vinculum*) was a standard one capable of several constructions. Unlike the scholastics (and Barbeyrac to a degree), Pufendorf refused to derive human society from man's community with God, deriving it instead from the need for peace and the cultivation of sociability. In what follows, Pufendorf thus treats conscience and the fear of God not as the foundation of natural law, but as a psychological factor useful for securing adherence to it.

† ———. *Cogi qui potest, nescit mori.*   Seneca Hercul. fur. ver. 425.
                                                          [Barbeyrac's note 2, p. 68.]

belong to him that possesses the Government; especially when he may easily persuade himself, that his Enterprise is just, either because He that at present sits at the Helm of Government is guilty of Mal-Administration, or that himself thinks he could manage it by many degrees to better purpose. An *Occasion* too cannot long be wanting for such Attempts, either from the Prince's Want of Circumspection in the care of his Person, (and indeed in such a State of Things *who shall guard even the Guards themselves?) or from a powerful Conspiracy, or, in time of foreign War, from a Defection to the Enemy. Beside *private* Men would be very prone to wrong one another; for the Proceedings in *human Courts* of Judicature being govern'd by *Proofs* of Matter of Fact, all those *Wickednesses* and *Villanies* which could be *secretly* acted and without Witnesses, if any thing were to be gain'd by them, would be accounted *Dexterities of Wit*, in the practice of which a Man might enjoy some Self-satisfaction. Again, no Man would be found that would do Works of *Charity* or of *Friendship*, except with probable Expectation of Glory or Profit. From whence it would follow, that, supposing no Punishment from above, one Man not being able to place any solid Confidence in the Troth of another, they must every one always live anxiously in a mutual *Fear* and *Jealousy*, lest they be cheated or harm'd each by his Neighbour. The *Governours* also would have as little Inclination, as the *Governed*, to Actions that are *brave* and *honourable*; for those that govern not being obliged by any Tie of Conscience, would put all Offices, and even Justice itself to sale; and in every thing seek their own *private Profit* by the Oppression of their Subjects; from whom they being always fearful of a *Rebellion*, they must needs know, there can be no surer Means to preserve themselves, than by rendring them as *heartless* and as *weak* as possible. The *Subjects* also, on the other side, standing in fear of the Violences of their Rulers, would always be seeking Opportunities to *rebel*, tho' at the same time they must be mutually distrustful and fearful of each other. The same would be the Case

---

*———. *Pone seram, cohibe, sed quis custodiet ipsos Custodes?*

Juv. Sat. VI. ver. 346, 347.
[Barbeyrac's note 3, p. 68.]

of *married Persons;* upon any slight Quarrel, they would be suspicious lest one should make away the other by Poison or some such *clandestine* Way; and the whole Family would be liable to the like Danger. For it being plain, that without *Religion* there could be no *Conscience;* it would not be easy to discover such *secret Villanies;* they being such as mostly are brought to light by the incessant pricking of the *Conscience,* and *internal Horrors* breaking forth into outward Indications. From all which it appears, how much it is the Interest of Mankind, that all Means be used to check the spreading of *Atheism* in the World; and with what *vain Folly* those Men are possess'd, who think to get the Reputation of being notable *Politicians,* by being seemingly inclin'd to *Looseness* and *Irreligion.*

~ CHAPTER V ~

Of the Duty of a Man towards Himself [19]

Although the *Love of himself* be so deeply fix'd in the Mind of Man, as to put him always under a Sollicitous Care of Himself, and upon Endeavours by all means to procure his own Advantage; so as, upon Consideration *hereof,* 'twould seem superfluous to find out *Laws* to oblige

I. Man liable to Obligation to Himself.

19. Despite the English editors' publicity claim to have made many useful additions to Pufendorf's text, the only substantial ones are to be found in this chapter. The added material begins with the second paragraph of section II and continues through sections III–IX, which consist of material on the care of the self taken from Pufendorf's *Law of Nature and Nations,* II.iv. The ultimate source of this reconstruction is Immanuel Weber, who claims to have introduced the interpolations with Pufendorf's approval, when undertaking the first German translation in 1691. Tooke's translation, which appeared in the same year, did not borrow them. Barbeyrac's first French edition of 1707 did, however, and it is from here that the editors of the 1716/35 English edition borrowed their reconstruction. Thus their wording of the added paragraphs is clearly an English translation of Barbeyrac's French.

him to the same: *yet in *other* Respects it is necessary, that he be bound
to the Observation of some certain *Rules* touching *Himself.* For, not being born for himself alone, but being therefore furnish'd with so many
excellent *Endowments,* that he may set forth his *Creator's* Praise, and be
rendred a fit Member of *Human Society;* it follows hence, that it is his
Duty, to cultivate and improve those Gifts of his Creator which he finds
in himself, that they may answer the End of their *Donor;* and to contribute all that lies in his Power to the Benefit of *Human Society.* Thus,
though true it is, that the *Ignorance* of any Man is *his own* Shame and
his own Loss; yet we accuse not the Master of Injustice, who chastises
his Scholar for *Negligence* in not learning those Sciences of which he is
capable.

L. N. N. l. 1. c. 4.

And since Man consists of two Parts, a *Soul* and a *Body,* whereof the
first supplies the Part of a *Director,* the other that of an *Instrument* or
subordinate Minister; so that our Actions are all performed by the Guidance of the *Mind,* and by the Ministration of the *Body;* we are hence
obliged to take care of both, but especially the former.

II. The general Obligation that every one lies under to take care of his Soul.

The *Care of the Soul* consists, in general, in the right Formation of
the Mind and Heart; that is, not only in framing to our selves true and
just Opinions concerning all those Things to which our Duties bear
any reference, and in making a true Judgment of, and setting a right
Value upon, those Objects which commonly excite our *Appetites;* but
also in regulating the Dispositions of our Minds; in reducing and conforming them to the Dictates of right Reason; in employing our Time

---

*The Duties of every Man, which directly and solely respect himself, have their
immediate Foundation in that *LOVE* which every Man by Nature hath *OF HIM-
SELF;* which was before laid down as one of the grand Principles of Natural Right,
and which not only obliges a Man to preserve himself, as far as possibly he can, without prejudice to the Laws of Religion or Sociality; but also to put himself into the
best Condition he can, and to obtain all the Happiness of which he is innocently
capable. *See L. N. N. Lib.* II. *Cap.* III. §15. [Barbeyrac's note (I.1, p. 71) in fact refers
to the "three great principles of natural right"—love of oneself, of God, and of society—continuing his attempt to evade Pufendorf's subordination of these to the
need for security and the cultivation of sociability.]

and Pains in the Prosecution of honest Arts and Sciences; and, in one word, in getting our selves possest of all those Qualities which are necessary for us to lead an *honest* and a *sociable* Life.[20]

Among all the *Opinions* then, which it highly concerns all Men firmly to *settle* in their Minds, the chief are those which relate to ALMIGHTY GOD, as the great Creator and Governour of the Universe, such as are represented in the foregoing Chapter. The full Persuasion of these *great Truths* being not only the principal Ground of *the Whole Duty of Man to God,* but the Foundation of all those Virtues which we are to exercise toward our Neighbour, and the true Source of all that Quiet of Conscience and Tranquillity of Mind, which is one of the greatest Blessings of Life. Since no sober and considering Man can deny these Truths, we must diligently avoid and utterly reject all those Opinions, which contain in them any thing *contrariant* to Principles so important. By which I mean not only *Atheism* and *Epicurism,* but all other Sentiments which are prejudicial to Human Society, or destructive of good Manners; such being incompatible with true Religion, and overturning the very Foundation of the Morality of Human Actions; of which kind there are many Instances.[21]

III. Particular Duties to which this Care of our Soul obliges us.

1. To settle in our selves right Opinions of Religion. L. N. N. l. 1. c. 4. §7.

The first I shall mention is the Stoical Conceit of *Fate* or *Destiny,* and (which nearly resembles it) *Judicial Astrology;* by which it being supposed, that all things happen in the World by an internal and inevitable Necessity, Men must be looked upon as the simple Instruments only of their own Actions; for which, consequently, they are no more accountable upon this Presumption, than a Clock is answerable for the Motion of its Wheels.

Another Opinion there is very nearly allied to this, which supposes the unalterable Consequences of Causes, and of Effects; or the great Chain of Things, established by the Creator, to stand by such an Im-

20. The interpolated sections begin here.
21. The following duties related to the care of the soul, taken from *LNN,* II.iv.4–5, represent a characteristically Lutheran rejection of "fatalistic" philosophical rationalism and "ritualistic" Catholicism.

moveable Decree, that even GOD has left Himself no Liberty of interposing in particular Cases.

Most pernicious likewise is that Conceit, which makes GOD allow
a kind of Market of Sins, so as to suffer them to be bought off with
Money, to be commuted for with Offerings, with the Observance of
some vain Ceremonies, or the Utterance of some set Forms of Speech,
without Amendment of Life, and an honest Endeavour to become
Good Men. To this may be joyned, the sottish Imagination of such,
who fancy that Almighty GOD is delighted with such Inventions of
Men, such Institutions and Ways of Living, as are disagreeable to Human and Civil Society, as it is regulated by the Dictates of Reason and
the *Laws of Nature.*

All superstitious Notions, such as debase and dishonour the Divine
Nature and Worship, are carefully to be avoided, as contrary to true Religion.

The same thing must be said of the Notions of those Men, who imagin that the bare Exercise of Piety towards GOD in Acts of Devotion,
as they are called, is sufficient, without any Regard had to Honesty of
Life, or to those Duties which we are to practice towards our Neighbour. Nor is the Conceit of others less Impious, who fancy, that a Man
may be able, not only to fulfil his own Duty towards GOD, but even
exceed what is required of him, and thereby transfer some of his Merits
on others; so that one Person's Negligence in his Duty, may be supply'd
from the Works of *Supererogation,* that is, the Over-righteousness of another. Of the same Stamp is that shameful Opinion of some others, that
imagine, that the Wickedness of some Actions is overlooked and excused by GOD, on the Account of the Dexterity, the Humour, or the
Gallantry of the Persons who do them; as if such Sins passed only as
Jests and Trifles in the Cognisance of Heaven. No less wicked is it to
believe, that those Prayers can please GOD, by which a Man desires,
that others may suffer an undeserved Evil, for the occasioning or promoting an Advantage to himself; or to imagine, that Men may treat, in
the worst manner they please, such as are of a different Persuasion from
them in Religious Matters. Not to mention some other such like Opin-

ions, which carry indeed the Pretence of Piety, but in reality tend to the Destruction of Religion and Morality.

When we have thus arm'd our Minds against all false Opinions of the Divine Nature and Worship, the main Concern behind is, for a Man accurately to examine his own Nature, and to study to *know himself.*[22]

IV. 2. To arrive at a true Knowlege of our selves. The Duties that result from such a knowledge. L. N. N. l. 2. c. 4. §5.

From this Knowledge of himself, rightly pursued, a Man is brought acquainted with his own Original; he comes to know perfectly his Condition here, and the Part he is to bear in the World. Hereby he will perceive, that he does not exist of himself, but owes his Being and Life to a Principle infinitely superior to him; that he is endowed with Faculties far more noble than he sees enjoy'd by the Beasts about him; and farther, that he was not born by himself, nor purely for his own Service, but that he is a Part of Human kind. From thus knowing a Man's self he must necessarily conclude, that he lives in Subjection to Almighty GOD, that he is obliged, according to the Measure of the Gifts he hath received from his Maker, to serve and honour Him; and moreover, to behave himself towards his Equals in such a manner, as becomes a Sociable Creature. And in as much as GOD hath bestowed on him the Light of Reason and Understanding, to guide him in the Course of his Life, it evidently follows, that he ought to make a right Use of it: And consequently *not to act at random, without End or Design, but, whatever he undertakes, to propose thereby to himself some particular End, in its self both possible and lawful, and to direct his own Actions suitably to that End; as also to use such other Means as he shall find proper for the compassing it.* Again, from hence it follows, that since Truth and Right are always uniform and without alteration, so *a Man ought always to form the same Judgments of the same Things, and when he hath once judged truly, to be always constant in his Mind and Resolution.* Farther it follows, that a

---

22. Despite Pufendorf's objections to Stoic fatalism, the advice on care of the self in sections IV–VIII contains a compendium of neo-Stoic rules for cultivating the self and restraining the passions and desires in accordance with the limited ends of personal and civil tranquillity.

Man's Will and Appetite ought not to get the Superiority over his Judgment, but follow and obey it, never making resistance to its Decrees; or, which amounts to the same thing, *Men ought to form no Judgments but upon mature Deliberation, nor ever to act against their Judgments so formed.*

L. N. N. l. 2. c. 4. §7.　Besides, by considering and knowing himself, a Man will rightly apprehend his own Strength and Power: He will find that it is of a finite nature, having certain Limits beyond which it can never extend it self; and therefore, that there are many Things in the World which he can no ways manage or compass, many that he can no ways hinder or resist, and other Things again not absolutely above Human Power, but which may be prevented and intercepted by the Interposition of other superior Powers. Again, another Sort of Things there are, which though we cannot compass by our bare Strength, yet we may, if it be assisted and supported by Dexterity and Address.

What seems to be most free from outward Restraint, and most within our own Power is our *Will;* especially so far as it is concerned in producing and exerting Actions suitable to our Species of Being, as we are reasonable Creatures. Hence it follows, that *every Man ought to make it his main Care and Concern, rightly to employ all his Faculties and Abilities, in conformity to the Rules of right Reason.* For this is the Standard by which we are to rate the Worth of every Person, and to measure his intrinsical Goodness and Excellency.

As to other Matters which lie without us, before he enters upon the Pursuit of them, *A Man should diligently examine, Whether they do not surpass his Strength? Whether they tend to a lawful End?* and, *Whether they are worth the Labour which must be spent in obtaining them?* When, upon mature Deliberation, he is resolved to engage in any such Affairs, a wise Man will indeed use his best Efforts to bring his Design about; but if he finds those Endeavours ineffectual, he will not strive against the Stream, and drive on his Designs with vain Hope, but quit his Pursuit without Grief or Anger at his Disappointment. From these Considerations this further Consequence may be drawn; That Man, as he is guided only by the Light of Reason, ought principally to aspire after that Happiness in this World, which arises from the prudent Government of his Faculties, and from those Assistances and Supports which the Divine Providence he knows will afford him in the universal Administration of things. Hence he will not leave things to meer Hazard and Chance, while there is room for Human Caution and Foresight. But then, since human Foresight is very weak in discovering future things, which are so far from being under our Guidance, that they frequently fall out beyond our Hopes and Expectations: Hence it is plain, that we ought neither too securely to trust to our present Condition, nor to spend too much Care and Anxiety on what is to come: and for the same reason, Insolence in Prosperity and Despair in Adversity are to be both avoided, as equally dangerous and equally absurd.

Another necessary Improvement of our Mind and Understanding is, *To be able to set a just Price on those Things which are the chief in moving our Appetites.* For, from this Knowledge it is that the degree of Desire is to be determined, with which we may seek after them.

V. 3. To regulate the measure of our Desires in proportion to the Just value of the things we desire. How we ought to seek for Honour or Esteem. L. N. N. l. 2. c. 4. §9.

Among these, that which bears the greatest sway, and appears with most splendor, and which most forceably moves Elevated and Noble Souls, is the Opinion of Worth and Excellency; an Opinion from whence springs what we usually call *Glory* or *Honour:* In respect to which we are to form and temper our Minds in the following manner.

We must use our utmost Care and Endeavour to procure and preserve that kind of *Esteem* that is *simply* so called, that is, the Reputation of being Good and Honest Men; and if this Reputation be assaulted by the Lies and Calumnies of Wicked Men, we are to use all possible Pains to wipe them off; but if that be not in our Power, we are to comfort our selves with the Testimony of a good Conscience, and with the Assurance, that our Integrity is still known to GOD.

As for that *Esteem,* which is oft-times called *Intensive,* or *Esteem of Distinction,* but more commonly *Honour* or *Glory,* we are no otherwise to pursue it, than as it redounds from such worthy Actions as are conformable to Right Reason, and productive of the Good of Human Society; but even then good Heed is to be taken, that hereby our Mind do not swell with Arrogance and Vain-glory. If at any time we have no Opportunity, or want an Occasion of shewing our Worth, without being able to procure one, we must bear this ill Fortune with Patience, since there is nothing in it that can be charged upon our Default. To value our selves upon, and make our boasts of what is empty, vain, and trifling, is most impertinent and ridiculous; but it is abominably Wicked, as well as extremly Foolish, to aspire to Fame and to Honours by evil Arts, and by Deeds repugnant to Reason; and to desire Preheminence above others, only to be able to insult over them, and to make them obnoxious to our Pleasure.

VI. In what manner we may desire Riches.

The *Desire of outward Possessions, Riches, and Wealth,* does also prevail greatly in the Minds of Men; and no wonder, since Men have not only need thereof for their own Support and Preservation in the World, but also often lie under an indispensible Duty to provide them for others. But then, because our Wants are not infinite, but lie in a very narrow Compass, and since Nature is not wanting in a plentiful Provision for the Necessities of her Sons; and lastly, since all that we can heap together must, at our Death, fall to others; we must moderate our Desire and our Pursuit of those Things, and govern our selves in the Use of them according to the just Occasions of Nature, and the modest Demands of Temperance and Sobriety. We must do no dishonest or base Thing for the procuring them; we must not increase them by sordid Avarice, nor squander them away by profuse Prodigality, nor in any ways make them subservient to vicious and dishonest Purposes. Farther, since Riches are of a very perishable Nature, and may be taken from us by many Accidents and Casualties, we must, with respect to 'em, put our Mind in so even a Temper, as not to lose it self if it should happen to lose them.

VII. In what manner we may desire Pleasures.
L. N. N. l. 2. c. 4. §11.

The Desire of *Pleasures* does as strongly excite the Minds of Men as that of *Honour* or *Riches:* In reference to these we must observe, that there are *Innocent Pleasures* and *Criminal Pleasures.* The latter of which must be always avoided; but it is by no means a Fault to enjoy the former, provided it be done with moderation, and in conformity to the Rules of Temperance and Sobriety. As there is no Fault to avoid, as much as may be, unnecessary Grief and Pain, because they tend to the Destruction of the Body; so Reason, on the other side, is so far from forbidding us the Enjoyment of moderate Recreation and innocent Pleasure, that it directs us to entertain our Senses with such Objects as are, in this manner, agreeable and delightful to them, since hereby the Mind is unbent and refresh'd, and render'd more active and vigorous. But then, in the Enjoyment of these lawful and innocent Gratifications, great Care is to be taken, that we enjoy them to such a Degree only, that we be not thereby weakened and enervated; that neither the Vigour of the Body or Soul be thereby lessen'd; that they waste not nor consume our Wealth, when it might be better and more usefully laid out; and that they steal not our Time from better and more necessary Employments. Lastly, This must be an inviolable Rule, that no Pleasure must be purchased at so dear a Rate, as the Neglect or Transgression of our Duty; nor ought any to be receiv'd that brings after it Loss, Disgrace, Sorrow, or Repentance.

Lastly, The chief Care incumbent on us, in order to improve and well cultivate our Mind, is, to use the utmost Diligence, *To gain the Mastery over our Passions;* to maintain the Sovereignty of our Reason over the Motions and Affections of our Minds; the greatest Part of which, if they gain the Ascendant, and grow masterless, do not only impair the Health of the Body, and the Vigour of the Soul, but cast such a Cloud on the Judgment and Understanding, as to wrest them violently from the Ways of Reason, and of Duty. So that the natural Principle of Prudence and Probity amongst Men, may be justly said to be founded in calming and cooling the Passions. But let us briefly speak of them in particular. *VIII. 4. We ought to subject our Passions to the Government of our Reason. L. N. N. l. 2. c. 4. §21.*

JOY is in it self a Passion most agreeable to Nature; but strict Care is to be taken, that it break not out on improper Occasions, that it shew not itself in Matters vain or trifling, base or indecent.

SORROW, like a Canker, wastes both the Body and Soul: it is therefore as much as possible to be remov'd and expell'd, nor ever to be admitted, even moderately, unless when by the Ties of Humanity, we are obliged to express our Concern, or Pity at the Misfortunes, or at the Deaths of others; and as it is requisite to the great Duty of Repentance.

LOVE is a Passion of a benevolent and friendly Nature to Mankind;

but yet it is to be so wisely managed and moderated, that it be not fix'd upon an unworthy Object; that we take not unlawful Ways to satisfy its Demands; that it keep within due Bounds, so as not to degenerate into Disease and Disquiet, if the beloved Object is not to be obtained.

HATRED is a Passion pernicious, as well to the Person who employs it, as to those against whom it is employ'd; it is therefore diligently to be quenched and stifled, lest it betray us to Injuries, and Breach of Duty against our Neighbours. And when any Persons do really deserve our Aversion, we must even then take care not, on their Account, to create Uneasiness and Disquiet to our selves.

ENVY is a most deform'd Monster, sometimes producing ill Effects in others, but always in the Envious Person, who, like Iron cankered with Rust, not only defiles, but destroys himself continually.

HOPE, although in it self a Passion mild, easy, and gentle, yet is it also to be brought under due Regulation. We must be careful not to direct it to Things vain or uncertain; nor, by placing it on Objects out of our Reach, and beyond our Power, make it tire it self to no purpose.

FEAR, as it is a dangerous Enemy to Men's Minds, so is it a Passion altogether useless and unprofitable. It is indeed by some esteemed the Parent of good Caution, and consequently, the Occasion of Safety; but this good Caution may owe it self to a much better Principle, it may arise without the Assistance of Fear, from a wary Circumspection, and a Prudence alike untouched with Anxiety or with Consternation.

ANGER is the most violent, as well as the most destructive of all the Passions, and is therefore to be resisted with our utmost Strength and Endeavour. It is so far from exciting Men's Valour, and confirming their Constancy in Dangers, as some alledge, that it has a quite contrary Effect; for it is a Degree of Madness, it renders Men blind and desperate, and runs them headlong into their own Ruin.

DESIRE OF REVENGE is nearly related to *Anger;* which, when it exceeds a Moderate Defence of our selves and Concerns, and a just Assertion of our Rights against the Invaders of them, turns, beyond Dispute, into a Vice.

In such Duties as we have reckoned up doth that Culture of the Mind chiefly consist, which all Men are indispensably obliged to look after: But there is still behind a more peculiar Culture and Improvement of the Mind, consisting in the various Knowledge of Things, and *the Study of Arts and Sciences.* This Knowledge, it is true, cannot be said to be absolutely necessary to the Discharge of our Duty in general, but yet must by all be allowed to be exceedingly useful to supply the Necessities and promote the Conveniencies of Human Life, and therefore by every one to be followed, according as his own Capacity and Occasion will permit. IX. How far the Study of Arts and Sciences is necessary. L. N. N. l. 2. c. 4. §13.

No one disputes the *Usefulness of those Arts,* which supply the Necessities, or contribute to the Convenience of Human Life.

As to *Sciences;* some may be stiled *Useful;* others *Curious,* and others again *Vain.*

In the Number of *useful Sciences,* I reckon *Logick,* which teaches to reason justly, closely, and methodically; those *Sciences which have any respect to Morality, Physick, and all such Parts of Mathematicks as lay the Foundation of those practical Arts,* which serve to procure and augment the Necessaries or Conveniencies of Life.

By *Curious,* or *Elegant Sciences,* I understand such as are not indeed of so necessary Use, as to render the Life of Man less sociable, or less convenient upon the Want of them; but yet such as serve to gratify and please an innocent Curiosity, to polish and adorn our Wit, and to embellish and render our Understanding more compleat: Such *Sciences* are, *Natural and Experimental Philosophy, the more fine and subtile Parts of Mathematicks, History, Criticism, Languages, Poetry, Oratory,* and the like.

By *Vain Sciences,* I mean such as are made up of false and erroneous Notions, or are employ'd about frivolous, trifling, and unprofitable Speculations; such are *the Amusements of old Philosophers, the Dreams of Astrologers,* and *the Subtilties of the School-men.*

To employ Labour and Pains in these last Sort of Studies is highly unworthy of any Man, and an unpardonable Waste of his Time. But whosoever would not deserve to be accounted an useless Lump on Earth, a Trouble to himself and a Burthen to others, ought, as far as he has Means and Opportunity, to employ himself in some of the afore-mention'd *Arts* and *Sciences*. Every one at least ought, in a proper Time, *to take upon himself some honest and useful Employment,* agreeable to his natural *Inclinations,* suitable to the *Abilities* of his *Body* and *Mind, Extraction,* and *Wealth;* or according as the just *Authority* of his *Parents,* the *Commands* of his *Superiours,* or the *Occasion* and *Necessity* of his own *private Circumstances* shall determine.[23]

X. Wherein consists the Care of the Body. Altho' the Care of our Soul, which we have been explaining, is the most difficult, as well as the most necessary Part of our Charge in this Life, yet ought we by no means to neglect *the Care of our Body;* these two constituent Parts of us being so strictly united and ally'd to each other, that no Injury or Hurt can come to the one, but the other must likewise bear its Part in the Suffering.

We must therefore, as far as possible, continue and increase the *natural Strength* and *Powers* of our Bodies, by convenient *Food* and proper *Exercise;* not ruining them by any *Intemperate Excess* in Eating or Drinking, nor wasting and consuming them by unnecessary or immoderate *Labours,* or by any other Abuse or Misapplication of our *Abilities.* And upon this Account, *Gluttony, Drunkenness,* the immoderate Use of *Women,* and the like, are to be avoided: And besides, since unbridled and exorbitant *Passions,* not only give frequent Occasion to disturb *Human Society,* but are very hurtful even to the Person *himself;* we ought to take care with our utmost to quell *them,* and subject *them* to Reason. And because many Dangers may be escap'd, if we encounter 'em with *Courage,* we are to cast off all *Effeminacy* of the Mind, and to put on *Resolution* against all the terrible Appearances that any Event may set before us.

23. This marks the end of the sections on the care of the self added by Weber and subsequently copied by Barbeyrac and thence the editors of the 1716/35 edition. The following section, X, on the care of the body, was section III in Pufendorf's original Latin text and in Tooke's first English edition.

And yet, because no Man could give *himself* Life, but it must be ac-counted as the bounteous Favour of *God,* it appears, that Man is by no means vested with such a Power over his own *Life,* as that he may put an *End* to it when he pleases; but he ought to tarry, till he is call'd off by Him who placed him in this Station. Indeed, since Men both can and ought to be serviceable to one another, and since there are some Sorts of Labour, or an Overstraining in any, which may so waste the Strength of a Man, that old Age and Death may come on much sooner than if he had led an easy and painless Life; there is no doubt but that a Man may, without any Contravention to this Law, chuse that Way of living which may with some probability make his Life the *shorter,* that so he may become more useful to Mankind. And whereas sometimes the Lives of *many* will be lost, except some Number of Men expose themselves to a Probability of losing their own on their behalf; in this Case the lawful *Governour* has Power to lay an Injunction on any *private* Man under the most grievous Penalties, not to decline by Flight such Danger of losing his Life. Nay farther, he may of *his own Accord* provoke such Danger, provided there are not *Reasons more forcible* for the contrary; and by thus Adventuring he has hopes to save the Lives of *others,* and those *others* are such as are worthy so dear a Purchase. For it would be silly for any Man to engage his Life together with another to *no purpose;* or for a Person of *Value* to die for the Preservation of a *paltry Rascal.* But for any other Cases, there seems nothing to be required by the *Law of Nature,* by which he should be persuaded to prefer another Man's Life before his own, but that all things rightly compared, every Man is allowed to be *most dear* to *himself.* And indeed all those who voluntarily put an end to their own Lives, either as *tir'd* with the many *Troubles* which usually accompany this Mortal State; or from an *Abhorrence* of *Indignities* and *Evils* which yet would not render them scandalous to *Human Society;* or thro' *Fear,* or *Pains,* or *Torment,* by enduring which with Fortitude, they might become useful Examples to others; or out of a vain *Ostentation* of their *Fidelity* and *Bravery;* All these, I say, are to be certainly reputed *Sinners against the Law of Nature.*

XI. Whether a Man has the Power of his own Life.

XII. Self-
Defence mod-
erated.

But whereas it often happens that this *Self-Preservation,* which the tenderest Passion and exactest Reason thus recommends to Mankind, does
seem to interfere with our Precepts concerning *Society,* then when our
own Safety is brought into Jeopardy by another, so far that either we
must perish, or submit to some very grievous Mischief, or else we must
repel the Aggressor by force and by doing him Harm; Therefore we are
now to deliver, *With what Moderation the Defence of our selves is to be
tempered.* This Defence of our selves then will be such as is, either *without any Harm* to him from whom we apprehend the Mischief, by rendring any Invasion of us formidable to him and full of Danger; or else
by *hurting* or *destroying* him. Of the *former* way, [whether (in *private*
Men) by *keeping off* the Assailant, or by *Flight, &c.*] there can be no
Doubt but that 'tis lawful and altogether blameless.

XIII. We may
repel force by
force, even so
far as to kill an
unjust Aggres-
sor. L. N. N.
l. 2. c. 5. §2.

But the *latter* may admit of Scruple, because Mankind may seem to
have an *equal Loss,* if the *Aggressor* be killed, or if I lose *my* Life; and
because one in the same Station with my self will be destroyed, with
whom it was my Duty to have lived in *Civil Society:* Beside, that a *forcible Defence* may be the Occasion of *greater Outrages,* than if I should
betake my self to flight, or patiently *yield* my Body to the Invader. But
all these are by no means of such Weight as to render this Sort of Defence unlawful. For when I am dealing fairly and friendly with *another,*
it is requisite that he shew himself ready to do the *like,* or else he is not
a fit Subject of such good Offices from me. And because the End of the
Law of Society is the *Good of Mankind,* therefore the Sense thereof is to
be taken, so as effectually to preserve the Welfare of every *Individual* or
particular Man. So that if another Man make an *Attempt* upon my Life,
there is no Law that commands me to *forgoe* my own Safety, that so he
may practise his Malice with *Impunity:* And he that in such case is *hurt*
or *slain,* must impute his Mischief to his own *Wickedness,* which set me
under a Necessity of doing what I did. Indeed otherwise, whatsoever
Good we enjoy either from the Bounty of *Nature,* or the Help of our
own *Industry,* had been granted to us in vain, if we were not at liberty
to *oppose* the Violences of Ruffians, who would wrongfully ravish all
from us; and *honest* Men would be but a ready Prey for *Villains,* if they

were not allowed to make use of *Force* in defence of themselves against the others Insults. *Upon the whole then, it would tend to the *Destruction* of Mankind, if *Self Defence* even with *Force* were prohibited to us.

Not however that hence it follows, that as soon as any *Injury* is threatned us, we may *presently* have recourse to *Extremities;* but we must first try the *more harmless Remedies;* for instance, we must endeavour to keep out the Invader by cutting off his Access to us; to withdraw into strong Places; and to admonish him to desist from his outragious Fury. And it is also the Duty of a prudent Man to put up a *slight Wrong,* if it may conveniently be done, and to *remit* somewhat of his Right, rather than, by an unseasonable Opposition of the Violence, to expose himself to a *greater Danger;* especially if that Thing or Concern of ours upon which the Attempt is made, be such as may easily be made amends for or repaired. †But in Cases where by these or the like means I cannot secure my self, in order to it I am at liberty to have recourse even to *Extremities.*

XIV. Extremities last to be used. L. N. N. l. 2. c. 5. §3.

But that we may clearly judge, whether a Man contains himself within the Bounds of an *unblameable Defence of himself,* it is first to be examined, whether the Person be one who is in a State of *Natural Liberty* or *subject to no Man,* or one who is obnoxious[24] to some *Civil Power.* In the *first* Case, if another shall offer Violence to me, and cannot be brought to change his malicious Mind and live quietly, I may repel him even by *killing* him. And this not only when he shall attempt upon my *Life,* but if he endeavour only to *wound* or *hurt* me, or but to *take away* from me my Goods, without meddling with my Body. For I have no Assurance but from these *lesser Injuries* he may proceed to *greater;* and he that has once professed himself my Enemy (which he doth whilst he injures me without Shew of Repentance) gives me, as far as 'tis in his

XV. Self-Defence how far justifiable in a supposed state of Natural Liberty.

---

* See *Grotius de Jure Belli & Pacis, Lib.* I. & *Chap.* 2. *Lib.* II. *c.* 1. §3. *Et seq.*
† *Grotius de Jure Belli & Pacis, Lib.* 1. *cap.* 1.
24. Here and elsewhere Tooke uses "obnoxious" in the early modern (Latin) sense of "subject to." The distinction he draws is thus between self-defense where there is no prevailing law or civil authority and self-defense where these conditions prevail.

Power to give, a full Liberty of proceeding against him, and resisting him in such manner as I shall find most necessary for my own Safety. And indeed the *Sociality* necessary to Human Life would become unpracticable, if a Man may not make use even of *Extremities* against him who shall irreclaimably *persist* in the Commission tho' but of *meaner Wrongs*. For at that rate the most *modest* Persons would be the continual Laughing-stock of the *vilest* [25]Rakehels.[26]

XVI How the Right of Self-defence is limited in a State of Civil Society. L. N. N. l. 2. c. 5. §4. But in *Civil Society,* those who are Subjects to the *Civil Power,* may then only use Violence in the Defence of themselves, when the Time and Place will not admit of any Application to the Magistrate for his Assistance in repelling such Injuries by which a Man's Life may be hazarded, or some other most valuable Good which can never be repaired, may be manifestly endangered.

XVII. Of the Time when in a State of Nature Self defence may be allowable. As for the time when Men may put in practice their *just Right* of *Self-defence,* it may be learnt from the following Rules.

Altho' every one, under that Independence in which all Men are supposed to be in a *State of Nature,* may and ought to presume, that all Men are inclined to perform towards him all those Duties which the *Law of Nature directs,* until he has evident Proof to the contrary: Nevertheless, since Men have *natural Inclinations* to that which is ill, no one ought to rely so securely on the Integrity of another, as to neglect taking all necessary Precautions to render himself secure, and placed, as far as may be, out of the Reach of other Men's ill Designs. It is but *common Prudence* to stop up all Avenues against those from whom we apprehend Hostilities, to be provided with serviceable Arms, to raise Troops, to get Succour and Assistance, in case of need, by Alliances and Confederacies, to have a watchful Eye over the Actions and Behaviour of those whom we have reason to apprehend to be our Enemies; and, in a word, to use all other Precautions of this Nature, which appear neces-

25. Hellish rakes.
26. In Pufendorf's original and Tooke's first English edition a further paragraph begins here. Barbeyrac moved this to the bottom of section XVII, and the English editors show their fidelity to Barbeyrac's text by altering Tooke's version accordingly.

sary to prevent our being surprized or found unprovided. The Jealousy and Suspicion which we ought to have of each other, from our Knowledge of the Pravity of Human Nature, will justifie our acting thus far; but then it must stop here: it must not put us upon using Violence to our Neighbours, under pretence of disabling them from injuring us, and of preventing their making a mischievous Use of that superior Power we see them have; especially if we find that this Increase of Power in them, and their Superiority over us, was the Product of their innocent Industry, or the Gift of Providence, and not the Result of Injury and Oppression.

*Nay, if our Neighbour, whom we see powerful enough to hurt us, should shew an Inclination to use that Power mischievously, by actually injuring others, yet shall not this justifie our Assaulting him by way of prevention, till we have good Evidence, that he designs us also Mischief; unless we are under some prior Engagement or Alliance, to support the Persons we see thus injuriously attacked by a superior Power. In this Case we may with greater Vigour oppose the Invader, and take the Part of our injured Ally; since we have very good Reason to apprehend, that when by his superior Power he has oppressed him, he will apply the same Force against us; and that the first Conquest he makes is to be the Instrument of another that he intends.

But when we have evident Proof that another does actually intend, and has taken proper Measures to do us an Injury, altho' he has not openly declared such his Intention; then we may fairly put our selves on our Defence, and anticipate the Aggressor before he compleats the Preparations he is making to do us the designed Mischief: Provided notwithstanding we have endeavoured, by friendly Advice, to move him to lay aside his ill Purposes so long, that there remains no Hopes of his being prevailed upon to do so by fair and gentle Means: In using which friendly Advice and gentle Means, care must be taken, that it be not done when it may prove a Prejudice and a Disadvantage to our own Affairs. He who first forms the Design to do an injurious Act, and first

---

* See *Grotius de Jure Belli & Pacis, Lib. 2. cap. 1.* §17, &c. and *c.* 22. §5.

makes Preparation to bring it about, is to be accounted the Aggressor; altho' it may perhaps so fall out, that the other using greater Diligence, may prevent him, and so commit the first open Acts of Hostility. It is not absolutely necessary to a justifiable *Self-defence,* that I receive the first Stroke, or that I only ward off and avoid the Blows that are aimed at me.[27]

But farther: In a *State of Nature* of which we are speaking, a Man has not only a Right to repel a present Danger with which he is menaced, but also, after having secured himself from the Mischief intended him, he may pursue his Success against the Aggressor, till he has made him give him *satisfactory Security of his peaceable Behaviour for the time to come.* Concerning which Caution and Security, the following Rule may be usefully observed: *If a Man having injured me, shall presently after, repenting of what he had done, come voluntarily and ask my pardon, and offer Reparation of the Damage; I am then obliged to be reconciled to him, without requiring of him any farther Security than his Faith and Promise to live hereafter in Peace and Quietness with me.* For when of his own accord any Person takes such measures, it is a satisfactory Evidence, that he has altered his Mind, and a sufficient Argument of his firm Resolution to offer me no Wrong for the future. *But if a Man having injured me, never thinks of asking Pardon, or of shewing his Concern for the Injuries he has done me, till he is no longer in Condition to do them, and till his Strength fails him in prosecuting his Violences; such an one is not safely to be trusted on his bare Promises, his Word alone being not a sufficient Warrant of the Sincerity of his Protestations.* In such Case, in order to our farther Security, we must either cut off from him all Power of doing Mischief, or else lay upon him some Obligation of greater Weight and Force than his meer Promise, sufficient to hinder him from appearing ever after formidable to us.

27. The following paragraph originally stood as the final paragraph of section XV (i.e., section VIII in Pufendorf's original). It is not clear why Barbeyrac moved it.

But among Men who live in a *Community*,[28] the Liberties for *Self-defence* ought not to be near so large. For here, tho' I may know for certain, that another Man has *armed* himself in order to set upon me, or has openly *threatned* to do me a Mischief; this will by no Means bear me out in *assaulting* him; but he is to be *informed* against before the Civil Magistrate, who is to require *Security* for his good Behaviour. The Use of *Extremities* in repelling the Force being then only justifiable, when I am *already* set upon, and reduced to such *Streights,* that I have no Opportunity to require the *Protection* of the Magistrate, or the *Help* of my Neighbours; and even then I am not to make use of *Violence,* that by the Slaughter of my Adversary I may *revenge* the Injury, but only because without it my *own Life* cannot be out of *Danger.*

XVIII. When and how far a Man may defend himself with arm'd force in a State of Civil Society.

Now the Instant of *Time,* when any Man may with Impunity *destroy* another in his own Defence, is, when the Aggressor, being *furnished* with Weapons for the Purpose, and *shewing* plainly a *Design* upon my Life, is got into a *Place* where he is very capable of doing me a Mischief, allowing me some time, in which it may be necessary to prevent rather than be prevented; although in *foro humano* a little *Exceeding* be not much minded in regard of the great Disturbance such a Danger must be thought to raise in the Spirit of Man. And the *Space of Time* in which a Man may *use Force in his own Defence,* is so long as till the Assailant is either *repulsed,* or has *with-drawn* of his own accord, (whether in that Moment *repenting* of his wicked Design, or for that he sees he is like to *miss* of his Aim) so that for the present he cannot hurt us any more, and we have an Opportunity of retiring into a Place of Safety. *For as for *Revenge* of the Wrong done, and *Caution* for future Security, that be-longs to the Care of the *Civil Magistrate,* and is to be done only by *his* Authority.

Of the Time when in a State of Civil Society Self-defence may be allowable.

---

28. Here and elsewhere in the discussion of self-defense, Tooke again opts for "community" in place of Pufendorf's "state" (*civitas*).

* *Grotius de Jure Belli & Pacis, Lib.* 2. *Cap.* 1. §5.

XIX. Whether a Man may use his Right of Self-defence against one that assaults him by mistake. L. N. N. l. 2. c. 5. §5.

Farthermore,[29] both in a *State of Nature,* and in a *Civil State,* it is lawful for every Man to defend himself, if the *Precautions* before-mentioned be taken against him who attempts to take away his Life; whether it be *designedly,* and with a *malicious Intention,* or *without any particular Design* against the Party assaulted: As suppose a Mad-man, or a Lunatick, or one that mistakes me for some other Person who is his Enemy, should make an Attempt on my Life, I may justifiably use my Right of *Self-Defence;* for the Person from whom the Attempt comes, whereby my Life is hazarded, hath no Right to attack me, and I am by no means obliged to suffer Death unnecessarily; on which account it is altogether unreasonable that I should prefer *his* Safety to *my own.*

XX. How the most just Self-defence ought to be managed: and of Duels.

Nevertheless though true it is, that we ought not to take away another Man's *Life,* when it is possible for us after a more convenient way to avoid the Danger we are in; yet in consideration of that *great Perturbation of Mind,* which is wont to be occasion'd upon the Appearance *of imminent Mischief,* it is not usual to be *over-rigorous* in the Examination of these Matters; for it is not likely that a Man *trembling* under the *Apprehension* of Danger, should be able to find out so exactly all those *Ways of escaping,* which to one who *sedately* considers the Case may be plain enough. Hence, though it is *Rashness* for me to come out of a *safe* Hold to him who shall *challenge* me; yet, if another shall set upon me in an *open* Place, I am not streight obliged to betake my self to *Flight,* except there be at hand such a Place of *Refuge* as I may withdraw into without

---

29. The opening word is incongruous because, far from continuing the thought of the preceding section, this one contradicts it, indicating circumstances in which individuals may defend themselves regardless of the civil magistrate. In fact this section (XIX) is not in its original location. It was originally Pufendorf's section X, which means that it should be located between sections XV and XVI in Barbeyrac's augmented version of Chapter V. In relocating this section Barbeyrac evidently intended it to undermine Pufendorf's transfer of the right of self-defense to the civil magistrate. That this was Barbeyrac's intent is clear from the long note (XIX.1, p. 99) that he added near the end of this section in his translation, the burden of which is to justify a subject's right of defence against the unjust aggression of the civil magistrate himself. In choosing not to include this incendiary note, the editors largely defeated the purpose of Barbeyrac's rearrangement of Pufendorf's text.

Peril: Neither am I always bound to *retire;* because then I turn my defenceless Back, and there may be hazard of falling; beside, that having once lost my Posture, I can hardly recover it again. But as the Plea of *Self-defence* is allow'd to that Person who shall thus encounter Danger, when he is going about his lawful *Business,* whereas if he had staid at Home he had been safe enough; so it is denied to him who being challenged to a *Duel,* shall by appearing *set himself* in that Condition, and except he kill his Adversary, himself must be slain. *For the *Laws* having *forbidden* his venturing into such *Danger,* any Excuse on account *thereof* is not to be regarded.

What may be done for the Defence of *Life* may also for the *Members;*[30] so as that he shall be acquitted for an *honest Man* who shall *kill* a Ruffian, that perhaps had no farther Intention than to *maim* him, or give him some *grievous Wound:* For all Mankind does naturally abhor to be *maimed* or *wounded;* and the cutting off any, especially of the more noble Members, is often not of much less value than Life itself; beside, we are not sure beforehand, whether upon such *wounding* or *maiming* Death may not follow; and to endure this is a Sort of *Patience* that surpasses the ordinary Constancy of a Man, †to which no man is regularly obliged by the Laws, only to gratifie the outragious Humour of a Rogue.

> XXI. Defence of Members. L. N. N. l. 2. c. 5. §10.

Moreover, what is lawfully to be done for Preservation of *Life,* ‡is adjudged to be so for *Chastity:* Since there cannot be a more horrid *Abuse* offered to an honest Woman, than to force her out of that which being kept undefiled is esteemed the greatest *Glory* of their Sex; and to put upon her a Necessity of raising an Offspring to her Enemy out of her own Blood.

> XXII. Defence of Chastity. L. N. N. l. 2. c. 5. §11.

---

*See *Grotius de Jure Belli & Pacis, Lib.* 2. *Cap.* 1. §15.

30. The "members" or limbs of the body.

†See *Grotius de Jure Belli, & Pacis, Lib.* 2. *Cap.* 1. §6.

‡Mr. Budaeus denies this (in the 2d Part of his *Elements of Practical Philosophy, chap.* 4. *sect.* 3.) and his Reason is, That there is no *Proportion between the Life and the Honour of any Person.* But can any Violation be too great for a Woman to expect

XXIII. De-
fence of Goods
or Estate.
L. N. N. l. 2.
c. 5. §16.

As for *Defence of Goods or Estate,* this may, among those who are in a
State of *Natural Liberty,* go as far as the *Slaughter* of the Invader, *provided what is in Controversie be not a *Thing contemptible.* For without
Things necessary we cannot keep our selves alive; and he equally declares
himself my Enemy, who wrongfully seizes my *Estate,* as he that attempts
upon my *Life.* But in *Communities,* where what is ravished from us may,
with the Assistance of the *Civil Authority,* be recovered, this is not regularly allowed; unless in such case when he that comes to take away
what we have, cannot be brought to *Justice:* On which account it is, that
we may lawfully kill *Highwaymen* and *Night-robbers.*

XXIV. Self De-
fence in him
that first in-
jur'd. L. N. N.
l. 2. c. 6. §19.

And thus much for *Self-Defence* in those who without Provocation are
unjustly invaded by others: But for him who has *first* done an *Injury* to
another, he can only then rightly *defend* himself with *Force,* and *hurt*
the other *again,* when having *repented* of what he has done, he has offered *Reparation* of the Wrong and *Security* for the future; and yet he
who was *first injured,* shall, out of ill Nature, *refuse* the same, and endeavour to *revenge* himself by Violence; [shewing hereby that he seeks
not so much *Reparation* and *Right* to himself, as *Mischief* to the other.]

---

from a Man that is arriv'd to such a Pitch of Brutality? Besides, *Honour* is a *Good*
whose Loss is not only irrecoverable, but which, among civiliz'd Nations, is placed
in the same Degree of Value with Life it self. After all, does not such an Act of Hostility as this, give her a perfect Right to have recourse to Extremities against a Man,
who to satisfie his brutish Passion, irreparably stains the Honour and takes away the
Liberty of an honest Woman? See *Grotius de Jure Belli & Pacis, lib.* 2. *cap.* 1. §7.
[Barbeyrac's XXII.1, p. 102.]

   *The Author I just now quoted pretends in the same place, that *no one can jus-
tifiably kill a Thief, unless he attempts to steal from him so considerable a Part of his
Substance, as that he could not live upon the Remainder.* But this learned Author has
said nothing to invalidate the Principles, and confute the Reasons alledged to the
contrary by our Author, in his large Work of *The Law of Nature and Nations,* of
which this is an Abridgment. See *Lib.* 2. *Cap.* 5. §16. [Barbeyrac's XXIII.1, p. 102.]

Lastly, *Self-Preservation* is of so much regard, that, if it cannot otherwise be had, in many Cases it exempts us from our Obedience to the standing Laws; and on this Score it is, that *Necessity* is said to *have no Law*. For seeing Man is naturally inspired with such an earnest Desire to preserve himself, it can hardly be presumed that there is any Obligation laid upon him, to which he is to sacrifice his *own Safety.* For tho' not only *God,* but the *Civil Magistrate,* when the Necessity of Affairs requires it, may lay upon us so strict an Injunction, that we ought rather to die than vary a Little from it; yet the *general Obligation* of Laws is not held to be so rigorous. For the Legislators, or those who first introduced *Rules* for Mankind to act by, making it their Design to promote the *Safety* and *common Good* of Men, must regularly be supposed to have had before their Eyes the Condition of *Human Nature,* and to have considered how *impossible* it is for a Man *not* to shun and keep off all Things that tend to his own *Destruction.* Hence those Laws especially, called *Positive,* and all *Human Institutions* are judged to except *Cases of Necessity;* or, not to oblige, when the Observation of them must be accompanied with some Evil which is *destructive* to *Human Nature,* or not tolerable to the *ordinary Constancy* of Men; unless it be *expressly* so ordered, or the *Nature* of the Thing requires, that even *that* also must be undergone. Not that Necessity *justifies* the Breach of a Law and Commission of Sin; but it is presumed, from the favourable Intention of the Legislators, and the Consideration of Man's Nature, that *Cases of Necessity* are not included in the general Words of a Law. This will be plain by an Instance or two.

XXV. Self Preservation in Cases of Necessity. L. N. N. l. 2. c. 6.

I. THOUGH otherwise Man have no such Power over his own *Members,* as that he may lose or maim any of them at his pleasure; yet he is justifiable in *cutting off* a gangren'd Limb, in order to save the *whole Body;* or to preserve those *Parts* which are *sound;* or lest the other Members be rendred *useless* by a dead and cumbersome Piece of Flesh.

XXVI. Cutting off Members. L. N. N. l. 2. c. 6. §3.

XXVII. One
lost to save
many.

II. If in a *Shipwrack* more Men leap into the Boat than it is *capable* of carrying, and no one has more Right than another to it; they may *draw Lots* who shall be cast overboard; and if any Man shall *refuse* to take his chance, he may be thrown over without any more ado, as one that seeks the Destruction of *all.*

XXVIII. One
hastens the
Death of an-
other to save
himself.
L. N. N. l. 2.
c. 6. §4.

III. If *two* happen into imminent Danger of their Lives, where *both* must perish; one may, as he sees good, hasten the Death of the other, that he may save *himself.* For instance, If I, who am a skilful Swimmer, should fall into some deep Water with another who could not swim at all, and he clings about me; I not being strong enough to carry *him* off and *my self* too, I may put him off with *force,* that I may not be drowned together with him; tho' I might for a little while be able to keep him up. So in a Shipwrack, if I have got a Plank which will not hold *two,* and *another* shall endeavour to get upon it, which if he does, we are *both* like to be drowned, I may keep him off with what *violence* I please. And so if *two* be pursued by an Enemy meaning to kill them, *one* may, by shutting a Gate or drawing a Bridge after him, secure *himself,* and leave the *other* in great Probability of *losing* his Life, supposing it not to be possible to save *both.*

XXIX. An-
other de-
stroyed or hurt
to the same
end.

IV. Cases also of *Necessity* may happen, where one may *indirectly* put another in Danger of *Death,* or some *great* Mischief, when at the same time he means no harm to the Person; but only, for his own *Preservation,* he is forced upon some Action which probably may do the other a Damage; always supposing that he had rather have chosen any *other* Way, if he could have found it, and that he make that Damage as *little* as he can. Thus, if a stronger Man than I pursues me to take away my Life, and one meets me in a narrow Way thro' which I must flee, if, upon my Request, he will not stand out of the Way, or he has not time or room so to do, I may throw him down and go over him, tho' it be very likely that by the Fall he will be very much hurt; except he should be one who has such peculiar Relation to me, [suppose my *Parent, King,* &c.] that I ought for his Sake rather to surrender my self to the Danger. And if he who is in the Way cannot, upon my speaking to him, get out of the Way, suppose being lame or a Child, I shall be excused who try to leap over him, rather than to expose my self to my Enemy by delaying. But if any one shall, out of *Wantonness* or *cross Humour,* hinder me or deny to give me the Liberty of escaping, I may immediately by any Violence throw him down, or put him out of my Way. And those who in these Cases get any *Harm,* are to look upon it not as a *Fault* in the Person that did it, but as an unavoidable *Misfortune.*

V. IF a Man, not through his own Fault, happen to be in *extreme Want of Victuals and Cloaths* necessary to preserve him from the Cold, and cannot procure them from those who are wealthy and have great Store, either by Intreaties, or by offering their Value, or by proposing to do Work equivalent; he may, without being chargeable with *Theft* or *Rapine,* furnish his Necessities out of their Abundance, either by force or secretly, especially if he do so with a Design to pay the Price, as soon as he shall have an Opportunity. For it is the Duty of the *opulent* Person to succour another who is in such a *needy* Condition. And tho' regularly what depends upon *Courtesie* ought by no means to be extorted by *Force,* yet the *Extreme Necessity* alters the Case, and makes these Things as *claimable,* as if they were absolutely *due* by a formal Obligation. But it is first incumbent upon the Necessitous Person to try all Ways to supply his Wants with the *Consent* of the Owner, and he is to take care that the Owner be not thereby reduced to the *same Extremity,* nor in a little time like to be so; and that *Restitution* be made; *especially if the Estate of the other be such as that he cannot well bear the Loss.

XXX. Case of extreme Want. L. N. N. l. 2. c. 6. §5.

VI. LASTLY, the *Necessity* of our own Affairs seems sometimes to justifie our destroying the *Goods of other Men;* 1. Provided still, that we do not bring such Necessity upon our selves by our *own Miscarriage:* 2. That there cannot be any *better* Way found: 3. That we cast not away that of our Neighbours which is of *greater Value,* in order to save our own which is of *less:* 4. That we be ready to pay the *Price,* if the Goods would

XXXI. Destroying other Men's Goods to save our own. L. N. N. l. 2. c. 6. §8.

---

* See *Grotius de Jure Belli & Pacis, lib. 2. cap. 2. §6. lib. 3. cap. 17. §1, 2. seq.*

not otherwise have been destroyed, or to bear our share in the Damage done, if the Case were so that *his* must have perished together with *ours,* but now by the Loss of them *ours* are preserved. And this sort of Equity is generally found in the *Law*-Merchant.[31] Thus in case of *Fire,* I may pull down or blow up my Neighbour's House, but then those whose Houses are by this means saved, ought to make good the Damage proportionably.

ᗧᐧᗤ   C H A P T E R   V I   ᗧᐧᗤ

Of the Duty of one Man to another, and first of doing no Injury to any Man

I. Reciprocal Duties of two Sorts.

We come now to those Duties which are to be practis'd by *one Man towards another.* Some of these proceed from that *common Obligation* which it hath pleas'd the Creator to lay upon all Men in general; others take their Original from some certain *Human Institutions,* or some *peculiar,* *adventitious or accidental *State* of Men. The *first* of these are *always* to be practis'd by *every* Man towards *all* Men; the *latter* obtain

---

31. The *leges nauticae* (*lex mercatoria*), or "law of the sea."

*This *Status adventitius* is that State of Life we come into in consequence of some Human Constitution; whether we enter into it at our Birth immediately, or whether it happens after our Birth. Such are, for example, all those Conditions of Life where the Duties and Relations are reciprocal; such as a *Parent* and his *Child,* an *Husband* and a *Wife,* a *Master* and a *Servant,* a *Sovereign* and his *Subject.* &c. [Barbeyrac's I.1, p. III.]

only among those who are in such *peculiar* Condition or State.[32] Hence those may be called *Absolute,* and these *Conditional Duties.*

Among those Duties we account *Absolute,* or those of every Man to-wards every Man, this has the first Place, *that *one do no Wrong to the other;* and this is the *amplest* Duty of all, comprehending *all Men* as such; and it is at the same time the *most easy,* as consisting only in an *Omission* of acting, unless now and then when unreasonable Desires and Lusts are to be *curb'd.* It is also the *most necessary,* because without it *Human Society* cannot be preserv'd. For I can live *quietly* with him that does me *no Good,* or with whom I have no manner of Correspondence, provided he doth me *no Harm.* Nay this is all we desire from the *greatest Part* of Mankind; the doing mutually *good Offices* lying but among a few. But I can by no means live *peaceably* with him that *wrongs* me; Nature having instilled into every Man such a tender Love of *himself* and what is his *own,* that he cannot but by all possible means *repel* those Men who shall make any Attempt upon one or t'other.

II. No wrong
to be done.
L. N. N. l. 3.
c. 1.

---

32. The key to understanding Pufendorf's division of duties to others lies in his doctrine that duties attach not to human beings as such—that is, not to a human substance or essence—but to a particular condition, state, or status that humans occupy. This is defined at the beginning of Book II: "By 'state' [*status*] in general, we mean a condition in which men are understood to be set for the purpose of performing a certain class of actions" (Tully, ed., *Duty,* p. 115). All of the states of man and their associated duties are thus understood to be imposed or instituted, rather than to be expressions of an essence. The common or universal duties to others attach to man's natural status which was imposed by God. These are discussed in Chapters VI (to harm no one), VII (to treat others as equals or fellow humans), and VIII (to practice benevolence). The artificial or adventitious statuses are those men have imposed on themselves via pacts, which means that their duties are conditional on particular institutional arrangements. These states are those of linguistic communication, property ownership, marriage, parenthood, and, especially, the political state. In between the natural and adventitious duties to others come the duties relating to pacts, discussed in Chapter IX of Book I.

* See *Grotius de Jure Belli & Pacis, lib.* 2. and the whole 17th Chapter.

III. So to do a Crime.

By this Duty are fenced not only what we have by the Bounty of *Nature;* such as our Laws, Bodies, Limbs, Chastity, Liberty; but whatsoever by any *Human Institution* or *Compact* becomes our Property; so as by this it is forbidden to take away, spoil, damage, or withdraw, in whole or in part, from our Use, whatsoever by a lawful Title we are possess'd of. Whence all those Actions are hereby made Crimes, by which any Wrong is done to others, as Murther, Wounding, Striking, Rapine, Theft, Fraud, Violence, whether practis'd directly or indirectly, mediately or immediately, and the like.

IV. Reparation of Wrong a necessary Consequence from thence.

Farther, hence it follows, That *if any Harm or Damage be done to another, he who is truly chargeable as Author of the Wrong, ought, as far as in him lies, to make Reparation:* For otherwise the Precept would be to no purpose, That no Man shall be hurt nor receive damage; if when he has actually sustain'd a Mischief, he must put it up quietly, and he who did the Injury shall enjoy *securely* the Fruit of his Violence without *Reparation.* And setting aside this *Necessity of Restitution,* the Pravity of Man's Nature is such, that they would never forbear *injuring* one another, and it would be very hard for him who has suffered Wrong, to compose his Mind so as to live peaceably with the other, till *Reparation* were made.

V. Damage how to be accounted.
L. N. N. l. 3. c. 1. §3.

Tho' the Word *Damage* may seem properly to belong to Loss in Goods, yet we take it here in the large Sense, that it may signifie all Manner of *Harm, spoiling, diminishing,* or *taking away* what is already ours, or *intercepting* that which by an *absolute Right* we ought to have, whether it be bestowed upon us by Nature, or given us by Man and Human Laws; or lastly, the *Omission* or *Denial* of paying what by a *perfect Obligation* is due to us. But if *such* Payment only be stopt, as was *not due* by any *perfect Obligation,* it is not looked upon as a Damage that ought to be made good: For it would be unmeet to account it a *Wrong* suffered if I receive not such Stipends; and unreasonable for me to demand as my *Right,* what I cannot expect from another but under the name of a *Free Gift,* and which I can by no means call *my own,* till after I have received it.

Under the Head of *Damage* liable to Reparation, we must also comprise not only a Mischief, Loss or Interception of what is ours or due to us; but also such *Profits* as do naturally accrue from the Thing, or have already accrued, or may fairly be *expected,* if it was the Right of the Owner to receive them; allowing still the Expenses necessary for gathering in such Profits. Now the Value of *Profits,* thus in *Expectation* only, is to be high or low, according as they are certain or uncertain, and will be sooner or later received. And lastly, that also is to be called *Damage,* which upon a Hurt given, does of Natural Necessity *follow* thereon.

VI. Damage in expectations.

One Man may damnifie[33] another not only *immediately* or by *himself,* but also by *others:* And it may happen that a Damage immediately done by *one Man* may be chargeable upon *another,* because he contributed somewhat to the Action, either by doing what he ought not, or not doing what he ought to have done. Sometimes among *several Persons* who concurred to the same Fact one is to be accounted the *Principal,* others but *Accessories;* sometimes they may all be *equally Parties.* Concerning whom it is to be observed, that they are so far obliged to *repair* the Wrong as they were indeed the *Causes* thereof, and by so much as they contributed to doing *All* or *Part* of the Damage. But where any one did not actually assist in the Trespass committed; nor was antecedently a Cause of its being done, nor had any Advantage by it; there, though upon Occasion of the Injury done, he may be *blame worthy,* yet he cannot be any ways obliged to *Restitution:* And of this Sort are such as *rejoyce* at their Neighbour's Misfortunes, such as *commend* the Commission of Outrages, or are ready to *excuse* them, who *wish* or *favour* the Practice of them, or who *flatter* the Actors therein.

VII. Damage mediately or immediately done. L. N. N. l. 3. c. 1. §4.

Where *many* have joined in an Action from whence Damage has come, he in the *first* place shall be chargeable with *Reparation,* by whose *Command* or powerful *Influence* the others were put upon the Action; and he who immediately perpetrates the Thing, to which he could not decline his helping Hand, shall be esteemed but only as the *Instrument.*

VIII. Damage done by many. L. N. N. l. 3. c. 1. §5.

33. Inflict loss.

He who *without any constraint* concerned himself in the Enterprize shall be *chiefly liable,* and then the rest who assisted in it. But this so, as that if *Restitution* be made by the former, then the latter are cleared, (which in *Penal Cases* is otherwise.) If *many in Combination* have committed an Injury, all are obliged for each one single, and each one single is obliged for all; so as that if *all* are seized, they must each pay their Shares to make good the Loss; and if all escape but *one,* he shall be obliged to pay for all; but where some amongst them are *insolvent,* those who are *able* must pay the Whole. If many, *not in Combination,* concur to the same Thing, and it can plainly be discerned *how much* each of them contributed to the doing of the Mischief; each shall only be accountable for so much as *himself* was the Cause of. But if *one shall pay* the whole, they are *all discharged* for the same.

IX. Damage by Negligence.
L. N. N. l. 3.
c. 1. §6.

Not only he who out of an *evil Design* does wrong to another, is bound to Reparation of the Damage, but he who does so thro' *Negligence* or *Miscarriage,* which he might easily have avoided. For it is no inconsiderable Part of *social Duty,*[34] to manage our Conversation with such *Caution* and *Prudence,* that it does not become *mischievous* and *intolerable* to others; in order to which, Men under some Circumstances and Relations, are obliged to more exact and watchful *diligence:* The slightest Default in this point is sufficient to impose the Necessity of *Reparation;* unless the Fault lay rather more in him who was harmed, than in him who did it; or unless some great Perturbation of Mind, or some Circumstance in the Matter, would not allow the most deliberate Circumspection; *as, when a Soldier in the Heat of Battle in handling his Arms shall hurt his Comrade.

X. Damage by Chance.

But he who by *meer Chance,* without any Fault of his own, shall do Harm to another, is not obliged to *Reparation.* Because nothing in this Case being done which can be chargeable upon him, †there is no Reason, why he who *unwillingly* did a Mischief should rather suffer, than he to whom it was done.

34. Here Tooke's "social Duty" translates Pufendorf's *socialitas,* or "sociability."
* See *Grotius de Jure Belli & Pacis, lib.* 3. *c.* 1. §4.
† See *Grotius de Jure Belli & Pacis, lib.* 3. *c.* 1. §5.

It is also agreeable to Natural Equity, if *my Vassal,* though not by my
Desire, do Wrong to another, that either I make it good, or surrender
him to the Party injured. For 'tis true, this *Vassal* is *naturally obliged* to
Reparation; but he not having wherewith, and his Body being the *Property* of his Patron, it is but just that such Patron either *repair* the Loss
sustained, or *deliver* him up. Otherwise such a Bond-man would be at
liberty to do what Mischief he listed, if Amends cannot be had from
him, because he is the Owner of nothing, no not of the Body he bears;
nor from his *Patron.* For, let him beat the Slave never so severely, or
punish him with the closest imprisonment, that gives *no Restitution* to
the Person wronged.

XI. Damage by a Vassal.

The same seems to be just in the Case of our *Cattle* or any *living Creature* we keep, that, when they *against* our Wills and by a Motion of their
own, contrary to their *Natures,* do a Mischief to another, we either
make *Reparation,* or *give up* the same. For if I am hurt by any Animal
that lives in its *Natural Liberty,* I have a Right, by what means I can, to
give my self Satisfaction by *taking* or by *killing* it; and this Right doubtless cannot be taken away by its being in the Possession of another. And
whereas the Owner of this Animal makes some *Gain* by it, but I have
suffered *Loss* by the same; and whereas the *Reparation* of *Wrong* is more
to be favoured than procuring *Gain;* it appears that I may with reason
demand Satisfaction from the *Owner,* or if the Animal be not worth so
much, then that *it* at least be delivered to me on Account of the Damage sustained.

XII. Damage by Cattle.

Thus then, he who without any *evil Intention* does an Injury to another,
ought of his own accord to offer *Reparation,* and to protest himself to
have done it *unwillingly,* lest the injured Person take him for his *Enemy,*
and endeavour to *retaliate* the Mischief. But he, who with a *naughty
design* shall wrong his Neighbour, is not only bound to offer *Reparation,*
but to declare his *Repentance* for the Fact and to beg *Pardon.* On the
other side, the *wronged Party* having Satisfaction made him, is obliged,
upon the *Repentance* of the other, and at his *Request,* to grant him *Pardon.* For he that will not be content when *Reparation* is made him, and
a fit *Submission* offered, but still seeks to revenge himself by Force, does

XIII. Recapit-ulation.

nothing else but gratifie his own ill Nature, and so disturbs the common Peace of Men without cause. And upon that account *Revenge* is by the *Law of Nature* condemned, as proposing no other End, than doing Mischief to those who have hurt us, and pleasing our selves in their Sufferings. Moreover, there is great Reason that Men should be the more apt to pardon *each others* Offences, upon a consideration how often themselves transgress the *Laws of God,* and have therefore daily so much need of begging Forgiveness of *Him.* [Not still but that the *Publick* may inflict a *Punishment* on the Aggressor, tho' he have given satisfaction to the *Private* Man, if the Act was *Criminal,* and in its Nature *Evil.*]

ᛜᛜ C H A P T E R   V I I ᛜᛜ

The Natural Equality of Men to be acknowledged

I. Equality of Mankind. Man is a Creature not only most sollicitous for the *Preservation* of Himself; but has of Himself also so nice an *Estimation* and *Value,* that to diminish any thing thereof does frequently move in him as great Indignation, as if a Mischief were done to his *Body* or *Estate.* Nay, there seems to him to be somewhat of *Dignity* in the Appellation of **Man**: so that the last and most efficacious Argument to curb the Arrogance of insulting Men, is usually, *I am not a Dog, but a Man as well as your self.* Since then Human Nature is the *same* in us all, and since no Man will or can cheerfully join in Society with any, by whom he is not at least to be esteemed equally as a Man and as a Partaker of the same Common Nature: It follows that, among those *Duties which Men owe to each other,* **L. N. N. I. 3.** this obtains the *second* Place, That *every Man esteem and treat another,* **c. 2. §1.** as naturally *equal to himself, or as one who is a Man as well as he.*

Now this *Equality* of Mankind does not alone consist in this, that Men of ripe Age have almost the same *Strength,* or if one be weaker, he may be able to kill the stronger, either by *Treachery,* or *Dexterity,* or by being better furnished with *Weapons;* but in this, that though Nature may have accomplished one Man beyond another with various Endowments of Body and Mind; yet nevertheless he is obliged to an Observation of the *Precepts* of the *Law Natural* towards the meaner Person, after the same manner as *himself* expects the same from *others;* and has not therefore any greater Liberty given him to insult upon his Fellows.[35] As on the other side the Niggardliness of *Nature* or *Fortune* cannot of themselves set any Man so low, as that he shall be in worse Condition, as to the Enjoyment of *Common Right,*[36] than others. But what *one Man* may rightfully demand or expect from *another,* the same is due to *others* also (Circumstances being alike) from *him;* and whatsoever *one* shall deem reasonable to be done by *others,* the like it is most just he practise *himself:* For *the Obligation of maintaining Sociality among Mankind equally binds every Man;* neither may one Man more than another violate the *Law of Nature* in any part. Not but that there are other *popular Reasons* which illustrate this *Equality;* to wit, that we are all descended of the *same Stock;* that we are all born, nourished, and die after the *same Manner;* and that God has not given any of us a *certain Assurance* that our happy Condition in the World shall not at one time or other be *changed.* Besides, the Precepts of the Christian Religion tell us that God favours not Man for his Nobility, Power, or Wealth, but for *sincere Piety,* which may as well be found in a *mean* and *humble* Man, as in those of *high degree.*

II. Wherein this Equality consists.
L. N. N. l. 3. c. 2. §2.

35. For Pufendorf equality arises neither from a common ability to inflict harm (Hobbes) nor from the universal possession of a soul or rational faculties (the scholastics), but from the fact that all men are subject to the same duties of sociability.

36. Pufendorf's Latin is *communis juris,* which Weber renders as *Gemeinen Rechte,* Barbeyrac as *Droits commun à tous les Hommes,* while Silverthorne opts for "common law."

III. This
Equality
should make
us benevolent,
courteous and
complaisant to
each other.
L. N. N. l. 3.
c. 2. §4.

Now from this *Equality* it follows, *That he who would use the Assistance of others in promoting his own Advantage, ought to be as free and ready to use his Power and Abilities for their Service, when they want his Help and Assistance on the like occasions.* For he who requires that other Men should do him Kindnesses, and expects *himself* to be *free* from doing the like, must be of opinion that those other Men are below himself and not his *Equals.* Hence as those Persons are the *best Members* of a Community, who without any difficulty *allow* the same things to their Neighbour that themselves *require* of him; so those are altogether *uncapable of Society,* who setting a high Rate on themselves in regard to others, will take upon them to act any thing towards their Neighbour, and expect greater Deference and more Respect than the Rest of Mankind; in this insolent manner demanding a greater portion unto themselves in those things, to which all Men having a common Right, they can in reason claim no larger a Share than other Men: Whence this also is an universal Duty of the *Law Natural, That no Man, who has not a peculiar Right, ought to arrogate more to himself, than he is ready to allow to his Fellows, but that he permit other Men to enjoy Equal Privileges with himself.*

IV. It ought to
make us ob-
serve exact
Justice in dis-
tributing to
each his own.
L. N. N. l. 3.
c. 2. §5.

The same *Equality* also shews what every Man's behaviour ought to be, when his business is to *distribute Justice*[37] among others; to wit, *that he treat them as* Equals, *and indulge not that, unless the Merits of the Cause require it, to one, which he denies to another.* For if he do otherwise, he who is discountenanced is at the same time affronted and wronged, and loses somewhat of the Dignity which Nature bestowed upon him. Whence it follows, that Things which are in common, are of right to be *divided* by equal Parts among those who are equal: Where the Thing will not admit of *Division,* they who are equally concerned, are to use it *indifferently;* and, if the Quantity of the Thing will bear it, as *much as* each Party shall think fit: But if this cannot be allowed, then it is to be used after a *stated* manner, and *proportionate* to the Number of the

---

37. Originally *jus,* which might here be better translated as "right."

Claimants; because 'tis not possible to find out any other Way of observing *Equality*. But if it be a Thing of that nature as not to be capable of being *divided*, nor of being possest in *common*, then it must be used by *turns;* and if this yet will not answer the point, and it is not possible the rest should be satisfied by an *Equivalent*, the best Way must be to determin Possession by *Lot;* for in such Cases no fitter Method can be thought on, to remove all Opinion of Partiality and Contempt of any Party, without debasing the Person whom Fortune does not favour.

The Consideration of this *Natural Equality* among Men, ought to take from us all *Pride;* a Vice that consists herein, When a Man, without any Reason, or, without sufficient Reason, prefers himself to others, behaving himself contemptuously and haughtily towards them, as being in his Esteem base Underlings, unworthy of his Consideration or Regard. We say, *without any Reason.* For where a Man is regularly possest of some *Right,* which gives him a Preference to other Men; he may lawfully *make use of,* and *assert* the same, so it be without vain Ostentation and the Contempt of others; as on the contrary every one is with good reason to *yield* that *Respect* and *Honour* which is *due* to *another.* But for the Rest, *true Generosity* has always for its Companion a *decorous Humility,* which arises from a Reflection on the Infirmity of our Nature, and the Faults, of which our selves either have been, or may hereafter be guilty, which are not less heinous than those which may be committed by other Men. The Inference we ought to make from hence is, that we do not over-value our selves with regard to others, considering that *they* equally with us are endowed with a *free Use of their Understanding,* which they are also capable of managing to as *good Purpose;* the *regular Use* whereof is that alone which a Man can call *his own,* and upon which the *true Value* of Himself depends. But for a Man, without any Reason, to set a high esteem upon himself, is a most *ridiculous Vice;* first, because 'tis in it self *silly,* for a Man to carry it high for nothing at all; and then, because I must suppose all *other Men* to be Coxcombs, if I expect from them a great Regard, when I deserve none.

V. This Equality a sufficient Remedy against Pride. L. N. N. l. 3. c. 2. §6.

VI. And
against rude
unmannerly
and contemp-
tuous Behav-
iour. L. N. N.
l. 3. c. 3. §7.
The Violation of this Duty is yet carried farther, if a Man shew his *Contempt* of another by outward Signs, Actions, Words, Looks, or any other abusive way. And this Fault is therefore the more grievous, because it easily excites the Spirits of Men to Anger and Revenge: So that there are many who will rather venture their *Lives* upon the spot, much more will they break the Publick Peace, than put up an *Affront* of that nature; accounting that hereby their Honour is wounded, and a Slur is put upon their Reputation, in the untainted Preservation of which consists all their *Self-satisfaction* and *Pleasure* of Mind.

∽ CHAPTER VIII ∽

Of the mutual Duties of Humanity

I. Doing good
to others.
L. N. N. l. 3.
c. 3.
Among the Duties of one Man towards another, which must be practis'd for the sake of *Common Society,* we put in the *third* place this, *That every Man ought to promote the Good of another, as far as conveniently he may.* For all Mankind being by Nature made, as it were, *akin* to each other; such a Relation requires more than barely abstaining from offering Injury and doing Despight to others. It is not therefore sufficient that we neither hurt nor despise our Fellows, but we ought also to do such *good Offices* to others, or mutually to communicate the same, as that common *brotherly Love* may be kept up among Men. Now we become beneficial to our Neighbour, either *indefinitely* or *definitely;* and *that* either parting with *something* or *nothing* our selves.

II. Benefactors
of the first
Sort. L. N. N.
l. 3. c. 3. §2.
That Man *indefinitely* promotes the Good of others, who takes such necessary care of his *Mind* and *Body,* that he may be able to perform such Actions as may be profitable to his Neighbour; or who by the *Acuteness* of his *Wit* finds out something that may be of Advantage to Mankind. So that those are to be accounted guilty of a *Breach* of this

Duty, who betaking themselves to no *honest Calling* spend their Lives in Sloth, as if their Souls were given them but to serve as Salt to keep their Bodies from stinking, or as if they were born but to make up a Number, and eat their Share: And such as, being *content* with the Estates their *Ancestors* have left 'em, think they may give themselves up to *Idleness* without blame, because they have whereon to live by the Industry of others: And those who *alone* enjoy what they have got, not bestowing any Part upon others: Finally, all those who, like Hogs, do Good to no one till they *die;* and all that Sort of Wretches who only serve to load the Earth with their useless Weight.

On the other side, to those who make it their Business to deserve well of Mankind, the Rest of the World *owe* thus much, that they don't envy 'em, nor lay any Rubs in their way, while by their noble Actions they seek the Universal Good: And if there be no Possibility for themselves to *imitate* 'em, they at least ought to pay a *Regard* to their *Memory* and promote their *Honour,* which perhaps is all they shall get by their Labours. *III. Such deserve Honour as make themselves useful to the Publick. L. N. N. l. 3. c. 3. §3.*

Now *not to do* readily all that *Good* to others which we can do without Detriment, Labour, or Trouble to our selves, is to be accounted detestable *Villany* and *Inhumanity.* The following are wont to be called *Benefits which cost nothing,* or which are of Advantage to the Receiver, without being a Charge to the Bestower. Such as, to allow the Use of the running Water; the letting another light his Fire by mine; the giving honest Advice to him that consults me; the friendly Directing a wandring Man to the right Way, and the like. So, if a Man have a mind to quit the Possession of a Thing, either because he has too much, or because the keeping of it becomes troublesome, why should he not rather leave it fit for Use to others, (provided they are not Enemies) than to mar or destroy it? Hence it is a Sin for us to *spoil Victuals,* because our *Hunger* is satisfied; or to *stop up,* or cover a *Spring,* because we have quenched *our Thirst,* or to destroy *Buoys* set up to discover Shelves and *IV. Good done to others without any charge or cost to the Benefactor.*

Sands, or *Mercuries in Roads, when our selves have made use of them. Under this Head may be comprehended also the *little Alms* bestow'd by the Wealthy upon those who are in Want; and that *Kindness* which we justly shew to *Travellers,* especially if under Necessities, †and the like.

V. Good done to others with an Expence to the Benefactor. L. N. N. l. 3. c. 3. §15.

But it is a higher Degree of Humanity, out of a singular Favour *to do a good Turn freely,* which costs either *Charge* or *Pains,* that so another may either have his Necessities relieved, or acquire some considerable Advantage. And these, by way of Excellence, are called *Benefits,* and are the fittest Matter for rendring Men Illustrious, if rightly tempered with Prudence and Magnanimity. The *Dispensation* of which, and the *Manner,* are to be regulated according to the *Condition* of the *Giver* and *Receiver.* Wherein Care is first of all to be taken; 1. *That the Bounty we are about to exercise do not more Hurt than Good to the Person to whom we design a Kindness, and to others:* Next, 2. *That our Bounty be not greater than consists with our Ability:* Then, 3. *That the Worthiness of Men be regarded in our Distribution, and Preference given to the Well-deserving.* We must therefore consider *how far* each stands in need of our Help, and observe the Degrees of *Relation* among Men; moreover, 'tis to be observ'd *what* every one wants most, and what they can or cannot compass *with* or *without* our *Assistance.* ‡The *Manner* also of exercising Acts of Kindness will render them more acceptable, if they be done *chearfully, readily,* and *heartily.*

VI. Gratitude. L. N. N. l. 3. c. 3. §6.

And then he who *receives* a Benefit ought to have a *grateful Mind,* by which he is to make it manifest, that it was *acceptable* to him, and that for its sake he has a *hearty Respect* to the Donor, and that he wants nothing but an *Opportunity* or an *Ability* of making, if possible, a *Requital* of the full value or more. For it is not absolutely necessary that the Returns we make be *exactly tantamount* to the Courtesy we receive, but our *Good-will* and *hearty Endeavour* are in lieu to be accepted. Not but

---

* Inscribed Posts set up in Highways to direct Travellers.
† See *Grotius de Jure Belli & Pacis, lib.* 2. *cap.* 2. §11, 12. *seq.*
‡ *Grotius de Jure Belli & Pacis, Lib.* 2. *Cap.* 5. §10.

that sometimes he who pretends to have done me a Kindness, may, notwithstanding, have no Reason to say, he has *obliged* me thereby; as if a Man shall drag me out of the Water, into which he pushed me before; in such a Case I owe him no thanks.

Now by how much the more *Benefits* are apt to oblige and place Engagements on the Minds of Men, by so much ought the Party who is *beholden* to be the more eager to return his *Thanks*. If it be but because we ought not to suffer our Benefactor, who out of a good Opinion he had of us has done us a Kindness, to think worse of us; and because we should not receive any Favour, but with a Design to endeavour, that the Giver shall never have Cause to repent of what he has done for us. For, if for any particular Reason we are not willing to be beholden to such or such a Man, we may civilly *avoid* the Accepting of the *Courtesy.* And truly if no grateful Returns were to be made upon the Receipt of Benefits, it would be unreasonable for any Man to cast away what he has, and to do a good Turn where beforehand he is sure it will be slighted. By which means all Beneficence, Good-Will, and Brotherly-Love would be lost among Men; and there would be no such things as doing *Kindnesses frankly,* nor any Opportunities of procuring *mutual Friendships,* left in the World.

VII. Thanks.

And though the *ungrateful Man,* cannot be precisely said to do a *Wrong;* yet the Charge of *Ingratitude* is look'd upon as more base, more odious, and detestable than that of *Injustice;* because 'tis judged a Sign of an *abject* and *rascally Soul* for a Man to shew himself unworthy of the good Opinion, which another had entertain'd of his Probity, and not to be mov'd to some Sense of Humanity by *Benefits,* which have a Power to tame even the Brutes. But, let *Ingratitude* be never so abominable, yet simply considered as it is a bare *Forgetting* of a Courtesy, and a *Neglect* of making a due Return upon occasion, Courts of Judicature take no cognizance of it; for it would lose the Name of *Bounty,* if it were redemandable by Law, as Money lent is; because then it would be a *Credit.* And whereas it is a high Instance of *Generosity* to be grateful, it would cease to be a *generous* Action, when so to do could not be avoided. Be-

VIII. Ingratitude. L. N. N. l. 3. c. 3. §17.

side that it would take up the Business of all Courts, by reason of the great Difficulty in making an Estimate of all the Circumstances, which either would enhance or lessen the Benefit: And that it was to this End I bestow'd it, (to wit, that I did not therefore demand a Promise of Re-payment,) that so the other might have an Occasion of shewing his Gratitude, not for Fear of Punishment, but out of Love to Honesty; and to manifest, that it was not in Hopes of Gain, but only out of mere Kindness that I was liberal of that, which I would not take care should be reimburs'd to me. But for him who improves his *Ingratitude,* and not only gives no thanks to, but injures his Benefactor; *this shall cause an *Aggravation* of his *Punishment,* because it plainly demonstrates the profligate Villany and Baseness of his Mind.

✸ CHAPTER IX ✸

The Duty of Men in making Contracts

I. Contracts. From the Duties *Absolute* to those that are *Conditional* we must take our *Passage,* as it were, through the *intermediate Contracts;* [38] for, since all Duties, except those already mentioned, seem to presuppose some Covenant either expressed or implied; †we shall therefore in the next place treat of the *Nature of Contracts,* and what is to be observed by the Parties concerned therein.

---

*See *Grotius de Jure Belli & Pacis, Lib.* 2. *Cap.* 20. §20.

38. Pufendorf's term is pacts (*pacta*), or agreements. Duties in relation to pacts are transitional between the natural and adventitious duties because it is through pacts that men institute the statuses to which these latter duties attach.

†Compare herewith the whole Eleventh Chapter of the Second Book of *Grotius de Jure,* &c.

Now it is plain that *it was absolutely necessary for Men to enter into mutual Contracts.* For though the Duties of *Humanity* diffuse themselves far and near thro' all the Instances of the Life of Man; yet *that* alone is not Ground sufficient, whereon to fix all the Obligations which may be necessary to be made *reciprocal* between one and another. For all Men are not endowed with so much Good Nature as that they will do all good Offices to every Man out of *meer Kindness,* except they have some certain Expectation of receiving the *like* again: And very often it happens, that the Services we would have to be done to us by *other Men* are of that Sort, that we cannot with *Modesty* desire them. Frequently also, it may not *become* one of my Fortune, or in my Station, to be *beholden* to another for such a Thing. So that many times another cannot give, neither are we willing to accept, unless that other receive an *Equivalent* from us; and it happens not seldom, that my Neighbour *knows not* how he may be serviceable to my occasions. Therefore, that these *mutual good Offices,* which are the Product of *Sociality,* may be more freely and regularly exercised, it was necessary that Men should agree among themselves, concerning what was to be done on this side and on that, which no Man from the *Law of Nature* alone could have assured himself of. So that it was beforehand to be adjusted what, this Man doing *so* by his Neighbour, he was to expect *in lieu* of the same, and which he might lawfully *demand.* This is done by means of *Promises* and *Contracts.*

II. The Necessity of 'em.

With respect to this general Duty it is an Obligation of the *Law of Nature,* that *every Man keep his Word,* or fulfil his Promises and make good his Contracts. For without this, a great Part of that Advantage, which naturally accrues to Mankind by a *mutual Communication* of good Offices and useful Things, would be lost. And were not an exact Observance of one's Promise *absolutely necessary,* no Man could propose to himself any *Certainty* in whatever he design'd, where he must depend upon the Assistances of *others.* Besides that Breach of Faith is apt to give the justest Occasions to Quarrels and Wars. For if, according to my Agreement, I perform my Part, and the other falsifie his Word, whatsoever I have *done* or *deposited* in Expectation of his Performance, is *lost.* Nay, though I have done *nothing* as yet, yet it may be a Mischief for me

III. Veracity.
L. N. N. l. 3.
c. 4. §2.

by this Disappointment to have my *Affairs* and *Purposes confounded,* which I could have taken care of some other way, if this Man had not offered himself. And there is no reason I should become ridiculous, only for having trusted one whom I took to be an honest and a good Man.

IV. Distinction between what is due on Courtesy or Humanity, and what in particular Contract or Promise. L. N. N. l. 3. c. 4.

But it is to be observed, that such Things as are due to me only of *Courtesie,* differ from those which I can claim on account of a *Contract* or *Promise,* in this respect chiefly: That, 'tis true, I may fairly desire the honest Performance of the *first:* But then, if the other shall neglect my Request, I can only charge him with *Rudeness, Cruelty* or *hard dealing;* but I cannot *compel* him to do me reason either by my own Power or by any superior Authority. Which I am at liberty to do in the *latter* Case, if that be not freely performed which ought to have been according to an *absolute Promise* or *Covenant.* *Hence we are said to have an *imperfect Right* to those things, but to these our Claim is *perfect;* as also that to the Performance of the *first* we lie under an *imperfect,* but to the *other* under a *perfect* Obligation.

V. Obligations different. L. N. N. l. 3. c. 5.

Our Word may be given, either by a *single Act,* where one Party only is obliged; or by an *Act reciprocal,* where more than one are Parties. For sometimes *one Man* only binds himself to do somewhat; sometimes *two* or *more* mutually engage each other to the Performance of such and such things. The former whereof is called a *Promise,* the latter a *Covenant* or *Contract.*

VI. Promises imperfect. L. N. N. l. 3. c. 5. §6.

Promises may be divided into *imperfect* and *perfect.* The former is, when we mean indeed to be obliged to make good our Word to him to whom we promise; but we intend not to give him a Power of *requiring* it, or of making use of force to compel us to it. As, if I say thus, I really design to do this or that for you, and I desire you'll believe me. Here I seem more obliged by the Rules of *Veracity* than of *Justice;* and shall rather appear to have done the promised Service out of a Regard to *Constancy*

---

*See *Grotius de Jure Belli & Pacis, Lib.* 1. *cap.* 1. §4. *seqq.*

and *Discretion,* than to *Right.* Of this Sort are the Assurances of great Men who are in favour, whereby they *seriously,* but not upon their *Honours,* promise their Recommendation or Intercession, their Preferring a Man, or giving him their Vote, which yet they intend shall not be demanded of them as Matters of *Right,* but desire they may be wholly attributed to their *Courtesie* and *Veracity;* that the Service they do may be so much the more acceptable, as it was uncapable of *Compulsion.*

But this is called a *perfect Promise,* when I not only oblige my self by my Word, but I give the other Party Authority to *require* at my hands the Performance of what I stipulated, as if 'twere a Debt.

VII. Promise perfect.

Moreover, that *Promises* and *Contracts* may have a full Obligation upon us to *give* and to *do* somewhat, which before we were at liberty *not* to have done; or to *omit* that which we had a Power to *do,* 'tis especially requisite that they be made with our *free Consent.* For whereas the making good of any *Promise* or *Contract* may be accompanied with some *Inconvenience,* there can be no readier Argument why we should not *complain,* than we *consented* thereto of our own accord, which it was in our power not to have done.

VIII. No Obligation where the voluntary Consent of Parties is wanting. L. N. N. l. 3. c. 6.

And this *Consent is usually made known by outward *Signs,* as, by *Speaking, Writing,* a *Nod,* or the like; tho' sometimes it may also be plainly intimated without any of them, according to the Nature of the thing and other Circumstances. So *Silence* in some Cases, and attended with some Circumstances, passes for a *Sign* expressing *Consent.* To this may be attributed those *tacit Contracts,* where we give not our formal Consent by the Signs generally made use of among Men; but the Nature of the Business, and other Circumstances make it fairly supposable. Thus frequently in the principal Contract, which is *express,* another is included which is *tacit,* the Nature of the Case so requiring: And it is usual, in most Covenants that are made, that some *tacit Exceptions* and *imply'd Conditions* must of necessity be understood.

IX. Consent express or tacit. L. N. N. l. 3. c. 6. §16.

---

* See *Grotius de Jure Belli & Pacis, Lib.* II. *Cap.* 4. §4. *Lib.* III. *c.* 1. §8. *c.* 24. §1, 2.

X. Who capa-
ble of giving
Consent.
L. N. N. l. 3.
c. 6. §4.

But to render a Man capable of giving a valid *Consent,* 'tis absolutely requisite, that he have so far the *Use of his Reason,* as fully to *understand* the Business that lies before him, and to know whether it be *meet* for him, and whether it lie in his *Power* to perform it; and having consider'd this, he must be capable of giving *sufficient* Indications of his *Consent.* Hence it follows, that the Contracts and Promises of *Ideots* and *Madmen* (except such whose Madness admits of lucid Intervals) are

L. N. N. l. 3.
c. 6. §4.

null and void: And the same must be said of those of *Drunken Men,* if they are besotted to that degree as that their Reason is overwhelm'd and stupify'd. For it can never be accounted a *real* and *deliberate Consent,* if a Man, when his Brains are disorder'd and intoxicated, shall on a sudden and rashly make foolish Engagements, and give the usual Demonstrations of Consent, which at *another* time would have *obliged* him: and it would be a Piece of *Impudence* for any Man to exact the Performance of such a Promise, especially if it were of any considerable weight. But if one Man shall lay hold on the *Opportunity* of another's being drunk, and craftily making an *advantage* of his Easiness of Temper under those Circumstances, shall procure any Promise from him, this Man is to be accounted guilty of a *Cheat* and *Knavery:* Not but that, if, after the Effects of his Drink are over, he shall *confirm* such Promise, he shall be *obliged;* and this not with regard to what he said when *drunk,* but to his Confirmation when *sober.*

XI. Consent in
young Persons.
L. N. N. l. 3.
c. 6. §5.

As for *Consent* in *young Persons,* it is impossible for the *Laws Natural* to determine so nicely the *exact Time* how long Reason will be too weak in them to render 'em capable of making Engagements; because Maturity of Discretion appears earlier in some than in others; Judgment therefore must be made hereof by the *daily Actions* of the *Person.* Though this is taken care for in most Commonwealths, by *Laws* prescribing a certain *Term* of years to all in general; and in many Places it is become a commendable Custom to set these under the *Guardianship* of wiser Men, whose Authority must be had to any Contracts they make, till the other's youthful Rashness be a little abated. For Persons of this Age, however perhaps they may well enough understand what they do, yet for the most part act with too much Vehemence and Rashness; are too free and easie in their Promises, eager and over confident in their Hopes, proud of being thought generous and liberal, ambitious and hasty in contracting Friendships, and not furnished with prudent Caution and necessary Diffidence. So that he can hardly pass for an *honest* Man, who makes any advantage of the *Easiness* of this Age, and would gain by the *Losses* of *young people,* who for want of Experience could not foresee, or place a true Estimate thereon.

Another Thing which invalidates *Consent,* and by consequence the Promises and Pacts that are built upon it, is *Errour* or Mistake; thro' which it comes to pass, that the Understanding is cheated in its Object, and the Will in its Choice and Approbation. Concerning *Error,* these three Rules are deligently to be observ'd. (I.) *That when to my Promise, some* Condition *is supposed, without the Consideration whereof I should not have made such Promise; the same shall, without the* other, *have no Obligation upon me.* For in this Case the Promiser does not engage *absolutely,* but upon a *Condition,* which not being made good, the Promise becomes null and void. (2.) *If I am drawn into a Bargain or Contract by a* Mistake, *which Mistake I find, before as we use to say Bulk is broke,*[39] *or any thing done in order to the Consummation thereof, it is but Equity*

---

*Provided this Error concerns something essential to the Bargain made; that is to say, that it does necessarily and naturally concern the Affair in hand, or respects plainly the Intention of those who contract, notified sufficiently at such time as the Contract was made: And on both Sides allowed as a Reason without which such Contract had never been made; otherwise, as the Errour had no Influence on the Contract to be made, so can it not disannul it when made, whether it be executed or not. An Example will make the meaning hereof plain. Suppose I imagin that I have lost my Horse and that I shall never recover him again; and buy another, which otherwise I wouldn't have done: If I happen afterwards, contrary to Expectation, to find my own again, I can't oblige the Person I bought the new one from to take it again, altho' at that time he shou'dn't have sent me the Horse, or have receiv'd the money agreed for: Unless when we bargain'd, I had expressly and formally made this a Condition of annulling such Agreement: For without such formal Stipulation, the Agreement stands good against me, altho' I might (in way of Discourse only) mention, that I would not have bought this Horse, had I not lost my other. See *L. N. N. lib.* 3. *c.* 6. §7. See also *Grotius de Jure Belli &. Pacis, lib.* 3. *cap.* 23. §4. [Barbeyrac's XII.1, p. 147.]

39. Roughly, "before the cargo is unloaded."

that I should be at liberty to retract; especially if upon the Contract making, I plainly signify'd for what *Reason* I agreed to it; more particularly,
if the other Party suffers no *Damage* by my going off from my Bargain,
or, if he does, that I am ready to make *Reparation.* But when, as was
said afore, Bulk is broke, and the *Mistake* is not found till the Covenant
is either wholly or in part already performed, the Party who is under an
Errour cannot retract, any farther than the other shall of *Courtesy* release
to him. (3.) *When a* Mistake *shall happen concerning the* Thing, *which is
the* Subject *of the Contract, such Contract is invalid, not for the sake of the
Mistake, but because the Laws and Terms of the Agreement are not really
fulfilled.* For in Bargains of this nature, the *Thing* and all its *Qualifications* ought to be known, without which Knowledge a fair Agreement
cannot be supposed to be made. So that he who is like to suffer Wrong
by any Defect therein, either may throw up his Bargain, or force the
other to make the Thing as it should be, or else to pay him the Value,
if it happen'd through his Knavery or Negligence.

**XIII. Guileful
Contracts.
L. N. N. l. 3.
c. 6. §8.** But if a Man be drawn into a Promise or Bargain by the *Craft* and
fraudulent Means of another; then the Matter is thus to be considered.
(1.) *If a* third *Man were guilty of the Cheat, and the Party with whom the
Bargain is driven was not concerned in it, the Agreement will be valid:* But
we may demand of him who practis'd the Knavery, so much as we are
Losers by being deceiv'd. (2.) *He who knavishly procures me to promise or
contract with him, shall not set me under any Obligation.* (3.) *If a Man
will indeed come freely with a plain* *Design *to drive a Bargain, but in the
very* Action *shall perceive a Trick put upon him; suppose in the* Thing *bargain'd for, its Qualities or Value; the Contract shall be so far naught, as to
leave it in the Power of him who is deceiv'd, either to relinquish his Bargain, or to require Satisfaction for his Loss.* (4.) *If unfair Dealing chance to
be us'd in some things not* essential *to the Business, and which were not*
expressly under regard, *this weakens not the Agreement, if, for the* rest, *it
be regularly made;* tho' perhaps *one Party* might have a Secret and sly
Respect to some such thing, at the very time of driving the Bargain, and

---

*See *Grotius de Jure Belli & Pacis, Lib.* 2. *cap.* 17. §17.

cunningly conceal'd such his View till the Contract were perfectly transacted.

Whensoever *Fear* is to be consider'd in Promises or Bargains, it is two-fold, and may either be call'd a *probable Suspicion* lest we should be deceiv'd by another, and this because he is one who is very much addicted to unjust Practices, or has sufficiently intimated his fraudulent Design; or else a *panic Terror of the Mind,* arising from some grievous Mischief threatned, except we make such a Promise or Contract. Concerning the first Sort of *Fear,* (or *Mistrust* rather) these Things are to be observ'd. (1.) *He who trusts the Engagements of one who is* notoriously negligent *of his Word and Troth, acts very imprudently; but, for that Reason only can have no Remedy, but shall be obliged.* (2.) *When a Bargain is fully made and compleated, and a Man hath no new Reasons to apprehend any knavish Designs from the other Party, it shall not be sufficient to invalidate the Agreement that the other was, on other Occasions before this Agreement, known to have been trickish and deceitful.* For since our Knowledge of such his former Behaviour did not prevent our making the Agreement with him, it ought not to prevent our making it good to him. (3.) *Where* after *the Bargain made, it appears plainly that the other Person intends to elude* his *Part of the Contract, as soon as I have perform'd* mine; *here I cannot be forced to comply* first, *till I am secure of a Performance on the other side.*

XIV. Contracts suspicious. L. N. N. l. 3. c. 6. §9.

As for the other Sort of *Fear,* these Rules are to be observ'd. (1.) *If a Man has taken an Obligation upon him, thro' Fear of Mischief threatned by a* third *Person, neither at the Instigation, nor with the Confederacy of the Party to whom the Engagement was made, he stands firmly bound to perform what he promis'd.* For there appears no Fault in him to whom the Promise was made, which can render him uncapable of acquiring a Right to the Performance of it; on the contrary, he may justly challenge a Requital, in that he lent his Assistance to the other, in warding off the Danger he apprehended from the *third* Person. (2.) *All such* Covenants *that are made out of* Fear *or* Reverence *of our lawful Superiours, or by the* Awe *we have for those to whom we are very much beholden, shall be firm*

XV. Contracts thro' Fear. L. N. N. l. 3. c. 7. §11.

and good. (3.) *Those* Bargains *which are* wrongfully *and* forcibly *extorted from a Man by the Person to whom the Promise or Agreement is made, are invalid,* For the *Violence* he unjustly uses to set me under that *Fear,* renders him uncapable of pretending to any Right against me on account of such Action of mine. And whereas in all other Cases, every Man is bound to Reparation of what Wrong he shall do to another: this *Restitution to which he is bound is understood as it were to take off any Obligation from such Promise, since if what was promised were paid, it ought to be immediately restored.

XVI. Consent mutual. L. N. N. l. 3. c. 6. §15. Moreover not only in Contracts, but in Promises the *Consent* ought to be *reciprocal;* that is, both the Promiser and he to whom the Promise is made must agree in the Thing. For if the latter shall not *consent,* or refuse to *accept* of what is offered, the thing promised remains still in the Power of the Promiser. For he that makes an *offer* of any thing, cannot be supposed to intend to *force* it upon one that is *unwilling* to receive it, nor yet to *quit* his own Title to it; therefore when the other *denies* Acceptance, he who proffered it loses nothing of his Claim thereto. If the Promise was occasion'd by a *Request* before made, the same shall be accounted to oblige so long, as till such Request be expressly *revok'd;* for in that case the thing will be understood to be *accepted beforehand;* provided yet that what is offer'd be proportion'd to what was desired. For if it be not, then an *express Acceptance* is requisite; because it may often do me no good to answer my Request by halves.

XVII. Impossible Engagements. L. N. N. l. 3. c. 7. As for the *Matter* of our Promises and Contracts, it is absolutely necessary, that what we promise, or make a Bargain for, be *in our Power* to make good, and that so to do be not prohibited by any Law; otherwise we engage our selves either *foolishly* or *wickedly.* Hence it follows that *no Man is obliged to do Things impossible.* But if it be a Thing which at the time of the Bargain making was possible, and yet afterwards by

---

*There was no need to have recourse to this Duty of Restitution, thereby to shew the Invalidity of such Contracts. For the want of Liberty in the Person promising, and the want of Capacity in the Person obtaining by force the Promise, of creating to himself thereby any Right to the Thing promised, are sufficient to shew the plain Nullity of the Agreement thus obtained. [Barbeyrac's XV.1, p. 152.]

some Accident, without any Fault of the Contracter, became altogether impossible, the Contract shall be null, if there be nothing as yet done in it; but if one Party have perform'd somewhat towards it, what he has advanced is to be restor'd to him, or an Equivalent given; and if this cannot be done, by all means it is to be endeavour'd that he suffer no loss thereby. For in Contracts that is principally to be regarded which was *expressly* in the Bargain; if this cannot be obtain'd, it must suffice to give an *Equivalent;* but if neither can this be had, at least the *utmost Care* is to be taken that the Party undergo no Damage. But where any Man shall *designedly,* or by some very *blameable Miscarriage,* render himself uncapable of making good his Part of the Bargain, he is not only obliged to use his utmost Endeavour, but ought also to be *punish'd,* as it were, to make up the amends.

It is also manifest, that we cannot set our selves under any Obligation to perform what is *unlawful.* For no Man can engage himself farther than he hath *lawful Authority* so to do. But that Legislator who prohibits any Action by a Law takes away all legal Power of undertaking it, and disables any Man from obliging himself to perform it. For it would imply a Contradiction, to suppose, that from a Duty enjoyn'd by the Laws should arise an Obligation to do that which the same Laws forbid to be done. So that he transgresses who promises to do what is unlawful, but he is doubly a Transgressor who performs it. Hence also it follows, that neither are those Promises to be kept, the Observation of which will be *mischievous* to him to whom they are made; because it is forbidden by the *Law-Natural* to do hurt to any Man, even though he do foolishly desire it. And if a Contract be made to do some *filthy* and *base* Thing, neither shall be obliged to fulfil it. If such filthy Thing be done by one Party pursuant to the Bargain, the other shall not be bound to give the Reward agreed for; *but if any thing be already given on that account, it cannot be demanded again.

XVIII. Unlawful Engagements.
L. N. N. l. 3. c. 7. §6, 7.

---

*This determination seems not altogether just, because he who had parted with his Goods, had parted with them by an act invalid and of no effect. See *L. N. N. l. 3. c. 7.* §9. [Barbeyrac's XVIII.1, p. 155.]

XIX. Engage-
ments con-
cerning other
men, L. N. N.
l. 3. c. 7. §10.
And then, it is plain, that such Engagements and Bargains as we shall make of what belongs to other Men are altogether insignificant, so far as they are not ours, but subject to the Will and Direction of others. But if I promise thus; *I will use my Endeavour that such a Man* (always supposing him to be one not absolutely under my Command) *shall do so or no:* Then I am obliged by all methods morally possible, (that is, so far as the other can fairly request of me, and as will consist with Civility) to take pains to move that Person to perform what is desired. Nay we cannot promise to a third Man *Things* in our own possession, or *Actions* to be done by our selves, to which another has acquir'd a Right, unless it be so order'd, as not to be in force till the time of that other's Claim is *expir'd.* For he who by *antecedent* Pacts or Promises has already transferr'd his Right to another, has no more such Right left to pass over to a *third* Person: And all manner of *Engagements* and *Bargains* would be easily eluded, if a Man after having contracted with one, might be at liberty to enter a Treaty with another, wherein Disposals should be made contrary to the *first* Agreement, and with which it is impossible *this* should consist. Which gives foundation to that known Rule, *First in Time, prior in Right.*

XX. Condi-
tions various
L. N. N. l. 3.
c. 8. §1.
Beside all which it is to be chiefly observ'd concerning Promises, that they are wont to be made *positively* and *absolutely;* or *conditionally,* that is, when the Validity thereof lies upon some *Event* depending on Chance or the Will of Man.

Now *Conditions* are either *possible* or *impossible;* and the former are subdivided into *Casual* or fortuitous, which *we* cannot cause to be or not to be; or *Arbitrary,* or such as are in the Power of him to whom the Promise is made, that they are or are not comply'd with; or else *Mixt,* the fulfilling of which depends partly on the Will of the Person receiving the Promise, and partly on Chance.

Impossible Conditions are either such as are *naturally* or *morally* so, that is, some Matters by the Nature of Things *cannot* be done; others by the Direction of the Laws *ought not* to be done. Such Conditions then as these being annex'd, do, according to the plain and simple Construction of the Words, render the Promise *Negative,* and therefore null; tho' it is true it may be so provided by Law, that if to Affairs of great

Concernment any such *impossible Conditions* should be annex'd the Agreement may remain good, rejecting these Conditions as if they had never been made; that so Men may not have busied themselves about that which otherwise can signifie nothing.

Lastly, we promise and contract, not only in our *own Persons,* but often-times by the *Mediation* of other Men, whom we constitute the *Bearers* and *Interpreters* of our Intentions; by whose Negociations, if they deal faithfully by us in following the Instructions we gave, we are firmly obliged to those Persons who transacted with them as our Deputies.

XXI. Media-
tory Contracts.
L. N. N. l. 3.
c. 9 §1.

And thus we have done with the *Absolute* Duties of Man, by which, as it were, we naturally pass to the *Conditional* Duties of Men. And these do all presuppose some Human Institution, founded upon an *Universal Agreement,* and so introduced into the World, or else some peculiar State or Condition. And of this Sort of Institutions, there are three chiefly to be insisted on, to wit, *Speech* or *Discourse, Property* and the *Value* of Things, and the *Government* of Mankind. Of each of these, and of the Duties arising therefrom we shall next discourse.

XXII. Conclu-
sion.

ↁↃↀ C H A P T E R   X   ↁↃↀ

The Duty of Men in Discourse

How useful and altogether necessary an Instrument of Human Society *Discourse*[40] is, there is no Man can be ignorant; since many have made that only an Argument to prove Man to be by Nature design'd for a *Social Life.* Now that a *lawful* and *beneficial Use* may be made hereof for the Good of the same Human Society, the *Law* of *Nature* has given

I. General
Rule. To de-
ceive no one
by any means
established to
express our
Thoughts.

40. In Pufendorf's Latin the word is *sermo,* meaning "conversation" or "discourse," which Barbeyrac translates as *parole* and Silverthorne as "language."

Men this for a Duty, *That no Man deceive another either by Discourse, or any other Signs which customarily are accepted to express our inward Meaning.*

II. Uniform Signification of Words. L. N. N. l. 4. c. 1.

But that the Nature of *Discourse* may be more throughly understood, it must first be known, that there is a two-fold Obligation respecting *Discourse,* whether exprest with the Voice, or written in *Characters.* The first is, that those who make use of the *same Language,* are obliged to apply such certain *Words* to such certain *Things,* according as Custom has made them to signify in each Language. For since neither any *Words* nor any particular *Strokes* form'd into *Letters* can *naturally* denote any certain *Thing* (otherwise all Languages and Characters for writing would be the same; and hence the Use of the Tongue would be to no purpose if every Man might call every *Thing* by what *Name* he pleas'd;) it is absolutely necessary among those who speak the same Language, that there be a *tacit Agreement* among them, that this certain Thing shall be so, or so call'd, and not otherwise. So that unless an *uniform Application* of *Words* be agreed upon, 'twill be impossible for one Man to gather the Meaning of another from his Talk. By virtue then of this *tacit Compact,* every Man is bound in his common Discourse to apply his Words to *that Sense,* which agrees with the *receiv'd Signification* thereof in that Language: From whence also it follows, that albeit a Man's *Sentiments* may differ from what he expresses in Words, yet in the Affairs of Human Life he must be look'd upon as *intending* what he *says,* tho', as was said, perhaps his inward Meaning be the clear contrary. For since we cannot be inform'd of another's *Mind* otherwise than by outward *Signs,* all Use of Discourse would be to no purpose, if by *mental Reservations,* which any Man may form as he lists, it might be in his power to elude what he had declar'd by Signs usually accepted to that end.

III. Discourse to be plain. L. N. N. l. 4. c. 1. §6.

The other Obligation which concerns *Discourse,* consists in this, that every Man ought by his *Words* so to express to another his *Meaning,* that he may be plainly understood. Not but that it is in a Man's power to be *silent,* as well as to *speak;* and whereas no Man is bound to tell every one all that he bears in his Mind; it is necessary that there be some *peculiar Obligation* that shall engage him first to speak, and then so to speak as that another shall fully understand his Meaning. Such Obligation may arise from a *particular Compact,* or some *common Precept of the Law Natural,* or from the *Nature of the present Affair,* in which Speech is made use of: For oftentimes a *Bargain* is made expressly with a Man, that he shall disclose to me all that he knows in some Matter; as suppose I desired to be instructed in any Science: Frequently also I may be *commanded* by some Precept of the *Law of Nature* to communicate my Skill to another, that by this Means I may be helpful to him, or that I may save him from Mischief, or that I may not give him some Cause or Occasion of receiving a Harm: And lastly, the *present Case* may require me to declare my Opinion in a Matter wherein another is concerned; as it often happens in Contracts of the greatest Importance.

But because it cannot *always* happen, that upon any of these Heads I am *obliged* to signify my Thoughts upon any Matter, it is plain that I am not bound to disclose in Words any more than another has a *Right* either *perfect* or *imperfect* to require. So that I may, by holding my Tongue, lawfully conceal what he has no just Claim to the Knowledge of, or to the Discovery whereof I lie under no Obligation, however earnestly it be desir'd. *IV. Silence. L. N. N. l. 4. c. 1. §7.*

Nay, since *Speech* was not only ordain'd for the Use of *others,* but *our own* Benefit also; therefore whensoever my private Interest is concern'd, and it occasions Damage to no Body else, I may so order my Words, that they may communicate a Sense different from that which I bear in my Mind. *V. Counterfeit Discourse.*

Lastly, because oftentimes those to whom we talk upon some Matters may be so disposed, that from a *downright* and *plain Discourse* they would perceive the true State of the Case, which ought rather to be *conceal'd,* because a full Knowledge would not procure the good End we drive at, but be a *Detriment* to 'em; we may in such Cases use a *figurative* or *shadow'd* way of *Speech,* which shall not directly represent our Meaning and plain Sense to the Hearers. For he who would and ought *VI. Figurative Speech.*

to benefit another, cannot be bound to attempt it after such a manner, as shall incapacitate him from obtaining his End.

VII. Verity.
L. N. N. l. 4.
c. 1. §8.

From what has been said may be gather'd wherein that *Verity* consists, for their Regard to which good Men are so much celebrated; to wit, that our *Words* do fitly represent our *Meaning* to any other Person who *ought* to understand 'em, and which it is our *Duty* to *express plainly* to him, either by a perfect or imperfect Obligation; and this to the end either that he upon knowing our Minds may make to himself some Benefit thereby, or that he may avoid some undeserv'd Evil, which he would incur upon a wrong Understanding of the Case. Hence by the Bye it is manifest, that it is not always to be accounted *Lying*, when even for the nonce a Tale is told concerning any Thing in such a manner as does not exactly quadrate with the Thing it self, nor with our own Opinion of it; and consequently, that the Congruity of *Words* with *Things,* which constitutes the *Logical* Verity, is not in all Points the same with *Moral Truth.*

VIII. A Lye.

On the contrary that is rightly call'd a *Lye,* when our Words bear a different Signification from that which we think in our Minds, whereas the Person to whom we direct our Discourse has a *Right* to understand the Thing as it *really* is, and we are under an *Obligation* of making our Meaning *plain* to him.

IX. Innocent
Untruths.
L. N. N. l. 4.
c. 1. §11.

From what is said it appears, *that those are by no Means chargeable with *Lying*, who entertain *Children* or the like with Fables and fictitious Discourses for their better Information, they being suppos'd uncapable of the naked Truth. As neither are those who make Use of a *feign'd Story* to some *good End,* which could not be attain'd by speaking the *plain Truth;* suppose, to protect an Innocent, to appease an angry Man, to comfort one who is in Sorrow, to encourage the Fearful, to persuade a nauseating Patient to take his Physick, to soften the Obstinate, or to divert the evil Intention of another, and the like; or, if the Secrets and

---

* See *Grotius de Jure Belli, &c. lib. 3. cap. 1. §9. seqq.*

Resolutions of a Community[41] are to be kept from publick Knowledge, we may raise false Rumours in order to conceal 'em, and to mislead the importunate Curiosity of others; or, if we have an Enemy, whom by open Force we cannot Annoy, we may, by way of Stratagem, make Use of any lying Tales to do him Mischief.

On the other side, if any Man be *bound* in Duty to signifie *plainly* his *true Meaning* to another, he is not without Blame, if he discover only a *part* of the Truth, or amuse him with *ambiguous* Discourse, or use some *mental Reservation* not allow'd in the common Conversation of Men.

X. Equivocation and mental Reservation. L. N. N. l. 4. c. 1. §14.

∞ CHAPTER XI ∞

The Duty of those which take an Oath

All Men agree in the Opinion, That an *Oath* gives a great additional Confirmation to all our Assertions, and to those Actions which depend upon our Discourse. An *Oath* is, *A Religious Asseveration, by which we disavow the Divine Clemency, or imprecate to our selves the Wrath of God if we speak not the Truth.* Now when an All-wise and an Almighty *Witness* and *Guaranty* is invok'd, it causes a strong Presumption of the Truth, because no Man can easily be thought so Wicked, as to dare rashly to call down upon himself the grievous Indignation of the Deity. Hence it is the Duty of those that take an Oath, *To take the same with awful Reverence, and religiously to observe what they have sworn.*

I. An Oath. L. N. N. l. 4. c. 2.

41. This is Tooke's English euphemism for Pufendorf's *arcana reip[ublicae]*, appropriately translated by Barbeyrac as *secrets de l'Etat* (*secrets of state*).

*Compare herewith the whole 13*th* Chapter of the 2*d* Book of *Grotius de Jure*, &c.

II. The End and Use. Now the *End* and *Use* of an Oath is chiefly this, To oblige Men the more firmly to speak the Truth, or to make good their Promises and Contracts out of an Awe of the Divine Being, who is infinitely Wise and Powerful; whose Vengeance they imprecate to themselves when they Swear, if they wittingly are guilty of Deceit; whereas otherwise the Fear of what *Men* can do may not be sufficient; because possibly they may have Hope to oppose or escape their Power, or to beguile their Understandings.

III. Swearing by what. L. N. N. l. 4. c. 2. §3. Since GOD alone is of infinite Knowledge and of infinite Power, it is a manifest Absurdity to swear by any other Name but the Name of GOD only; that is, in such a Sense, as to invoke it for a Witness to our Speech, and for an Avenger of our Perjury: But if in the Form of Oaths any other Things, that we hold Dear, or have in Veneration or Esteem, be mention'd, it is not to be understood that such Things are invok'd as Witnesses to our Truth or Avengers of our Falsehood; but GOD only is herein invok'd, with a Desire, that if we swear falsely, he would be pleas'd to punish our Crime, in these Things especially for which we are most nearly and tenderly concern'd.

IV. Forms how to be accommodated. L. N. N. l. 4. c. 2. §4. In Oaths the *Form* which is prescrib'd, (by which the Person swearing invokes GOD as a Witness and an Avenger) is to be *accommodated to the Religion of the said Swearer;* that is, to that Persuasion and Opinion of GOD which he is of. For 'tis to no Purpose to make a Man swear by a God, whom he does not *believe,* and consequently does not *fear.* But no Man supposes himself to take an Oath in any other Form, nor under any other Notion, than that which is consonant to the Precepts of *his Religion,* which, in his Opinion, is the *true.* Hence also it is, that he who swears by *false Gods,* which yet himself takes to be true ones, stands obliged, and if he falsifies is really guilty of Perjury; because whatever his peculiar Notions were, he certainly had some Sense of the Deity before his Eyes; and therefore by wilfully forswearing himself he violated, as far as he was able, that Awe and Reverence which he ow'd to Almighty GOD.

That an Oath may be *binding,* 'tis necessary it be taken with *deliberate Thoughts,* and a *real Design:* Whence he shall not be obliged by an Oath who meerly *recites* it; or speaking in the *first Person,* dictates the concept formal Words thereof to another who is to say after him. But he who shall *seriously* behave himself as one that is about to *swear solemnly,* shall be obliged, whatsoever *mental Reservations* he all the while may harbour in his Mind. For otherwise all Oaths, nay, all Methods of mutual Obligation by the Intervention of the plainest Significations would be of no Use to human Life, if any Man by his *tacit Intention* could hinder such an Act from obtaining such an Effect as it was first instituted to produce.

V. Delibera-tion necessary. L. N. N. l. 4. c. 2. §5.

We ought likewise carefully to observe, that Oaths do not of themselves produce a new and peculiar Obligation, but are only apply'd as an *Accessional Strength,* and an additional Bond to an *Obligation,* in its nature valid before. For whenever we swear, we always suppose some Matter, upon non-performance of which we thus imprecate the Vengeance of Heaven. But now this would be to no purpose, unless the Omission of the Thing suppos'd had been before unlawful, and consequently, unless we had before been obliged. Tho' indeed it frequently happens, that we comprehend in one Speech, both the *principal Obligation* and the *additional Bond* of the *Oath;* as thus, *As God help me, I'll give you a hundred Pounds.* Where the Oath is not superfluous, albeit 'tis added to a Promise that might have been valid of it self. Because tho' every good Man believes a bare Promise to oblige, yet 'tis look'd upon to be the more firm when 'tis reinforced with an Imprecation of Vengeance from above upon a Failure. Hence it follows, that any Acts which were before attended with some inward *Flaw,* hindring any Obligation to arise from them, cannot be made obligatory by the Accession of an Oath; as neither can a *subsequent* Oath avoid a *former legitimate Engagement,* or annul that Right which *another* may claim thereby; thus a Man would swear in vain not to pay another Person what is justly due to him: Nor will an Oath be of any Validity, where it appears, that 'twas made by the Juror upon *Supposition* of a Thing to be done which was not *really so;* and that he would not have so sworn, had not he *believ'd* it to be done;

VI. Oaths how obliging. L. N. N. l. 4. c. 2. §6.

especially if he were *cajol'd* into such his Error by the *Craft* of him to whom the Oath was made: *Neither shall he, who by setting me under *panick Fear* forces me to take an Oath, have any good Title to require my Performance. Farthermore, an Oath shall have no Obligation upon me to do any *unlawful Act,* or to *omit* the performing any *Duty* enjoyn'd by the Laws of God or Man. Lastly, an Oath cannot *alter* the Nature or Substance of the Contract or Promise to which it is annex'd: Hence it cannot oblige to *Impossibilities.* Again, a *Conditional* Promise, by the Addition of an Oath, is not changed into a *Positive* and *Absolute* Promise: In like manner, it is no less requisite to Promises confirm'd by Oaths, than to others which are not so confirm'd, that they be accepted by the other Party: So that he who obtains a Right by any Covenant, may equally release the Performance of it, whether it was sworn to or not.

VII. Punishment. L. N. N. l. 4. c. 2. §12.   But the taking of an *Oath* has this Effect among Men, for the sake of that Invocation of God which is therein made use of, whose Wisdom no Man's Cunning can elude, and who suffers not the Man that mocks Him to escape unpunish'd; that not only a *heavier Punishment* is assign'd to him who forswears himself, than to him who barely breaks his Word; but it puts them in mind to avoid all *Deceit* and *Prevarication* in the Matters which it is added to confirm.

VIII. Strict Interpretation. L. N. N. l. 4. c. 2. §14.   Not yet that *all Oaths* are to be consider'd in their greatest *Latitude,* but that sometimes they must be interpreted in the *narrowest Sense,* if so it be, that the Subject-matter seem to require it: For instance; if the Oath be made to promote some *malicious Design* against another, to execute something *threatned,* and not to perform somewhat *promis'd.* Neither does an Oath exclude *tacit Conditions* and *Limitations,* provided they are such as plainly result from the Nature of the Thing; as suppose, I have sworn to give another whatsoever he shall request, if he ask what it is *wicked* or *absurd* for me to grant, I am not at all obliged. For he who indefinitely promises any Thing to him that desires, before he

---

* *Grotius de Jure Belli & Pacis, Lib.* 3. *cap.* 19. §5.

knows what he is like to ask, presupposes the other will crave nothing but what is *honest,* and morally *possible,* not Things absurd or mischievous to himself or any Body else.

This is also to be noted, that in Oaths *the Sense of all the Words thereof is to be such as he shall acknowledge himself to take them in, who accepts the Oath,* that is, *to whom* the other Party swears. For the Oath is to be look'd upon to be made for *his* sake, and not for the sake of the *Juror.* Whence it is *his* Part to dictate the *Form* of the Oath, and this to do in Words as *plain* as is possible, so that himself may signify in what *Sense* he conceives them; and the Person swearing may profess that he well understands his *Meaning,* and then those Words are *distinctly* to be express'd, that so no room may be left for Cavils or Shuffling.

IX. Sense of an Oath. L. N. N. l. 4. c. 2. §15.

Oaths may most fitly be *distinguish'd* according to the *Use* they are apply'd to in Human Life. *Some are annex'd to *Promises* and *Contracts,* thereby to procure a *strict and religious Observance* of the same; others are apply'd to the *Confirmation* of any Man's *Assertion* concerning a Matter of Fact not altogether evident, and where the Truth cannot by other Means be more conveniently search'd out; such are the Oaths administred to *Witnesses,* and those who are privy to another Man's doings; sometimes also two *Adversaries,* or *Litigants,* may, with the Consent of the Judge, or the Concession of one Party, by taking such or such an Oath put an end to their *Law-Suit.*

X. Oaths divided.

---

*These are call'd Obligatory or Promissory Oaths, (*Juramenta Promissoria:*) the other Assertory or Affirmative Oaths, (*Assertoria.*) [Barbeyrac's X.1, p. 172.]

CHAPTER XII

Duties to be observ'd in acquiring
Possession of Things

I. Other Crea-
tures useful to
Man.

Whereas such is the Condition of Man's Body, that it cannot be *supported* and *preserved* from that which would destroy its Fabric, without the Assistance of *Things without* him; and whereas by making Use of *other Creatures*[42] his Life may be render'd much more *comfortable* and *easie;* we may safely gather, that it is the Will of the supreme Moderator of the World, that he be allow'd to apply such other Creatures to his Service, and that he may even destroy many of them for his Occasions. *Neither doth this hold, as to *Vegetables* only, which have no Sense of the Loss of their Beings; but it reaches even the *innocent Animals,* which though they die with Pain, yet are kill'd and devour'd by Men for their Sustenance without Sin.

L. N. N. l. 4.
c. 3. §2.

II. Possession
introduced.

Farther, all these *outward Things* are understood to have been left in the Beginning by God *indifferent to the claim of all Men;* that is, so that none of them were the Property of this Man rather than that. Not but that Men were at liberty to *dispose* Things so, as should seem requisite to the Condition of Mankind, and the Conservation of Peace, Tranquillity and good Order in the World. Hence it was, that at first, while the Human Race was but of a small Number, †it was agreed, That *whatever any one did first seize should be his, and not be taken from him*

L. N. N. l. 4.
c. 4. §5.

---

42. Meaning not just animals but created things in general.
* See *Grotius de Jure Belli & Pacis, lib.* 2. *cap.* 2. §2. *seqq.*
† There was no need of any Convention, either exprest or tacit for this purpose. The Right of the first Occupant is necessarily concluded to be conformable to his Intention who bestows any Thing in common to many, provided, that in possessing one's self of that which no one has a particular Right, we content our selves with a modest Proportion, not engrossing the Whole, but leaving what is sufficient for the Occasions and Use of others. See *L. N. N. l.* 4. *c.* 4. §4. [Barbeyrac's note (II.1, p. 174) dissents from Pufendorf's treatment of all property rights as adventitious or

by another; provided however, *that he only possesses himself out of the common Store of what is sufficient for his private Service, but not so as to destroy the whole Fund, and so prevent a Stock for future Uses.* But afterward, when Mankind was multiply'd, and they began to bestow *Culture* and *Labour* upon those Things which afforded them Food and Raiment; for the prevention of Quarrels; and for the sake of good Order, those *Bodies* or *Things* also, which produced such Necessaries, *were divided among particular Men,* and every one had his proper Share assign'd him, with this general Agreement, That *whatsoever in this first Division of Things, was yet left unpossest, should for the future be the Property of the first Occupant.* *And thus, God so willing, with the previous Consent, or at least by a tacit Compact of Man, *Property, or the Right to Things,* was introduced into the World.

Now from *Property* flows a Right, whereby the Substance, as it were, of any Thing so belongs to One, that it cannot after the *same* manner *wholly* belong to Another. From whence it follows, that we may at our own Pleasure dispose of those Things which are our Property, and hinder all other People from the Use of them; unless by Agreement they have procur'd from us some special Right. Although in Communities it does not always happen that Properties are kept so unmix'd and absolute, but are sometimes circumscrib'd and limited by the Municipal Laws thereof, or by Orders and Agreements of Men among themselves.[43] But when any certain Thing belongs jointly to more Persons

III. Property what. L. N. N. l. 4. c. 4. §2.

----

conditional on "social" contracts. Barbeyrac views the property right of the first occupant as a natural and unconditional expression of his liberty. Pufendorf rejects the notion of natural rights, which he regards as a mortgage on sovereignty, treating rights instead as capacities arising from instituted offices and obligations.]

*See *Grotius de Jure Belli & Pacis, lib.* 2. *cap.* 3. §1.

43. The preceding sentence provides a good example of the manner in which Tooke's anglicization adapts Pufendorf's statist jurisprudence to the image of a community governed by common law. In Pufendorf's original it is the state (*civitas*) that may set limits to private ownership of property, which is done not through "Municipal laws" but at the direction of civil government (*imperium civile*) or as a result of human agreements. Barbeyrac opts for *sociétez civiles* in which the limits are set by *les Loix & par la volonté du Souverain* or else by human conventions (p. 175).

than one after the same manner, then it is said to be *common* to those several Persons.

IV. All things
not possessed.

But as Things did not *all at once* become the Possessions of Men, but successively, and according as the State of Mankind seem'd to require; so it was not necessary neither that *every Thing* in the World should be

L. N. N. l. 4.
c. 5. §2.

claim'd by one Man or other, but, the Peace of Mankind being preserv'd, *some Things may, and some Things ought to continue, as at the Beginning, common to all.* For there are Things which are, indeed, very advantagious to Man, but then since they are *inexhaustible,* so that every Man may have the Benefit of 'em, and yet no single Person can have the less Use of them, it would be foolish, and to no purpose, for any one to enclose or lay claim to 'em. Such are the Light of the Sun, the Air, the running Water, and the like: Among which also may be accounted the vast Ocean flowing between great Continents, for so much of it as is very far distant from the Shore. Because 'tis not only more than sufficient for the promiscuous Use of all Men, but 'tis morally impossible for any single Nation to guard it. *For where a Thing is of that Nature, that other Men cannot by any Means be hinder'd from the Use of it, it is not only in vain to divide or lay claim to it, but it is apt to give Occasion for insignificant Quarrels.

V. Property
twofold.
L. N. N. l. 4.
c. 6.

The Methods of acquiring Property are either *Original* or *Derivative:* The *Original Ways* of obtaining Property, are those by which the Property of Things was first introduced: The *Derivative Ways* are those, by which a Property already settled passeth from one Man to another. Again, the *Original Way* of acquiring Property is twofold; either, first, *simple and absolute;* as when we obtain *Dominion* and *Property* over the Body or Substance of the Thing: Or, secondly, *primitive and respective;* as when we add to a Thing already our own some farther Improvement and Increase.

---

* See *Grotius de Jure Belli & Pacis, l.* 3. *c.* 2. §3.

After it had been covenanted among Mankind that Things should be *appropriated* to this or that Man, it was also agreed, That what Things soever had *not fallen* within that *first Division,* should thereafter become the Property of the *first Occupant,* that is, of him, *who before any other, should actually seize it with a Design of possessing the same. So that even at this time the Original Method of acquiring Property in many Things is only *Premier Seisin,* or the first Occupancy. After this manner Titles are made to desolate Regions, which no Man ever claim'd, which become his who *first enters* upon 'em with an Intention of making them his own, provided he cultivate them and assign *Limits* how far he propounds to occupy. But when any Number of Men *jointly* possess themselves of any Tract of Land, 'tis customary to assign to each Member of the Company a *Share,* and to account what is left undivided to belong to the Society in *common.* †By this *first* Occupancy also are gain'd all the wild Beasts, Birds, and Fishes living in the Sea, Rivers, or Lakes thereunto appertaining; as well as what by the Sea shall be thrown upon the Shore; except *particular Laws* inhibit the promiscuous Seizure of the same, or assign them to some certain Claimant. These, if we would make our own, we must actually *seize* 'em, and take 'em into our *Possession.* By this Occupancy also we may rightfully acquire Possession of Things whereof the *Property* which any other Person could have is *extinct.* As for instance, in Things which are cast away with Intention of the Owner not to have 'em any more, or in Things which at first we lost unwillingly, but in Time relinquish'd and forewent. ‡To which may be added what the Lawyers call *Treasure trove,* or Money found, the

VI. Premier Seisin

L. N. N. l. 4. c. 6. §3, 4.

---

*That whereon the first Occupant properly grounds his Right is, his giving open Notice, before any other, of his Design and Intention to preserve to his own Use this or that Thing, which he has made himself the first Possessor of. If therefore he has given any such fair and significant Notice of such his Intention; or if any others, who might with him have a common Right to the Thing, shall freely and significantly set forth their Intention to depart from their Share, or Part of the Thing in favour of this Claimant: He then comes to have the Original Property in the Thing, even before he may have taken actual Possession of it. See *L. N. N. l. 4. c. 6.* [Barbeyrac's VI.1, p. 177.]

†See *Grotius de Jure Belli, &c. L.* II. *c.* 8. §2. *seqq.*

‡See *Grotius de Jure Belli & Pacis, lib.* 2. *c.* 8. §2. *seq.*

Owner whereof is not known, which goes to the Finder, except by the special Laws of a Country it be otherwise provided.

VII. Accessional Improvements. L. N. N. l. 4. c. 7.

Moreover, there are many Things capable of being possess'd which continue not always in the same State, but soon after several manners *increase* of themselves or inlarge their Substance; to others some *external Additions* are made; many bring forth *Fruit,* and not a few by Man's Labour and Workmanship admit of *Improvement.* All these are comprised under the Head of *Accessional* Advantages, and may be divided into two Sorts; for *some* without the Help of a Man accrue from *Nature* alone; while *others* either wholly or in part are to be attributed to *Human Industry.* *Concerning both which this is to be the Rule, To him who is the Owner of the *Thing,* to the same belong the *Improvements* and *Accessional* Advantages; and he who has form'd any Matter of his own into such or such a *Fashion,* is Owner of that *Form* or *Fashion.*

VIII. Services.

L. N. N. l. 4. c. 8.

But Cases often happen, where, either by Contract, or some different Way, another Man may get a Right to receive a certain *Profit* out of Things that are *ours,* or to prohibit us the Using even of what is *our own* to *every* Purpose. These Rights are wont to be call'd *Services,* and they are of two Sorts, either *Personal,* where the Advantage from what belongs to another Man comes to the Person *immediately;* or *Real,* where such Benefit is receiv'd from that which is another's by the Means or *Mediation* of that which is ours; among which are accounted the Right of receiving Profits, of making use of what is another's, of living in such a Place, of commanding the Work of Servants. The *Real Services* are again subdivided into such as regard the *City* or the *Country;* the first Sort are the supporting my Neighbour's House or Wall which cannot but bear upon mine, affording the Benefits of Lights, not stopping them up, allowing Prospects, carrying off the Rain-Water, and the like: The *latter* are Liberty of Passage for Men or Cattle, Leave to derive or

---

*See *Grotius de Jure Belli & Pacis, Lib.* 2, *cap.* 8.

draw Water, or to water Cattle, or to graze 'em for a time, &c. All which Services have been introduced for the Preservation of good *Neighbourhood.*

Among the *derivative* Methods of acquiring Property, some are when by the Disposal of the Law Things are devolv'd from one upon another; others are when Possession is transferr'd by the *former Owner;* and this sometimes affecting the same in *whole,* and sometimes in *part.*

IX. Derivative Property. L. N. N. l. 4. c. 9.

The *Whole of an Estate by the Death of the former Owner generally passes by *Succession* to the *next Heir* of the Intestate. For it being repugnant to the common Inclinations of Men, and altogether disserviceable to the Peace of Mankind, that such Possessions should be accounted as *foregone* and *relinquish'd,* and as left to be a Prey to any who shall seize 'em, which such Owner had, while he liv'd, taken so much Care and Pains to get: Hence, by the Dictates of *Reason* it has obtain'd among all civiliz'd Nations, that if any Man dies, not having *dispos'd* of what he had, the same shall *devolve* to those, whom, according to the *general Inclination* of Mankind, he must be thought to have holden most dear to him. And these, regularly consider'd, are those who *descend* from us, as our *Children,* &c. after them those who are of the same *Consanguinity,* according as they are nearly ally'd. And tho' there may be many, who either for having receiv'd *Benefits,* or from some *particular Affection,* have a greater Respect for Persons not at all by *Blood* related to them, than for the nearest *Kin;* yet for Peace sake it is necessary, without taking Notice of the peculiar Case of some Few, rather to follow the *universal Propensity* of Man, and to observe that *Method* of Succession which is most plain, and least obnoxious to *Controversies;* which would be very apt to arise, if the *Benefactors* and *Friends* of the deceased might be admitted to contest Succession with the next of *Kin.* So that if a Man has a mind to prefer those to whom he stands obliged by Kindnesses,

X. Inheritance to those who die intestate. L. N. N. l. 4 c. 11.

---

* See *Grotius de Jure Belli, & c. l.* 2. *c.* 7. §3. *seqq.*

or such as he has on any other account a Love for, he is to make such Disposals openly and expressly.

XI. Children
Heirs. l. 4.
c. 11. §3. Whence it follows, that the next *Heirs* to any Man are his *Children,* which are given by Nature to Parents to be carefully bred and educated, and for whom every Parent is supposed to wish a most plentiful Provision, and to design to leave whatsoever he shall die possess'd of. But by *Children* are *chiefly* understood such as are born in lawful Matrimony: For to these much Favour is due from *Reason* itself, from the *Honour* and *Decency* of the married Life, and from the *Laws* of all civiliz'd Countries, above the *Illegitimate.* All which Considerations obtain yet with these Exceptions, to wit, unless the Father has sufficient Reason not to *acknowledge* such a one for his Son, or *disinherits* him for some heinous Wickedness. In the same Case with *Children* are also to be consider'd Progeny of *lower Degrees,* as Grand-children, whom the Grandfather is bound to bring up, and who have Right to share his Inheritance together with the Uncles on both sides; and this, because there can be no Reason, that the Misery of losing their deceased Parent should be aggravated by being excluded from their Proportion of Inheritance in the Estate of their Grand-father. Upon failure of *Heirs descendant,* 'tis reasonable the Goods of Children revolve to their *Parents;* and that to those who are Fatherless, Motherless, and Childless their *Brethren* should succeed; and upon Default of these, the *next of Kin* to the deceas'd ought to inherit. Tho' in order to prevent Contentions, to which on this score great Occasions are frequently given, and that this Matter may be settled for the publick Good, in most Communities the *Order of Succession* is found to be accurately stated; and such Directions of the Government it is most safe for every private Man to follow in this case, unless very weighty Causes force him to the contrary.

Another *derivative* Method of acquiring Property justifiable by Law, was by the *Romans* call'd *Usucaptio,* by the Modern's *Prescription;* by which he who by honest Means and a just Title hath gotten Possession of what was really another's, and hath also held it for a considerable time, without being disturb'd or oppos'd, obtains the full Property of the Thing thus possess'd, so as to extinguish all the *Right* and *legal Claim* of the former Owner.

XII. Of Pre-scription.[44] L. N. N. l. 4. c. 12.

The Reasons on which this *Right of Prescription* is grounded, are, First, The former Proprietor having for so long time neglected claiming what was his, is judged voluntarily to have relinquish'd all Right and Title to it; it being reasonable to believe, that in a sufficient Space of time he could not want Opportunities, had he had Inclinations to put in his Claim: Secondly, The Preservation of the Peace of Society demands, that he who by *honest* Methods comes to the *Possession* of what he has, should not be perpetually liable to have taken from him, what became his Purchase by a *fair and honest Title;* especially it being much more grievous to the *present Possessor* to be turn'd out of a Possession honestly acquir'd, than to the *former Owner* not to be put into Possession of what he had long since lost the *Hopes* and *Expectations* of. The Rules of *Natural Equity* are sufficient to determine what time shall suffice to create *Prescription* in particular Cases: However, it is much better, for the Prevention of *Strife* and *Controversies,* that certain limited times, according to Reason and Convenience, should be stated and mark'd out by all Communities, whereby it may be determined what shall make a good *Prescription.*

The Whole also of an Estate may, by an Act of the former Proprietor, upon his Death be pass'd away by his †*Last Will* and *Testament;* for this has been allow'd by most Nations, that for some kind of Ease to our Thoughts of Mortality, a Man yet alive may, if Death happen, transfer what he has of outward Goods to some Person that he loves best. Now

XIII. Last Will. L. N. N. l. 4. c. 10.

---

44. This section on prescription (*usucapio*) was originally Pufendorf's final section (section XV), where it remains in Tooke's first edition. It was relocated here by Barbeyrac, without explanation.

* See the whole 4*th Chap.* of the 2*d* Book of *Grotius de Jure Belli, &c.*

† See *Grotius de Jure Belli, &c. lib.* 2. *cap.* 6. §14.

whereas in the most ancient Times it seems to have been customary, that the dying Man upon the Approach of his End *openly declar'd* his Heirs, and with his own Hands *deliver'd* such or such Portions into the Hands of them who were to receive; yet afterwards, for good Reasons, another manner of *Bequeathing* was approved by many People; to wit, that a Man may at any time, when himself thinks good, make his own Will, and either declare it *openly*, or keep it *close* in Writing; which Will also he may at his Pleasure *alter*, and of which the Heirs he has named or written down cannot make any Use till the Testator be *dead*. Not but that such *Last Wills*, of how much Authority soever they are among Men, yet are to be order'd with Consideration of the Party's *various Relations* to Men, and of the Good of the *Community*; the Neglect whereof has given Occasion for the *Laws* oftentimes to provide and give Rules for making them; from which prescribed *Directions*, if any Man depart, he has no Reason to *complain*, that Regard was not had to his *Last Will*.

XIV. Gift.   While Men are yet living, Things are transferr'd by the Act of the first Proprietor, either *Gratis* or *Freely*; or else by the Mediation of some *Contract*. The former Way of Transferring is call'd *Gift:* And of the latter, which is *Contracting*, we shall speak hereafter.

XV. Forcible Possession.   Sometimes also Things change their Owner without the Consent, and even *against the Will* of the same Owner; and this is mostly in Communities, by way of *Fine*, when sometimes *all* the Estate of a Convict, sometimes such a *Portion* only shall be forfeited, and the same shall be given either to a private Person who has suffer'd Wrong, or applied to the Uses of the Publick. So in *War* Goods are *forcibly* taken from the Possessor, who parts with them very *unwillingly*, by an Enemy who is too strong for him, and become the true *Property* of the Seizer; not but that the first Owner has still a Right with a greater Force, whenever he can, to recover them, so long as till by subsequent Treaties of Peace he does in effect renounce his Pretences thereto.

L. N. N. l. 4. c. 6. §14 l. 2. c. 16. §13.

CHAPTER XIII

The Duties which naturally result from
Man's Property in Things

Property in Things being established among Men, these Duties natu-
rally arise. *EVERY *Man is obliged to suffer another, who is not a declared
Enemy, quietly to enjoy whatsoever Things are his; and neither by Fraud or
Violence to spoil, imbezzel, or convert them to his own Use.* Whence it ap-
pears, That Theft, Rapine, removing of Boundaries, and the like
Crimes, which tend to the Invading and Incroaching upon other Mens
Properties, are forbidden.

I. We must
conscientiously
abstain from
invading our
Neighbours
Property.
L. N. N. l. 4.
c. 13.

When *any Thing, that belongs to another, falls into our Hands, although
it be fairly on our Part, that is, without Trick or Fraud of ours; yet if it
belongs to another Person, and we have Possession of it, we are obliged to
take care, as far as in us lies, to return it to its right Owner.* By this is not
to be understood, That when we have procur'd any Thing to our selves
by fair and honest Means, and enjoy it by a rightful Title, we are to
make groundless Doubts and Scruples about the Validity of our Right,
and make Proclamation, as it were, That we are in Possession of such a
Thing; that, if possibly it should belong to another Person, the Proprietor might come and demand it. It is enough that, if we come to the
Knowledge that what we possess is another Person's, we then give notice to the Proprietor, that it is in our Possession, and that we are ready
to deliver it up to the right Owner. And in this Case, we are not bound
to restore it, unless we are repay'd the necessary Charges we have been
at in procuring, or preserving it; which we may justly demand to be
reimbursed, or stop the Thing 'till Satisfaction be made. And the Duty
of *Restitution* of which we are speaking, is so indispensably necessary,
that it sets aside all private Ingagements or Contracts to the contrary,
and takes away all Right that may seem to arise from any such private

II. Restitution
to be made if
we possess
what belongs
to another.
L. N. N. l. 4.
c 13. §2.

* See *Grotius de Jure Belli & Pacis, Book* II. *Ch.* 10.

Obligations: As for Instance, Should a *Thief* trust and deposite with me, upon my Promise of Redelivery, somewhat that he has stollen, I being altogether ignorant of the Matter; if after this, the *Right Owner* appears, the same is to be restor'd to *him,* and not to the *Thief.*

III. Restitution Part consum'd. L. N. N. l. 4. c. 13. §6.
But *if any Thing belonging to another, which yet we came by fairly and honestly, be wasted and consum'd, 'tis our Duty to restore only so much to the Owner as we have made Profit or Advantage to our selves from it.* All that lies upon us to do herein, being to refund so much as we have gain'd thereby, that so we may not be the richer by another Man's undeserved Loss.

IV. Conclusions. First. L. N. N. l. 4. c. 13. §7.
From these Premises, we may deduce the following Conclusions: 1. *A Presumptive Owner,* (or one who without any Covin[45] on his Part, becomes the Possessor of what belongs to another Man) *is not obliged to make any Restitution, if the Thing perishes;* because neither the Thing it self is in his Power, neither has he receiv'd any Gain or Advantage thereby.

V. Second. L. N. N. l. 4. c. 13. §8.
2. SUCH a Presumptive Owner is obliged *to make Restitution, not only of the Thing it self, but also of the Fruits and Profits, which are in being at the Time.* For to whomsoever the *Thing* really belongs, to the same likewise the *Profits* and *Advantages* thence arising do accrew. Nevertheless, it is lawful for the Possessor to deduct what Charges he has been at upon the Thing, or upon its Culture and Improvement, by means whereof it has produced those Fruits and Profits.

VI. Third. L. N. N. l. 4 c. 13. §9.
3. A Presumptive Owner is obliged *to make Restitution of the Thing, and of the Fruits and Profits of it that are consumed, if otherwise he would have consum'd as much of his own, and can recover the Value thereof from him of whom he received Possession.* For otherwise he would inrich himself, whilst by spending what belongs to another, he spares his own.

45. Fraud.

4. A Presumptive Owner is not oblig'd *to make good the Fruits and Profits which he might have made of the Thing in his Possession, but neglected so to do:* Because he has not the Thing it self, nor any Thing in Lieu thereof, and he must be consider'd, to have done by it, as he would have done by that which was *truly* his own.

VII. Fourth.
L. N. N. l. 4.
c 13. §10.

5. IF a Presumptive Owner *makes a Present or Donation of any Thing belonging to another, which was given to himself, he is not bound to restore it;* unless he had been *obliged* in Duty to have given the like Value. For in such a Case, he would be a Gainer, by saving what he must have given of his own.

VIII. Fifth.
L. N. N. l. 4.
c. 13. §11.

6. IF a Presumptive Owner *makes over what he hath purchased of another Man, upon a valuable Consideration, he is not bound to make Restitution;* unless so far as he has made any Advantage by it.

IX. Sixth.
L. N. N. l. 4.
c. 13. §12.

7. A Presumptive Owner is obliged *to restore that which belongs to another, tho' he bought it upon a valuable Consideration;* nor can he demand of the *true Owner* the Price he paid for it, but only of him from whom he had it; unless so far as the Charges which the Owner must necessarily have been at, in regaining the Possession of his Right; or that otherwise he did freely promise some Reward for the Recovery.

X. Seventh.
L. N. N. l. 4.
c. 13. §13.

Whosoever happens to *find* any Thing belonging to another, which, 'tis probable, the right Owner lost against his Will, he cannot take it up with an Intention to detain it from him when he requires it. But if the Owner appear not, he may fairly keep it himself.

XI. Things found.
L. N. N. l. 4.
c. 13. §15.

Of the Price and Value of Things

I. Price.
L. N. N. l. 5.
c. 1. §1.

After *Property* was introduced into the World, all Things not being of the same *Nature,* nor affording the same *Help* to Human Necessities; and every Man not being sufficiently provided with such Things as were necessary for his Use and Service, it was early brought into Practice among Men to make *mutual Exchanges* of one Thing for another. But because it very often happened, that Things of a *different Nature* and *Use* were to be transferred; lest either Party should be a Loser by such *Exchanging,* it was necessary, by a common Agreement or Consent among themselves, to assign to Things a certain *Quantity* or *Standard,* by which those *Things* might be compar'd and reduced to a Balance between each other. The same also obtained as to *Actions,* which it was not thought good should be done *gratis* by one Man for another. And this *Quantity* or *Standard* is that which we call *Price* or *Value.*

II. Price two-fold. L. N. N.
l. 5. c. 1. §3.

This *Price* is divided into *Common* and *Eminent;* The *First* is in *Things* or *Actions* which come within the compass of *ordinary Commerce,* according as they afford either Usefulness or Delight to Mankind. But the other is in *Money,* as it virtually contains the Value of all Things and Works, and is understood to give them their common Estimate.

III. Common
Value.
L. N. N. l. 5.
c. 1. §4.

The natural Ground of the *Common Value,* *is that †*Fitness* which any Thing or Action has for supplying, either mediately or immediately, the *Necessities* of Human Life, and rendring the same more *easie* or more *comfortable.* Hence it is we call those Things which are not of any *Use* to us, *Things of no Value.* There are nevertheless some *Things most useful*

---

* See *Grotius de Jure Belli & Pacis,* l. 2. c. 12. §14.
† Our Author here gives an imperfect Account of the proper and intrinsick Value of Things. For Things capable of Valuation or Price, ought not only to be of some Use and Service to human Life, if not really, yet at least in the Opinion and Fancy

to Human Life, which are not understood to fall under any *determinate Price* or *Value;* either because they are or ought to be exempted from Dominion and Property, or because they are not capable of being exchanged, and therefore cannot be traded for; or else, because in Commerce they are not otherwise regarded than as Appendages to be supposed of course to belong to another Thing. Besides also, when the Law of God or Man places some Actions above the Reach of Commerce, or forbids that they should be done for a Reward, it is to be understood that the same Laws have set them without the Bounds of Price or Valuation. Thus the Upper Regions of the *Air,* the *Sky,* and the *Heavenly Bodies,* and even the vast *Ocean* are exempt from Human Property, so that no Rate or Value can be put upon them. So there is no Rate or Price to be set upon a *Freeman,* because Freemen come not within the Compass of Commerce. Thus, the Lying open to the Sun, a clear and wholesome Air, a pleasant Prospect to the Eye, the Winds, Shades, and the like, consider'd separately in themselves, bear no Price, because they cannot be enjoy'd and purchas'd separately from the Lands they belong to; but yet of what Moment they are in raising the Value of Lands and Tenements to be purchas'd, no Man is ignorant. So likewise 'tis unlawful to set any Rate or Price on *Sacred Actions,* to which any moral Effect is assign'd by *Divine Institution;* which Crime is call'd *Simony.* And it is great Wickedness in a *Judge* to expose *Justice* to Sale.

Now there are various Reasons, why the Price of one and the same Thing should be *increas'd* or *diminish'd,* and why one Thing should be preferr'd before another, though it may seem to be of *equal* or *greater Use* to Human Life. For here the *Necessity* of the Thing, or its extraordinary *Usefulness,* is not always regarded; but, on the contrary, we see those Things are of the least Account or Value, without which Human

IV. Inhansing or Debasing a Price. L. N. N. l. 5. c. 1. §6.

---

of those who desire them; but also they ought to be of such a Nature, as not to be sufficient for the Occasions and Demands of every one. The more any Thing is useful or scarce, in this Sense, the greater is its intrinsick Price or Value. Nothing can be more useful to human Life than Water, yet it never bears any Price or Value, unless in such Places, or under such Circumstances, as make it not sufficient for every one's Use, or difficult to be come at. [Barbeyrac's III. 1, p. p. 193–94.]

Life is least able to subsist; and therefore, not without the singular Providence of Almighty God, *Nature* has been very *bountiful* in providing
plentiful Store of those Things. But the *Rarity* or *Scarceness* of Things
conduces chiefly to the inhansing their Value; which is the more look'd
upon, when they are brought from remote Countries. And hence the
wanton Luxury of Mankind has set *extravagant Rates* upon many
Things which Human Life might very well be without; for Instance,
upon *Pearls* and *Jewels*. But the Prices of Things, which are of *daily Use,*
are then chiefly rais'd when the *Scarcity* is join'd with the *Necessity* or
Want of them. The Prices of *Artificial Things,* besides their *Scarceness,*
are for the most Part inhans'd by the ingenious *Contrivance* and Curiosity of *Art,* that is seen in them, and sometimes by the Fame and Re-
nown of the Artificer, the Difficulty of the Work, the Want of Artists in
that Way, and the like. The Prices of *Works* and *Actions* are rais'd by
their Difficulty, Neatness, Usefulness, Necessity, by the Scarcity, Dignity, and Ingenuity of the *Authors* of them; and lastly, by the Esteem
and Reputation which that Art has gotten in the World. The *Contrary*
to these are wont to *diminish* the Price of Things. Sometimes again,
there may be some certain Thing, which is not *generally* much esteem'd,
but only by some *particular Persons,* out of a peculiar Inclination; for
Example, because he, from whom we had it, is mightily *belov'd* by us,
and that it was given as a *Token* of his particular Affection to us; or because we have been *accustom'd* thereto, or because it is a *Remembrancer*
of some remarkable Accident, or because by the Help thereof, we have
escap'd any extraordinary *Danger,* or because the Thing was made by
Our selves. And this is called *The Estimate of singular Affection.*

V. Particular
Prices Legal.
L. N. N. l. 5.
c. 1. §8.

But there are other Circumstances likewise to be consider'd in *stating*
the Rates and Prices of *particular Things.* And among those indeed,
who live in a Natural Independance on any other, the Prices of particular Things are determin'd no otherwise, than by the *Will* of the *Persons contracting;* since they are intirely at their own Liberty to make over
or to purchase what they please, nor can they be controlled in their
Dealings by any superior Authority. But in States and Governments the
Prices of Things are determin'd two several Ways: The *First* is by an *Order* from the *Magistrate,* or some *particular Law;* the *Second* is by the

common *Estimate* and *Judgment* of Men, or according as the *Market* goes, together with the *Consent* and *Agreement* of those who contract among themselves. The former of these by some is call'd the *Legal,* the other the *Vulgar Price.* Where the *Legal Rate* is fix'd for the sake of the *Buyers,* as it is for the most part, there it is not lawful for the *Sellers* to exact *more;* though they are not forbidden, if they will, to take *less.* So where the Rate of any *Labour* or *Work* is tax'd by the Publick Magistrate for the sake of those who have Occasion to hire, it is not lawful for the Workman to demand *more,* though he be not prohibited to take *less.*

But the *Vulgar* Price, which is not fix'd by the Laws, admits of a certain *Latitude,* within the Compass whereof more or less may be, and often is, either taken or given, according to the *Agreement* of the Persons *dealing;* which yet for the most part, goes according to the Custom of the *Market.* Where commonly there is Regard had to the Trouble and Charges which the Tradesmen generally are at, in the bringing home and managing their Commodities, and also after what manner they are bought or sold, whether by Wholesale or Retail. Sometimes also on a sudden the Common Price is alter'd by reason of the *Plenty* or *Scarcity* of *Buyers, Money,* or the *Commodity.* For the *Scarcity* of Buyers and of Money, (which on any particular Account may happen) and the Plenty of the Commodity, may be a Means of *diminishing* the Price thereof. On the other hand, the Plenty of Buyers and of Money, and the Scarcity of the Commodity, *inhanses* the same. Thus as the Value of a Commodity is lessen'd, if it *wants* a Buyer, so the Price is augmented when the Possessor is solicited to sell what otherwise he would not have parted with. Lastly, it is likewise to be regarded, whether the Person offers *ready Money,* or desires *Time* for Payment; for Allowance of *Time* is Part of the *Price.*

VI. Vulgar Price. L. N. N. l. 5. c. 1. §9.

But after Mankind degenerated from their primitive Simplicity, and introduced into the World several kinds of Gaining, it was easily discern'd, that that *Common* and *Vulgar* Price was not sufficient for the dispatching the Business of Men, and for the carrying on of Commerce, which then daily increas'd. For at first all Kind of Trading consisted only in *Exchanging* and *Bartering,* and the Labours of others could no

VII. Price eminent. L. N. N. l. 5. c. 1. §12.

otherwise be valued than by Work for Work, or some Thing given in Hand for Recompence. But after Men began to desire so many several Things for *Convenience* or *Pleasure,* it was not easie for every one to become Master of That which another would be willing to take in Exchange, or which might be of equal Value to the Things he wanted from him. And in civiliz'd States or Societies, where the Inhabitants are distinguish'd into *several Stations,* there is an absolute Necessity there should be different Degrees and Sorts of Men, which, if that simple and plain Way of *bartering* of *Things* and *Works* had been still in Use, could not, or at least, not without great Difficulty, support themselves. Hence most Nations, which were pleased with a more sumptuous Way of Living, thought fit, by Publick Consent, to set an *Eminent Price* or *Value* upon some Certain Thing, whereby the *Common* and *Vulgar* Prices of other Things should be measured, and wherein the same should be virtually contain'd. So that by Means of this *Thing,* any one may purchase to himself whatsoever is to be sold, and easily manage and carry on any Kind of Traffick and Bargain.

VIII. Gold, Silver, &c. L. N. N. l. 5. c. 1. §13. For this purpose, most Nations chose to make use of the nobler Kind of *Metals,* and such as were not very Common; because these being of a very compacted Substance, they cannot easily be *worn out,* and admit of being *divided* into many minute Parts; nor are they less proper to be *kept* and *handled;* and for the *Rarity* of 'em are equivalent to many other Things. Altho' sometimes for Necessity, and by some Nations for Want of *Metals,* other *Things* have been made Use of instead of *Money.*

IX. Coin. L. N. N. l. 5. c. 1. §14. Moreover, in Communities, it is only in the Power of the Chief Magistrates[46] to assign the *Value* of *Money;* and thence *Publick Stamps* are wont to be put upon them. Nevertheless, in the assigning thereof, respect is to be had to the Common Estimate of the *Neighbouring Nations,* or of those with whom we have any *Traffick* or *Commerce.* For

46. In Pufendorf's Latin this occurs in the "state" (*civitas*), not "Communities," at the direction of the "sovereign" (*summus imperator*) rather than the "Chief Magistrates."

otherwise, if the State should set *too high a Value* on their Money, or if they should not give it a *just* and *true Alloy*, all Commerce with Foreign Nations, which could not be carried on by *Exchange* or *Barter* alone, would be at a Stand. And for this very Reason, the Value of Money is not rashly to be *alter'd*, unless a very great Necessity of State require it. Tho' as Gold and Silver grow more plentiful, the *Value* of *Money*, in Comparison to the Price of Land, and Things thereon depending, is wont, as it were insensibly and of its self, to grow lower.

♺ CHAPTER XV ♺

Of those Contracts in which the Value of Things is pre-supposed; and of the Duties thence arising

A *Pact* or *Agreement* in general, is the Consent and Concurrence of Two or more in the same *Resolution*. But because oftentimes simple *Agreements* are contra-distinguish'd to *Contracts*, the Difference seems chiefly to consist herein, That by *Contracts* are understood such Bargains as are made concerning *Things* and *Actions*, which come within the compass of *Commerce*, and therefore suppose a *Property* and *Price* of Things. But such Covenants as are concluded upon, about other Matters, are called by the common Term of *Pacts* or *Agreements*.

    *Although even to some of these is promiscuously given the Name of *Pacts* and *Contracts*.

I. Pacts and Contracts. L. N. N. l. 5. c. 2. §1.

---

  * *Grotius de Jure Belli & Pacis, lib.* 2. *cap.* 12.

II. General Division of Contracts. L. N. N. l. 5. c. 2. §8. Contracts may be divided into *Gratuitous* and *Chargeable.* The former Sort affords *gratis* some Advantage to one of the Parties contracting: the latter subjects each of the Parties contracting to some Charge, or lays upon them some Condition or Obligation equally burdensome to them both; in which Case, nothing is done or delivered by either Party, but with a Prospect of receiving an Equivalent.

III. L. N. N. l. 5. c. 4. §1. Of *Gratuitous* Contracts, there are three Sorts; a *Commission,* a *Loan,* and a *Charge.*

A *Commission* is, *When any one takes upon himself* gratis, *and in mere good Will, to transact the Business of his Friend, who requests this Trouble of him on the Account of Friendship only.* And this may be done two Ways; first, When the Method of transacting the Business is *prescribed* to the Person who is so kind as to undertake it; and, secondly, When it is wholly left to his *Judgment* and *Discretion.*

But as no one would commit the Management of his Affairs to any one but a Friend, and one of whose Honesty and Integrity he has a good Opinion; so he who undertakes this Trust, ought to be careful not to abuse this Confidence reposed in him; but to execute it with the greatest Care, and with the utmost Fidelity. But then, on the other hand, he who has given him this Commission, ought to prevent its being any Loss to him that executes it, by repaying him any Expences he is at in the Execution of it, and likewise by satisfying him for any Loss he may suffer in his own Affairs, while he spends his Pains and Time thus in Friendship to him.

IV. Of Loans. L. N. N. l. 5. c. 4. §6. When *we give to another the free Use of what is ours, without any Consideration for the Use of it,* this is called a *Loan;* and the Rules to be observed in this Case, are:

1. WE must take all possible Care most diligently to look after and preserve intirely the Thing lent us.

2. WE must put it to no other Uses, nor detain it any longer Time, than the Proprietor is willing.

3. WE must restore it to the Owner intire, and in the same Condition

we received it; or at least with no other Detriment than what it must of Necessity receive by the common and ordinary Use of it.

4. If after a Thing is lent us for a certain Time, something, not foreseen at the Time it was lent, should fall out, so that the Proprietor wants it before the Time he had lent it us for, we are to restore it without Delay, as soon as ever it is required of us.

5. If the Thing lent us, comes to any Damage, or is destroyed by any unforeseen and unavoidable Accident, and not by any Fault of ours, we are not obliged to make it good, if it be reasonable to think, it would have been in the same manner damaged or destroyed, had it been in the Proprietor's Custody, as it was in ours. But if it lay in our Power to have prevented such Damage or Loss, then we ought to make Restitution to the Proprietor to the full Value, *since it is very unreasonable in us to make any one lose what is his, only for being so kind to us, as for our sakes, to deprive himself of the Use of it.

He that lends any Thing to another, lies under no other Obligation to the Person he lends it to, but this only; If the Borrower has been at any necessary Charge, more than what the ordinary Use of the Thing requires, in preserving it, then this extraordinary Expence ought to be made good to him by the Proprietor.

The Third and Last Sort of gratuitous Contracts, is a *Charge, Trust,* or *Deposit:* Which is, *When we commit any Thing of our own, or which we have any manner of Title to, or Interest in, to the Trust and Care of another Person, to keep the same* Gratis: And what the Person's Duty is, to whom the Deposit is made, will easily be understood.

V. Deposit or Trust. L. N. N. l. 5. c. 4. §7.

1. The Thing thus trusted in his Hands, must be carefully looked after, nor must any Use be made of it, without the Knowledge and Consent of the Proprietor, if it can in any ways receive Damage by such using it; as also if it be any Profit or Benefit to the Proprietor to have it

---

*There is, in Cases of this Nature, always a tacit Agreement, by Virtue of which, he that borrows any Thing, ingages to restore the Thing lent, either in Kind, or to make Amends by something of equal Value. *See L. N. N. l. 5. c. 4.* §6. [Barbeyrac's IV.1, p. 204.]

kept concealed from any one's Sight: And if the Person intrusted shall take the Liberty of using it, he ought to make good any Damage or Disadvantage that shall accrue from the Use of it to the Owner. Likewise, it is not just to untye, unseal, or otherwise open any Thing we are intrusted withal, that is sealed or ty'd up, or to take it out of any Box, Chest, or other Thing in which the Owner had inclosed and secured it, when he put it into our Hands.

2. WE ought immediately to restore any Thing deposited with us, as soon as ever the Proprietor claims it; at least, unless the Redelivery of it, at such Time it is so claimed, should be a real Prejudice to the Claimant, or to some other Person. But to deny that we have it, when the Owner comes to reclaim what he trusted us with, is a most infamous Piece of Wickedness, and even more base than Theft it self: And it is yet a more detestable Crime, to withold or disown a *miserable Deposit;* that is, what is put into our Hands in the Time of any Misfortune, during the Danger of Fire, or in the Midst of Tumults and Confusions, or the like Calamities.

He who makes the Deposit on his Part, ought to re-imburse, to the Person with whom it is made, all the Charges that he has necessarily laid out upon the Thing deposited, while it continued in his Hands.

VI. Equality in all chargeable Contracts. L. N. N. l. 5. c. 3. §1. In all *Contracts that are purely chargeable,* and have nothing gainful in them, where the Law or the Market hath fix'd the Prices of Things, a *just Equality* is to be observed, that is, one Party ought to receive as much Benefit as the other; and if it happens, that one receives less than the other, he has a Right to demand the Rest, which if denied him by the other Party, he is at Liberty to set aside the Contract.

Now to find out and adjust this *Equality,* it is necessary that the Parties contracting be each of them alike thoroughly acquainted with the Commodity about which they are treating, and with the several Qualities of it; and therefore whosoever is going, by way of Contract, to make over the Property of a Thing to another, is indispensably obliged to expose not only the good Qualities of it, but also, to the best of his Knowledge, the Faults and Defects of it; since otherwise no just Price or real Value of the Thing can be assign'd. But this is not to be extended to minute and circumstantial Matters, which affect not the Substance of the Thing; nor need the Faults already known to the Buyer, be mention'd to him; for if, knowing the Faults, he purchases the Thing, such Defects do not annull the Contract, which shall stand good, and the Buyer must be contented with the Inconvenience he has consented hereby to bring on himself.

The Equality we have been mentioning, is so absolutely necessary in all *chargeable Contracts,* that although in making such a Contract, all the Faults of the Thing contracted for, have been fairly expos'd, and nothing demanded more than was really believed to be the just Value of the Thing; yet if afterwards there appears to have been an Inequality, without any Fault of the Contractors, (as suppose some Defect or Blemish lay undiscover'd, or there was some Mistake in the Price) it ought to be corrected, and he that has too much, must make Amends to the Sufferer. In *notorious Abuses* of this Kind, the Laws of every Country have made Provision for Reparation; but in lesser Breaches of this Duty, they are silent, for the avoiding a Multitude of unnecessary Suits, supposing herein, that every Body will take Care, in his own Concerns, not to be impos'd upon.

VII. If an Inequality is discover'd after the Bargain is made, it must be redress'd. L. N. N. l. 5. c. 3. §9.

Now among *chargeable Contracts,* or Covenants which imply somewhat to be done or given on both Parts, the most ancient, and that whereby Trading and Commerce was carried on before the Invention of Money, was *Permutation* or *Bartering,* whereby, on each Side, something was given for some other Thing equivalent thereto. Altho' at this Day, since the Invention of Money, that Sort of *Exchange* is chiefly practis'd among Merchants, whereby Things are not simply compar'd between themselves, but they are first reduced to Money, and afterwards deliver'd as so much Money. But *reciprocal Donation* is a different Sort of a Thing from the Contract of Barter; for in this there is no Necessity that an *Equality* should be observ'd.

VIII. Bartering L. N. N. l. 5. c. 5. §1.

IX. Buying
and Selling.
L. N. N. l. 5.
c. 5. §2.

Buying and *Selling,* is, When for Money the Property of any Thing is acquired, or else such a Right as is equivalent thereto; of which Kind this is the most plain and obvious; When the Buyer, after the Value is agreed upon, immediately pays down the Price, and the Seller thereupon delivers the Commodity. Yet oftentimes the Agreement is made so, that the Commodity shall be immediately delivered, and the Price thereof paid at a certain Time. And sometimes the Price is agreed upon, but the Delivery of the Thing or Commodity is to be within a certain Time limited. In which Case, it seems but Equity, that before the Time be elaps'd, the Seller should stand to the Hazard of it; but if, after the Time is elaps'd, the Buyer makes Delay, and neglects the taking it away, then, if the Commodity perishes, the Buyer shall stand wholly to the Loss thereof. Now to this of Buying and Selling, are wont to be added several other Kinds of Bargains: As that which is term'd *Addictio in diem,*[47] whereby any Thing is sold with this Proviso, That it may be lawful for the Seller to accept of better Terms, offered by another within a certain Time. So also the *Lex Commissoria,*[48] which is such a Condition in any Contract, as not being perform'd within a Time limited, the Bargain becomes void. So likewise any Kind of Recalling, or Privilege of Recanting a Bargain, which is to be either so understood, That if the Price be laid down within a certain Time limited, or at any Time whatever is offer'd, the Buyer shall be obliged to restore it again to the Seller; or else so, as if the Thing be offer'd again, the Seller is bound to return back again the Price thereof; or so as if the Buyer be willing to sell the same again, the first Seller should have the Refusal of it, before any other, which is likewise call'd *Jus Protimeseos,* or the Right of Preemption. It is also customary that the Seller should reserve to himself a certain Portion of the Lands which he sells, or some Use or Acknowledgement for the same.

There is another Way of Buying, which they call *Per Aversionem,*[49]

47. Provisional sale.
48. Forfeiture clause.
49. Buying a job lot.

when several Things of different Prices are not valued singly, but at Hap-hazard, and, as it were, in the Lump.

In that Way of Sale, which is call'd an *Auction,* the Thing is adjudged to that Person who, among several Bidders, offers most.

Lastly, There is another Way of Buying, whereby not any certain Thing is bought, but only the probable Hopes and Expectation thereof which implies something of *Chance;* so as neither the Buyer, if his Expectation fails him, nor the Seller, though it much exceed, hath any Reason to complain.

Hiring and *Letting,* is, *When the Use of a Thing, or any Labour is granted to another, upon a certain Consideration.* X. Hiring and Letting. L. N. N. l. 5. c. 6. §1.

1. THE usual Method is to agree beforehand, how much shall be received for doing the Thing propos'd; yet if any one makes no actual Bargain for what he undertakes to perform, or for the Use of any Thing he lends, he is suppos'd to expect so much as the common Custom allows, and for that to refer himself to the Honesty and Justice of the Person hiring.

2. HE who lets out a Thing, ought to take care, that it be in a serviceable Condition, and must therefore be content to undergo all Charges necessary to render it fit for Use. On the other Hand, the Person who hires the Thing, ought to be a good Husband in the Use of it; and if it be lost or damaged by his Fault, he is responsible for it. And for the same Reason, he who is hired to do any Work, if by his Fault it be spoil'd or damaged, must make it good.

3. IF a Man be hired only for some transient Business, which does not require his constant Attendance to perform, and any Mischance hinders him from performing what he undertook, he can have no Title to the *Wages* agreed for: But if a Man takes another into his Service for a continu'd Time, and he should, by Sickness or other Misfortune, be hinder'd from doing what he undertook, in common Humanity, he ought neither to be discarded, nor have his Wages refus'd or abated.

4. WHEN any Thing let out happens wholly to perish; from that Time, the Person hiring is no longer obliged to pay the Wages or Stipend agreed on. But if the Thing let out, has a known, certain, and de-

termin'd Use assigned to it, for which Use the Owner is obliged to make it fit and serviceable; in this Case, if by any Misfortune it becomes less fit and proper for this Use, the Owner is obliged to abate of the agreed Price in such Proportion as the Thing falls short of the design'd Use. Thus, for Instance, I *hire* a House to dwell in, which my *Landlord* is obliged to make habitable; if, in this Case, the Violence of a Storm, or my Neighbour's Fire, should intercept the Use of it, I may fairly with-hold, in Proportion, so much of the *Rent* as I suffer by Want of the Use of the House. But if the Profit or Increase of the Thing farmed out be uncertain, and have any Thing of Chance attending it, wherein, as a large Increase happens to the Advantage of the Hirer, so a small one is to his Loss; in such Case there can be nothing deducted from the Pension in Strictness of Law, upon the Account of Barrenness, especially since a Dearth of one Year may be recompenced by the Plenty of another: Unless those Accidents, which prevent the Increase, do but very rarely happen, and the Person hiring be presumed not to have intended to run any manner of Risk; and if so, it is but equitable that his Rent be abated, when such uncommon and unforeseen Accidents happen.

XI. Things lent. L. N. N. l. 5. c. 7. In a Contract of *Things* lent, Something is given to a certain Person upon this Condition, That he be obliged to restore the same *Kind* after a certain Time in the same *Quantity* and *Quality*. Now those Things which are usually lent, are called *Fungibiles*, that is, such Things as are capable of being repaid in Kind, though not in *Specie;*[50] because any Thing of that Kind may so perform the Part of another Thing, that he who receives any Thing of that *Kind* in the same *Quantity* and *Quality*, may be said to have receiv'd the *same*, which he gave. The same Things are likewise determined and specified by Number, Weight, and Measure, in which Respect also they are commonly called *Quantities*, as they are contra-distinct to *Species*. Now a Thing is lent either *gratis*, so

---

50. Added by Tooke, "in Specie" is a now archaic legal term meaning the precise or actual form of something. The idea is that fungibles are items that may be repaid by any acceptable thing, rather than by something exactly the same as the loaned item.

as no more is to be received than was deliver'd; or else for some Profit or Advantage, which is call'd *Usury;* and which is no Ways repugnant to the Law of Nature, provided it be moderate, and proportionable to the Gain, which the other Person makes of the Money or the Thing lent; or to that Gain I my self might have made with the same Money; or to the Loss I suffer by the Want of the present Use of it; or, lastly, that it be not exacted of *Poor Men,* to whom a Thing lent, is sometimes as good as an *Alms.*

In a Contract of *Partnership,* Two or more join together their *Money, Wares,* or *Works,* with an Intention that every one should receive a proportionable Share of the Profit; and if there happens to be any Loss, that likewise must be born ratably[51] by each Party. In which Kind of Society, as all Parties are obliged to Faithfulness and Industry; so no Party must break off the Partnership before the Time, or to the Detriment of his Partner. But when the Time of the Partnership is expired, after the Gain and Loss is allow'd, each Party is to receive what Stock he put in. But if one Person puts in *Money* or *Goods,* and the other contributes his *Labour,* we must consider, after what Manner such a Contribution was made. For when one Man's *Labour* is only concern'd about the Managing and Disposing of the other Person's *Money* or *Goods,* the Shares of the Gain are so to be determin'd, as the Profit of the *Money* or *Commodity* bears Proportion to the Value of the *Labour;* the *Principal* still remaining the Property of him only, who first contributed it. But when any Labour is bestow'd in the *Improvement* of any Commodity, which is put in by another, he is suppos'd to have such a Share in the Thing it self, as is proportionable to the *Improvement* it has received. Again, when Men ingage all that they have in any Joint-Stock, as each of the Partners must faithfully bring into the Account the Profits they have made; so also every one of them is to be maintain'd out of the Joint-Stock according to their Condition. But when the Partnership is broken off, the Division of the Goods is made ratably, according as each Party at first brought in; without any Regard had, by whose Goods any

XII. Partnership. L. N. N.
l. 5. c. 8.

---

51. That is, in a rateable or proportionate manner.

Gain or Loss happened to the Company, unless before-hand it was otherwise agreed.

XIII. Contracts upon Chance.
L. N. N. l. 5. c. 9.

There are likewise several Contracts which imply a *Chance:* Amongst which may be reckon'd **Wagers,* when the Certainty of any Event, which is not yet known by either Party, is affirmed by one, and denied by the other, a Certain Value being laid on both Sides, it is adjudg'd to that Person, to whose Assertion the Event is found to agree. Hitherto may also be referr'd all Sorts of † *Games,* wherein we play for any Thing of Value. Among which, those have the least Chance which contain a Trial of *Wit, Dexterity, Skill,* or *Strength.* In some of these *Skill* and *Chance* have both a like Share. In others, *Chance* does chiefly determine the Matter. Altho' it is the Part of the Civil Magistrate[52] to consider how far such Kind of Contracts may be tolerated, as consistent with the publick or private Good: Among these we may reckon the various Sorts of *Lotteries;* as either when several Men, having paid for a Thing by Money laid down jointly, refer it to a Decision by Lot, which of them shall have the Whole; or when a Box or Pot of Lots is made Use of, into which a certain Number of Lots or Papers, both Blanks and Prizes are put, and for some set Price, Liberty is granted of drawing them out, so that the Person drawing, may receive the Prize mark'd upon the Lot. To these Contracts, the receiv'd Methods of ‡ *Insurance* have some kind of Affinity, which are such Bargains whereby is undertaken the securing

---

* A Wager shall be deem'd Good, though one of the Parties, who lay the Wager, knows perfectly the Truth of what he lays upon; unless he pretends himself ignorant or doubtful about it, in order to draw the other Party on to lay with him. See *L. N. N. l. 5. c. 9.* §4. [Barbeyrac's XIII.1, p. 215.]

† To make Games, and other Contracts, in which there is Hazard, lawful, it is not only necessary that what both Parties playing run the Risk of losing, be equal; but also, that the Danger of losing, and the Hope of gaining, on both Sides, bear a just Proportion with the Thing plaid for. [Barbeyrac's XIII.2, p. 215.]

52. This is Tooke's rendering of Pufendorf's *rector civitatis,* or "ruler of the state," which Barbeyrac translates without embarrassment as *Souverain.*

‡ The Insurer may demand more or less, according as there is more or less Hazard run. But the Contract shall be null, if, at the Time of making thereof, the Insurer knew, that the Goods were safe arrived, or if the Owner of the Goods at that Time, knew that the Goods were lost. [Barbeyrac's XIII.3, p. 216.]

from, and making good any Damage, so that the Insurer, for a certain Sum of Money paid down, takes upon himself, and is obliged to satisfie for whatsoever Losses or Damages any Commodities may undergo in their Transportation to remote Countries; so that if it shall happen that they be lost, he is bound to pay the Owner the Value of them.

For the rendring of Contracts and Covenants more firm and secure, *Sureties* and *Pledges* are frequently made Use of. *A *Surety* is, when another Person, who is approv'd of by the Creditor, takes upon himself the Obligation of the principal Debtor; so that unless he makes Payment, the other must make it good; yet so, that the principal Debtor is obliged to repay him, and save him harmless. And altho' the Surety cannot stand bound for a greater Sum than the principal Debtor, yet nothing hinders but that the Surety is more firmly ty'd than the other, because more is rely'd upon his Credit, than upon that of the principal Debtor. Yet in course, the principal Debtor is to be call'd upon before the Surety, unless he has wholly taken the Obligation upon himself; and such a Person in the Civil Law is commonly called *Expromissor,* or an Undertaker. Now if several Persons be Security for one, each of them is to be call'd upon for his Proportion only; unless by Accident, any one of them becomes insolvent, or is not to be found: For in such a Case, the others must be charged with his Share.

> XIV. Sureties and Pledges. L. N. N. l. 5. c. 10. §8,9, &c.

'Tis likewise oftentimes customary for the Debtor to deliver, or make over to the Creditor for the securing his Debt, some certain Thing, which is call'd a *Pledge* or a *Mortgage,* until the Debt be paid. The Intent of which is, not only that the Debtor should be excited to make Payment out of a Desire of recovering what belongs to him; but also that the Creditor should have some Prospect how he may be satisfied. And upon this Account, Pledges ought regularly to be of equal, or greater Value than the Debt it self. Now the Things which may be offer'd as Pledges, are either Improveable, or not Improveable: As to the former Kind, there is commonly added a Covenant called *Pactum*

> XV. Pledge or Mortgage. L. N. N. l. 5. c. 10. §13.

---

* *Grotius de Jure Belli & Pacis,* l. 3. c. 20. §59.

αντιχρησεωσ,[53] which impowers the Creditor to enjoy the Fruits and Profits of that Pledge, instead of *Interest:* Now as to the other Sort, the *Lex Commissoria* takes Place; which provides, That the Pledge shall be forfeited to the Creditor, if Payment be not made within a certain Time limited: And this is no ways unreasonable, when the Pledge is not of greater Value than the Debt, together with the Use for the intermediate Time, and provided the Overplus be restored to the Owner. But as the Creditor is obliged to restore the Pledge upon Payment of the Debt; so in the mean Time he ought to be as careful in the preserving thereof, as if it were really his own. And when there is no *Pactum* αντιχρησεωσ, and the Thing be of that Nature, as to receive any Damage by Use, or if it be any way for the Debtor's Advantage, he ought not to make Use of it without his Consent. Now a *Mortgage* differs from a *Pledge* in this, That a *Pledge* consists in the Delivery of the Thing, but a *Mortgage,* though the Thing be not deliver'd, holds good by the bare Assignation of a Thing altogether immoveable, from which, Payment not being made, the Creditor may receive Satisfaction for his Debt.

And thus what the Duties of Persons contracting are, will plainly appear from the End and Nature of these Contracts.

✎ CHAPTER XVI ✎

The several Methods by which the Obligations arising from Contracts are dissolved

I. Fulfilling or
Payment.
L. N. N.
l. 5 c. 11.

Among the several Ways of discharging Obligations arising from Contracts, and by which likewise the Duties and Offices which proceed from thence do utterly expire, the chiefest and most natural of all, is the *Fulfilling* or *Payment* of what was agreed upon. Where, although generally he that is the *Debtor,* is obliged to make the Payment; yet, if it be

53. Antichresis.

perform'd by any other in *his Name* who contracted the Obligation, the same is dissolv'd; since 'tis no ways material by what Person the Thing is perform'd. Yet with this Proviso, That he who pays for another, without any Intention of bestowing it upon him, may demand from the same again what he laid out upon his Account. Moreover, Payment must be made to that Person to whom it is due, or else to one whom he has *appointed* to receive the Debt in his Name. And lastly, *That very Thing* must be perform'd or paid which was agreed upon, not any Thing else instead thereof, intire and not mangled, nor in Parcels, nor by Piece-meal; and likewise at the *Place* and *Time* appointed: Altho' frequently the *Courtesie* of the Creditor, or the *Inability* of the Debtor, may be the Occasion of prolonging the Time of Payment, or receiving a Debt by little Sums at once, or else of accepting of one Thing for another.

Obligations are likewise taken away by *Compensation which is an Adjusting or Balancing the Credit and the Debt, one against the other; or when the Debtor is therefore discharged, because 'tis manifest that the Creditor himself stands indebted to him for something that is of the same Kind, and of the same Value. Especially since in those *Things* (called *Res Fungibiles,* that is) which admit of being repaid in *Kind,* tho' not in *Specie,* an Equivalent is look'd upon to be the same Thing; and where the Debt is mutual, since I must presently return back as much as I have received, for the declining of unnecessary Payments, it seems to be the most convenient Way so to order the Matter, that each Party may keep what he has. Now it is evident, that those Things aforementioned, may very properly be brought to a Balance, of which the Time for Payment is either present, or past. But it is not so in other Things or Performances, which are of a different Nature; unless they are estimated on both Sides, and reduced to Money.

II. Compensation. L. N. N. l. 5. c. 11. §5.

---

* *Grotius de Jure Belli & Pacis,* l. 3. c. 19. §15.

III. Release.
L. N. N. l. 5.
c. 11. §7.

An Obligation also ceases when the Thing is *released* and *forgiven* by him to whom it was due, and whose Interest it was that the Obligation should have been perform'd. And this is done either *expressly*, by some certain Tokens declaring his Consent; as by giving a Discharge, by giving up or cancelling the Bonds and Writings; or else *tacitly*, if he himself hinders, or is any ways the Occasion that what is owing to him cannot be paid.

IV. Breaking
off mutually.
L. N. N. l. 5.
c. 11. §8.

Those Obligations are likewise sometimes dissolved, which imply some Performance on both Sides, *by a mutual Breaking off* before any Thing on either Side be done in the Contract; unless this be expressly forbidden by the Laws. But if any Thing is performed by one of the Parties, the Obligation in this Case cannot be cancelled, unless he who perform'd his Part, releases the other, or has Amends made him some other Way.

V. Falseness on
one Side.
L. N. N. l. 5.
c. 11. §9.

Besides, an Obligation is not indeed properly dissolv'd, but rather broken off by the *Falseness* of either Party; for when the one does not perform what was agreed upon, neither is the other obliged to make good what he undertook upon a Prospect of the other's performing. For as to the main Things which are to be performed in Contracts, the former are always included in the latter by way of *Condition;* as if it should be said, I will perform this, if you perform that first.

VI. Case al-
tered. L. N. N.
l. 5. c. 11. §10.

Obligations likewise cease when that *State of Things* upon which they chiefly depended, is either *alter'd* by the Party who was obliged to perform somewhat, or by him to whom, or for whose Sake it was to be done.

VII. Time.
L. N. N. l. 5.
c. 11. §11.

Sometimes also *Time* it self puts an End to some Obligations, whose Duration depends upon a certain precise Day; unless it be prolong'd by the *express* or *tacit Consent* of each Party. Yet there is a Necessity that the Power of exacting the Obligation within the Time limited, should stand good.

Any one may make over by *Assignment,* his Debtor to his Creditor, provided he approves him, that he, instead of the other, may discharge the Debt. Where indeed there is required the Consent of the Creditor, but not of that third Person who is the Debtor, whom I may turn over without his Knowledge or Consent, to the other Person that is to accept him. For it is no great Matter *to whom* any Person makes Payment; but *from whom* the Debt is to be required, is very material.

VIII. Assignment. L. N. N. l. 5. c. 11. §13.

Lastly, By *Death* those Obligations expire, which were founded in the Person of the Deceas'd; for the *Subject* being gone, the *Accidents* must necessarily follow, and the Performance is hereby rendred impossible in Nature. Yet oftentimes the Obligation that lay on the Deceas'd, is continued to the Survivors; and this, either when the Survivor takes it upon him of his own Accord to preserve the Reputation of the Deceased, or for other Reasons; or when the Goods of the Deceased being made over to the Heir, the Incumbrance goes along with them.

IX. DEATH. L. N. N. l. 5. c. 11. §12.

෨ CHAPTER XVII ෨

Of Meaning, or Interpretation

As in all Commands and Directions which Men receive from their Superiors, no other Obligation is derived on them from thence, but such as is conformable to the Will and *Intention* of the Superior; so likewise, when any Man of his own free Will, sets himself under any Obligation, he is bound only to that which himself *intended,* when he entered into that Obligation. But then, because one Man cannot make a Judgment of another Man's Intention, but by such Signs and Actions as are apparent to the Senses; hence, therefore, every one, *in foro humano,*[54] is

I. Rules for Interpretation necessary. L. N. N. l. 5. c. 12.

---

54. "In the human forum"; i.e., regardless of how things appear in the sight of God.

adjudged, To be *obliged to that Thing, which he may fairly be supposed to have suggested by a right Interpretation of the outward Signs made by him.* Wherefore 'tis of great Use for the true Understanding both of Laws and Covenants, and for the better Discharging the Duties thence arising, that there should be laid down **Certain Rules for the true Interpretation of Words,* especially they being the most common and ordinary Signs whereby we express our Mind and Intention.

II. Popular Terms. L. N. N. l. 5. c. 12. §3. Concerning *Common* and *Vulgar Terms,* this is the Rule: Words are generally to be taken in their most proper and receiv'd Signification, which they have not so much from Analogy and Construction of Grammar, or Conformity of Derivation, as by Popular *Use* and *Custom,* which is the Sovereign Comptroller and Judge of Speech.

III. Terms of Art. L. N. N. l. 5. c. 12. §4. Terms *of Art* are to be explain'd according to the Definitions of Persons knowing in each Art. But if those Terms are differently defin'd by several Persons, for the avoiding of Disputes, 'tis necessary that we express in Vulgar Terms, what we mean by such a Word.

IV. Conjectures. L. N. N. l. 5. c. 12. §6. But for discovering the genuine Meaning of Words, 'tis sometimes necessary to make Use of *Conjectures,* if either the Words in themselves, or the Connexion of them, be ambiguous, and liable to a double Interpretation; or if some Parts of the Discourse seem to contradict the other, yet so as by a fair and true Explanation they may be *reconcil'd.* For where there is a plain and manifest Contrariety, the latter Contract[55] vacates the former.

* *Grotius de Jure Belli & Pacis, l. 2. c. 16.*

55. The word "Contract" has been added, unnecessarily, by the English editors. Tooke's wording was "the later part must be accounted to *contradict* that which went before," which, while not entirely perspicuous, is closer to Pufendorf's original *posterius derogabit prioribus,* "the later passage supersedes the earlier."

Now Conjectures of the Mind, and the right Meaning thereof in an ambiguous or intricate Expression, are chiefly to be taken *from the Subject Matter, from the Effects and the Accidents* or Circumstances. As to the *Matter,* this is the Rule: Words are generally to be understood according to the Subject Matter. For he that speaks is suppos'd to have always in View the Matter of which he discourses, and therefore agreeably thereunto, the Meaning of the Words is always to be applied.

V. Taken from the Subject Matter. L. N. N. l. 5. c. 12. §7.

As to the *Effects* and *Consequences,* this is the Rule: When Words taken in the literal and simple Sense, admit either of none, or else of some absurd Consequences, we must recede so far from the more receiv'd Meaning, as is necessary for the avoiding of a Nullity or Absurdity.

VI. From the Consequences. L. N. N. l. 5. c. 12. §8.

Farthermore, most probable Conjectures may be taken from the *Circumstances;* because of Consequence every one is presum'd to be consistent with himself. Now these Circumstances are to be consider'd either as to their *Place,* or only as to the *Occasion* of them. Concerning the former of these, this is the Rule: If the Sense in any Place of the Discourse be express'd plainly and clearly, the more obscure Phrases are to be interpreted by those plain and familiar ones. To this Rule there is another nearly related: In the Explaining of any Discourse the Antecedents and Consequents must be carefully heeded, to which those Things that are inserted between are presum'd to answer and agree. But concerning the *latter,* this is the Rule: The *obscure* Expressions of one and the same Man are to be interpreted by what he has deliver'd more clearly, though it was at another Time and Place; unless it manifestly appears that he has changed his Opinion.

VII. From Circumstances. L. N. N. l. 5. c. 12. §9.

It is likewise of very great Use for finding out the true Meaning, in Laws especially, to examine into the *Reason of that Law,* or those Causes and Considerations which induced the Legislator to the making thereof; and more particularly when it is evident, that that was the *only Reason* of the Law. Concerning which, this is the Rule: That Interpretation of the Law is to be followed, which agrees with the Reason of that Law; and the contrary is to be rejected, if it be altogether inconsistent with

VIII. The Reason of the Thing. L. N. N. l. 5. c. 12. §10.

the same. So likewise when the sole and adequate Reason of the Law ceases, the Law it self ceases. But when there are several Reasons of the same Law, it does not follow, that if one of them ceases, the whole Law ceases too, when there are more Reasons remaining, which are sufficient for the keeping it still in Force. Sometimes also the Will of the Law-giver is sufficient, where the Reason of the Law is conceal'd.

IX. Words of various Signifi-cation. L. N. N. l. 5. c. 12. §11. Moreover, it is to be observ'd, That many Words have *various Significations,* one Meaning being of great Latitude, and the other more *strict* and *confin'd;* and then the subject Matter is sometimes of a *favourable* Nature, sometimes *invidious,* sometimes between both or *indifferent.* Those are *favourable* where the Condition is equal on both Sides, where Regard is had to the publick Good, where Provision is made upon Transactions already ratified, and which tend to the promoting of Peace, and the like. The *Invidious,* or more distastful, is that which ag-grieves one Party only, or one more than the other; that which implies a certain Penalty; that which makes any Transaction of none Effect, or alters what went before; that which promotes Wars and Troubles. That which is between both and *Indifferent* is, That indeed which makes some Change and Alteration in the former State of Things, but 'tis only for the sake of Peace. Concerning these, this is the Rule: That those Things which admit of a *favourable* Construction, are to be taken in the largest and most comprehensive Meaning; but those Things which are capable of an unpleasing Construction, in the most literal and strictest Sense of the Words.

X. Conjectures extended. L. N. N. l. 5. c. 12. §11. There are likewise some Kind of Conjectures which are elsewhere to be fetch'd than from the Words, and which are the Occasion that the In-terpretation of them is sometimes to be *extended,* and at other times to be *confin'd:* Although 'tis more easie to give Reasons why the Explana-tion thereof should be *confin'd* and *limited,* than *extended.* But the Law may be *extended* to a Case which is not express'd in the Law, if it be apparent, that the Reason which suits to this Case, was particularly re-garded by the Law-giver amongst other Considerations, and that he did design to include the other Cases of the like Nature. The Law also ought to be *extended* to those Cases wherein the Subtlety of ill Men have found out Tricks in order to evade the Force of the Law.

Now the Reason why some Expressions deliver'd in general Terms should be *restrain'd*, may happen either from the *original Defect of the Will*, or from the Repugnancy of some *emergent Case* to the Will and Intention. That any Person is to be presum'd not at first to have intended any such Thing, may be understood, XI. Conjectures limited. L. N. N. l. 5. c. 12. §19.

1. FROM the *Absurdity*, which otherwise would follow from thence; and which, 'tis believ'd, no Man in his Wits could design. Hence general Expressions are to be restrain'd, inasmuch as such Absurdity would thence otherwise arise.

2. FROM *Want of that Reason* which might chiefly cause him to be of that Mind. Hence in a general Expression, those Cases are not comprehended, which do no ways agree with the sole and adequate Reason of the Law.

3. FROM *Defect of Matter*, which always he that speaks, is suppos'd to have consider'd. And therefore all those general Words are to be regarded with relation to the same.

Now that an emergent State of Things is repugnant to the Intention of the Person who made the Constitution, may be discover'd either from *Natural Reason,* or else from some declared Mark and *Signification* of his Meaning. XII. Emergent Cases. L. N. N. l. 5. c. 12. §21.

The first happens, when we must exclude *Equity,* if some certain Cases be not exempted from the universal Law. For *Equity* is the Correcting of what is defective in the Law by reason of its *Universality.*

And because all Cases could neither be foreseen, nor set down, because of the infinite Variety of them; therefore when general Words are apply'd to special Cases, those Cases are to be look'd upon as exempt, which the Law-giver himself would likewise have exempted, if he had been consulted upon such a Case.

But we must not have Recourse to *Equity,* unless there be very sufficient Grounds for it. The Chiefest of which, is, If it be evident, that the Law of Nature would be violated, if we followed too closely the Letter of that Law.

The next Ground of Exception is, That though it be not indeed unlawful to keep to the very Words of the Law; yet, if, upon an impartial Consideration, the Thing should seem too grievous and burdensome, either to Men in general, or to some certain Persons; or else, if the Design be not of that Value, as to be purchas'd at so dear a Rate.

XIII. Exception with Regard to Time. L. N. N. l. 5. c. 12. §23. Lastly, There are also some certain Signs of the Legislator's Will, from whence it may be certainly collected, That a Case ought to be excepted from the general Expressions of the Law; as when the Words of the Legislator in another Place, though not directly opposite to the Law now supposed to be before us, (for that would be a Contradiction) yet, by some peculiar Incident, and unexpected Event of Things, happen to oppose it in the present Case; or, which amounts to the same Thing, When there are two different Laws, which don't interfere, and which easily may and ought to be observ'd at different Times, but can't both of them be satisfy'd, when by some Chance, they call for our Obedience at the same Instant: In this Case we must observe some certain Rules to know which Law or Pact ought to give Place to the other, where both cannot be fulfill'd.

1. THAT *which is only permitted gives place to that which is commanded.**

2. THAT *which ought to be done at this present Time, is preferable to that which may be done at any other Time.*

3. *A Law forbidding the doing any Thing, is to be preferr'd before a Law directing the doing any Thing:* †Or when an *affirmative* Precept can't be

---

*1. This Rule is not true, unless we suppose the *Permission* general, and the *Command* particular. For it is certain, on the contrary, that a particular Permission takes Place of a general Command; the Permission in this last Case, being an Exception to the Command; as in the former Case, the Command restrains the Extent of the Permission. [Barbeyrac's XIII.1, p. 233.]

†3. Here, likewise, it must be distinguish'd, whether these Laws forbidding or commanding, be general or particular, as was laid down in the foregoing Note. [Barbeyrac's XIII.2, p. 233.]

satisfy'd but at the Expence of a *negative* one, then the Performance of the *Affirmative,* shall be deferr'd or put off, 'till it ceases to clash with that other which is *Negative.* Thus I am commanded to be charitable, and I am commanded not to steal: If I have not wherewith to be charitable, unless I steal to give away, I lye under no Obligation to be charitable at that Time.

4. In *Covenants and Laws, which are in other respects Equal, that which is particular and applicable to the present Case, takes Place of that which is General.*

5. When *two Duties happen to interfere at the same Point of Time, that which is founded upon Reasons more honourable and beneficial is to be preferr'd.*

6. When *two Covenants, one upon Oath, the other not, can't be perform'd both together, the former ought to take Place of the latter.**

7. An *Obligation imperfectly mutual, gives Place to one that is perfectly mutual and binding on both sides.* †Thus what I owe upon Contract, ought to be paid before what is due from me upon free Promise or Gratitude.

8. What *I am obliged to do out of Gratitude, must be preferr'd before what I am obliged to out of Generosity.*

---

* 6. This Rule is not true, unless in such Case, where all other Circumstances are exactly equal. For when two Covenants are directly opposite, the latter shall be binding, whether the former be upon Oath, or not. But if the Two Covenants are not directly opposite, but only in some Respects different, the particular one shall be preferr'd before the general one. [Barbeyrac's XIII.3, p. 234.]

† 7. These Two last Rules are comprehended in the *Fifth,* of which they are, as is obvious, only Consequences. [Barbeyrac's XIII.4, p. 234.]

Book II

CHAPTER I

Of the Natural State of Men

I. Condition of MAN. L. N. N. l. 1. c. 1. §6, &c.

In the next Place, we are to inquire concerning those Duties which are incumbent upon a Man with Regard to that *particular State* wherein he finds himself ordained by Providence to live in the World. What we mean by such *State,* is in general, that *Condition* or *Degree* with all its Relatives, in which Men being placed, they are therefore supposed to be obliged to these or those Performances: And such *State,* whatever it be, has some peculiar Rights and Offices thereunto belonging.[1]

II. Twofold. Natural and Adventitious. L. N. N. l. 2. c. 3. §24.

The *State* of MAN then may be distinguish'd into either *Natural* or *Adventitious*. The natural State, by the Help of the Light of natural Reason alone, is to be considered as Threefold, Either as it regards *God our Creator,* or as it concerns *every single Man* as to *Himself,* or as it affects *other Men;* concerning all which we have spoken before.

> 1. Tooke's rendering of this crucial paragraph differs significantly from Pufendorf's original. Pufendorf wrote not of duties attaching to a particular state ordained for man by providence, but of those arising from the diverse statuses (*ex diverso statu*) man occupies in social life. This definitively Pufendorfian viewpoint results from his doctrine that civil duties attach not to a human essence, or *telos,* but to statuses instituted by man. Silverthorne's rendering is broadly accurate: "We must next inquire into the duties which fall to man to perform as a result of the different states in which we find him existing in social life. By 'state' [*status*] in general, we mean a condition in which men are understood to be set for the purpose of performing a certain class of actions. Each state also has its own distinctive laws [*jura*]" (*Man & Citizen,* p. 115). Only Silverthorne's choice of "laws" for *jura* is questionable. Here perhaps Tooke's "Rights and Offices" better captures the spirit of Pufendorf's formulation.

The Natural State of Man consider'd in the *first* mention'd Way, is that Condition wherein he is placed by the Creator pursuant to his Divine Will, that he should be the most excellent Animal in the whole Creation. From the Consideration of which *State,* it follows, That Man ought to acknowledge the AUTHOR of his Being, to pay Him Adoration, and to admire the Works of His Hands; and moreover, to lead his life after a different Manner from that of the Brutes. So that the contrary to this State is *the Life and Condition of Brutes.*

III. Natural State Three-fold. First.

In the *second* Way we may contemplate the Natural *State* of Man, by seriously forming in our Minds an Idea of what his Condition would be, if every one were left **alone* to himself without any Help from *other* Men.[2] And in this Sense, the *Natural State* is opposed to *a Life cultivated by the Industry of Men.*

IV. Second. L. N. N. l. 2. c. 2. §2.

After the *third* Way we are to regard the Natural State of Man, according as Men are understood to stand in respect to one another, merely from that common Alliance which results from the *Likeness* of their *Natures,* before any mutual Agreement made, or other Deed of Man perform'd, by which one could become obnoxious[3] to the Power of an-

V. Third.

---

* *See* Book I. Chap. III. §3. *and the* References *made to it.* [Barbeyrac's marginal note (a), p. 236.]

2. At this point, following Barbeyrac, the English editors have deleted Pufendorf's characterization of the life of man imagined in the absence of the mutual assistance and industry through which he compensates for his natural weakness (*imbecillitas*). In Tooke's original edition the deleted passage runs "especially considering the present circumstances under which we at this time find Human Nature: Which would certainly be much more miserable than that of a Beast, if we think with our selves, with what weakness man enters this World, so that he must immediately perish, except he be sustained by others, and how rude a Life he must lead, if he could procure nothing for himself, but by means of his own single Strength and Skill. But 'tis plain, that we owe it all to the aid of *other persons,* that we are able to pass through so many Infirmities from our Infancy to Manhood; that we enjoy infinite number of Conveniences; that we improve our Minds and Bodies to such a degree as to be useful to our selves and our Neighbour." Barbeyrac had ideological misgivings about the bleakness of Pufendorf's picture of the state of nature, believing that it gives too great a role to the civil state in securing man's happiness, hence too much power to the civil sovereign.

3. In the early modern (Latin) sense of "subject to the authority of another."

other. In which Sense, those are said to live reciprocally in a *State of Nature*, who acknowledge no *common Superior*, and of whom none can pretend Dominion over his Fellow, and who do not render themselves known to each other, either by the doing of good Turns or Injuries. And in this Sense it is, That a *Natural State* is distinguish'd from a *Civil State*, that is, *The State of Man in a Community.*[4]

VI. Consider'd again Two ways L. N. N. l. 2. c. 2.

Moreover, the Property of this *Natural State* may be consider'd, either as it is represented to us *notionally* and by way of *Fiction,* or as it is *really* and *indeed.* The *former* is done, when we imagine a certain Multitude of Men at the Beginning to have started up into Beings all at once without any Dependence upon one another, as it is fabled of the *Cadmean* Harvest of Brethren;[5] or else when we form a Supposition, that all the mutual Ties, by which Mankind are one way or other united together, were now dissolv'd; so that every Man might set up for himself apart from the Rest, and no one Man should have any other Relation to his Fellow, but the Likeness of their Natures. But the true State of Nature, or that which is *really* so, has this in it, that there is no Man who has not some peculiar Obligations to *some* other Men, though with all the rest he may have no farther Alliance than that they are Men, and of the same Kind; and, beside what arises from thence, he owes them no Service at all. Which at this Time is the Case of many Kingdoms and Communities, and of the Subjects of the same, with respect to the Subjects of the other;[6] and the same was anciently the State of the Patriarchs, when they liv'd independently.

4. "The State of Man in a Community" is Tooke's addition. Pufendorf's sentence ends at "Civil State."

5. Ovid's myth of Cadmus, in which men spring from the ground where the dragon's teeth have been scattered.

6. In other words, even today states exist in a state of nature with regard to other states; for the civil condition, with its entire array of duties and rights, is internal to the particular state.

It is then taken for manifest, that all Mankind never were universally   VII Paternal
and at once in the former *Natural State;* for those Children who were   Authority.
begotten and born of the Protoplasts, or first created Man and Woman,
(from whom the whole Human Race derives its Original, as the *Holy
Scriptures* tell us) were subject to the *Paternal Authority.* Not but that
this Natural State arose afterwards among some People; for Men at
first, in order to spread over this wide World, and that they might find
for themselves and their Cattle more spacious Abodes, left the Families
of their Fathers, and roaming into various Regions, almost every single
Man became himself the Father of a Family of his own; and the Posterity of these again dispersing themselves, that *peculiar Bond* of Kindred,
and the Natural Affections thence arising, by little and little were extinct, and no other Obligation remain'd, but that common one, which
resulted from the Likeness of their Natures: 'Till afterwards, when
Mankind was vastly multiplied, they having observ'd the many Inconveniences of that loose Way of living, the Inhabitants of Places near one
another, by Degrees join'd in Communities,[7] which at first were small,
but grew soon greater, either by the voluntary or forced Conjunction of
many which were lesser. And among these Communities, the State of
Nature is still found, they being not otherwise obliged to each other,
than by the common Tie of Humanity.

Now it is the chief *Prerogative* of those who are in the State of Nature,   VIII. Natural
that they are subject and accountable to none but GOD only; in which   Liberty.
respect also, this is call'd a State of *Natural Liberty,* by which is understood, that a Person so circumstanced without some antecedent human
Act to the contrary, is to be accounted absolutely in his own Power and
Disposition, and above the Controll of all mortal Authority. Therefore
also any one Person is to be reputed *equal* to any other, to whom himself is not subject, neither is that other subject to him.

7. That is, "states" (*civitates*). Barbeyrac's formulation, according to which men
gradually bring themselves under *Gouvernement Civil* (p. 239), is an improvisation
on the theme.

And farthermore, whereas Man is indued with the Light of Reason, by the Guidance whereof he may temper and regulate his Actions, it follows, That whosoever lives in a State of Natural Liberty, depends not on any other for the Direction of his Doings; but is vested with a Right to do, according to his own Judgment and Will, any Thing he shall think good, and which is consonant to sound Reason.

And whereas Man, from that universal Inclination which is implanted in all living Creatures, cannot but, in order to the Preservation of his Person and his Life, and to the keeping off whatsoever Mischiefs seem to threaten the Destruction thereof, take the utmost Care and Pains, and apply all necessary Means to that End; and yet whereas no Man in this Natural State has any superiour Person, to whom he may submit his Designs and Opinions, therefore every one in this State makes use of his own Judgment only, in determining concerning the Fitness of Means, whether they conduce to his Self Preservation or not. For though he may give ear to the Advice of another, yet it is in his Choice, whether he will approve or reject the same. But that this absolute Power of Governing himself be rightly managed, it is highly necessary, That all his Administrations be moderated by the Dictates of true Reason, and by the Rules of the Law of Nature.

IX. Its Inconveniences.

L. N. N. l. 1. c. 3. §3.

And yet this Natural State, how alluring soever it appears to us with the Name of LIBERTY, and flattering us with being free from all manner of Subjection, was clogg'd, before Men join'd themselves under Governments, with many *Inconveniences;* whether we suppose every single Man as in that Condition, or only consider the Case of the Patriarchs or Fathers of Families, while they liv'd independent.[8] For if you form in your Mind the Idea of a Man, even at his full Growth of Strength

8. Barbeyrac deleted the following evocation of man's miserable condition in the state of nature (to the end of the paragraph), his second such deletion. (See note 2, p. 167.) Further, to reinforce his unauthorized intervention, he added a footnote to Pufendorf's ensuing praise of the civil state, accusing him of exaggerating its virtues. In declining to follow Barbeyrac on this occasion, the English editors perhaps display a degree of detachment from his more intense ideological engagement with Pufendorf's text.

and Understanding, but without all those Assistances and Advantages by which the Wit of Man has rendred Human Life much more orderly and more easie than at the Beginning; you shall have before you, a naked Creature no better than dumb, wanting all Things, satisfying his Hunger with Roots and Herbs, slaking his Thirst with any Water he can find, avoiding the Extremities of the Weather, by creeping into Caves, or the like, exposed an easie Prey to the ravenous Beasts, and trembling at the Sight of any of them.

'Tis true, the Way of Living among the Patriarchs, might be somewhat more comfortable, even while they contain'd their Families apart; but yet it could by no Means be compar'd with the Life of Men in a *Community;* not so much for the Need they might have of Things from abroad, which, if they restrain'd their Appetites, they might perhaps well enough bear withal; as because in that State they could have little Certainty of any continu'd Security.

And, that we may comprehend all in a few words, In a *State of Nature,* every Man must rely upon his own single Power; whereas in a *Community,* all are on his Side: There no Man can be sure of enjoying the Fruit of his Labour; here every one has it secur'd to him: There the *Passions* rule, and there is a continual Warfare, accompanied with Fears, Want, Sordidness, Solitude, Barbarity, Ignorance, and Brutishness; here *Reason* governs, and here is Tranquillity, Security, Wealth, Neatness, Society, Elegancy, Knowledge, and Humanity.

Now though it was the Will of Nature itself, that there should be a Sort of *Kindred* amongst all Mankind, by Virtue of which they might be obliged at least not to hurt one another, but rather to assist and contribute to the Benefit of their Fellows; yet this Alliance is found to be but of little Force among those who live promiscuously in a State of

X. Uncertainty of the State of Nature.[9]

9. In Pufendorf's original text and in Tooke's original translation, this important section, on the limited degree to which natural law binds man in the state of nature, was the final one in the chapter (sec. XI). In it, Pufendorf signals his relation to Hobbes's famous account of the state of nature as the "war of all against all." Against Hobbes, Pufendorf argues that even in the state of nature men should be bound by the natural law of sociability. In denying that men can in fact live by this law in the

Natural Liberty; so that any Man who is not under the same Laws and Possibilities of Coercion with our selves, or with whom we live loosely and free from any Obligation in the said State, is not indeed to be treated as an *Enemy,* but may be look'd upon as a *Friend,* not too freely to be *trusted.* And the Reason hereof is, That Man not only is accomplish'd, with an Ability to do Mischief to his Like, but for many Causes has also a Will so to do: For some, the Pravity of their Natures, Ambition, or Covetousness, incite to make Insults upon other Men; others, though of a meek and modest Nature, are forced to use Violence either in defending themselves from imminent Outrages, or by way of Prevention.

L. N. N. l. 1.
c. 3. §4.

Beside that, a Rivalship in the Desire of the same Thing in some; and in others, Competition for Priority in one Quality or other, shall set them at Variance. So that in this State, 'tis hardly possible but that there should be perpetual Jealousies, Mistrusts, Designs of undoing each other, Eagerness to prevent every one his Fellow, or Hopes of making Addition to his own Strength by the Ruin of others.

Therefore as it is the Duty of every *honest* Man to be content with his own, and not to give Provocation to his Neighbour, nor to covet that which is his; so also it behoves him who would be as *wary* as is needful, and who is willing to take Care of his own Good, so to take all Men for his Friends, as not to suppose yet but that the same may quickly become his Enemies; so to cultivate Peace with all Men, as to be provided though it be never so soon changed to Enmity. And for this Reason, happy is that Commonwealth, where in Times of Quietness, Consideration is had of Requisites for War.

---

absence of civil authority, however, Pufendorf comes close to the Hobbesian viewpoint. If others are natural friends, they are unreliable ones, and in peace we should be prepared for war. In reversing the order of Pufendorf's final two sections, Barbeyrac prevents this being Pufendorf's final word on the natural condition.

Beside, in the *Natural State,* if any one either will not voluntarily make good what he has *covenanted* to do, or does another an *Injury,* or if upon any other Account some Dispute arise; there's no Man has Authority to force the naughty Person to perform his Bargain, to cause him to repair the Wrong, or to determine the Controversy; as there is in *Communities,* where I may have recourse for Help to the Civil Magistrate.

XI. Most convenient Remedy in Controversies.
L. N. N. l. 5. c. 13.

And here, because Nature allows not that upon every Occasion we should betake our selves to *violent Means,* even though we are very well satisfy'd in our Consciences of the Justice of our Cause; therefore we are first to try, whether the Matter may not be composed after a milder Way, either by an amicable Reasoning of the Point in Question between the Parties themselves, or by a free and unconditional Compromise, *or *Reference* of the Debate to *Arbitrators.* And these Referees are to manage the Matter with an equal Regard to both Sides, and in giving their Award, they are to have an Eye only to the Merits of the Cause, setting aside all partial Animosity or Affection. For which Reason, it is not best to chuse any Man an Arbitrator in such a Cause wherein he shall have greater Hopes of Profit or particular Reputation, if one Party get the better, rather than the other; and consequently where it is his Interest that that Litigant, at what Rate soever, gain the Point. Hence also there ought not to be any underhand Bargain or Promise between the Umpire and either of the Parties, by which he may be obliged to give his Judgment on the behalf of the same.

Now in this Affair, if the Arbitrator cannot find out the Truth in Fact, neither from the Confessions of the Parties, nor from apparent Writings, nor any other manifest Arguments and Signs; he must then inform himself by the Testimonies of Witnesses; whom, though the Law of Nature obliges, especially being usually reinforced by the Religion of an Oath, to speak the Truth; yet it is most safe not to admit the Evidence of such as are so peculiarly affected to one Party, that their Consciences will be forced to struggle with the Passions either of Love,

---

*See *Grotius de Jure Belli & Pacis, lib. 2. cap. 23. §6,* &c.

Hatred, Desire of Revenge, any violent Affection of the Mind, or else some strict Friendship or Dependance; all, or any of which every Man is not endued with Constancy enough to surmount.

Controversies also are frequently made an end of by the *Interposition* of the common *Friends* of each Party, which to do, is deservedly accounted among the best Actions of a good Man. For the rest, in the *Natural State,* when Performances are not made good by either Side of their own Accord, the other seeks his Due after what manner he likes best.

ɷɷ   C H A P T E R   I I   ɷɷ

Of the Duties of the Married State

I. Matrimony.
L. N. N. l. 6.
c. 1.

Among those States of Man which we have call'd *Adventitious,* or in which a Man is placed by some antecedent human Act, MATRIMONY obtains the first Place. *Which also is the chief Representation of the Social Life, and the Seed-Plot of Mankind.

II. Instituted
by Nature.

And, first, it is certain, That that ardent Propensity found to be in both Sexes to each other, was not implanted in them by the All-wise CREA-TOR, merely that they might receive the Satisfaction of a vain Pleasure; for had it been so, nothing could have been the Occasion of greater Brutishness and Confusion in the World; but that hereby Married Persons might take the greater Delight in each other's Company; and that both might with the more Chearfulness apply themselves to the necessary Business of Propagation, and go through those Cares and Troubles which accompany the Breeding and Education of Children. Hence it follows, That all Use of the Parts destin'd by Nature for this Work, is

* *Grotius de Jure Belli & Pacis, l. 2. c. 5. §9. &c.*

contrary to the Law Natural, if it tends not to this End. On which Account also, are forbidden all Lusts for a different *Species,* or for the same Sex; all filthy Pollutions; and indeed, all Copulations out of the State of Matrimony, whether with the mutual Consent of both Parties, or against the Will of the Woman.

The *Obligation* under which we lye to contract *Matrimony,* may be consider'd either with respect to *Mankind* in general, or to our particular *Station* and *Relation* in the World. The Strength of the former of these, consists in this, That the Propagation of Mankind, neither can nor ought to be kept up by promiscuous and uncertain Copulations, but is to be limited and circumscribed by the Laws of *Wedlock,* and only to be endeavour'd in a married State: For without this no Man can imagine any Decency or orderly Society among Men, nor any Observation of the Civil Rules of Life.

III. Obligation to Matrimony. L. N. N. l. 6. c. 1. §3.

But Men *singly* consider'd, are obliged to enter the Matrimonial State, when a convenient Occasion offers it self; whereto also not only a mature Age, and an Ability for Generation-Work[10] is necessary, but there ought beside to be a Possibility of lighting on a Person of the like Condition, and a Capacity of maintaining a Wife, and the Posterity she shall bring forth; and that the Man may be such a one as is fit to become the Master of a Family.

Not still, but that any Man is excepted from this Duty, who betakes himself to a chaste SINGLE LIFE, finding his Constitution accommodated thereto, and that he is capable in that, rather than in the Married State, to be useful to Mankind, or to the Commonwealth; especially also, if the Case be so, that there is no Fear of the Want of People.

Between those who are about to take upon themselves the Married State, a *Contract* ought, and is wont to intervene, which, if it be *Regular* and *Perfect,* consists of these Heads:

IV. Matrimonial Contract. L. N. N. l. 6. c. 1. §9.

First, Because the Man (to whom it is most agreeable to the Nature of both Sexes, that the Contract should owe its Original) intends

---

10. I.e., the capacity to procreate.

hereby to get himself Children of his own, not spurious or supposititious; therefore the Woman ought to *plight her Troth*[11] to the Man, That she will permit the Use of her Body to no other Man but to him; the same, on the other Hand, being requir'd of the Husband.

And, Secondly, Since nothing can be more flatly contrary to a Social and Civil Life, than a vagabond, desultory, and changeable Way of Living, without any Home, or certain Seat of his Fortunes; and since the Education of that which is the Off-spring of both, is most conveniently taken Care of by the joint Help of both Parents together: And whereas continual Cohabitation brings more of Pleasure and Comfort to a Couple who are well match'd, whereby also the Husband may have the greater Assurance of his Wife's Chastity; therefore the Wife does moreover ingage her Faith to her Husband, That she will *always cohabit* with him, and join her self in the strictest Bond of Society, and become of the same Family with him. And this mutual Promise must be supposed to be made from the Husband to her of the like Cohabitation, the Nature of this State so requiring.

But because it is not only agreeable to the natural Condition of both Sexes, that the Case of the Husband should be the more Honourable of the two; but that he should also be the Head of the Family, of which himself is the Author; it follows, That the Wife ought to be subject to his Direction in Matters relating to their mutual State and to their Household. Hence it is the Prerogative of the Husband, to chuse his Habitation, and she may not against his Will, wander abroad, or lodge apart.

Yet it does not seem essentially necessary to Matrimony, that the Man should have Power of Life and Death, or of inflicting any grievous Punishment, as neither of disposing at his Pleasure of all the Estate or Goods of his Wife: But these Points may be settled between the Married Couple, by peculiar Agreements, or by the municipal Laws of the Place.

---

11. I.e., the woman must promise to be sexually faithful.

Now tho' 'tis manifestly repugnant to the Law of Nature, that one Woman should have more Men than one at once; yet it obtain'd among the *Jews* of old, and many other Nations, that one Man might have two or more Wives. Nevertheless, let us allow never so little Weight to Arguments brought from the primitive Institution of Marriage deliver'd in *Holy Writ;* *yet it will appear from *right Reason,* That 'tis much more decent and fit for one Man to be content with one Woman. Which has been approved by the Practice of all the Christians through the World, that we know of, for so many Ages.

V. One Man and one Woman.
L. N. N. l. 6. c. 1. §19.

Nor does the Nature of this strict Union tell us less plainly, That the Bond of *Matrimony ought to be perpetual,* and not to be unloosed, but by the Death of one Party; except the *essential Articles* of the principal Matrimonial Covenant be violated, either by *Adultery,* or a wicked and dishonest *Desertion.* But for *ill Dispositions,* which have not the same Effect with such *lewd Desertion,* it has obtained among Christians, that a Separation from Bed and Board shall be sufficient, without allowing any Ingagement in a new Wedlock. And one great Reason hereof, among others, is this, That too free a Liberty of Divorce might not give Incouragement to either Party to cherish a stubborn Temper; but rather, that the irremediable State of each, might persuade both to accommodate their Humours to one another, and to stir them both up to *mutual* Forbearance. For the rest, if any essential Article of the Matrimonial Contract be violated, the *wronged Party* only is discharged from the Obligation; the same still binding the other, so long as the former shall think good.

VI. Contract perpetual.
L. N. N. l. 6. c. 1. §20, 21.

Any Man may contract with any Woman, where the Law makes no special Prohibition, if their Age and Constitution of Body render them capable of Matrimony, except some *Moral Impediment* be in the Way: Presupposing, That he or she is under a Moral Impediment, who are already married to some other Person.

VII. Moral Impediments.
L. N. N. l. 6. c. 1. §27.

* See *Element. jurisprud. universal.* l. 11. §7. *Apol.* §29. *Eris Scandica.* P. 48. & seq. p. 109.

VIII. Kindred
L. N. N. l. 6.
c. 1. §28.

And it is accounted a Moral Impediment of lawful Matrimony, if the Parties are *too nearly allied by Blood or by Affinity.* On which Score, even by the Law of Nature, those Marriages are accounted incestuous and wicked, which are contracted between any Persons related in the *Ascending* or *Descending* Line. And for those in the other *transverse Order,* as with the Aunt, either on the Father's or Mother's Side, the Sister, *&c.* As also those in *Affinity,* as, with the Mother-in-law, Step-Mother, Step-Daughter, *&c.* Not only the positive Divine Law, but that of most civiliz'd Nations, with whom also all Christians agree, does abominate. Nay, the Special Laws of many Countries forbid Marriage even in the more remote Degrees, that so they may keep Men from breaking in upon those which are more sacred, by setting the Barrier at a greater Distance.

IX. Ceremony.

Now as the Laws are wont to assign to other Contracts and Bargains some *Solemnities,* which being wanting, the Act shall not be adjudged of Validity: So also it is in Matrimony, where the Laws require, for the sake of Decency and good Order, that such or such *Ceremonies* be performed. And these, though not injoined by the Law Natural, yet without the same, those who are Subjects of such a Community,[12] shall not consummate a legal Matrimony; or at least, such Contract shall not be allowed by the Publick to be effectual.

X. Mutual
Duties.

It is the Duty of a *Husband* to love his Wife, to cherish, direct and protect her; and of the *Wife* to love and honour her Husband, to be assistant to him, not only in begetting and educating his Children, but to bear her Part in the Domestick Cares. On both sides, the Nature of so strict an Union requires, That the Married Couple be Partakers as well in the good as ill Fortune of either, and that one succour the other in

---

12. The reference to "Subjects of such a Community" is Tooke's innovation. Pufendorf refers only to those subject to the "civil laws" (*leges civiles*), which he is here treating as supplementary to the natural laws dictating monogamous perpetual unions. We recall that by civil laws Pufendorf means the positive laws of a particular state—here, the laws prescribing the form of marriage ceremonies—which should accord with the end of natural law (social peace) but are not the same.

all Cases of Distress; moreover, That they prudently accommodate their Humours to each other; in which Matter, it is the Wife's Duty to submit.

:∞: CHAPTER III :∞:

Duty of Parents and Children

From MATRIMONY proceeds POSTERITY,[13] which is subjected to the *Paternal Power,* *the most Ancient and the most Sacred Kind of Authority, whereby Children are obliged to reverence their Parents, to obey their Commands, and to acknowledge their Pre-eminence.

I. Paternal Authority. L. N. N. l. 6. c. 2.

The Authority of Parents over their Children, hath its chief Foundation on a *Twofold Cause.*

II. Its Foundation Twofold.

First, Because the Law of Nature it self, when Man was made a Sociable Creature, injoin'd to *Parents the Care of their Children;* and lest they should herein be negligent, Nature implanted in them a most tender Affection for their Issue. Now that this Care may be rightly managed, it is requisite that they have a Power of ordering the Actions of their Children for their Good; because these, as yet, understand not, for want of *Discretion,* how to govern themselves.

Next, This Authority is also grounded on the *tacit Consent of their Offspring.* For it may fairly be presum'd, that if an Infant, at the Time of its Birth, had the Use of its Reason, and saw that its Life could not be preserv'd without the Care of the Parents, to which must be join'd a Power over it self, it would readily consent to the same, and desire for it self a comfortable Education from them. And this Power is *actually*

13. Children.
* *Grotius de Jure Belli & Pacis,* l. 2. c. 5. §1, &c.

in the Parents, then when they breed and nurse up the Child, and form him as well as they can, that he may become a fit Member of Human Society.

III. Which
Parent has
greater Right.
L. N. N. l. 6.
c. 2. §4.

But whereas the Mother concurs no less than the Father to the Generation of Children, and so the Offspring is common to both, it may be inquir'd, *Which hath the greatest Right thereto?* Concerning which Point we are to distinguish: For if the Issue were begotten *not in Matrimony,* the same shall be rather the Mother's, because here the Father cannot be known, except the Mother discover him. Among those also who live in a State of *Natural Liberty,* and above Laws, it may be agreed, that the Mother's Claim shall be preferr'd to that of the Father. But in *Communities,*[14] which have their Formation from Men, the Matrimonial Contract regularly commencing on the Man's Side, and he becoming the Head of the Family, the *Father's Right* shall take Place, so as though the Child is to pay the Mother all Reverence and Gratitude, yet is it not obliged to obey her, when she bids that to be done which is contrary to the just Commands of the Father. Yet upon the Father's Decease, his Authority over his Child, especially if not of Age, seems to devolve upon the *Mother,* and if she marry again, it passes to the *Step-Father,* he being esteemed to succeed to the Trust and Care of a Natural Father. And he who shall allow liberal Education to an Orphan or a forsaken Child, shall have a Right to exact *filial Obedience* from the same.

IV. Paternal
Authority dis-
tinguish'd.
L. N. N. l. 6.
c. 2. §6.

But that we may handle more accurately the *Power of Parents over their Children,* we must distinguish, first, between *Patriarchs,* or Chiefs of independent Families; and such as are *Members of a Community;*[15] and then betwixt the *Power* of a *Father,* as *Father,* and his Power as *Head of his Family.* And whereas it is injoyn'd by Nature to a *Father as such,* That he bring up his Children well, in order to render 'em fit Members of Human Society, so long as 'till they can take Care of themselves;

---

14. Again, in Pufendorf this is "state" (*civitas*) and in Barbeyrac *Sociétez Civiles.*
15. Tooke's "Members of a Community" evades the political force of Pufendorf's original "who have submitted to the state" (*qui in civitatem subierunt*).

hence he has so much Power given him over them, as is necessary for this End; which therefore by no means extends it self so as to give the Parents Liberty to destroy their unborn Offspring, or to cast away or kill it when it is born. For though it is true, the Issue is of the Substance of the Parents, yet it is placed in a Human State equal to themselves, and capable of receiving Injuries from them. Neither also does this Authority vest them with the Exercise of a Power of Life and Death, upon Occasion of any Fault, but only allows them to give moderate Chastisement; since the Age we speak of is too tender to admit of such heinous Crimes as are to be punished with Death. But if a Child shall stubbornly spurn at all Instruction, and become hopeless of Amendment, the Father may turn him out of his own House, and abdicate or renounce him.

Moreover, This Power, thus nicely taken, may be considered according to the *diverse Age of Children.* For in their *early Years,* when their Reason is come to no Maturity, all their Actions are subject to the Direction of their Parents. During which Time, if any Estate fall to the young Person, it ought to be put into the Possession, and under the Administration of the Father, so that the Property be still reserved to the Child; tho' it may be reasonable enough that the Profits arising therefrom should be the Father's till the other arrive at Manhood. So also any Advantage or Profit that can be made by the Labour of a Son, ought to accrew to the Parent; since with the Latter lies all the Care of maintaining and of educating the Former.

V. Childhood.
L. N. N. l. 6.
c. 2. §7.

When Children are come to *Man's Estate,* when they are indued with a competent Share of Discretion, and yet continue themselves a Part of the Father's Family, then the Power which the Father hath comes differently to be considered, either as he is a *Father,* or as *Head* of the Family. And since in the former Case he makes his End to be the Education and Government of his Children, it is plain, That when they are of *ripe Years,* they are to be obedient to the Authority of their Parents, as wiser than themselves. And whosoever expects to be maintain'd upon what his Father has, and afterwards to succeed to the Possession of the same,

VI. Manhood.
L. N. N. l. 6.
c. 2. §11.

is obliged to accommodate himself to the Methods of his Paternal Household; the Management whereof ought to be in his Father's Power.

VII. Patriarchs Power abridged. L. N. N. l. 6. c. 2. §6.

Patriarchs, or *Heads* of independent Families, before they join'd in Communities,[16] acted in many Cases after the manner of *Princes,* in their Houses. So that their Progeny, who continued a Part of their Families, paid the highest Veneration to their Authority. But afterward, this Family-Royalty (as well as some other private Rights) was moderated for the Benefit and Order of Communities; and in some Places more, in others less of Power was left to Parents. Hence we see that, in some Governments, Fathers have in Criminal Cases a Power of Life and Death over their Children; but in most it is not allowed, either for fear Parents should abuse this Prerogative to the Detriment of the Publick, or to the unjust Oppression of those so subjected; or, lest thro' the Tenderness of Paternal Affection, many Vices should pass unpunished, which might break forth one time or other into publick Mischiefs; or else, that Fathers might not be under a Necessity of pronouncing sad and ungrateful Sentences.

VIII.[17] Marriage with Parents Consent. L. N. N. l. 6. c. 2. §14.

And as the Father ought not to *turn his Child out of his Family,* while he stands in Need of Education and Assistance from him, without the most weighty Reasons; so also ought not the Son or Daughter leave the Parent's House without his Consent. Now whereas Children frequently leave their Father's Family on Occasion of Matrimony; and since it much concerns Parents what Persons their Children are married to, and from whom they are to expect Grand-Children; hence it is a Part of filial Duty, herein to *comply with the Will of the Parents,* and not to marry without their Consent. But if any do actually contract Matri-

---

16. Again, Pufendorf's term is "states" (*civitates*).

17. In Pufendorf's original text, as in Tooke's first edition, this was section X. The English editors have followed Barbeyrac in their reordering of this and the following two sections, locating Pufendorf's original section VIII (on the piety due to parents) as the present section IX, and Pufendorf's original section IX (on education) as the present section X.

mony against their Liking, and consummate the same, such Marriage seems not to be void by the Law of Nature, especially if they intend to be no longer burthensome to their Parents, and that for the rest their Condition be not scandalous. So that if in any Country such Marriages are accounted null and void, it proceeds from the Municipal Laws of the Place.

But when a *Son* or *Daughter have left their Father's House,* and either have set up a new Family of their own, or joined to another; the Paternal *Authority* indeed ceases, but Piety and Observance is for ever due, as being founded in the Merits of the Parents, whom Children can never or very seldom be supposed to requite. Now these Merits do not consist in this only, That a Parent is to his Child the Author of Life, without which no Good can be injoyed; but that they bestow also a chargeable and painful Education upon them, that so they may become useful Parts of Human Society; and very often lay up somewhat for them, in order to make their Lives more easie and comfortable.

IX. Piety ever due to Parents. L. N. N. l. 6. c. 2. §12.

And yet, though the Education of Children be a Duty laid upon Parents by Nature it self, it hinders not but that, either in Case of Necessity, or for the Benefit of the Children, the Care thereof may by them be *intrusted with another;* so still that the Parent reserve to himself the Oversight of the Person deputed. Hence it is, that a Father may not only commit his Son to the *Tutorage* of proper Teachers; but he may give him to another Man to *adopt* him, if he perceives it will be advantagious to him. And if he have no other Way to maintain him, rather than he should die for Want, he may *hire* him out for Wages, or *sell* him into some tolerable Servitude, reserving still a Liberty of redeeming him, as soon as either himself shall be able to be at the Charge, or any of his Kindred shall be willing to do it. But if any Parent shall inhumanly expose and forsake their Child, he who shall take it up and educate it, shall have the *Fatherly Authority* over it; so that the Foster Child shall be bound to pay filial Obedience to his *Educator.*

X. Education intrusted. L. N. N. l. 6. c. 2. §6.

XI. Duty of Parents. The Duty of *Parents* consists chiefly in this, That they maintain their Children handsomly, and that they so form their Bodies and Minds by a skilful and wise Education, as that they may become fit and useful Members of Human and Civil Society, Men of Probity, Wisdom, and good Temper. So that they may apply themselves to some fit and honest Way of Living, by which they may, as their Genius and Opportunity shall offer, raise and increase their Fortunes.

XII. Duty of Children. On the other Hand, 'tis the Duty of *Children* to honour their Parents, that is, to give them Reverence, not only in outward Shew, but much more with a hearty Respect, as the Authors not only of their Lives, but of many other invaluable Benefits to 'em; to obey 'em; to be assistant to 'em to their utmost, especially if they are Aged, or in Want; not to undertake any Business of Moment, without paying a Deference to their Advice and Opinion; and, lastly, To bear with Patience their Moroseness, and any other their Infirmities, if any such be.

ௐ CHAPTER IV ௐ

The Duties of Masters and Servants

I. Servile State how begun. L. N. N. l. 6. c. 3. After Mankind came to be multiplied and it was found how conveniently Domestic Affairs might be managed by the Service of other Men, *it early became a Practice to *take Servants into a Family,* to do the Offices belonging to the House. These at first probably offer'd themselves, driven thereto by Necessity, or a Consciousness of their own Want of Understanding; but upon being assur'd that they should constantly be supplied with Food and Necessaries, they devoted all their Services for ever to some Master: And then Wars raging up and down the World,

* *Grotius de Jure Belli & Pacis.* lib. 2. cap. 5. §27, &c.

*it grew a Custom with most Nations, that those *Captives,* to whom they granted their Lives, should be made Slaves ever after, together with the Posterity born of them; though in many Countries, no such Servitude is in Use; but all Domestic Offices are perform'd by mercenary Servants hired for a certain Time.

Now as there are several *Degrees,* as it were, of *Servitude,* so the Power of the Masters, and the Condition of the Servants do vary. To a *Servant hired* for a Time, the Duty of the Master is to pay him his *Wages;* the other making good on his Part the *Work* as agreed for: And because in this Contract the Condition of the Master is the better, therefore such Servant is also to pay Respect to his Master according to his Dignity; and if he have done his Business knavishly or negligently, he is liable to Punishment from him; provided it go not so far as any grievous Maiming of his Body, much less so far as Infliction of Death. II. A Temporary Servant.
L. N. N. l. 6.
c. 3. §4.

But to such a Servant as *voluntarily offers himself to perpetual Servitude,* the Master is obliged to allow perpetual Maintenance, and all Necessaries for this Life; it being his Duty on the other hand to give his constant Labour in all Services whereto his Master shall command him, and whatsoever he shall gain thereby, he is to deliver to him. In thus doing, however, the Master is to have a Regard to the Strength and Dexterity of his Servant, not exacting rigorously of him what is above his Power to do. Now this Sort of Servant is not only subject to the Chastisement of his Master for his Negligence, but the same may correct his Manners, which ought to be accommodated to preserve Order and Decency in the Family: But he may not sell him against his Will; because he *chose this* for his Master of his own Accord, and not another; and it concerns him much with whom he serves. If he have been guilty of any heinous Crime against one not of the same Family, he is subject to the Civil Power, if he live in a Community; but if the Family be independent, he may be expell'd. But if the Crime be against the same III. A Voluntary Perpetual Servant.

---

* *Grotius de Jure Belli & Pacis,* lib. 3. cap. 14. §1, &c.

Family, it being independent, the Head thereof may inflict even Capital
Punishment.

IV. Captive   Captives *in War* being made *Slaves,* are frequently treated with greater
Slaves L. N. N.   Severity, something of a hostile Rage remaining towards 'em, and for
l. 6. c. 3. §7   that they attempted the worst upon us and our Fortunes. But as soon
as there intervenes a *mutual Trust,* in order to Cohabitation in the Family, between the Victor and the vanquish'd Person, all past Hostility is
to be accounted as forgiven: And then the Master does Wrong even to
a Servant thus acquir'd, if he allow him not Necessaries for Life, or exercise Cruelty to him without Cause, and much more if he take away
his Life, when he has commited no Fault to deserve it.

V. Alienable   It is also the Practice to pass away our Property in such *Slaves* who are
taken in War, or bought with our Money, to whom we please, after the
same manner as we do our other Goods and Commodities; so that the
Body of such Servant is holden to be a Chattel of his Master. And yet
here *Humanity* bids us not to forget that this Servant is a MAN, however, and therefore ought not to be treated as we do our Moveables, use
'em or abuse 'em, or destroy 'em as we list. And when we are minded
to part with him, we ought not to deliver him into the Hands of such,
as we know will abuse him inhumanly and undeservedly.

VI. Offspring   Lastly, 'Tis every where allow'd, That the *Progeny* of Parents who are
of Slaves.   Bondmen, are also in a *servile State,* and belong as Slaves to the Owner
L. N. N. l. 6.   of their Mother. Which is justified by this Maxim, That whosoever is
c. 3. §9.   Proprietor of the Body, is also Proprietor of whatsoever is the Product
thereof, and because such Issue had never been born, if the Master had
executed the Rigor of War upon the Parent; and for that the Parent having nothing she can call her own, the Offspring cannot otherwise be
brought up but at her Master's Charge. Whereas, therefore, the Master
afforded such Infant Nourishment, long before his Service could be of
any Use to him; and whereas all the following Services of his Life could
not much exceed the Value of his Maintenance, he is not to leave his
Master's Service without his Consent. But 'tis manifest, That since these
Bondmen came into a State of Servitude not by any Fault of their

own, there can be no Pretence that they should be otherwise dealt withal, than as if they were in the Condition of perpetual hired Servants.

❀   C H A P T E R   V   ❀

The Impulsive Cause of Constituting Communities[18]

Altho' there be hardly any Delight or Advantage, but what may be obtain'd from those Duties, of which we have already discours'd; it remains, nevertheless, that we inquire into the Reasons, why Men, not contenting themselves with those primitive and small Societies, have founded such as are more ample, call'd COMMUNITIES.[19] For from these Grounds and Foundations is to be deduced the Reason of those Duties, which merely relate to the Civil State of Mankind.

I. This Inquiry necessary. L. N. N. l. 7. c. 1.

Here, therefore, it suffices not to say, That Man is *by Nature inclin'd to Civil Society,* so as he neither can nor will live without it.[20] For since, indeed, it is evident, that Man is such a Kind of Creature, as has a most tender Affection for himself and his own Good; it is manifest, that when he so earnestly seeks after Civil Society, he respects some partic-

II. Difficulty herein. L. N. N. l. 7. c. 1. §2.

18. Originally: On the Impulsive Cause Constituting the State (*civitas*).

19. The infelicity of Tooke's use of "community" for "state" becomes a particular problem from here on, as Pufendorf begins to *contrast* "primitive" communities (*societas*)—family, household, clan—with the state (*civitas*), whose appearance marks man's transition from the natural to the civil condition.

20. Here begins Pufendorf's important criticism of Aristotle's conception of man as the political animal (*zoon politikon*). In treating man as a "rational and social animal" whose virtues can only be realized in the *polis,* Aristotle and his scholastic followers naturalize the state. For Pufendorf, however, the state is an artificial arrangement for preventing man's mutual predation, which means that it is civil discipline rather than natural virtue that makes the good citizen.

ular Advantage that will accrue to him thence. And altho' without Society with his Fellow-Creatures, Man would be the most miserable of all Creatures; yet since the natural Desires and Necessities of Mankind might be abundantly satisfied by those primitive Kind of Societies, and by those Duties to which we are obliged, either by Humanity or Contracts; it cannot immediately be concluded from this natural Society between Man and Man, that his Nature and Temper does directly incline him to the forming of Civil Communities.

III. Twofold Inquiry. L. N. N. l. 7. c. 1. §4. Which will more evidently appear, if we consider, What Condition Mankind is placed in by the Constitution of *Civil Communities:* What that Condition is, which Men enter into when they make themselves Members of a Civil State:[21] What Qualities they are which properly intitle them to the Name of *Political Creatures,* and render them good Patriots or Subjects to the State.[22] And, lastly, What there is in their Frame and Constitution, which seems, as we may say, to indispose them for living in a *Civil Community.*[23]

IV. Natural State. Whosoever becomes a *Subject,*[24] immediately loses his Natural Liberty, and submits himself to some Authority, which is vested with the Power of Life and Death; and by the Commands of which, many Things must be done, which otherwise he would have been no ways willing to do, and many Things must be let alone, to which he had a strong Inclination: Besides, most of his Actions must terminate in the Publick Good, which in many Cases seems to clash with Private Men's Advantage. But Man by his *Natural* Inclinations is carried to this, To be subject to no one, to do all Things as he lists, and in every thing to consult his *single* Advantage.

21. Section IV following.
22. Section V below. Note Tooke's interpolation of the republican formula "good Patriots." This blunts the edge of Pufendorf's original "good citizen" (*bonus civis*), which he used as a polemical redescription of Aristotle's "Political Creatures" (*animal politicum*).
23. Section VI below.
24. Originally "citizen" (*civis*).

But we call him a (*Political Animal* or) *True Patriot,* and Good Subject,[25] who readily obeys the Commands of his Governours; who endeavours with his utmost to promote the Publick Good, and next to that, regards his Private Affairs; nay, more, who esteems nothing profitable to himself, unless the same be likewise profitable to the Community; lastly, who carries himself fairly towards his Fellow-Subjects. But there are few Men to be found, whose Tempers are naturally thus well inclin'd. The greater Part being restrain'd merely for fear of Punishment; and many continue all their Lifetime ill Subjects and unsociable Creatures.

V. The Qualities of a good Member of the Community.

Farthermore, there is no Creature whatsoever more fierce or untameable than Man, or which is prone to more Vices that are apt to disturb the Peace and Security of the Publick. For besides his inordinate Appetite to Eating, Drinking, and Venery, to which Brute Beasts are likewise subject, Mankind is inclin'd to many Vices, to which Brutes are altogether Strangers; as is the unsatiable Desire and Thirst after those Things which are altogether superfluous and unnecessary, and above all to that worst of Evils, AMBITION; also a too lasting Resentment and Memory of Injuries, and a Desire of Revenge increasing more and more by Length of Time; besides an infinite Diversity of Inclinations and Affections, and a certain Stiffness and Obstinacy in every one to indulge his own particular Humour and Fancy. Moreover, Man takes so great Delight in exercising his Cruelty over his Fellow Creatures, that the greatest Part of the Evils and Mischiefs, to which Mankind is obnoxious,[26] is wholly owing to the merciless Rage and Violence of Men to each other.

VI. How Men naturally disturb and hinder the Benefits of Society. L. N. N. l. 1. c. 3. §4.

25. "True Patriot" is again Tooke's innovation, intended to add some republican warmth to Pufendorf, who writes not of patriots and community but of citizens disciplined by the state.

26. I.e., is liable or subject.

VII. Reason of Change. L. N. N. l. 7. c. 1. §7. Therefore the genuine and principal Reason which induced Masters of Families to quit their own natural Liberty, and to form themselves into Communities,[27] was, That they might provide for themselves a Security and Defence against the Evils and Mischiefs that are incident to Men from one another.[28] For as, next under God, one Man is most capable of being helpful to another; so nothing is able to create Man more Distress, and work him more Mischief, than Man himself; and those Persons have entertain'd a right Conception of the Malice of Men, and the Remedy thereof, who have admitted this as a common Maxim and Proverb; That *unless there were Courts of Judicature, one Man would devour another.* But after that, by the Constituting of Communities, Men were reduced into such an Order and Method, that they might be safe and secure from mutual Wrongs and Injuries among themselves, it was by that means provided, that thereby they might the better enjoy those Advantages, which are to be reap'd and expected from one another; to wit, That they might from their Childhood be brought up and instructed in good Manners, and that they might invent and improve several Kinds of Arts and Sciences, whereby the Life of Man might be better provided and furnished with necessary Conveniences.

VIII. Farther Penalties. L. N. N. l. 7. c. 1. §8. And the Reason will be yet more cogent for the Constituting of Communities, if we consider, that other Means would not have been capable of curbing the Malice of Men. For although we are enjoyn'd by the Law of Nature not to do any Injury one to another; yet the Respect and Reverence to that Law is not of that Prevalence as to be a sufficient Security for Men to live altogether quietly and undisturbed in their Natural Liberty.

For although by Accident, there may be found some few Men of that moderate quiet Temper and Disposition, that they would do no Injury

---

27. Pufendorf uses "state" (*civitas*) throughout.

28. This is a central expression of Pufendorf's secularization of political philosophy. By rejecting the Aristotelian conception of the state as nature's vehicle for realizing human virtues, and by viewing it instead as a device for providing man with security against man, Pufendorf detaches the state from all transcendent moral and religious goals.

to others, tho' they might escape unpunish'd; and there may be likewise some others, that in some measure bridle in their disorderly *Affections* thro' fear of some Mischief that may ensue from thence; yet, on the contrary, there are a great Number of such, as have no Regard at all to Law or Justice, whenever they have any Prospect of Advantage, or any Hopes, by their own subtle Tricks and Contrivances, of being too hard for, and deluding the injur'd Party. And as it behoves every one, that would take care of his own Safety, to endeavour to secure himself against this Sort of Persons; so no better Care and Provision can be made, than by means of these Communities and Civil Societies. For altho' some particular Persons may mutually agree together to assist each other; yet unless there be some Way found out, whereby their Opinions and Judgments may be united together, and their Wills may be more firmly bound to the Performance of what they have agreed upon, it will be in vain for any one to expect and rely upon any certain Succour and Assistance from them.

Lastly, Altho' the Law of Nature does sufficiently insinuate unto Men, that they who do any Violence or Injury to other Men, shall not escape unpunished; yet neither the Fear and Dread of a Divine Being, nor the Stings of Conscience are found to be of sufficient Efficacy to restrain the Malice and Violence of all Men.[29] For very many Persons, thro' the Prejudice of Custom and Education, are, as it were, altogether deaf to the Force and Power of Reason. Whence it comes to pass, that they are only intent upon such Things as are present, taking very little Notice of those Things which are future; and that they are affected only with those Things which make a present Impression upon their Senses. But since the Divine Vengeance is wont to proceed on but slowly; from whence many ill Men have taken Occasion to refer their Evils and Misfortunes to other Causes; especially since they very often see wicked Men enjoy a Plenty and Abundance of those Things wherein the vulgar

IX. Advantage of Penalties. L. N. N. l. 7. c. 1. §11.

29. Once again we take note of the fact that, despite wishing them to be viewed as divine commands, Pufendorf denies natural laws all effective sanctions, until the advent of the state.

Sort esteem their Happiness and Felicity to consist. Besides, the Checks of Conscience, which preceed any wicked Action, seem not to be of that Force and Efficacy, as that Punishment which follows the Commission of the Fact, when, that which is done, cannot possibly be undone. And therefore the most present and effectual Remedy, for the quelling and suppressing the evil Desires and Inclinations of Men, is to be provided by the Constituting of Civil Societies.

∽ CHAPTER VI ∽

Of the Internal Frame and Constitution of any State or Government

I. Conjunction necessary.
L. N. N. l. 7. c. 2.

The next Enquiry we are to make, is upon what Bottom Civil Societies have been erected, and wherein their *Internal Constitution* does consist. Where, in the first Place, this is manifest, That neither any Place, nor any Sort of Weapons, nor any Kind of brute Creatures can be capable of affording any sufficient and safe Guard or Defence against the Injuries to which all Men are liable, by reason of the Pravity of Mankind: From such Dangers, Men alone can afford an agreeable Remedy by joining their Forces together, by interweaving their Interests and Safety, and by forming a general Confederacy for their mutual Succour; that therefore this End might be obtain'd effectually, it was necessary that those who sought to bring it about, should be firmly joined together and *associated* into *Communities.*

II. Numbers Necessary.
L. N. N. 1. 7. c. 2. §2.

Nor is it less evident, that the Consent and Agreement of *Two* or *Three* particular Persons cannot afford this Security against the Violence of other Men: Because it may easily happen, that such a Number may conspire the Ruin of those *few Persons,* as may be able to assure themselves of a certain Victory over them; and 'tis very likely they would with the greater Boldness go about such an Enterprise, because of their certain Hopes of Success and Impunity. To this end therefore it is necessary, that a very considerable *Number* of Men should unite together, that so the Overplus of a few Men to the Enemies, may not be of any great Moment to determine the Victory to their Side.

Among those many, which join together in order to this End, it is absolutely requisite that there be a *perfect Consent and Agreement concerning the Use of such Means as are most conducive to the End aforesaid.* For even a great Multitude of Men, if they do not *agree* among themselves, but are divided and separated in their Opinions, will be capable of effecting but very little; Or, although they may agree for a certain Time, by reason of some present Motion or Disposition of the Mind; yet as the Tempers and Inclinations of Men are very variable, they presently afterwards may divide into Parties. And although by Compact they engaged among themselves, that they would employ all their Force for the common Defence and Security; yet neither by this Means is there sufficient Provision made, that this Agreement of the Multitude shall be permanent and lasting: But something more than all this, is requisite, to wit, That they who have once entered into a mutual League and Defence for the Sake of the Publick Good, should be debarr'd from separating themselves afterwards, when their private Advantage may seem any ways to clash with the Publick Good.[30]

III. Agreement to be perpetual. L. N. N. 1. 7. c. 2. §3.

But there are two Faults, which are chiefly incident to Human Nature, and which are the Occasion that many who are at their own Liberty, and independent one upon the other, cannot long hold together for the promoting of any Publick Design. The One is the *Contrariety* of Inclinations and Judgments in determining what is most conducive to such an End; to which in many there is join'd a *Dulness* of Apprehending which, of several Means propos'd, is more advantagious than the rest;

IV. Faults herein how remedied. L. N. N. 1. 7. c. 2. §5.

30. The condition of achieving collective security is thus that men give up their individual right to determine the best means of achieving security, which henceforth belongs to the sovereign or government of the state.

and a certain *Obstinacy* in defending whatsoever Opinion we have embraced. The other is a certain *Carelesness* and *Abhorrence* of doing that freely, which seems to be convenient and requisite, whensoever there is no absolute Necessity, that compels them, whether they will or no, to the Performance of their Duty. The First of these Defects may be prevented by a lasting Uniting of all their Wills and Affections together. And the Latter may be remedied by the constituting of such a Power as may be able to inflict a present and sensible Penalty upon such as shall decline their Contributing to the Publick Safety.

V. Union of Wills. The Wills and Affections of a great Number of Men cannot be united by any better means, than when every one is willing to submit his Will to the Will of one particular *Man,* or one Assembly of Men; so that afterwards whatsoever he or they shall will or determine concerning any Matters or Things necessary for the Publick Safety, shall be esteemed as the Will of *All* and every particular Person.[31]

VI. And of Forces. Now such a Kind of Power, as may be formidable to All, can by no better means be constituted among a great Number of Men, than when All and every one shall oblige themselves, to make Use of their Strength after that Manner, as he shall command, to whom All Persons must submit and resign the Ordering and Direction of their united Forces: And when there is an Union made of their Wills and Forces, then this Multitude of Men may be said to be animated and incorporated into a firm and lasting Society.[32]

---

31. In other words, the individual or assembly that exercises sovereignty is regarded as "representing" the will of all only in the very limited sense that anything decided by the sovereign power pertaining to security will be *deemed* the will of all.

32. Tooke's reluctance to transmit Pufendorf's view of the state as the supreme and autonomous political entity is clear when we compare this sentence with Silverthorne's accurate rendering: "Only when they have achieved a union of wills and forces is a multitude of men brought to life as a corporate body stronger than any other body, namely a state [*civitas*]" (*Man & Citizen,* p. 136).

Moreover, that any Society may grow together after a regular Manner, there are required Two *Covenants,* and One Decree, or *Constitution.*[33] For, first, Of all those many, who are supposed to be in a Natural Liberty, when they are joined together for the forming and constituting any Civil Society, every Person enters into Covenant with each other, That they are willing to come into one and the same lasting Alliance and Fellowship, and to carry on the Methods of their Safety and Security by a common Consultation and Management among themselves: In a Word, That they are willing to be made Fellow Members of the same Society.[34] To which Covenant, it is requisite, that All and singular Persons do consent and agree, and he that does not give his Consent, remains excluded from such Society.[35]

VII. Other Requisites. Two Covenants. The First. L. N. N. 1. 7. c. 2. §6.

After this *Covenant,* it is necessary, that there should be a *Constitution* agreed on by a publick Decree, setting forth, what *Form* of *Government* is to be pitched upon. For 'till this be determined, nothing with any Certainty can be transacted, which may conduce to the publick Safety.

VIII. Constitution.

After this Decree concerning the *Form* of *Government,* there is Occasion for another *Covenant,* when he or they are nominated and constituted upon whom the Government of this Rising Society is conferr'd; by which Covenant the Persons that are to govern, do oblige themselves to take Care of the Common Safety, and the other Members do in like manner oblige themselves to yield Obedience to them; whereby also all Persons do submit their Will to the Will and Pleasure of him or them, and they do at the same Time convey and make over to him or them the Power of making Use of, and applying their united Strength, as shall seem most convenient for the Publick Security. And when this

IX. The other covenant. L. N. N. 1. 7. c. 2. §8.

---

33. "Constitution" is Tooke's Whiggish innovation. In Pufendorf's account, sovereignty is formed prior to the decree determining the form of government. This decree may take the form of a constitution—by including certain basic laws limiting the sovereign's exercise of power—but it need not.

34. Originally: to become "fellow citizens" (*concives*).

35. Originally: is to remain outside the future "state" (*civitas*).

Covenant is duly and rightly executed, thence, at last, arises a *complete* and *regular Government.*

X. A Community defined.
L. N. N. 1. 7.
c. 2. §13.

A CIVIL Society and Government, thus constituted, is look'd upon as if it were but *One Person,* and is known and distinguished from every particular Man by one *Common Name;* and it has peculiar Rights and Privileges, which neither each One alone, nor Many, nor All together can claim to themselves, without him, who is the Supreme, or to whom the Administration of the Government is committed.[36] Whence a Civil Society is defined to be, One Person morally incorporated, whose Will containing the Covenants of many united together, is looked upon and esteemed as the Will of All; so that he is in a Capacity of making Use of the Strength and Power of every particular Person for the Common Peace and Security.

XI. How subjected to One.
L. N. N. 1. 7.
c. 2. §14.

Now the Will and Intention of any Constituted Government or Society exerts it self, as the Principle of Publick Actions, either by one particular Person, or by one Council or Assembly, according as the Power of Managing Affairs is conferr'd on him, or on such an Assembly. Where the Government of the State is in the Power of One Man, the said Society is supposed to will, whatsoever shall be the Will and Pleasure of that Man, allowing that he is in his perfect Senses; and it being about those Affairs which only relate to Government.[37]

36. In viewing agency or personhood as an instituted office—rather than as flowing from a moral nature or essence—Pufendorf is able to treat the state as an independent "moral person," bearing rights and duties irreducible to those of natural man.

37. This qualification is central to Pufendorf's construction of the *limits* of sovereignty and the state. Given that the sovereign is a persona instituted for the sole purpose of maintaining security and social peace—"those Affairs which only relate to Government"—the state has no rights or powers in areas lying outside this domain; for example, in the areas of family life and religion, unless particular incidents should threaten social peace.

But when the Government of a State is conferr'd upon a *Council*, consisting of several Men, every one of them retaining his own Natural Free-Will, that regularly is esteemed to be the Will and Pleasure of the State, whereto the *Major Part* of the Persons, of whom the Council is composed, does give their Assent; unless it be expressly declared, how great a Part of the Council consenting is required to represent the Will of the Whole. But where two differing Opinions are equally balanced on both sides, there is nothing at all to be concluded upon, but the Affair still remains in its former State. When there are several differing Opinions, that shall prevail which has more Voices than any of the other differing Opinions, provided so many concur therein, as otherwise might have represented the Will and Pleasure of the Whole, according to the Publick Constitutions.

XII. How to many. L. N. N. 1. 7. c. 2. §15.

A STATE or Government being thus constituted, the Party on whom the Supreme Power is conferr'd, either as it is a single Person, or a Council consisting of select Persons, or of All in General, is called a MONARCHY, an ARISTOCRACY, or a FREE STATE; the rest are looked upon as *Subjects* or *Citizens,* the Word being taken in the most comprehensive Sense: Although, in Strictness of Speech, some call only those *Citizens,* who first met and agreed together in the forming of the said Society, or else such who succeeded in their Place, to wit, *House-holders* or *Masters of Families.*

XIII. Various Forms of Government. L. N. N. 1. 7. c. 2. §20.

Moreover, Citizens are either *Originally* so; that is, such as are born in the Place, and upon that Account claim their Privileges: Or else *Adscititious;* that is, such as come from Foreign Parts.

Of the first Sort, are either those who at first were present and concerned in the forming the said Society, or their Descendants, whom we call *Indigenae,* or Natives.

Of the other Sort are those who come from Foreign Parts in order to settle themselves there. As for those who come thither only to make a short Stay, although they are for that Time subject to the Laws of the Place; nevertheless, they are not looked upon as Citizens, but are called *Strangers* or Sojourners.

XIV. Govern-
ment from
GOD. L. N. N.
l. 7. c. 3.

Not that what we have delivered concerning the Original of Civil Societies, does any ways hinder, but that CIVIL GOVERNMENT may be
truly said to be from GOD. For it being his Will, that the Practices of
Men should be ordered according to the *Law of Nature;* and yet upon
the Multiplication of Mankind, Human Life would have become so
horrid and confused, that hardly any Room would have been left for
the same to exert its Authority; and seeing the Exercise thereof would
be much improved by the Institution of Civil Societies; therefore (since
He who commands the End, must be supposed to command likewise
the Means necessary to the said End) GOD also, by the Mediation of
the Dictates of Reason, is to be understood antecedently to have willed,
That Mankind, when they were multiplyed, should erect and constitute
Civil Societies, which are, as it were, animated with a Supreme Authority. The Degrees whereof He expressly approves in Divine Writ, ratify-
ing their Divine Institution by a peculiar Law, and declaring, That
Himself takes them into his especial Care and Protection.

✄ CHAPTER VII ✄

Of the several Parts of Government[38]

I. L. N. N. l. 7.
c. 4.

What are the Constituent *Parts* of Supreme Power, and by what *Methods* it exerts its Force in Civil Societies, may easily be gather'd from the
Nature and End of the said Societies.

38. Here Tooke uses "Government" to translate Pufendorf's phrase "sovereign
power" (*summum imperium*), which Barbeyrac renders as *Souveraineté*. Given the
centrality of the concept to Pufendorf's construction of political authority, the fact
that Tooke uses sovereignty (in its political sense) only twice in his entire translation
is a good indication of the lexical and ideological changes made to Pufendorf's absolutist vocabulary.

In a Civil Society all Persons are supposed to have submitted their Will to the Will and Pleasure of the Governours, in such Affairs as concern the Safety of the Publick, being willing to do whatsoever they require. That this may be effected, it is necessary, that the Governors do *signify* to those who are to be governed, what their Will and Pleasure is concerning such Matters. And this they do, not only by their *Commands,* directed to particular Persons about particular Affairs; but also by certain general *Rules,* whence all Persons may, at all Times, have a clear and distinct Knowlege of what they are to do or omit. By which likewise it is commonly defined and determined what ought to be looked upon to be each Man's Right and Property, and what does properly belong to another; *what is to be esteemed Lawful, and what Unlawful in any Publick Society; what Commendable, or what Base; what every Man may do by his own Natural Liberty, or how every one may dispose and order his own particular Rights towards the Advancement of the common Peace and Tranquillity: In fine, what, and after what manner, every one by Right may lay Claim to from another. For it conduces very much to the Peace and Prosperity of any Civil Society, that all these Things should be clearly and plainly laid down and determined.

II. Will of the Supreme to be made known. L. N. N. l. 7. c. 4. §2.

Moreover, this is the Chief *End* of Civil Societies, That Men, by a mutual Agreement and Assistance of one another, might be secured against the Injuries and Affronts, which may, and very often do, befall us by the Violence of other Men. Now that this End may the better be obtained by those Men, with whom we are link'd together in the same Society; it is not sufficient, that they should mutually agree among

III. *Penalty.* L. N. N. l. 7. c. 4. §3.

---

*That is to say, In such Matters as are neither commanded nor forbidden by any Divine Law, whether it be Natural or Revealed. See *Law of Nature and Nations.* Book VIII. Chap. I. §2, &c. [In this note (II.1, p. 284) Barbeyrac seeks to restrict the sovereign's legislative power to matters left indifferent by divine law, natural and positive (*adiaphora*). Yet it is clear that Pufendorf intends that this power be broader, including in particular the right to determine which natural laws will be enacted as positive civil laws and which will be left as "imperfect" (moral) duties. It should also be noted that Pufendorf writes not of the sovereign's right to determine the lawful in "any Public Society," but only in the state (*quid in civitate pro licito*).]

themselves not to injure one another: Nor is it enough, that the bare Will and Pleasure of the Supreme Magistrate should be made known to them; but 'tis likewise requisite, that there should be a certain Fear and Dread of *Punishment,* and a Power and Ability of inflicting the same. Which *Punishment* or *Penalty,* that it may be sufficient for this End, is to be so ordered, that there may plainly appear a greater Damage in violating the Laws, than in observing them; and that so the *Sharpness* and *Severity* of the Penalty, may outweigh the *Pleasure* and *Advantage* gotten, or expected by doing the Injury: Because it is impossible but that of two Evils Men should chuse the least. For although there are many Men who are not restrained from doing Injuries by any Prospect of Punishment hanging over their Heads; yet that is to be looked upon as a Case that rarely happens, and such as, considering the present Condition and Frailty of Mankind, cannot be wholly avoided.

IV. *Controversies.* L. N. N. l. 7. c. 4. §4. Because also it very often happens, that many Controversies do arise about the *right Application* of the Laws to some particular Matters of Fact, and that many Things are to be nicely and carefully considered in order to determine whether such a Fact may be said to be against Law; therefore, in order to the Establishment of Peace and Quietness amongst the Subjects, it is the Part of the supreme Governour to take Cognizance of, and determine the *Controversies* arising between Subject and Subject, and carefully to examine the Actions of particular Persons, which are found to be contrary to Law, and to pronounce and execute such Sentence as shall be agreeable to the same Law.

V. **Power of Peace and War.** L. N. N. l. 7. c. 4. §5. But that those, who by mutual Agreement have constituted a Civil Society, may be safe against the Insults of Strangers, the supreme Magistrate has Power to *assemble,* to *unite* into a Body, and to *arm,* or, instead of that, to list as many Mercenaries as may seem necessary, considering the uncertain Number and Strength of the Enemy, for the maintaining the publick Security; and it is likewise intirely left to the Discretion of the same Magistrate, to make Peace whenever he shall think convenient.

And since, both in Times of Peace and War, *Alliances* and *Leagues* with other Princes and States are of very great Use and Importance, that so the different Advantages of divers States and Governments may the better be communicated to each other, and the Enemy, by their joint Forces, may be repulsed with the greater Vigour, or be more easily brought to Terms. It is also absolutely in the Power of the supreme Magistrate to enter into such *Leagues* and *Treaties* as he shall think convenient to each Occasion; and to oblige all his Subjects to the Observation of them, and at once to derive and convey down to the whole Civil Society, all the Benefits and Advantages thence arising.

Seeing also the Affairs of any considerable State, as well in Time of War as Peace, cannot well be managed by one Person, without the Assistance of subordinate *Ministers* and *Magistrates,* it is requisite that able Men should be appointed by the supreme Magistrate, to decide and determine in his Room[39] the Controversies arising between Subject and Subject; to inquire into the Councils of the Neighbouring Princes and States; to govern the Soldiery; to collect and distribute the publick Revenue: and, lastly, in every Place to take special Care of the Common Good. And from each of these Persons the supreme Magistrate may, and ought to exact the Performance of their Duty, and require an Account of their Behaviour in their respective Stations.

VI. Publick Officers. L. N. N. l. 7. c. 4. §6.

And because the Concerns of any Civil Society can, neither in Time of War nor Peace, be managed without *Expences,* the supreme Authority has Power to compel the Subjects to provide the same. Which is done several Ways; either when the Community appropriates a certain Portion of the Revenues of the Country they possess, for this Purpose; or when each Subject contributes something out of his own Estate, and, if Occasion requires, gives also his personal Help and Assistance; or when Customs are set upon Commodities imported and exported, (of which the first chiefly affects the Subjects, and the other Foreigners;) or, lastly, when some moderate Tax is laid on those Commodities which are spent.

VII. Taxes. L. N. N. l. 7. c. 4. §7.

39. I.e., on his behalf.

VIII. Publick Doctrines. L. N. N. l. 7. c. 4. §8. To conclude: Since the Actions of each Person are governed by his own particular Opinion, and that most People are apt to pass such a Judgment upon Things as they have been accustomed unto, and as they commonly see other People judge; so that very few are capable of discerning what is just and honest; upon this Account therefore it is expedient for any Civil Society, that such Kind of Doctrines should be publickly taught, as are agreeable to the right End and Design of such Societies, and that the Minds of the Inhabitants should be seasoned betimes with these Principles. *It does therefore belong to the supreme Magistrate to constitute and appoint fitting Persons to inform and instruct them publickly in such Doctrines.

IX. All these Parts concentered. Now these several Parts of Government are naturally so connected, that to have a regular Form suitable to any civil Society, all these Parts thereof ought radically to center in One.[40] For if any Part be wanting, the Government is defective, and uncapable of procuring its End. But if these several Parts be divided, so that some of them be radically here, and others there, hence of Necessity will follow an irregular and incoherent State of Things.

---

* *Apolog.* §6. *Eris Scandica.* P. 7, &c. *See also the* References *at* Lib. I. c. 4. §9.

40. Pufendorf's doctrine of the regular state—in which all the rights and powers of sovereignty are held by a single authority—was directed against the conception of multiple authorities in the Aristotelian doctrine of the "mixed republic," and against the reality of the German Empire, where lesser powers and estates claimed to exercise sovereignty rights on their own behalf. Pufendorf's conception of the regular state was a blueprint for the sovereign territorial state.

Of the several Forms of Government[41]

The Supreme Power consider'd either as it resides in a Single *Man,* or in a Select *Council* or *Assembly* of Men, or of *All* in General, produces diverse Forms of Government.

I. Diverse Forms. L. N. N. l. 7. c. 5.

Now the Forms of Government are either *Regular* or *Irregular.* Of the first Sort are those where the supreme Power is so united in one particular Subject, that the same being firm and intire, it carries on, by one *supreme Will,* the whole Business of Government. Where this is not found, the Form of Government must of Necessity be *Irregular.*

II. Regular and Irregular.

There are Three *Regular* Forms of Government:[42] The First is, When the supreme Authority is in *One Man;* and that is call'd a MONARCHY. The Second, When the same is lodged in a *select Number* of Men; and that is an ARISTOCRACY. The Third, When it is in a Council or Assembly of *Free-holders* and *Principal Citizens;* and that is a DEMOCRACY. In the First, he who bears the supreme Rule, is stil'd, A MONARCH; in the Second, the NOBLES; and in the Third, The PEOPLE.

III. Three Regular Forms. L. N. N. l. 7. c. 5. §2.

---

41. Here Tooke uses "Government" to translate Pufendorf's *respublica.* While accurate enough in itself, this leads to a degree of confusion in the present context, because of Tooke's propensity to also use "government" to translate Pufendorf's "state," or *civitas.* The problem is that in this chapter Pufendorf draws a crucial distinction between state (*civitas*) and form of government (*respublica*), identifying the former with the principle of sovereignty—that is, the principle of a supreme unified political authority—and the latter with the three governmental forms (monarchical, aristocratic, democratic) in which sovereignty can be exercised.

42. One of the most distinctive features of Pufendorf's construction of sovereignty and the state is that it is neutral between the three standard forms of government: monarchy, aristocracy, and democracy. In tying the legitimacy of sovereignty to the achievement of security and social peace—rather than to the representation of a prior moral will (God's or the people's)—Pufendorf can accept the legitimacy of all three forms of government, to the extent that each succeeds in exercising supreme political power in the interests of security.

IV. Forms compar'd. L. N. N. l. 7. c. 5. §9. In all these Forms, the Power is indeed the same. But in one Respect MONARCHY has a considerable Advantage above the rest; because in order to deliberate and determine, that is, actually to exercise the Government, there is no Necessity of appointing and fixing certain Times and Places; for he may deliberate and determine in any Place, and at any Time; so that a *Monarch* is always in a Readiness to perform the necessary Actions of Government. But that the *Nobles* and the *People,* who are not as one natural Person, may be able so to do, it is necessary that they meet at certain Times and Places, there to debate and resolve upon all publick Business. For the Will and Pleasure of a Council, or of the People, which results from the Majority of Votes concentring, can no otherwise be discover'd.

V. A distemper'd State L. N. N. l. 7. c. 5. §10. But, as it happens in other Matters, so in Governments also it falls out, That the same may be sometimes well, and at other times scurvily and foolishly managed. Whence it comes to pass, that some States are reputed *Sound,* and others *Distemper'd.* Yet we are not, on Account of these Imperfections, to multiply the several Species or Forms of Government, imagining that these several Defects make different Sorts of Governments; for these Vices or Defects, though different in themselves, do not, however, either change the Nature of the Authority it self, or the proper Subject in which it resides. Now these Defects or Vices in Government, do sometimes arise from the Persons who administer the Government; and sometimes they arise from the Badness of the *Constitution* it self. Whence the First are styl'd, Imperfections of the *Men,* and the Latter, Imperfections of the *State.*

VI. Monarchy L. N. N. l. 7. c. 5. §10. The Imperfections of the *Men* in a *Monarchy* are, when he who possesses the Throne, is not well skilled in the Arts of Ruling, and takes none, or but a very slight Care for the publick Good, prostituting the same to be torn in pieces and sacrificed to the Ambition or Avarice of evil Ministers; when the same Person becomes terrible by his Cruelty and Rage; when also he delights, without any real Necessity, to expose the Publick to Danger; when he squanders away, by his Luxury and profuse Extravagance, those Supplies which were given for the Support of the Publick; when he heaps up Treasure unreasonably extorted from his Subjects; when he is Insolent, Haughty, or Unjust; or guilty of any other scandalous Vice.

The Imperfections of the Men in an ARISTOCRACY are, When by Bribery and base Tricks, Ill Men and Fools get into the Council, and Persons much more deserving than they, are excluded: When the Nobles are divided into several Factions: When they endeavour to make the common People their Slaves, and to convert the publick Stock to their private Advantage. VII. Aristocracy.

The Imperfections of the Men in a DEMOCRACY are, when silly and troublesome Persons stickle for their Opinions with great Heat and Obstinacy; when those Excellencies,[43] which are rather beneficial than hurtful to the Common-wealth, are depress'd and kept under; when, thro' Inconstancy, Laws are rashly establish'd, and as rashly annull'd, and what but just now was very pleasing, is immediately, without any Reason, rejected; and when base Fellows are promoted in the Government. VIII. Men in a Democracy.

The Imperfections of the Men, which may promiscuously happen in any Form of *Government,* are, When those who are intrusted with the publick Care, perform their Duty either amiss, or slightly; and when the Subjects, who ought to make Obedience their Glory, grow restiff and ungovernable. IX. Men in any Government.

But the Imperfections of any *Constitution,* are, When the Laws thereof are not accommodated to the Temper and Genius of the People or Country; or, When the Subjects make use of them for fomenting intestine Disturbances, or for giving unjust Provocations to their Neighbours; or, When the said Laws render the Subjects incapable of discharging those Duties that are necessary for the Preservation of the Publick; for Instance, When thro' their Defect the People must of Ne- X. Faults in a Constitution.

43. Men of great talent.

cessity be dissolv'd in Sloth, or rendred unfit for the Injoyment of Peace and Plenty; or when the fundamental Constitutions are order'd after such a Manner, that the Affairs of the Publick cannot be dispatched but too slowly, and with Difficulty.

XI. How called.
L. N. N. l. 7.
c. 5. §11.

To these *distemper'd Constitutions,* Men have given certain Names; as a corrupt Monarchy, is call'd *Tyranny;* a corrupt Aristocracy, is styl'd An *Oligarchy,* or a Rump-Government; and a corrupt *Popular State,* is call'd An *Anarchy,* or a Rabble-Government. Altho' it often happens, that many by these Nick-names do not so much express the Distemper of such a Government, as their own natural Aversion for the present Governours and Constitution.

For, oftentimes, he who is dissatisfied with his *King,* or a *monarchical Government,* is wont to call, even a Good and Lawful Prince, a Tyrant and Usurper, especially if he be strict in putting the Laws in Execution. So he who is vex'd because he is left out of the *Senate,* not thinking himself Inferiour to any of the other Counsellors, out of Contempt and Envy, he calls them, A Pack of assuming Fellows, who tho' in no Respect they excell any of the Rest, yet domineer and lord it over their Equals, nay, over better Men than themselves.

Lastly, Those Men who are of a haughty Temper, and who hate a *Popular Equality,* seeing that all People in a *Democracy,* have an equal Right to give their Suffrages in Publick Affairs, tho' in every Place the common People makes the greatest Number, they condemn that as an *Ochlocracy,* or Government by the Rabble, where there is no Preference given to Persons of Merit, as they, forsooth, esteem themselves to be.

XII. An Irregular State.
L. N. N. l. 7.
c. 5. §12.

An *Irregular Constitution*[44] is, Where that perfect Union is wanting, in which the very Essence of a Government[45] consists: And that not through any Fault or Male-administration[46] of the Government, but because *this Form* has been receiv'd as good and legitimate by publick Law or Custom. But since there may be infinite Varieties of Errors in

44. Originally: *respublica* or "public administration" (government).
45. Originally: "state" or *civitas.*
46. I.e., maladministration.

this Case, it is impossible to lay down distinct and certain Species of Irregular Governments. But the Nature thereof may be easily understood by one or two Examples; for Instance, If in a State the Nobles and the People are each vested with a supreme and unaccountable Power; *Or if in any Nation the Nobles are grown so great, that they are no otherwise under the King, then as unequal Confederates.

We call those *Unions,* when several Constituted Societies by some special Tie are so conjoin'd, that their Force and Strength may be look'd upon in Effect as the united Force and Strength of one civil Society. Now these Unions may arise two several Ways; the one by a *Common Sovereign,* the Other by *League* or *Confederacy.*

XIII. Union of several Communities. L. N. N. l. 7. c. 5. §17.

Such a *Union* happens, by means of a common Sovereign, when diverse separate Kingdoms, either by Agreement, or by Marriage, or hereditary Succession, or Victory, come to be subject to the same King; yet so that they do not close into one Realm, but each are still govern'd by the same common Sovereign, according to their own fundamental Laws.

XIV. Union by a common Sovereign.

Another Sort of *Union* may happen, when several neighbouring States or Governments are so connected by a perpetual League and Confederacy, that they cannot exercise some Parts of the supreme Power, which chiefly concern their Defence and Security against Strangers, but by a general Consent of them All: Each Society, nevertheless, as to other Matters, reserving to it self its own peculiar Liberty and independency.

XV. Union by Confederacy. L. N. N. l. 7. c. 5. §18.

---

* *See* L. N. N. l. 7. c. 5. §14, &*c. Dissert. Accademic. de Rep. irregulari.* p. 301. & *in Append. ibid. p.* §29. *Eris Scandica.* p. 176, 187.

CHAPTER IX

The Qualifications of Civil Government[47]

I. Supreme Authority L. N. N. l. 7. c. 6.

It is always one Prerogative of the Government by which any Community is directed, in every Form of Commonwealth whatsoever, *to be invested with the supreme Authority:* *Whereby it has the Regulating of all Things according to its own Judgment and Discretion, and acts without Dependence upon any other Person †as Superiour, that can pretend to annul or countermand its Orders.

II. Unaccountable. L. N. N. l. 7. c. 6. §2.

For the same Reason, a Government so constituted remains *unaccountable to all the World;* there being no Authority *above* it to punish it, or to examine whether its Proceedings are right or no.

III. Above the Laws. L. N. N. l. 7. c. 6. §3.

And a *third Qualification* of like Nature with the former, is, That inasmuch as all civil Laws, of human Authority, derive both their Beginning and their Continuance from the Favour of the Government; it is impossible they should directly *oblige the very Power that makes them;* because the same Power would in Consequence be superiour to it self. Yet it is a happy Prospect, and a singular Advantage to the Laws, when a

---

47. Originally: "On the characteristics of civil authority" (*De affectionibus imperii civilis*). The central attributes of the sovereign authority are that it is supreme, unaccountable, above the law, and venerable.

* *Grotius de Jure Belli & Pacis,* lib. 1. cap. 3. §6, &c.

† This Restriction must be carefully observ'd; for tho' in a *limited Monarchy,* the Sovereign can't enact a Law without the Advice and Consent of his People represented in Parliament, yet notwithstanding, this Authority of the People is not equal, much less superiour, to that of the *Prince:* The Author's Account of the Nature of supreme Authority is imperfect; it ought to have comprehended distinctly what is equally agreeable to a *limited* and to an *Absolute Sovereignty.* [Barbeyrac's note (I.1, p. 298). In fact, Pufendorf discusses the distinction between absolute and limited sovereignty in sections V and VI. It is indeed difficult to see how a sovereign bound by basic (parliamentary) laws may be considered "supreme," unless of course monarch and parliament are considered jointly to be the sovereign authority, or unless the monarch is given the sole capacity to judge when he is acting in accordance with these laws.]

Prince conforms himself, of his own Pleasure, as Occasion serves, to practise the same Things that he commands his Subjects.

There is also a peculiar *Veneration* to be paid to the supreme Government under which we live; not only in obeying it in its just Commands, wherein it is a Crime to disobey, but in *induring its Severities* with the like Patience as the Rigour of some Parents is submitted to by dutiful Children. Wherefore, when a Prince proceeds to offer the most heinous Injuries imaginable to his People, let them rather undergo it, or every one seek his Safety by Flight, than draw their Swords upon the Father of their Country.

IV. Obedience due to it. L. N. N. l. 7. c. 8.

We find, in *Monarchies* and *Aristocracies* especially, that the Government is sometime *Absolute* and sometime *Limited*. An *Absolute* Monarch is one, who having no prescrib'd Form of Laws and Statutes perpetually to go by, in the Method of his Administration, proceeds intirely according to his own Will and Pleasure, as the Condition of Affairs and the publick Good in *his Judgment* seem to require.

V. An absolute Monarchy. L. N. N. l. 7. c. 6. §7.

But because a single Person may be subject to be *mistaken* in his Judgment, as well as to be seduced into evil Courses in the Injoyment of so vast a Liberty; it is thought convenient by some States, *to circumscribe the Exercise of this Power within the *Limits of certain Laws,* which are proposed to the Prince at his Succession to be the future Rule of his Government. And particularly when any extraordinary Concern arises, involving in it the Interest of the whole Kingdom, for which there can be no Provision extant in the Constitution foregoing; They then oblige him to ingage in nothing without the previous Advice and Consent of the People, or their *Representatives in Parliament;* the better to prevent the Danger of his swerving from the Interest of the Kingdom.[48]

VI. A limited Monarchy L. N. N. l. 7. c. 6. §9.

---

* *Grotius de Jure Belli & Pacis,* l. 1. c. 3. §14. &c.

48. It remains ambiguous here whether Pufendorf regards the king or "the king in parliament" as sovereign. Note that "Representatives in Parliament" is Tooke's Anglicization of Pufendorf's "deputies in assembly" (*deputatis in comitia convocatis*).

VII. Right and
Manner of
holding.
L. N. N. l. 7.
c. 6. §14.

We see likewise a Difference in the *Right and Manner of holding* some Kingdoms, from what it is in others. For those Princes especially who have acquired Dominions by Conquest, and made a People their own by Force of Arms, can *divide, alienate,* and *transfer* their Regalities[49] at Pleasure in the manner of a Patrimonial Estate. Others that are advanced by the Voice of the People, tho' they live in full Possession of the Government during their Reigns, yet have no Pretensions to such a Power. But as they attain'd to the Succession, so they leave it to be determin'd, either by the ancient Custom, or the fundamental Laws of the Kingdom: *For which Reason they are compared by some to Usufructuaries, or Life-Renters.

ΩΩ　C H A P T E R　X　ΩΩ

How Government, especially Monarchical, is acquired

I. Consent of
the Subject
free or forced.
L. N. N. l. 7.
c. 7.

Although the *Consent of the Subject* is a Thing to be required in Constituting of every lawful Government, yet it is not[50] always obtain'd the same way. For as it is sometimes seen, that a Prince ascends the Throne with the *voluntary Acclamations of the People;* so sometimes he makes himself a King by his *Army,* and brings a People to consent by *military Force.*

49. Royal rights.
* *Grotius de Jure Belli & Pacis,* l. 1. c. 3. §11. & l. 2. c. 7. §12.
50. The editors of the 1716/35 edition omitted the negative.

Which latter Method of acquiring a Government is called *Conquest;* it happening, as often as a victorious Prince, having Fortune on his Side and a just Cause, reduces a People by his Arms to such Extremities, as to compel them to receive him for their Sovereign. And the Reason of this Title is derived, not only from the Conqueror's Clemency in saving the Lives of all those whom, in Strictness of War, he was at Liberty to destroy, and instead thereof laying only a lesser Inconvenience upon them; but likewise from hence, That, when a Prince will choose to go to War with one that he has injured, rather than he will condescend to satisfie him in a just and equal Manner; *He is to be presum'd to cast himself upon the Fortune of War, with this Intention, that he does beforehand *tacitly* consent to accept of any Conditions whatsoever shall befal him in the Event.

II. Of Conquest. L. N. N. l. 7. c. 7. §3.

As for the *voluntary Consent of the People,* a Government is acquired by it, when in an *Election* the People, either in order to their Settlement, or at any Time after, do nominate such a One, to bear that Office, as they believe is capable of it. Who, upon Presentation of their Pleasure to him, accepting it, and also receiving their Promises of Allegiance, thereby actually enters upon the Possession of the Government.

III. Election. L. N. N. l. 7. c. 7. §6.

But betwixt this Election of a new Prince and the Death of the former, there uses in Monarchies that are already fix'd and settled, to intervene an *Interregnum;* which signifies an imperfect Kind of State, where the People keep together merely by Virtue of their *Original Compact:* Only that this is much strengthned by the common Name and Love of their Country, and the Settlement of most of their Fortunes there; whereby all good Men are obliged to preserve the Peace with one another, and study to restore their fallen Government again as soon as they can. Yet to prevent the Mischiefs which are apt to arise in an *Interregnum,* it is very convenient the Law should provide *Administrators,* to manage the publick Affairs during the Vacancy of the Crown.

IV. An Interregnum. L. N. N. l. 7. c. 7. §7.

---

* *Grotius de Jure Belli & Pacis,* lib. 3. cap. 8.

V. Succession.
L. N. N. l. 7.
c. 7. §11.

Now though, as is said, in some Monarchies, as every King dies, they proceed again to a *New Election:* yet in others, the Crown is conferr'd upon Conditions to descend to certain Persons *successively,* (without any intervening Election) for all Time to come. The Right to which Succession may either be determined by the *Order of the Prince,* or the *Order of the People.*

VI. Devisable
when L. N. N.
l. 7. c. 6. §16.

When Princes hold their Crowns in the Manner *of a Patrimony,* they have the Liberty of *disposing of the Succession as themselves please.* And their declared Order therein, especially if their Kingdoms are of their own Founding or Acquiring, shall carry the same Force with the last Testament of any private Man. They may divide, if they please, their Kingdom amongst all their Children, not so much as excepting the Daughters. *They may, if they think fit, make an Adoptive, or their Natural Son, their Heir, or one that is not in the least a-kin to them.

VII. Succes-
sion upon an
Intestate.

And when such an Absolute Monarch as this dies, without leaving Order for the Succession, it is to be presumed he did not thereby intend the Kingdom should expire with himself; but *first,* That it should devolve to his Children (before all others) because of the natural Affection of Parents to them: Then, *That* the same Monarchical Government should continue, which he recommended by his own Example. *That* the Kingdom be kept undivided, as one Realm; because any Division thereof must give Occasion to great Troubles, both among the Subjects and the Royal Family. *That* the Elder reign before the Younger, and the Male before the Female in the same Line: †And, lastly, *That* in Default of Issue, the Crown shall devolve upon the next in Blood.

VIII. Succes-
sion in the
People.
L. N. N. l. 7.
c. 7. §11.

But in those Monarchies, whose Constitution, from the very Beginning, was founded upon the voluntary Choice of the People, there the *Order of Succession must have an Original Dependance upon the Will of the same People.* For if, together with the Crown, they did confer upon the Prince the Right of appointing his Successor; whosoever shall be

---

* *Grotius de Jure Belli & Pacis,* Lib. 2. Cap. 7. §12, &*c.*
† *Grotius de Jure Belli & Pacis,* l. 2. c. 7. §12, &*c.*

nominated to the Succession by him, will have all the Right to injoy it. If they did not confer it upon the Prince, it is to be understood as reserved to themselves: Who, if they pleased, might make the Crown Hereditary to their Prince's Family; either prescribing the Order of Succession to be like other ordinary *Inheritances,* so far as can consist with the Publick Good; or set the same under any peculiar necessary *Limitations.*

When a People have barely conferr'd upon their King an Hereditary Right, without any thing farther express'd; tho' 'tis true, it may seem to be intended, that the Crown shall pass to the Heirs in the same common Order of Descent as private Inheritances do; yet the Publick Good requires, That the Sense of such a Publick Act shall be taken under some *Restrictions,* notwithstanding their not being particularly express'd. As, IX. Of Hereditary Kingdoms. L. N. N. l. 7. c. 7. §12.

1. IT is supposed, That the Kingdom shall continue inseparable, as one Realm.

2. THAT the Succession shall go to the Descendants of the first Prince of the Line. Excluding,

3. ILLEGITIMATE and Adopted Children, with all that are not born according to the Laws of the Realm.

4. THAT the Heirs Male be preferr'd before the Female in the same Line, tho' their Inferiors in Age. And,

5. THAT each Prince esteem his Succession, not as the Gift of his Predecessor, but as the Bounty of the People.

Now, because after a long Descent of Princes, there may easily arise Controversies almost inextricable, about the Person of the Royal Family, who approaches nearest in Kindred to the Prince deceased; therefore, for Prevention of such, in many Kingdoms they have introduced a *Lineal Succession,* of this Nature; *That* as every one descends from the Father of the Stem Royal,[51] they compose, as it were, a perpendicular Line; from whence they succeed to the Crown, according to the Priority of that Line to others: And tho', perhaps, the nearest of Kin to the X. A Lineal Succession. L. N. N. l. 7. c. 7. §13.

51. The royal stock or lineage.

Prince last deceased, may stand in a *New* Line, different from that of *His;* Yet there is no passing out of the Old Line thither, 'till Death has exhausted the same.

XI. By the Father's side, or the Mother's. The Series of Succession most regardable, are those Two, deduced from the several *Families of the Father and the Mother;* the Relation whereof is distinguish'd in the Civil Law by the Names of *Cognation* and *Agnation.* The First, called also the *Castilian Law,* does not exclude the Women, but only postpones them to Males in the same Line; for it recurs to them in the Case of the other's *Default.* But by the Second, which is sometimes styl'd the *French* or *Salick Law,* both the Women and all their Issue, even Males, are excluded for ever.

XII. Differences about Succession how to be determined. When, in a Patrimonial Kingdom, there arises a Dispute concerning the Succession, the most adviseable Way to determine it, is, To put it to the Arbitration of some of the Royal Family; And where the Succession originally depended upon the Consent of the People, there their Declaration upon the Matter, will take away the Doubt.

≫⊙≪ CHAPTER XI ≫⊙≪

The Duty of Supreme Governours

I. L. N. N. 1. 7. c. 9. If we consider what is the End and Nature of Communities, and what the Parts of Government, it will be easie from thence to pass a Judgment upon the Rules and Precepts, in the Observance of which, consists the Office of a Prince.[52]

---

52. Pufendorf's formulation is sharper and more "statist" than Tooke's Whiggish rendering, as we can gather by comparing Silverthorne's accurate translation of this sentence: "A clear account of the precepts that govern the office of the sovereign may be drawn from the nature and end of states and from consideration of the functions of sovereignty." (*Man & Citizen,* p. 151)

Before all Things, it is requisite, That he apply himself, with the utmost Diligence, to the Study of *whatever may conduce to give him a perfect Comprehension of the Affairs belonging to a Person in his Station:* because no Man can manage a Place to his Honour, which he does not *rightly* understand. He is therefore to be sequestred from those remote and foreign Studies, which make nothing to *this Purpose:* He must abridge himself in the Use of Pleasures and vain Pastimes, that would divert his Attention from *this Mark* and End.

II. Their proper Studies and Conversation. L. N. N. l. 7. c. 9. §2.

And for his more *familiar Friends,* instead of Parasites and Triflers, or such as are accomplished in nothing but Vanities, (whose Company ought utterly to be rejected;) let him make Choice of Men of Probity and Sense, experienced in Business, and skilful in the Ways of the World; being assured, that 'till he does thoroughly understand, as well the Condition of his own State, as the Disposition of the People under him, he will never be able to apply the general Maxims of *State Prudence,* to the Cases that will occur in Government, in such a Manner as they ought. More especially, let him study to be excellent in Virtues, that are of the greatest Use and Lustre in the Exercise of his vast Charge;[53] and so compose the Manners, and all the Actions of his Life, that they may be answerable to the Height of his Glory.

The most General Rule to be observed by Governours, is this; *The Good of the Publick is the Supreme Law of all.*[54] Because, in conferring the Government upon them, what is there else intended, but to secure the common End for which Societies were constituted in the Beginning? From whence they ought to conclude, That whatsoever is not expedient for the *Publick* to be done, ought not to be accounted expedient for *themselves.*

III. The Publick Good, the Supreme Law. L. N. N. l. 7. c. 9. §3.

53. Here Tooke fails to capture the meaning of Pufendorf's original formulation, which is that rulers should cultivate the virtues required by large-scale administration (*administratione maxime*).

54. The original Latin formula—*salus populi suprema lex est* (the welfare of the people is the supreme law)—derives from classical Greek political thought. Pufendorf gives this traditional doctrine a new use by restricting the people's welfare to their political security, setting aside all higher moral conceptions of the public good.

IV. Laws, Dis-
cipline, and
Religion.
L. N. N. l. 7.
c. 9. §5.

And it being necessary, in order to preserve a People at Peace with one another, that the Wills and Affections of them should be disposed and regulated, according as it is most proper for the publick Good; there ought to be some *suitable Laws* for the Purpose prescribed by Princes, and also a *publick Discipline* established with so much Strictness, that so, Custom, as well as Fear of Punishment, may be able to keep Men close to the Practice of their several Duties. *To which End it is convenient to take Care, that the Christian Religion, after the most pure and most uncorrupt Way, be profess'd by the Subjects of every Realm or Community; and that no Tenets be publickly taught in the Schools, that are contrariant to the Designs of Government.

V. The Laws
plain and few.

It will conduce to the Advancement of the same End, that in the Affairs which are wont to be most frequently negociated between Subject and Subject, the Laws which are prescribed be *clear* and *plain;* and *no more in Number* than will promote the Good of the Republick and its Members. For, considering that Men use to deliberate upon the Things they *ought,* or ought *not* to do, more by the Strength of their *Natural Reason,* than their Understanding in the *Laws;* whenever the Laws do so *abound* in Number, as not easily to be retained in Memory; or are so *particular* in their Matter, as to prohibit Things which are not prohibited by the Light of Reason; it must certainly come to pass, That innocent Persons, who have not had the least ill Intention to transgress the Laws, will be many times unwittingly hamper'd by them, as by Snares, to their unreasonable Prejudice, against the very End of Societies and Government.

---

*See *Dissertationes Academicae de Concord. Polit. cum Religione Christiana,* Lib. II. Pag. 449. And also *De Habitu Religionis Christianae ad Vitam Civilem:* Especially *Chapters* 7, 47, 49. [The editors have added this footnote to two of Pufendorf's larger discussions of the role of religion in civil life. At the center of these works lies Pufendorf's insistence that because they serve different ends—security and salvation—the state and the church must not be combined to form a state church or a church state.]

Yet it is in vain for Princes to make Laws, and at the same time suffer the Violation of them to pass with Impunity. They must therefore *cause them to be put in Execution,* both for every *honest Person* to injoy his Rights without Vexation, Evasions, or Delays; and also for every *Malefactor* to receive the Punishment due to the Quality of his Crime, according to the Intention and Malice in the committing it. They are not to extend their Pardons to any without sufficient Reason. For it is an unjust Practice, which tends greatly to irritate the Minds of People against the Government, not to use Equality (all Circumstances considered) towards Persons that are Equal in their Deservings.

VI. And duly executed. L. N. N. l. 7. c. 9. §6.

And as nothing ought to be Enacted under a *Penalty,* without the Consideration of some *Profit* to the Common-wealth, so in the *fixing of Penalties proportionably to that End,* it is fitting to observe a Moderation; with Care, that the Damage thence arising to the Subject on the one Hand, exceed not the Advantage that redounds to the Common-wealth on the other. In fine, to render Penalties effectual in obtaining the End intended by them, it is clear they should still be magnified to such a Degree, as, by their Severity, to out-weigh the contrary Gain and Pleasure, that is possible to proceed from chusing the Crime.

VII. Penalties. L. N. N. l. 7. c. 9. §7.

Moreover, inasmuch as the Design of People, in incorporating together in a Common-wealth, is their Security from Harms and Violence; it is the Duty of the supreme Magistrate to *prohibit any Injury of one Subject to another* so much the more severely, because, by their constant Cohabitation in the same Place, they have the fairer Opportunities to do them or to resent them: Remembring, that no Distinctions of Quality or Honour derive the least Pretence to the Greater to insult over the Less at their Pleasure. Neither has any Subject whatsoever the Liberty to seek his Satisfaction for the Injuries, he presumes are done him, in the Way of a private Revenge. For the Design of Government is destroyed by such a Proceeding as this.

VIII. Injuries. L. N. N. l. 7. c. 9. §8.

IX. Ministers
of State and
Judges.
L. N. N. l. 7.
c. 9. §9.

And although there is no one Prince, how ingenious soever in Business, that is able in his own Person to manage all the Affairs of a Nation of any considerable Extent, but he must have *Ministers to participate with him in his Cares and Counsels;* Yet as these Ministers borrow their Authority, in every Thing they do, from Him; so the Praise or Dispraise of their Actions returns finally upon Him also. For which Reason, and because according to the Quality of Ministers, Business is done either well or ill, there lies an Obligation upon a Prince to advance *honest* and *fit* Persons to Offices of Trust in the Government, and upon Occasion to examine into the Proceedings of the same; and as he finds them deserving, to reward or punish them accordingly, for an Example to others to understand, that there is no less *Fidelity* and *Diligence* to be used in managing the *publick* Business, than one would practise in any *private* Affair that relates to himself. So when wicked People are incouraged to put their Inclinations in Practice, upon the Hopes of escaping very easily unpunish'd under *Judges that are subject to Corruption;* it is a Prince's Duty to animadvert severely upon such Judges, as Favourers of Vice, against the *Safety* of the Subject, and *Quiet* of the Nation.[55] And though the Dispatching of the ordinary Affairs may be committed to the Ministers Care; yet a Prince is never to refuse to lend his Ear with Patience, when his Subjects present him with their Complaints and Addresses.

X. Of Taxes
and Duties.
L. N. N. l. 7.
c. 9. §10.

For Taxes and the like Duties, to which Subjects are upon no other Account obliged, than as they are *necessary* to support the publick Charge in Peace and War; it deserves to be the Care of Princes not to extort more, than either the *Necessities* or *signal Advantages* of the Nation[56] require; and so to alleviate and soften them in the Ways and Means of

55. Tooke's use of "nation" corresponds to nothing in Pufendorf's original passage, which speaks only of the "security of the citizens" (*securitas civium*). Tooke's "nation" belongs with his earlier use of "true Patriot" as a republican euphemism for Pufendorf's "good citizen." The notion of the nation as the spiritual homeland of true patriots is fundamentally at odds with Pufendorf's conception of the state as a territory governed by a sovereign authority in accordance with the end of security.

56. Having hit upon "nation" late in his translation, Tooke now proceeds to use it as one of the regular alternatives to Pufendorf's "state" (*civitas*) and "government"

laying them upon the Subject, that every one may find their Weight as little offensive as it can possibly be; being charged upon Particulars in a *fair* and *equitable Proportion,* without favouring of one Person, to deceive or oppress another. And let not the Money that is so rais'd be consumed by Princes in Luxury and Vanities, or thrown away in Gifts and needless Ostentation; but laid out upon the Occasions of the Nation; always foreseeing, that their *Expences* be made to answer to their *Revenue;* and in case of any Failure in the latter, so to order Things, that by prudent Frugality and retrenching unnecessary Expences, the Publick may not suffer Damage for want of a sufficient Treasure.

It is true, Princes have no Obligation upon them to find Maintenance for their Subjects, otherwise than Charity directs them to a particular Care of those, for whom it is impossible to subsist of themselves by Reason of some Calamity undeserved. Yet because the Money, that is necessary for the Conservation of the Publick, must be raised out of the Subjects Estates, in whose Wealth and Happiness the Strength of a Nation does consist; it therefore concerns Princes to use their best Endeavours, *that the Fortunes of their Subjects improve and flourish;* as particularly, by giving Orders, how the Products of the Earth and Water may be received in the most plentiful Measure; and that Men employ their Industry in improving such Matters as are of their own Growth, and never hire foreign Hands for those Works which they can conveniently perform themselves. That all Mechanick Arts and Merchandise, and in Maritime Places, Navigation be incouraged, as of great Consequence to the Commonwealth. That Idleness be banished from amongst them, and Frugality be restored by *Sumptuary Laws,* contrived on Purpose to avoid superfluous Expences; especially those, which occasion the transporting of Riches out of the Kingdom. Whereof, if the Prince is pleased to set an Example in his own Person, it is likely to prove of greater Force than all the *Laws* beside.

XI. Interest of the Subject to be advanced by Princes. L. N. N. l. 7. c. 9. §11.

(*respublica*). Tooke's language thus becomes capable of insinuating a gap between the interests of the nation and those of the state or prince, in keeping with Whig politics but quite at odds with Pufendorf's language and logic.

XII. Factions and Parties. L. N. N. l. 7. c. 9. §12. Farther, Since the *internal* Health and Strength of a Nation proceeds in a particular Manner from the *Unity that is among the People;*[57] and according as this happens to be more and more perfect, the Power of the Government diffuses it self through the whole Body with so much the greater Efficacy: It is for this Reason incumbent upon Princes, to hinder, as well the Growth of *publick Factions,* as of *private Associations* of particular Persons by Agreements amongst themselves. As also to see, that neither all, nor any of the Subjects, place a greater Dependance, or rely more for Defence and Succour on any other Person, within or without the Realm, under any Pretence whatsoever, whether Sacred or Civil,[58] than on their lawful Sovereign, in whom alone, before others, all their Expectations ought to be reposed.

XIII. Of War and Peace with foreign Nations. L. N. N. l. 7. c. 9. §13. Lastly, Since the Peace of Nations in reference to one another depends upon no very great Certainties; it ought to be the Endeavour of Princes to incourage *Valour and Military Studies* in their Subjects; having all things, as Fortifications, Arms, Men, and Money (which is the Sinews of Civil Affairs) ready prepared, in case of any Attack from abroad, to *repel* it: Though not voluntarily to *begin* one upon another Nation, even after sufficient Cause of War given, unless when invited by a very safe Opportunity, and that the Publick be in a good Condition conveniently to go thro' with the Undertaking. For the same Reason it is proper to observe and search into the Counsels and Proceedings of Neighbours with all Exactness, and to enter with them into *Leagues and Alliances* as prudently, as so great a Concern requires.

57. Tooke's substitution of "nation" for Pufendorf's "state" (*civitas*) and the "unity of the people" for Pufendorf's "union of citizens" (*unione civium*) is indicative of the emergence of a political language quite incapable of carrying Pufendorf's key distinctions between sovereignty and (form of) government, state and society.

58. This warning principally concerned Catholic citizens, whose duties to a transterritorial religious and political power Pufendorf regarded as incompatible with their loyalty to the territorial state and its secular sovereign.

Of the Special Laws of a Community, relating to the Civil Government[59]

It now remains, That we take a view of the respective *Parts* of Supreme Government, together with such *Circumstances* thereunto belonging, as we find are worthy to be observ'd. In the first Place, there are the *Civil Laws,* meaning the Acts and Constitutions of the highest *Civil* Authority for the Time being, ordained to direct the Subject in the Course of his Life, as to what Things he ought to do, and what to omit.

I. What they are. L. N. N. l. 8. c. 1. §1.

These are called *Civil,* upon two Accounts especially: That is, Either in Regard to their *Authority,* or their *Original.*[60] In the first Sense, all manner of Laws whatsoever, by the Force whereof Causes may be tried and decided in a Court of Civil Judicature, let their Original be what it will, may pass under that Denomination. In the other, we call only those Laws *Civil,* which derive their Original from the Will of the Supreme Civil Government, the Subjects whereof are all such Matters, concerning which neither the Laws of God or Nature have determined; yet a due Regulation and Settlement of them is found to be very conducive and advantagious to particular Commonwealths.

II. Why so called.

59. Tooke's chapter heading is a circumlocution for Pufendorf's "On the civil laws in particular" (*De legibus civilibus in specie*). Tooke has difficulty in rendering Pufendorf's "civil law" in part because of the English identification of this with (continental) *juscivile,* and in part because the notion of laws deriving from the civil sovereign is foreign to the English tradition of "judge-made" common law.

60. Their origin.

III. The Law of Nature to be reinforced by them.
L. N. N. l. 8. c. 1. §2.

As nothing therefore ought to be made the Subject of a Civil Law, but what relates to the *Good* of the Commonwealth that does ordain it; so it seeming in the highest Degree expedient towards the Regularity and Ease of living in a Community, That in particular *the Law of Nature should be diligently observed by all People;* it lies upon Supreme Governours to authenticate the said Law with the Force and Efficacy of a *Civil* Law.[61] For since indeed the Wickedness of a great Part of Mankind is arrived to a Degree, which neither the apparent Excellency of the Law of Nature, nor the Fear of God Himself, is sufficient to restrain; the most effectual Method remaining, to preserve the Happiness of living in a Community, is, by the Authority of the Government to inforce the *Natural* by the *Civil Laws,* and supply the Disability of the one with the Power of the other.

IV. The Penal Sanction.

Now the *Force and Power, which is in Civil Laws,* consists in this, That to the Mandatory Part of the Statute, concerning Things to be done or omitted, there is annexed a *Penal Sanction,* assigning the Punishment that is to be inflicted upon a Man by a Court of Justice for omitting what he ought to do, or doing what he ought to omit. Of which Kind of Sanctions, the Laws of Nature being of themselves destitute, the breaking of them does not fall under the Punishment of any Court in this World; but yet it is reserved for the Judgment of the Tribunal of GOD.

61. For Pufendorf, the civil law thus agrees with the natural law in two distinct but related ways. First, there is a broad agreement between the two because the end of the natural law, sociable existence, is achieved most fully in the state governed by the laws of a civil sovereign. Second, there is the agreement arising from the fact that the stability and tranquillity of the state are enhanced if its citizens act in accordance with the natural law (of sociability). This means that natural laws pertaining to social peace can be enacted and enforced as civil law, thereby, in effect, closing the gap between natural and positive law. Pufendorf thus neutralizes the scholastic and religious uses of natural law as a moral weapon against the civil state: first, by identifying the end of natural law with the end of the civil state (security), and, second, by subordinating natural law to positive civil law. For Barbeyrac's different view, see his two discourses in the appendix.

More particularly, it is inconsistent with the Nature of living in a Community, for any one by his *own* Force to exact and extort what himself accounts to be his Due. So that here the *Civil* Laws come in, to the Assistance of the *Natural*. For they allow the Creditor the Benefit of an *Action*, whereby the Debt that is owing to him by Virtue of a Law of Nature, with the Help of the Magistrate, may be demanded and recover'd in a Court of Justice, according to the Course of the Laws of the Nation: Whereas without such Inforcement of the said Laws, you can force nothing from a Debtor against his Will; but must intirely depend upon his Conscience and Honour. The Civil Laws admit of *Actions* chiefly in the Case of those Obligations that are contracted betwixt Parties by an express Bond or Covenant. For as to other Affairs, where the Obligation arises from some *indefinite* Duty of the Law of Nature, the Civil Laws make them not subject to an *Action* at all; on purpose to give occasion to good Men to exercise their Virtue, to their more extraordinary Praise, when it is evident, they do that which is just and honest without Compulsion. Beside that, frequently, the Point in Question may not be of Consequence enough to trouble a Court about it.

V. Of Actions

And whereas the Law of Nature commands many Things at large, in an indefinite Manner, and leaves the Application of them to every one in his own Breast; the Civil Laws being careful of the Honour and Tranquillity of the Community, prescribe a *certain Time, Manner, Place, Persons, and other Circumstances,* for the due Prosecution of those Actions, with the Proposal of a Reward upon Occasion, to incourage People to enter upon them. And when any Thing is obscure in the Law of Nature, the Civil Laws *explain* it. Which Explication the Subjects are obliged to receive, and follow, although their own private Opinions do otherwise lead them to a contrary Sense.[62]

VI. The Prosecution of them.

62. This restriction of political dissent to the domain of private opinion results from two central Pufendorfian doctrines: first, from the fact that, in order to achieve unity of political will, individuals have agreed that the government's decisions will be deemed to be those of all, even if they are not; second, because only the civil sovereign (the government) has the right to translate the natural law into civil laws.

VII. Form. So that there being thus a Number of Actions, left by the Law of Nature to be consider'd according to the Will and Judgment of each Person, which nevertheless in a Common-wealth ought to be regularly stated for the greater Decency and Quiet of the same; it uses to be the Care of the Civil Laws to reduce all those Actions, with their respective Concerns, to a *proper Form;* as we see it is in Wills, Contracts, and divers other Cases: from whence it comes, that they *limit* us (as they do) in the Exercise of several Rights, to the Use whereof the Law of Nature left us much at *Liberty.*

VIII. The Obedience due to the Civil Laws. For so far as the Civil Laws do not openly contradict the Law of GOD, the Subjects stand *obliged to obey them,* not merely out of Fear of Punishment, but by an internal Obligation confirm'd by the Precepts of the Law of Nature it self. This being one of them, amongst others, That *Subjects ought to obey their lawful Sovereigns.*

IX. And to the particular Commands of the Sovereign, L. N. N. l. 8. c. 1. §6. Nay, it is their Duty to obey even the *Personal Commands* of their Sovereigns, no less than they do the Common Laws of the Kingdom. Only here they must observe, whether the Thing commanded is to be done by them *as in their own Names,* in the Quality of an Action belonging *properly to Subjects to do;* or whether it be barely to undertake the *Execution* of an Affair for the Sovereign, in Consequence of that Authority which he has to command it. *In the latter Case, the Necessity that is imposed upon the Subject excuses him from Sin, tho' to command the Fact it self is a Sin in the Sovereign. But in the Other, for a Subject, as in his *own* Name, to do a Thing which is repugnant to the Laws of God

---

*This Distinction will by no means hold good; for if the Thing commanded by the Sovereign, be manifestly Criminal, Unjust, and Unrighteous, let it be commanded in what Way and Method it will, and inforced with the greatest Threats possible, it ought not to be comply'd with. See *L. N. N.* Lib. 1. Cap. 1. §24. [This shows the degree to which Pufendorf's construction of the citizen's civil duties separates these from the moral duties of the man and the Christian. Only the sovereign may determine whether his commands are in accord with the natural law, hence only the sovereign is responsible if they are not. Barbeyrac's footnote IX.1, p. 322, presumes to the contrary that ultimate responsibility rests in the conscience of each individual.]

and Nature, can never be Lawful. And this is the Reason, why, if a Subject takes up Arms in an unjust War, at the Command of his Sovereign, he sins not: Yet if he condemns the Innocent, or accuses and witnesses against them falsely upon the like Command, he sins. For as he serves in War, he serves in the Name of the Publick; but acting as a Judge, Witness, or Accuser, he does it in his Own.

ɞɷ CHAPTER XIII ɞɷ

Of the Power of Life and Death

The Civil Government, that is supreme in every State, has a Right over the Lives of its Subjects, either *indirectly,* when it exposes their Lives in Defence of the Publick; or *directly,* in the Punishment of Crimes.

I. Twofold.

For when the Force of Foreigners in an Invasion (which often happens) is to be repell'd by Force; or, That we cannot without the Use of Violence obtain our Rights of them; it is lawful for the Government, by its supreme Authority, to compel the Subjects to enter into its Service; not thereby purposely intending their Death, only their Lives are exposed to some Danger of it. On which Occasions, that they may be able to behave themselves with Skill and Bravery, it is fit they should be exercised and prepar'd for the Purpose. Now the Fear of Danger ought not to prevail with any Subject, to render himself uncapable of undergoing the Duties of a Soldier; much less ought it to tempt a Man that is actually in Arms, to desert the Station appointed him; who ought to fight it out to the last Drop of his Blood, unless he knows it to be the Will of his Commander, that he should rather preserve his Life than his Post; or if he be certain that the maintaining of such Post is not of so great Importance, as the Preservation of the Lives ingaged therein.

II. Indirectly.

L. N. N. l. 8. c. 2.

III. Directly. The Government claims a Power to take away the Lives of Subjects *di-*
L. N. N. l. 8.
c. 3. §1.   *rectly,* upon the Occasion of any heinous Crimes committed by them;
               *whereon it passes Judgment of Death by way of *Punishment:* As like-
               wise the Goods and Chattels of Criminals are subject to the Censure of
               the Law. So that here some general Things concerning the Nature of
               Punishments, come to be discours'd.

IV. Of Punish- Punishment is an Evil that is *suffered,* in Retaliation for another that is
ments L. N. N.
l. 8. c. 3. §4. *done.* Or, A certain grievous Pain or Pressure, imposed upon a Person
               by Authority, in the Manner of Force, with Regard to an Offence that
               has been committed by him. For although the *doing* of some Things
               may oftentimes be commanded in the Place of a Punishment, yet it is
               upon this Consideration, that the Things to be done are troublesome
               and laborious to the Doer, who will therefore find his Sufferings in the
               Performance of such Action. A Punishment also signifies its being in-
               flicted against the Wills of People: For it would not otherwise obtain its
               End; which is, to deter them from Crimes by the Sense of its Severity:[63]
               An Effect it never would produce, if it were only such, as an Offender
               is willing and pleas'd to undergo. As for other Sufferings, which happen
               to be undergone in Wars and Engagements; or which one bears inno-
               cently, being wrongfully and injuriously done him; the Former not be-
               ing inflicted by Authority, and the Other not referring to an antecedent
               Crime, they do neither of them import the proper Sense and Meaning
               of a *Punishment.*

---

* *Grotius de Jure Belli & Pacis,* l. 2. c. 20, & 21.

63. Pufendorf advances a secular conception of punishment in which severity is
tied to the state's interest in social peace and hence to the deterrent effect of the punishment, rather than to the notion of exacting retribution for a breach of the moral
order. This modern conception of punishment makes sense only in a desacralized
political order where security has replaced religious morality as the objective of law
and government.

By our *Natural Liberty,* we enjoy the Privilege to have no other Super-iour but G O D over us, *and only to be obnoxious[64] to Punishments Divine. But since the Introduction of *Government,* it is allow'd to be a Branch of the Office of those in whose Hands the Government is in-trusted, for the Good of all Communities; that upon the Representa-tion of the unlawful Practices of Subjects before them, they should have Power effectually to *coerce,* [punish and restrain] the same, that People may live together in Safety.

V. Inflicted by the Govern-ment. L. N. N. l. 8. c. 3. §7.

Neither does there seem to be any Thing of Inequality in this; that *he who* Evil *does* should Evil *suffer.* Yet in the Course of Human Punish-ments, we are not solely to regard the Quality of the Crime, but likewise to have an Eye upon *the Benefit of the Punishment:* By no means exe-cuting it on purpose to feed the Fancy of the Party injur'd, or to give him Pleasure in the Pains and Sufferings of his Adversary: Because such Kind of Pleasure is absolutely inhumane, as well as contrary to the Dis-position of a good Fellow-Subject.

VI. The Bene-fit of them.

*The Author here reasons on a false *Hypothesis.* He pretends, as is plain from what is here laid down, That no one can inflict any Punishment on another, unless he be his Superiour. Now in the State of Nature all are equal; and then all Natural Laws would be useless and insignificant, if a Power, in such Case, were no where lodged to punish those who violate them, either with Respect to any private Person, or to Mankind in general; the Preservation of which is the End of these Laws, to the Observation of which all Men stand under a common Obligation. In this indepen-dent State, every one has a Right to put these Laws in Execution, and to punish the Person who violates them. See *L. N. N.* Lib. 8. Chap. 3. §4. [In this note (V.1, p. 325) Barbeyrac rejects Pufendorf's treatment of punishment as a right belonging solely to the civil state and its sovereign; for this is a further sign of Pufendorf's tendency to collapse natural law into positive civil law. Conversely, by arguing that men possess the natural right to punish each other for breaches of the natural law in the state of nature, Barbeyrac maintains the theological view of punishment as retribution for breaches of the moral order—a view that permits individuals to punish a "tyranni-cal" sovereign.]

64. Liable or subject to.

The *Genuine End of Punishments in a State,* is, The Prevention of Wrongs and Injuries; which then have their Effect, when he who does the Injury is *amended,* or for the future *incapacitated* to do more, or others taking *Example* from his Sufferings are deterr'd from like Practices; or, to express it another way, That which a Government designs in the Matter of Punishments, is the *Good,* either of the Offender, or the Party offended, or generally of All its Subjects.

First, We consider the *Good of the Offender:* In whose Mind the Smart of the Punishment serves to work an Alteration towards Amendment, and corrects the Desire of doing the same again. Divers Communities leave such Kind of Punishments as are qualified with this End, to be exercis'd by Masters over the Members of their own Families. But it never was thought good they should proceed so far as to *Death,* because, he that is dead is past *Amendment.*

In the next Place, a Punishment intends the *Good of the Party offended:* securing him, that he suffer not the like Mischief for the future, either from the same or other Persons. He becomes secure from being again injured in like Manner by the same Person; first, By the Death of the Criminal; or, secondly, If he be allow'd Life, by depriving him of Power to hurt; as, by keeping him in Custody, taking his Arms, or other Instruments of Mischief, from him, securing him in some distant Place, and the like; or, thirdly, By obliging him to learn, at his own Peril, not to incur farther Guilt, or offend any more. But then to secure the Party offended from suffering the like Injury from other Hands, it is necessary that the Offender be punished in a most Open and Publick Manner, whereby the Criminal may become an Example to all others; and that his Punishment be accompanied with such Circumstances of *Form* and *Pomp,* as are apt to strike a Dread into as many as behold it.

In a Word, the *Good of all People* is intended by the Execution of Punishment in this Manner. For by this means, Care is taken, that he who has done a Mischief to one, shall do no such Mischief again to another: The Terrour of whose Example may also be an Antidote for the rest against the Temptations to his Crime: And this Good accrues after the same Manner as the former.

But if, together with the End of Punishments, we consider the Condition of Human Nature, we shall see, That *all Sins are not of that Quality,*
that they must necessarily fall under the Sentence of a Court of Justice. The
Acts of the Mind within it self, which are merely internal; such as, Thinking upon a Sin with Delight, coveting, desiring, resolving to do an ill
Thing, but without effect; though they should be afterwards made
known by a Man's own Confession, yet are all exempted from the
Stroke of human Punishments. For so long as those *internal* Motions
have not broken forth into Action, nor occasion'd the Prejudice of any
one, whom does it concern or profit to cause the Author to suffer for
the same?[65]

XI. Internal Acts of the Mind, not subject to them. L. N. N. l. 8. c. 3. §14.

It would also be over severe in Laws, to punish the more minute Lapses
which may daily happen in the Actions of Men; when, in the Condition of our Natures, the greatest Attention cannot prevent them.

XII. Nor minute Lapses.

There are many Instances of Actions more, of which the Publick Laws
dissemble the taking of any Notice, *for the sake of the Publick Peace.* As
sometimes, because a good Act shines with greater Glory, if it seems not
to have been undertaken upon Fear of human Punishment; or, perhaps,
it is not altogether worth the troubling of Judges and Courts about it;
or, it is a Matter extraordinarily difficult to be decided; or it may be
some old inveterate Evil, which cannot be removed, without causing a
Convulsion in the State.

XIII. And other Actions. L. N. N. l. 8. c. 3. §14.

In fine, it is absolutely necessary, That *all those Disorders of the Mind*
should be exempted from Punishment, that are the Effects of the common
Corruption of Mankind; such as Ambition, Avarice, Rudeness, Ingratitude, Hypocrisy, Envy, Pride, Anger, private Grudges, and the like. All
these of Necessity, must be exempted from the Cognizance of *Human*
Judicatures, so long as they break not out into publick Enormities; see-

XIV. Nor the Vices of the Mind.

65. Pufendorf's restriction of punishment to external acts capable of threatening
security is a key means of excluding the church from the state and establishing religious toleration. The "liberal" and absolutist dimensions of Pufendorf's thought
thus both flow from the same source: his restriction of sovereign power to the objective of social peace, over which it has sole disposition.

ing they abound to that Degree, that if you should severely pursue them with Punishments, there would be no People left to be the Subjects of Government.

XV. Of Pardon. L. N. N. l. 8. c. 3. §15. Farther, When there have been Crimes committed, which are punishable by the Civil Judicature, it is not *always* necessary to execute the Sentence of Justice upon them. For in some Cases a *Pardon* may possibly be extended to Criminals, with a great deal of *Reason,* (as it never ought to be granted without it;) and amongst other Reasons, *these* especially may be some: *That* the Ends, which are intended by Punishments, seem not so necessary to be attended to in the Case in Question: *Where* a Pardon may produce more *Good* than the Punishment, and the said Ends be more conveniently obtain'd another way: *That* the Prisoner can allege those excellent Merits of his own or of his Family towards the Common-wealth, which deserve a singular Reward: *That* he is famous for some remarkable rare Art or other; or, it is hoped, will wash away the Stain of his Crime by performing some Noble Exploit: *That* Ignorance had a great Share in the Case, tho' not altogether such as to render the Criminal blameless: Or, *That a particular* Reason of the Law ceases in a Fact of the same Nature with his. For these Reasons, and oftentimes for the *Number* of the Offenders, being very great, Pardons must be granted, rather than the Community shall be exhausted by Punishments.

XVI. The greatness of a Crime L. N. N. l. 8. c. 3. §18. To take an Estimate of the *Greatness of any Crime,* there is to be consider'd, first, The Object against which it is commited; how Noble and Precious *that* is: Then, The *Effects;* what Damage, more or less it has done to the Common-wealth: And next, The *Pravity* of the Author's Intention, which is to be collected by several Signs and Circumstances: As, Whether he might not easily have resisted the Occasions that did tempt him to it? and besides the common Reason, Whether there was not a peculiar one for his Forbearance? What *Circumstances* aggravate the Fact? or, Is he not of a Soul dispos'd to resist the Allurements of a Temptation? Inquiring yet farther, Whether he was not the *Principal* in the Commission? or, Was he seduced by the Example of others? Did he commit it once, or oftner, or after Admonition spent in vain upon him?

But for the precise *Kind and Measure of Punishment*, that is fit to be pronounced upon each Crime, it belongs to the Authority of the Government to determine it, with an intire Regard to the Good of the Common-wealth. Whence the *same* Punishment may, and oftentimes is, impos'd upon two *unequal* Crimes; understanding the Equality that is commanded to be regarded by Judges, to mean the particular Case of those Criminals, who being guilty of the same Kind of Fact, the one shall not be acquitted, and the other condemned without very sufficient Reason. And although Men ought to shew to one another all the Mercy and Tenderness that may be; yet the Good of the Nation,[66] and the Security of its Subjects, require, upon Occasion, when either a Fact appears most pernicious to the Publick, or there is need of a sharp Medicine to obviate the growing Vices of the Age, that the Government should *aggravate its Punishments:* which deserve at all times to be carried high enough, to be sufficient to controll the Propensity of Men towards the Sins against which those Punishments are levell'd. And let the Government observe, That no greater Punishments be inflicted, than the Law assigns, unless the Fact be aggravated by very heinous Circumstances.

XVII. Measure and Kind of Punishment. L. N. N. l. 8 c. 3. §24.

Moreover, Since the same Punishment, not affecting all Persons alike, meets with various Returns to the Design thereof, of restraining in them the Itch of Evil-doing, according to the Disposition of every one that incounters it; therefore both in the Designation of Punishments in general, and in the Application of them to Particulars, it is proper *to consider the Person of the Offender,* in Conjunction with as many Qualities as concur to augment or diminish the Sense of Punishment; as, Age, Sex, Condition, Riches, Strength, and the like.

XVIII. The Person of the Offender. L. N. N. l. 8. c. 3. §25.

66. Originally: "the safety of the state" (*salus civitatis*).

XIX. Effects of
one Man's
Crime upon
another.
L. N. N. l. 8.
c. 3. §33.

Not but that it frequently happens,[67] that the Crime of one *shall occasion the Inconvenience of many others,* even to the Intercepting of a future Blessing from them that they justly expected to receive. So when an Estate is confiscated for a Crime done by the Parents, the innocent Children are plunged into Beggary. And when a Prisoner upon Bail makes his Escape, the Bail is forced to answer the Condition of the Bond, not as a *Delinquent,* but because it was his voluntary Act to oblige himself to stand to such an Event.

XX. Crimes
done by Communities.
L. N. N. l. 8.
c. 3. §28.

From whence it follows, That as no Man in a Court of Civil Judicature, can properly be punish'd for another's Crime; so in the *Commission of a Crime by a Community,*[68] whoever does not consent to it, shall not be condemn'd for it; nor suffer the Loss of any Thing he does not hold in the Name and Service of the Community, farther than it is usual on these Occasions for the Innocent to feel the Smart of the *Common Misfortune.* When all those are dead, who did consent or assist towards the said Crime; then the Guilt thereof expires, and the Community returns to its pristine Innocency.

ଔ C H A P T E R X I V ଔ

Of Reputation

I. Defined.
L. N. N. l. 8.
c. 4. §1.

Reputation in General, is that *Value* set upon Persons in the World, on some account or other, by which they are compar'd and equaliz'd, preferr'd or postpon'd[69] to others.

---

67. Following Barbeyrac, the editors have reversed the order of Pufendorf's final two sections.

68. Tooke's all-purpose use of community is again potentially misleading. Here Pufendorf is concerned not with the political community or state (*civitas*) but with the private corporation (*universitas*) and the degree of liability of its members.

69. Meaning "subordinated to."

It is divided into *Simple,* and *Accumulative;* and may be consider'd as to both, either in a People living *at their Natural Liberty,* or united together under a Government.

II. Divided.

Simple *Reputation amongst a People in their Natural Liberty,* consists chiefly in this, That by their Behaviour, they have the Honour to be esteem'd, and treated with, as Good Men, ready to comport themselves in Society with others, according to the Prescription of the Law of Nature.

III. Simple Reputation in a State of Nature. L. N. N. l. 8. c. 4. §2.

The Praise whereof remains *Entire,* so long as no evil and enormous Fact is knowingly and wilfully done by them, with a wicked Purpose, to violate the Laws of Nature towards their Neighbour. Hence every one naturally is to pass for a Good Man, 'till the contrary is prov'd upon him.

IV. How preserved. L. N. N. l. 8. c. 4. §3.

The same is *diminish'd* by Transgression against the Law of Nature maliciously, in any heinous Matters; which serves also as a Caution for the future, to treat with him that does it, with greater Circumspection; though this *Stain may be wash'd off,* either by a voluntary Reparation of Damages, or the Testimonies of a serious Repentance.

V. Diminished, and repaired. L. N. N. l. 8. c. 4. §4.

But by a Course of Life directly tending to do Mischief, and the seeking of Advantages to themselves, by open and promiscuous Injuries towards others, the Reputation describ'd is *totally destroyed.* And till Men of this sort repent, and change their Ways, they may lawfully be used as Common Enemies, by every one, that is in any manner liable to come within the Reach of their Outrages: Since it is not impossible, even for those Men, to *retrieve their Credit;* if after they have repair'd all their Damages and obtain'd their Pardons, they renounce their vicious, and embrace for the time to come, an honest Course of living.

VI. Lost, and recovered. L. N. N. l. 8. c. 4. §5.

VII. Under
Government.
L. N. N. l. 8.
c. 4. §6.

Simple Reputation, with regard to such as live under Civil Government, is that Sort of Esteem, by which a Man is looked on at the lowest, as a common but a sound Member of the State: Or when a Man hath not been declar'd a corrupt Member, according to the Laws and Customs of the State, but is supposed to be a good Subject, and is look'd upon accordingly, and valu'd for such.

VIII. Lost by
an ill Condi-
tion of Life,
L. N. N. l. 8.
c. 4. §7.

Here therefore the same *perishes,* either by Reason *of the Course of a Man's Life,* or in *Consequence of some Crime.* The first is the Case of *Slaves;* whose Condition, tho' naturally having no Turpitude in it, in many Communities places them, if possible, below Nothing. As likewise that of *Panders, Whores,* and such like, whose Lives are accompanied with Vice, at least the Scandal of it. For tho', whilst the Community thinks fit publickly to tolerate them, they participate of the Benefit of the Common Protection; yet they ought however to be excluded the Society of Civil Persons. And we may conclude no less of others, who are employ'd in Works of Nastiness and Contempt, tho' *naturally* not including any Vitiousness in them.

IX. And his
Crimes.

By *Crimes* Men utterly lose their Reputation, when the Laws set a Brand of Infamy upon them for the same; either by Death, and so their Memory is set under Disgrace for ever; or by Banishment out of the Community, or by Confinement, being consider'd as scandalous and corrupt Members.

X. Otherwise
Indelible.
L. N. N. l. 8.
c. 4. §9.

Otherwise it is very clear, that the *Natural Honour of no Man can be taken from him solely by the Will of the Government.* For how can it be understood, that the Government should have a Power collated on it, which conduces in no Degree to the Benefit of the Common-wealth? So neither does it seem, as if a real Infamy can be contracted by executing the Commands of the Government, barely in the Quality of a Minister, or Officer.

Accumulative *Reputation* we call *that,* by which Persons, reciprocally equal as to their Natural Dignity, come to be preferr'd to one another according to those Accomplishments, which use to move the Minds of People to pay them Honour: For *Honour* is properly, the Signification of our Judgment concerning the Excellency of another Person.

XI. Accumula-
tive Reputa-
tion. L. N. N.
l. 8. c. 4. §11.

This Sort of Reputation may be consider'd, either as amongst those who continue in the *Liberty of a State of Nature,* or amongst the *Members of the same Common-wealth.* We will examine, what the *Foundations* of it are, and how they produce in People, both a *Capacity* to expect the being Honoured by others; and an *actual Right, strictly so called,* to demand it of them as their Due.

XII. Twofold.

The *Foundations of an Accumulative Reputation,* are in General reckoned to be all Manner of Endowments, either *really* containing, or such as are supposed to contain, some great Excellency and Perfection, which has plainly a Tendency in its Effects to answer the Ends of the Laws of Nature or Societies. Such are Acuteness and Readiness of Wit, a Capacity to understand several Arts and Sciences, a sound Judgment in Business, a steddy Spirit, immoveable by outward Occurrences, and equally superiour to Flatteries and Terrours: Eloquence, Beauty, Riches; but, more especially the Performing of good and brave Actions.

XIII. The
Grounds of it.
L. N. N. l. 8.
c. 4. §12.

All these Things together, produce a *Capacity* to receive Honour, *not a Right.* So that if any Person should decline the Payment of his Veneration to them, he may deserve to be taken Notice of for his Incivility, but not for an Injury. For a *perfect Right* to be honoured by others, that bear the Ensigns thereof, proceeds either from an Authority over them; or from some mutual Agreement; or from a Law that is made and approved by one Common Lord and Master.

XIV. The Dis-
tinction of a
Capacity and a
Right to it.
L. N. N. l. 8.
c. 4. §14.

Amongst *Princes* and *independent States,* they usually alledge, for *Honour and Precedence,* the Antiquity of their Kingdoms and Families, the Extent and Richness of their Territories, their Power Abroad and at Home, and the Splendour of their Styles. Yet neither will all these Pre-

XV. Amongst
Princes and
States.
L. N. N. l. 8.
c. 4. §20.

tences beget a *perfect Right* in any Prince or State to have the Precedence of others, unless the same has been first obtained by Concession or Treaty.

XVI. Amongst Subjects. L. N. N. l. 8. c. 4. §24.

Amongst *Subjects,* the *Degree of Honour is determined by the Prince,* who wisely therein regards the Excellency of each Person, and his Ability to advance the publick Good. And whatever Honour a Subject receives in this Nature, as he may justly *claim* it against his Fellow-Subject, so he ought no less to satisfie himself in the quiet Enjoyment of it.

❧ C H A P T E R   X V ❧

Of the Power of Governours over the Goods of their Subjects

I. Threefold. L. N. N. l. 8. c. 5. §1.

As it wholly lies at the Pleasure of supreme Governours, to appoint with what Restriction they will allow their Subjects to have Power over the Goods which *themselves* derive upon them; so also over the Goods of the Subjects *own acquiring* by their proper Industry or otherwise, the said Governours claim a *threefold Kind of Right,* resulting from the Nature, and as being necessary to the End, of Communities.[70]

II. By Laws. L. N. N. l. 8. c. 5. §3.

Their First, consists in this; That it belongs to them to *prescribe Laws* to the Subjects, about the Measure and Quality of their Possessions; and which way to transfer the same from Hand to Hand, with other Particulars of the like Nature; and how to apply them in the Use to the best Advantage of the whole Body.

70. Originally: sovereigns have three kinds of right over the property of citizens, in accordance with the nature and purpose of the state.

By the Second, they claim to appropriate to themselves, out of the Goods of the Subjects, a *Portion* by the Name of *Tribute* and *Customs*. And it is but reasonable, that since the Lives and Fortunes of all the Members are defended by the Community, the necessary Charges thereof should be defrayed by a general Contribution. For he must be very impudent indeed, who will enjoy the Protection and Priviledges of a Place, and yet contribute nothing in Goods or Service towards its Preservation. Only herein there will be great Occasion for Governours to accommodate themselves with Prudence to the querulous Temper of common People; and let them endeavour to levy the Money the most insensibly that they can: Observing first an Equality towards all, and then to lay the Taxes rather upon the smaller Commodities of various Kinds, than upon the Chief in a more uniform Way.

III. By Taxes and Customs. L. N. N. l. 8. c. 5. §4.

The Third, is a *Right of Extraordinary Dominion,* consisting in this; That upon an *urgent Necessity of State,* the Goods of any Subject, of which the present Occasion has need, may be taken and applied to *publick Uses,* tho' far exceeding the Proportion, that the Party is bound to contribute towards the Expences of the Common-wealth, For which Reason, as much (if it be possible) ought to be refunded to him again, either out of the publick Stock, or by the Contribution of the Rest of the Subjects.

IV. By Seisure for publick Use extraordinary. L. N. N. l. 8. c. 5. §7.

Beside these three Pretensions over the *private,* in divers Communities there are some particularly call'd, the *publick Estate;* which carry also the Name of the *Kingdom's, or the Prince's Patrimony,* according as they are distributed into the *Treasury* or the *Privy Purse.* The Latter serves for the Maintenance of the Prince and his Family; who has a Property in it during Life, and may dispose of the Profits thence arising at his Pleasure: But the Use of the Other is appropriated for the publick Occasions of the Kingdom; the Prince officiating therein as Administrator only, and standing obliged to apply all to the Purposes to which they

V. Publick Revenues unalienable. L. N. N. l. 8. c. 5. §9.

---

* *Grotius de Jure B. & P.* L. 1. c. 1. §6. L. 2. c. 14. §7. L. 3. c. 19. §7. *Junct.* l. 3. c. 1. §15.

are designed. And neither of the two *Patrimonies* can be *alienated* by the Prince without the People's Consent.

VI. Neither Royal Power nor Allegiance, alienable. L. N. N. l. 8. c. 5. §10.

Much less can a *whole Kingdom* (that is not held *patrimonially*) or any *Part* of it, be *alienated without their Consent to it:* And in the latter Case particularly the *Consent of that Part that is to be alienated.* As on the other Hand no Subject against the Will of his Community, can possibly *disingage himself from the Bonds of his Duty and Allegiance to it;* unless the Force of foreign Enemies reduces him to such a Condition, that he has no other Way to be safe.

❧ CHAPTER XVI ❧

Of War and Peace

I. Necessity of War sometimes. L. N. N. l. 8. c. 6. §2.

Altho' nothing is more agreeable to the *Laws of Nature,* than the mutual Peace of Men with one another, preserved by the voluntary Application of each Person to his Duty; living together in a State of Peace, being a peculiar Distinction of Men from Brutes; yet it is sometimes both *Lawful and Necessary to go to War,* when by means of another's Injustice, we cannot, without the Use of Force, preserve what is our own, nor injoy those Rights which are properly ours. But here common Prudence and Humanity do admonish us *to forbear our Arms there, where the Prosecution of the Injuries we resent, is likely to return more Hurt upon us and ours, than it can do Good.

---

* *Grotius de Jure Belli & Pacis,* l. 1. c. 2.

The *just Causes upon which a War may be undertaken,* come all to these: The Preservation of our selves, and what we have, against an unjust Invasion; and this Sort of War is called *Defensive.* The Maintenance and Recovery of our Rights from those that refuse to pay them: The Reparation of Injuries done to us, and Caution against them for the future. And this Sort of War is called *Offensive.*

II. Just Causes of War. L. N. N. l. 8. c. 6. §4.

Not that upon a Prince's taking himself to be injur'd, he is presently to have Recourse to Arms, especially if any Thing about the Right or Fact in Controversie remains yet under Dispute. †But first let him try to compose the Matter in *an amicable Way,* by Treaties, by Appeal to Arbitrators, or by submitting the Matter in Question to the Decision of a Lot; ‡and these Methods are the rather to be chosen by that Party who *claims* from another, because *Possession,* with any Shew of Right, is wont to meet with the most favourable Constructions.

III. Amicable Composition.

The *unjust Causes of War,* are either those which *openly to all the World are such;* as, Ambition and Covetousness, and what may be reduced thereto: Or §those that admit of a faint and imperfect *Colour* to be pretended in their Excuse. Of this Kind there is Variety: As, The Fear of a Neighbour's growing Wealth and Power; Conveniency of a Possession, to which yet no Right can be made out; Desire of a better Habitation; The Denial of common Favours; The Folly of the Possessor; The Desire of extinguishing another's Title, lawfully acquired, because it may be prejudicial to us; ‖and many more.

IV. Unjust Causes of War. L. N. N. l. 8. c. 6. §5.

And tho' the most proper Way of Acting in War, is by that of Force and Terrour, yet it is altogether as lawful to attack an Enemy by *Stratagems and Wiles,* provided that the Faith and Trust which you give him is inviolably observed. ˢIt is lawful to deceive him by Stories and feigned Narrations, not by Promises and Covenants.

V. Of Deceit in War. L. N. N. l. 8. c. 6 §6.

---

* *Grotius de Jure Belli & Pacis,* l. 2. c. 1, &c. to l. 2. c. 23.
† *Grotius de Jure Belli & Pacis,* lib. 2. cap. 23, 24.
‡ *Grotius de Jure Belli & Pacis,* lib. 2. c. 23. §12.
§ *Grotius,* l. 2. c. 24. §4.
‖ *Grotius,* l. 2. c. 1. §17. Cap. 22. §5.
ˢ *Grotius de Jure Belli & Pacis,* l. 3. c. 1. §6, &c.

VI. Violence:
L. N. N. l. 8.
c. 6 §7.

But concerning the *Violence* which may be used against him, and what belongs to him; we must distinguish betwixt what it is possible for him to *suffer without Injustice,* and what we may easily *inflict without the Breach of Humanity.* Whoever declares himself my Enemy, as he makes Profession by that very Act of enterprizing upon me the greatest Mischiefs in the World; so at the same Time he fully indulges me the Leave to imploy the utmost of my Power, without Mercy, against himself. *Yet Humanity commands me, as far as the Fury of War will permit, that I do my Enemy no more Harm, than the Defence or Vindication of my Right requires, with Care to my Security for the Time to come.[71]

VII. Solemn
and less sol-
emn War.
L. N. N. l. 8.
c. 6. §9.

We commonly divide War into *Solemn* and *less Solemn.* To a *Solemn* War it is required, That it be made on both Sides by the Authority of the Sovereign Governours; and preceeded by a publick Declaration. The *other* either is not publickly denounced, or, perhaps, is begun amongst private Persons. †To which latter Head belong also *Civil Wars.*

VIII. Power of
making War.
L. N. N. l. 8.
c. 6. §10.

As the *Power of making War,* in all Nations lies in the same Hands, that are intrusted with the Government; ‡so it is a Matter above the Authority of a *subordinate Magistrate* to ingage in, without a Delegation from thence, tho' he could suppose with Reason, that were they consulted upon the Matter, they would be pleased with it.

Indeed all Military Governours of fortified Places and Provinces, having Forces under them to command upon the Defence thereof, may understand it to be injoyn'd them by the very Design of their Imployments, to repel an Invader, from the Parts committed to their Trust, by

---

* *Grotius,* l. 3. c. 4. §2. Cap. 11, 12, &*c.*

71. In conceiving of the enemy only as someone who threatens the rights of the territorial sovereign, hence as someone who need be harmed only to the extent that it is necessary to defend these rights, Pufendorf is reflecting the secularized conception of the enemy that arose following the Thirty Years' War and the Peace of Westphalia (1648). The enemy was no longer a criminal or heretic on whom one waged war of annihilation, but a "just enemy" on whom one waged limited war in order to protect purely secular territorial rights.

† *Grotius de Jure Belli & Pacis,* l. 1. c. 3. §4.

‡ *Grotius,* &c. l. 1. c. 3. §1.

all the Ways they can. But they are not rashly to carry the War into an Enemy's Country.

In a State of Natural Liberty, a Person is assaulted by Force only for the Injuries that are done by himself. But in a Community, a War often happens upon the *Governour* or *the whole Body,* when *neither of them* has committed any Thing. To make this appear just, it is necessary, the Act of a Third Party must by some way or other pass upon them. Now Governours do partake of the Offences, not only of their proper Subjects, but of others that occasionally flee to them; if either the Offences are done by their *Permission,* or that they *receive and protect* the Offender. The Sufferance of an Offence becomes then blameable, when at the same Time that one knows of the doing it, he has a Power to hinder it. Things openly and frequently done by the Subjects, are supposed to be known to their Governours; in whom it is always presumed there is a Power also to prohibit, unless a manifest Proof appears of its Defect. Yet to make it an Occasion of War, to give Admittance and Protection to a Criminal, who flies to us for the Sake only of escaping his Punishment, is what must proceed rather by Virtue of a particular Agreement betwixt Allies and Neighbours, than from any *common Obligation;* unless the Fugitive, being in our Dominions, contrives Hostilities against the Common-wealth he deserts.

IX. Wars occasioned by protecting of Refugees. L. N. N. l. 8. c. 6. §12.

Another received Custom betwixt Nations, is, That the Goods and Estate of every Subject may be answerable to make good the Debts of that State of which they are originally Members; as also for all that Wrong which that State may offer to Foreigners, or that Justice it may refuse to shew them, insomuch, that the Foreign Nation, whose Subjects have been thus injur'd by this State, may retaliate the Wrong upon the Effects or Persons of such Subjects of this State, as may be found among them. And these Sorts of Executions are usually called *Reprisals,* *and commonly prove the Forerunners of War. Those States who are the Aggressors, and give just Cause for such Reprisals, ought to refund and

X. Reprisals. L. N. N. l. 8. c. 6. §13.

---

* *Grotius de Jure Belli & Pacis,* l. 3. c. 2. §4.

make Reparation to their Subjects upon whom they have thus brought Loss and Damage, by making them liable to have such Reprisals made upon them.

XI. Of Wars in the Defence of others.

L. N. N. l. 8. c. 6. §14.

A War may be made by a Person, not only *for himself, but for another.* In order to do this with Honesty, it is requisite, that He for whom the War is undertaken, shall have a just Cause; and his Friend, a probable Reason, why he will become an Enemy to *that other* for his sake. Amongst those, in whose Behalf it is not only lawful, but our Duty to make War, there is, in the first Place, *our Natural Subjects,* as well severally, as the universal Body of them; provided, that the War will not evidently involve the State in greater Mischiefs still. Next, there are the *Allies,* with whom we have engaged to associate our Arms by Treaty: Yet, therein not only giving the Precedence to our own Subjects, if they should chance to stand in need of Assistance at the same Juncture; but presupposing also, that the Allies have a just Cause, and begin the War with Prudence. *After our Allies, our *Friends* deserve to be assisted by us, even without our Obligation to do it by a special Promise. And where there is no other Reason, the common Relation alone of Men to Men, may be sufficient, when the Party imploring our Aid is unjustly oppressed, to engage our Endeavours, as far as with Convenience we are able, to promote his Defence.

XII. The Liberty of killing, &c. in War.

L. N. N. l. 8. c. 6. §18.

The *Liberty that is in War,* of killing, plundering, and laying all Things waste, extends it self to so very large a Compass, that tho' a Man carries his Rage beyond the *uttermost Bounds of Humanity,* yet in the Opinion of Nations, he is not to be accounted infamous, or one that ought to be avoided by Persons of Worth. †Excepting, that amongst the more Civilized World, they look upon some particular Methods, of doing Hurt to Enemies, to *be base;* as poisoning Fountains, or corrupting of Soldiers or Subjects to kill their Masters, *&c.*

* *Grotius de Jure Belli & Pacis,* l. 2. c. 25.
† *Grotius de Jure Belli & Pacis,* l. 3. c. 1, &c. c. 4. §15, &c.

Moveable *Things* are understood to be *Taken* in War then, when they are carried out of the Reach of the Enemy who before possessed them. *And *Things immoveable,* when we have them within our Custody so, that we can beat the Enemy away from thence. Yet the Right of the former Possessor to retake the same, is never utterly extinguished, till he renounces all his Pretensions to them by a subsequent Agreement. For without this, it will be always lawful, by Force, to retrieve again what by Force is lost. The Soldiers fight by the Authority of the Publick; and whatever they obtain from the Enemy, they get it not for themselves, but properly for the Community they serve. Only it is customary in most Places, to leave to them by Connivance the Moveables, especially those of small Value, that they take, in the Place of a Reward, or perhaps instead of their Pay, and for an Incouragement to them to be free of their Blood. When *Things immoveable* that have been lost to, are retaken *from* the Enemy, they return into the Possession of the former Owners: †And Moveables ought to do the same; but that amongst most People they are delivered over and foregone as a Prey to the Army.

XIII. Of things taken in War. L. N. N. l. 8. c. 6. §20.

Empire⁷² also or Government comes to be acquired by War, not only over the *particular or single Persons conquered,* but *intire States.* ‡To render this lawful, and binding upon the Consciences of the Subjects, it is necessary, That on the one Side the Subjects swear Fidelity to the Conqueror; and on the other, that the Conqueror cast off the State and Disposition of an Enemy towards *them.*

XIV. Conquest. L. N. N. l. 8. c. 6. §24.

The Proceedings of War are suspended by *a Truce;* which is an Agreement (the State and Occasion of the War remaining still the same as before,) to abstain on both Sides from all Acts of Hostility for some Time appointed. When that is past, if there be no Peace concluded in the *Interim,* they resume their Hostilities again, without the Formality of a new Declaration.

XV. Truce L. N. N. l. 8. c. 7. §3.

---

* *Grotius,* l. 3. c. 6.
† *Grotius de Jure Belli & Pacis,* l. 3. c. 9. §13.
72. I.e., *imperium* or rule.
‡ *Grotius de Jure Belli & Pacis,* l. 3. c. 7. &c. 15.

XVI. Treaties of Truce. Now *Truces* are either *such* as they consent to during the Continuance of the Expedition, whilst both Sides keep their Forces on foot; or *those,* on which they quite disband their Forces, and lay aside all Military Preparations. The first are seldom taken but for a small Time. The others they *may* and usually *do* take for a Continuance so long, as to carry the Face of a Peace; and sometimes also the very Name, with the Addition of some Term of Years, only to distinguish it from a *perfect Peace* indeed, which regularly is Eternal, and extinguishes the Causes of the War for ever. *Those that they call *tacit Truces,* oblige to nothing. For as on both Sides they lie quiet for their Pleasure, so, whenever they think fit, they may break out into Acts of Hostility.

XVII. Treaties of Peace. L. N. N. l. 8. c. 8. But when a Peace is mutually ratified by each Sovereign Governour, upon Articles and Conditions agreed betwixt themselves, which they ingage to observe and put in Execution faithfully by a Time prescribed; then a War is perfectly ended. †In Confirmation whereof, it is usual, not only for both Parties to take their Oaths and interchange Hostages; but for some others oftentimes, especially amongst the Assistants at the Treaty, to undertake the *Guaranty* of the same, with Promises of Aid to him who ever is first injured by the other, in Contravention to the Articles of the Peace that is made.

---

* *Grotius de Jure Belli & Pacis,* l. 3. c. 21. §1. &c.
† *Grotius,* l. 3. c. 20. §2, &c.

Of Alliances

Alliances[73] interchangeably passed betwixt Sovereign Governours, are of good Use both in Times of War and Peace. *They may be *divided,* in Respect of their Subject, either into such as *reinforce the Duty* already incumbent on us from the *Law of Nature;* or such as *superadd something* to the Precepts of the Law; at least, they determine their Obligation to such or such particular Actions, which before seemed indefinite.

I. Alliances twofold.
L. N. N. l. 8.
c. 9. §1.

By the *first* Sort are meant *Treaties of Peace,* wherein nothing more is agreed upon than the simple Exercise of Humanity towards one another, or a Forbearance of Mischief and Violence. Or, perhaps, they may establish a general Sort of Friendship betwixt them, not mentioning Particulars; or fix the Rules of Hospitality and Commerce, according to the Directions of the *Law of Nature.*

II. Treaties of Peace.
L. N. N. l. 8.
c. 9. §2.

The others of the latter Sort, are called *Leagues,* and are either *Equal* or *Unequal. Equal Leagues* are so far composed of the same Conditions on both Sides, that they not only promise what is *Equal* absolutely, or at least in Proportion to the Abilities of the Person; but they stipulate in such a Manner too, that neither Party is to the other obnoxious,[74] or in a worse Condition.

III. Equal Leagues.
L. N. N. l. 8.
c. 9. §3.

Unequal *Leagues* are those, wherein Conditions are agreed upon that are unequal, and render one Side worse than the other. †This Inequality may be either on the Part of the *Superiour,* or else of the *Inferiour Confederate.* For if the Superiour Confederate ingages to send the other Succours, unconditionally, not accepting of any Terms from him, or in-

IV. Unequal.
L. N. N. l. 8.
c. 9. §4.

---

73. Pufendorf's Latin term is *foedera,* which covers both treaties and alliances.
* *Grotius de Jure Belli & Pacis,* l. 2. c. 15.
74. Neither party is subordinate to the other.
† *Grotius de Jure Belli & Pacis,* l. 1. c. 3. §21.

gages to send a greater Proportion of them than He, the Inequality lies upon the *Superiour*. But if the League requires of the inferiour Confederate the Performance of more Things towards the Superiour, than the Superiour performs towards him, the Inequality there no less evidently lies on the Side of the *Inferiour*.

V. Conditions put upon Inferiours.
L. N. N. l. 8. c. 9. §5.

Amongst the Conditions required of an inferiour Ally, some contain a *Diminution of his Sovereign Power*, restraining him from the Exercise thereof in certain Cases without the Superiour's Consent. Others *impose no such Prejudice upon his Sovereignty*, but oblige him to the Performance of those we call *transitory* Duties, which once done, are ended altogether. As, to discharge the Pay of the other's Army; to restore the Expences of the War; to give a certain Sum of Money; to demolish his Fortifications, deliver Hostages, surrender his Ships, Arms, &c. And yet neither do some *perpetual* Duties *diminish the Sovereignty* of a Prince. As, to have the same Friends and Enemies with another, tho' the other be not reciprocally ingaged to have the same with him: To be obliged to erect no Fortifications here, nor to sail there, &c. To be bound to pay some certain friendly Reverence to the other's Majesty, and to conform with Modesty to his Pleasure.

VI. The Subject of Leagues.

Both these Sorts of Leagues, as well *Equal* as the *Unequal*, are wont to be contracted upon various Reasons, whereof such especially produce Effects of the strongest and most binding Complexion, as tend to the Conjunction of many Nations in a League that is to last for ever. But the *Common Subject* of the Leagues most in Use, is, either the Preservation of Commerce, or the Furnishing of Succours in a War, Offensive or Defensive.

VII. Real and personal Leagues.
L. N. N. l. 8. c. 9. §6.

There is another famous Division of Leagues into *Real*, and *Personal*. The *Latter* express such a near Regard to the Person of the Prince they are contracted with, that whenever he dies, they expire also. *Real Leagues* are those, which not being entred into in Consideration so much of any particular Prince or Governour, as of the Kingdom or

Common-wealth, continue in full Force, even after the Death of the first Contracters of them.

The next in Nature to *Leagues,* are the Agreements of a *Publick Minister,* made upon the Subject of the Affairs of the Prince his Master, without Orders for the same; which are usually called *Overtures.* The Conditions whereof impose no Obligation upon the Prince, till he shall please afterwards to ratifie them by his own Authority. And therefore, if, after the *Minister* has agreed upon the Compact absolutely, he cannot obtain his Prince's Confirmation of it; it lies upon himself to consider, what Satisfaction he ought to render to those, who, depending upon his Credit, have been deceived by him with insignificant Ingagements.

VIII. Sponsions.[75]
L. N. N. l. 8. c. 9. §12.

✽ CHAPTER XVIII ✽

The Duty of Subjects

The Duty of Subjects is either *General,* arising from the Common Obligation which they owe to the Government as *Subjects:* Or *Special,* upon the Account of some particular *Office* and *Imployment,* that the Government imposes upon them.

I. Twofold.
L. N. N. l. 7. c. 8. §10.

Their *General* Duty respects the Demeanour of themselves severally, towards their Governours, the Common-wealth,[76] and one another in particular.

II. General.

---

75. Unauthorized negotiations undertaken by lower officials.

76. In this chapter Tooke uses "commonwealth" rather than "community" to translate Pufendorf's *civitas.*

III. Towards their Governours. To their *Governours* they owe Honour, Fidelity, and Obedience. Beside that, they ought to entertain good and honourable *Thoughts* of them and their Actions, and *speak* accordingly; to acquiesce with Patience and Content under the present State of Things, not suffering their Desires to wander after Innovations; not adhering to any Persons, or admiring and honouring them, *more* than they do the Magistrates that are set over them.

IV. The Common-wealth; In Reference to the Common-wealth, their Duty is, to prefer the Happiness and Safety of it to the dearest Things they have in the World: To offer their Lives, Estates and Fortunes with Chearfulness towards its Preservation, and to study to promote its Glory and Welfare by all the Powers of their Industry and Wit.

V. One another. Towards *one another,* their Behaviour ought to be friendly and peaceable, as serviceable, and as affable as they can make it; not to give Occasion of Trouble by Moroseness and Obstinacy, nor envying the Happiness of any, or interrupting their lawful and honest Injoyments.

VI. Their special Duties. And as for their *peculiar Duties, as Officers,* whether they influence the whole Body of the Nation, or are employed only about a certain Part of it, there is this one general Precept to be observed for all; *That* no Person affect or take upon him any Imployment, of which he knows himself, by the Sense of his Disabilities (whether Want of Strength, Skill, Courage, *&c.*) to be unworthy and uncapable.

VII. The Duty of Privy-Counsellors. Particularly, let those who *assist at the Publick Counsels,* turn their Eyes round upon all Parts of the Common-wealth; and whatever Things they discover to be of Use, thereupon ingenuously and faithfully, without Partiality or corrupt Intentions, lay open their Observations. Let them not take their own Wealth and Grandure, but always the publick Good, for the End of their Counsels; nor flatter their Princes in their Humours to please them only. Let them abstain from Factions and unlawful Meetings or Associations; dissemble not any thing that they ought to speak, nor betray what they ought to conceal. Let them approve themselves impenetrable to the Corruptions of Foreigners; and not postpone the publick Business to their private Concerns and Pleasures.

Let the *Clergy,* who are appointed publickly to administer in *the Sacred Offices of Religion,* perform their Work with Gravity and Attention; teaching the Worship of God, in Doctrines that are most true, and shewing themselves eminent Examples of what they preach to others; that the Dignity of their Function, and the Weight of their Doctrine, may suffer no Diminution by the Scandal of their ill led Lives. <sub/> VIII. The Clergy.

Let such who are publickly imployed to *instruct the Minds of the People in the Knowledge of Arts and Sciences,* teach nothing that is false and pernicious; delivering their Truths so, that the Auditors may assent to them, not out of a Custom of hearing, but for the solid Reasons that attend them: And avoiding all Questions which incline to imbroil Civil Society; let them assure themselves, that whatever human Science or Knowledge returns no Good to us, either as Men or Subjects, the same deserves their Censure as *impertinent* Vanity. IX. Publick Readers.

Let those Magistrates, whose Office it is to *distribute Justice,* be easie of Access to all, and ready to protect the Common People against the Oppressions of the more mighty; administring Justice both to Rich and Poor, Inferiour and Superiour, with a perfect Equality. Let them not multiply Disputes unnecessarily; abstain from Corruption; be diligent in trying of Causes, and careful to lay aside all Affections that may obstruct *Sincerity* in Judgment; not fearing the Person of any Man while they are doing their Duty. X. Lawyers.

Let the *Officers of War* diligently Exercise their Men on all Occasions, and harden them for the enduring the Fatigues of a Military Life, and inviolably preserve good Discipline among them. Let them not rashly expose them to the Danger of the Enemy, nor defraud them of any of their Pay or Provisions; but procure it for them with all the Readiness they are able, and keep them in the Love of their Country, without ever seducing them to serve against it. XI. Officers of the Army.

XII. Soldiers. On the other Hand, let the *Soldiers* be content with their Pay, without plundering, or harrassing the Inhabitants. Let them perform their Duty couragiously and generously, in the Defence of their Country; neither running upon Danger with Rashness, nor avoiding it with Fear: Let 'em exercise their Courage upon the Enemy, not their Comrades: And maintain their several Posts like Men, preferring an Honourable Death before a Dishonourable Flight and Life.

XIII. Ambassadors and Envoys. Let the *Ministers of the Common-wealth in foreign Parts,* be cautious, and circumspect; quick to discern Solidities from Vanity, and Truths from Fables; in the highest Degree, Tenacious of Secrets, and obstinately averse to all Corruptions, out of their Care of the Good of the Common-wealth.

XIV. Officers of the publick Revenues. Let the *Officers for Collecting and Disposing of the Publick Revenue* have a Care of using needless Severities, and of increasing the Subjects Burthen for their own Gain, or through their troublesome and petulant Humours. Let them misapply nothing of the publick Stock; and satisfie the Persons who have Money to be paid out of it, without Delays unnecessary.

XV. The Continuance of the Duties aforesaid. L. N. N. l. 8. c. 11. All these *Particular* Duties of Subjects, *continue* during the Time of Employment: And when that ceases, the other expire also. But their *General Duties are in Force,* so long as ever Men continue to be Subjects; that is, 'till by either the *express* or *tacit* Consent of the Nation, they depart thence, to fix the Seat of their Fortunes elsewhere; that they are banished and deprived of the Rights of Subjects for their Crimes; or, being overcome in Battle, they are forced to yield to the Disposal of the Conqueror.

The END

INDEX

The Roman Numerals I *and* II, *signifie the* First *and* Second Book. *The first Figure after them directs to the* Chapter, *and the second Figure to the* Section *in that* Chapter.

A

ACCEPTANCE, of the Person to whom the Promise is made, necessary to make the Promise binding I. 9. 16.

Accessional Improvements, what they are, and to whom they belong I. 12. 7.

Accidents; Damages that come by Accidents not to be made good I. 6. 9.

Acquisition, the different Sorts of it I. 12. 5.

Action; what is meant by Human Actions I. 1. 2. What are the Principles of them I. 1. 3. What it is that makes Men chargeable with their Actions I. 1. 10. Actions involuntary or forced I. 1. 16. Mix'd Actions what I. 1. 16. Actions of other Men, how they may be chargeable on us I. 1. 18, 27. The different Qualities of Moral Actions I. 2. 11, 12, *&c.* What Actions above the Reach of Commerce I. 14. 3.

Actions at Law; for what Things a Man may or may not bring his Action II. 12. 5.

Advantage; in how many Ways Men may procure Advantages to others I. 8. 2, &c.

Adultery, dissolves the Marriage II. 2. 6.

Aggressor; we may not always use the last Extremity against an unjust Aggressor I. 5. 14. When the first Aggressor has a Right to defend himself I. 5. 24.

Alliances, and other publick Treaties consider'd and explain'd II. 17.

Ambassadors, their Duty II. 18. 13.

Antichresis; what Sort of Covenant so named I. 15. 15.

Arbitrators, what they are, and wherein their Duty consists II. 1. 11.

Aristocracy; what Sort of Government so called II. 6. 11. The Defects of such a Constitution II. 8. 7.

Arts; in what respect, and after what manner Arts are to be studied and cultivated 1. 5. 9.

Assignments of Debts, when they may properly be made I. 16. 8.

Astrology Judicial, a Science contrary to the true Principles of Religion and Morality I. 5. 3.

Atheists, are wholly inexcusable I. 4. 2. Whether they ought to be brought to Punishment I. 4. 2.

B

BARTER, what is meant by it I. 15. 8.

Beast; the Owner ought to make good the Damage his Beast has done; and in what manner this is to be done I. 6. 12. The Foundation of that Right which Man has over Beasts I. 12. 1.

Benefits, how they are to be managed I. 8. 5.

Body; wherein consists the Care that every Man ought to take of his own Body I. 5. 10.

Booty; to whom it belongs II. 16. 13.

Bounty; wherein the Bounty of any Action consists I. 2. 11.

C

CARES; All superfluous Cares ought to be banished I. 5. 4.

Celibacy, in what Respects allowable and justifiable II. 2. 3.

Chance; Nothing ought to be left to Chance, where Men can use their own Prudence and Foresight I. 5. 4. Of Contracts in the Performance of which Chance bears a Share I. 15. 13.

Charity. See *Humanity.*

Citizen; what a good Citizen is II. 6. 13. By what means Men may lose their Title of Citizens in a State II. 18. 15.

Commerce; The general Laws of Commerce I. 14. 6.

Community; How a Community may be punished II. 13. 20.

Compensation, what is meant by it, and how it takes away an Obligation I. 16. 2.

Complaisance, ought to be mutual I. 7. 3.

Condition; (State of Life) what Conditions of Life are infamous II. 14. 8.

Conditions; what they are on which the Validity of a Promise, or other Obligation, depends I. 6. 20.

Conquest; Of the Right obtain'd by Conquest II. 10. 2. II. 16. 14.

Conscience; Conscience rightly inform'd, what; and what a probable Conscience I. 1. 5. Doubting or scrupulous Conscience I. 1. 6.

Consent, what Signs are sufficient to express it I. 9. 9. What Conditions are required to make a true and perfect Consent I. 9. 10, 11, &c.

Constraint; How many Sorts of Constraints there are I. 1. 24.

Contempt; All such Behaviour is to be avoided that carries with it a Contempt of other Men I. 7. 6.

Contract, what is meant by it, and the different Sorts of them

Contradiction; How seeming Contradictions are to be reconcil'd I. 17. 4.

Controversies, how to be determin'd in a State of Nature II. 1. 11.

Convention, what is meant by it I. 9. 4. What Conditions requisite to make Conventions obligatory and valid I. 9. 8. Tacit Conventions what I. 9. 9.

Counsel; When we are chargeable for

the Ill that any one acts under the Influence of our Counsel and Direction I. I. 27.

Country; Desert Country, how it is made any one's Property I. 12. 6.

Courage, necessary for all Men, and the Reason why I. 5. 16.

Crime; How the Greatness of a Crime is to be rated II. 13. 16. Wherein one Man may suffer for the Crime of another II. 13. 19.

D

DAMAGE, what it is, and how to be repair'd I. 6. 5, &c.

Dangers, when Men may, and when they ought to expose themselves to them I. 5. 11.

Deceit, how far in Engagements and Promises, it destroys their Efficacy I. 9. 13.

Defence; How any one may, and ought to behave himself in his own Defence I. 5. 12, &c.

Degree; what Degrees of Kindred are prohibited in Marriage II. 2. 8.

Delegating, or *Assigning;* what is meant thereby, and when it may be done I. 16. 8.

Demesne of the Crown or State; that is, the publick Revenues, not alienable II. 15. 5.

Democracy; an Account of that Form of Government II. 16. 11. The Defects such a Government is chargeable with II. 8. 8.

Deposit, or *Loan;* what it is, and the Duty of those who receive them I. 15. 5.

Desert Country. Vide *Country.*

Desertion, of the Bed maliciously, dissolves the Marriage II. 2. 6.

Desire; How Men ought to regulate their Desires II. 5. 5.

Destiny, or *Fatality;* The Belief of it is contrary to the true Principles of Religion and Morality I. 5. 3.

Devotion, the false Notions some Men have of it I. 5. 3.

Diseases or *Distempers;* How far natural Diseases that disturb Mens Reason, excuse them from having what they do imputed to them I. 1. 15.

Dispensing; what that Power is, in whom lodg'd, and when to be exercis'd I. 2. 9.

Disquiet; All superfluous Disquiet ought to be banished I. 5. 4.

Dissimulation, not always a Crime I. 10. 5.

Division; Rules to be observ'd in dividing Things among them who have a common Right to them I. 7. 4.

Divorce, whether or no, and on what Occasions allowable II. 2. 6.

Domesticks. See *Servants.*

Dominion, extraordinary, what it is, and when to be exercis'd II. 15. 4.

Dreams; whether Men are answerable for any thing that they seem to consent to do in their Dreams I. 1. 26.

Drunkenness, whether any Excuse for ill Actions committed under its Influence I. 1. 15. I. 9. 10.

Duel, on no Account to be justified I. 5. 20.

Duty; what is meant by that Term I. 1. 1. The Notion the Stoicks had of it I. 1. *Note.* How many Sciences there are from whence Men may learn their Duty *Preface* §1. The different way Men may be called to the Performance of their Duties, according to their different Natures I. 2. 14. I. 9. 3. How many Sorts of Duties, generally speaking, are requir'd of Men by the Law of Nature I. 3. 13. I. 6. 1.

E

ELECTION, of a Sovereign Prince II. 10. 3, 5.

End, of Mens Actions I. 1. 9. How far the Will is concerned in bringing about this End I. 1. 9. What End Men should propose to themselves in their Actions I. 5. 4.

Engagement; (See Convention; Promise) The Necessity of entring into voluntary Engagements I. 9. 2. They are religiously to be observed when entred into I. 9. 3. How Engagements come to be render'd void I. 16.

Equality; wherein the Natural Equality of Men consists, and the Consequences of such their Equality I. 7. What Sort of Equality is to be observed in burdensome Contracts I. 15. 6, 7.

Equity; what is meant thereby I. 2. 10.

Esteem; how to be sought for I. 5. 5. What is Simple and what Accumulative Esteem II. 14. 2.

Error, what it is, and how many Sorts of it I. 1. 7. What the Effect of it is with respect to the Validity of Promises or Engagements I. 9. 12.

Events; how far Men are chargeable with them I. 1. 8.

Exchange, or Barter; what it is I. 15. 8.

F

FATALITY; the Belief of it contrary to the Principles of true Religion, and Morality I. 5. 3.

Fault; A simple Fault or Error, what I. 2. 15.

Favourable; what is meant by Matters of a Favourable Nature I. 17. 9.

Fear; Contracts made through Fear, how far obligatory I. 9. 14, 15.

Felicity; what Sort of it a Man may promise to himself in this World I. 5. 4.

Factions, in some Cases, may be made use of without Guilt I. 10. 16.

Fishery; The Right all Men have to take Fish I. 12. 6.

Flattery; We are answerable for the Faults of Men, when they are incited to commit them by our Flattery and Encouragement I. 1. 27.

Force only, suffices not to give a Right to bring an Obligation upon those who lye under the Power of this Force I. 2. 5. How the Forces or Powers of Men are restrain'd and limited I. 5. 4.

Freedom of the Will, (a Faculty of the Soul) wherein it consists I. 1. 9. What Use Men ought to make of it I. 5. 4.

G

GALLANTRY; The false Notions Men entertain of Sins of Gallantry I. 5. 3.

Glory; The false Notions Men usually take up of Glory I. 5. 5.

GOD, the Author of the Law of Nature I. 3. 11. What Ideas we ought to have of his Nature and Attributes I. 4. 2, &c. Wherein consists that Worship which we owe to Him I. 4. 6, 7.

Good; How many Acts of Good there are I. 1. 11.

Goods; (Wealth) whether we may kill him that comes to take them from us I. 5. 23. What Goods remain in Common for the Use of all Men I. 12. 4.

Goods of other Men; we are not to meddle with them I. 13. 1. In what Cases we may seize their Goods, indanger their Persons, or even their Lives I. 5. 28, 29. How far Bargains are valid entred into about Things belonging to other Men I. 9. 19. What is the Duty of him who is possess'd of Goods belonging to another Man I. 13. 2, &c.

Goods found; to whom they belong I. 12. 6. I. 13. 5.

Government; the different Forms of it, and the Defectiveness of each of them II. 8.

Grace; In what Cases Princes may shew Grace to Criminals in pardoning them II. 13. 15.

Gratitude; the Necessity of it, and the Characters of it I. 8. 6, &c.

H

HABITS; the great Power of them I. 1. 13.

Hazard; Nothing, where Men can use their own Prudence and Foresight, ought to be left to Hazard I. 5. 4. Of Contracts, in the Performance of which some Part must be left to Hazard I. 15. 13.

Hiring; Of the Nature and Rules of this Kind of Contract I. 15. 10.

Hirelings, for a Time, what is their Duty II. 4. 2. For Life, what Obligations they lye under I. 4. 3.

Honour. See *Esteem.*

Honour of Women, (Chastity) Whether a Woman may defend her Honour by killing him who comes to ravish her I. 5. 22.

Humanity; What is to be understood by the Laws of Humanity and Charity, as they are oppos'd to those of Justice; and wherein the Difference between them both consists I. 2. 14. I. 9. 3.

Humility; Wherein true Humility consists I. 7. 5.

I

IGNORANCE; what it is, and how many Sorts there are of it I. 1. 8. Invincible Ignorance wholly excuses what is done amiss I. 1. 20. Ignorance of a Law no Excuse for the Breach of it I. 1. 21.

Impossible; No body bound to do that which is impossible I. 1. 23. This Maxim is to be taken in a limited Sense *ibid. &* I. 9. 17.

Imposts, why laid, and how to be rais'd II. 11. 10.

Imputation; The fundamental Reason of the Imputation of human Actions I. 1. 16. Particular Rules whereby we may know when an Imputation does justly lye, or not I. 1. 17, &c.

Infamy; Whereby Men are branded with Infamy II. 14. 9.

Infants; why beaten and corrected I. 1. 25.

Ingratitude; the Baseness and Odiousness of it. I. 8. 7. Why it will not bear an Action I. 8. 7.

Injury; what it is I. 2. 15.

Insurances; What Sort of Contracts so stiled I. 15. 13.

Intemperance; Why vicious and Criminal I. 5. 10.

Interpretation; How Laws and Conventions ought to be interpreted I. 17.

Interregnum; What it is II. 10. 4.

Invidious; What is meant by Things odious or invidious I. 17. 9.

Justice; What it is, and how many Sorts there are of it I. 2. 13, &c.

K

KINGDOM; What is an Hereditary Kingdom II. 9. 7. Whether a Prince can alienate his Kingdom or any Part of it II. 15. 6.

Knowledge; How useful and necessary to every Man the Knowledge of himself is I. 5. 4.

L

LAW; What it is I. 2. 2. The Necessity of it I. 2. 1. How to be understood I. 2. 6. The Essential Part of it I. 2. 7. What the Matter of it ought to be I. 2. 8. How many different Sorts there are of Law in General I. 2. 16. Wherein the Reason of a Law is founded I. 17. 8. When the Terms of Law may be extended, and when restrained I. 17. 10, &c. Fundamental Laws of State, what II. 9. 6. What Laws are to be esteemed good II. 11. 5. Of the Nature and Power of Laws relating to a Civil Government II. 12.

Law of Nature; What it is, and the Necessity of it how to be understood I. 3. 1. In what the Funda-

mental Principle of it is placed I. 3. What it is that gives it the Force and Efficacy of a Law I. 3. 9, 10. In what Sense it may be said to be engraven on the Hearts of all Men I. 3. 12.

Legislator; How to be known I. 2. 6.

Liberty of the Will; What it is I. 1. 9. What Use Men ought to make of it I. 5. 4.

Life; Whether Men have the Power of their own Life I. 5. 11. The Power of Life and Death where II. 13.

Loans; What Obligation lies on them, to whom consumeable Things are sent for immediate Use I. 15. 11. What are the Duties of those, who have any Thing lent them freely for their Use. I. 15. 4.

Lotteries; wherein this Kind of Contract consists I. 15. 13.

Lying; what it is I. 10. 8.

M

MADNESS; Whether it takes away all Obligation from the Conventions and Agreements made by Men who are affected with it I. 9. 10.

Magistrates; their Duty II. 18. 10.

Maladies. See *Diseases.*

Man; From whence arises the great Difference which there is in the Desires and Carriage of Men I. 1. 11. I. 3. 6. How great the Love he naturally bears himself is I. 3. 2. The miserable Condition he would be in without the mutual Assistance of his Fellows I. 3. 3. The Vices he is naturally prone to I. 3. 4. The manifold Ways he has of doing Mischief to his Fellows I. 3. 5. His natural State requires that he should live in Society I. 3. 7. The Obligations he lies under to himself I. 5. 1. What Duties he is obliged to perform in respect to himself I. 5. 2, &c. How far his natural Powers are limited and restrained I. 5. 4. What he has most in his own Power *Ibid.* All Men are naturally equal I. 7. What Sort of Men are best form'd for Society I. 7. 3. The Foundation of that Right, which Man has over all other Creatures here below I. 12. 1.

Marriage; how constituted II. 2. 2. Who are obliged to enter into it II. 2. 3. When it is regular and perfect II. 2. 4. What Impediments properly hinder it II. 2. 7. What are the Duties of a married Life II. 2. 10.

Mediatory Contract; How far we are obliged to stand to Contracts made in our Name by Persons deputed by us I. 9. 21.

Members; we may preserve them at the Expence of his Life who goes about to maim them I. 5. 21. What Right every Man has over his own Members I. 5. 26.

Merchandise; he that sells them ought fairly to discover the hidden Faults of them I. 15. 6.

Mercenaries. See *Hirelings.*

Merit; Wherein true and solid Merit consists I. 5. 4.

Ministers; Publick Ministers of a Prince or State, how it may be known when they act by Order of their Sovereign I. 11. 9. What are their Duties II. 18. 7.

Minors; whether Contracts and Engagements made by them are valid I. 9. 10, 11. Whether they may contract Marriage without the Consent of Parents II. 3. 8.

Misfortunes, simply so call'd, what I. 2. 15.

Monarchy; its Constitution and Nature II. 6. 11. To what Defect it is liable II. 8. 6.

Money, its Original and Use I. 14. 7, &c.

Morality; the Principles of it naturally plain and evident I. 1. 4, 7.

Mortgages, what they are, and how many Sorts of them I. 15. 15.

N

NATURE; not the same with GOD I. 4. 3.

Natural Inclinations, do not unavoidably bring Men to commit Evil I. 1. 12.

Necessity, has no Law I. 5. 25. Several Cases of Necessity explain'd I. 5. 26, &c.

Negligence; Damage done by meer Negligence ought to be made good I. 6. 9.

O

OATHS; of the Nature of them, the End of imposing them, the Uses to be made of them, and the different Sorts of them I. 11.

Obligations; What is meant by an Obligation I. 2. 3. Why Men are subject to an Obligation I. 2. 4. Wherein the just Foundation of all Obligations is laid I. 2. 5. Perfect and imperfect Obligations, what I. 2. 14. I. 9. 3.

Occupant; How Men derive to themselves a Right to any Thing by *Pre-*

mier Seisin, or having the first Occupancy or Possession of it I. 12. 6.

Ocean; Why the Ocean cannot be
made the Property of any one I.
12. 4.

Ochlocracy; what is meant by it II.
8. 11.

Odious; What is meant by Things
odious or invidious I. 17. 9.

Offices; Good Offices ought to be mutual I. 7. 3. What are the Offices of
common Humanity I. 8.

Officers; The Duty of Officers in War
II. 18. 11.

Oligarchy; what it is II. 8. 11.

Omission; In what Respects Men are
chargeable for their Omissions I.
1. 22.

Opinions; How far a Sovereign has
Power over the Opinions of his
People II. 7. 8.

Outrage, ought to be commited
against no Body I. 7. 8.

P

PARDON, in what Cases it is proper
to bestow it on a Criminal II. 13.
15.

Parents; their Power over their Children; and what they are bound to
do for them II. 3.

Passions; how great the Power of them
is I. 1. 14. The Moral Difference
there is between those Passions,
which are raised from the Appearance of Good, and those rais'd
from the Appearance of Evil I. 1.
14. How they ought to be regulated
I. 5. 8.

Payment, of what, to whom, and in
what manner to be made I. 16. 1.

Peace; the Rights of Peace II. 16.

Penalties, their Nature, Use, and the
Rules which ought to be observed
in inflicting them II. 13.

Piety; wherein it consists I. 2. 13.

Play; What is the Obligation arising
from Contracts in Play or Gaming
I. 15. 13.

Pleasure; in what Manner and Degree
it may be pursu'd I. 5. 7.

Pledges; what they are, and how many
Sorts of them I. 15. 15.

Polygamy, whether on any Account allowable II. 2. 5.

Possessor; what Obligation he lies under that becomes, without any
Fault of his own, the Possessor of
that which is another Man's I. 13. 2.

Power, Legislative II. 17. 2. Coercive
II. 7. 3. Judiciary II. 7. 4. Power of
making Peace and War, and of
entring into Treaties and Alliances,
where placed II. 7. 5. Power of appointing Ministers and subordinate Magistrates II. 7. 6. To raise
Taxes and Subsides II. 7. 7. To take
Cognisance of the Doctrines publickly taught in a Kingdom II. 7. 8.
What is to be understood by Absolute Power II. 9. 5.

Power; (Might or Force) Whether if a
neighbouring Prince begins to
grow too powerful, it be lawful to
attack him under Pretence of preventing him, and keeping up a Balance of Power I. 5. 17.

Precedence; Wherein the Right of
Precedence is founded II. 14. 15.

Prescription; what it is, and wherein
the Right of it is founded I. 12. 12.

Price; wherein the Foundation of it is
laid, and what are the different
Sorts of it I. 14.

Pride; wherein the Vileness of it consists I. 7. 5.

Prince; Whether Self-Defence be allowable against the Person of a Prince I. 5. 19. How he ought to regulate the Value of his Coin I. 14. 9.

Professors, their Duty II. 18. 9.

Profession; Every one ought early to betake himself to some honest and useful Profession suitable to his Circumstances and Rank I. 5. 9. I. 8. 2.

Promise; What it is I. 9. 5. Imperfect what I. 9. 6. Perfect what I. 9. 7. What Conditions are requisite to make a Promise binding I. 9. 8, &c.

Property; By what means Property was first introduced among Men I. 12. 2. What is meant by it I. 12. 3. What Things Men may have a Property in, and what not I. 12. 4. The different Ways whereby Property is obtained I. 12. 5, &c.

Providence; In respect to Morality, the denying his Providence, is the same Thing as the denying the Existence of God I. 4. 4.

Publick; What Obligations all Men are under, to those who take Pains for the Publick Service I. 5. 17.

Q

QUALITIES; How far Men are answerable for their personal Qualities, whether they be natural or acquired I. 1. 19.

R

REASON; Whether Persons deprived of the Use of their Reason, are answerable for what they do I. 1. 2.

Contracts and Promises made by such Persons are invalid I. 9. 10.

Religion; An Abridgment of the System of Natural Religion I. 4. The Use of it in promoting Civil Society I. 4. 9. Opinions recited contrariant to the true Notions of Religion I. 5. 3. Duties of those who minister in the publick Worship II. 18. 8.

Reprisals; Wherein the Right of Reprisals consists II. 16. 10.

Reputation, by what Means sullied, and by what Means entirely lost II. 14. 5, 6.

Revenue; The Duty of those through whose Hands the Publick Revenue passes II. 18. 14. Publick Revenues are not alienable II. 16. 5.

Revenge; A very heinous Vice, and contrary to the Law of Nature I. 6. 13.

Riches; In what manner they may be innocently sought for I. 5. 5.

S

SALE, the Nature of it, the Rules by which this Contract is to be made, and the different Sorts of it I. 15. 9.

Sciences, how many Sorts there are of them, and how far the Study of them is necessary I. 5. 9.

Self-Love, one of the Fundamental Principles of the Law of Nature I. 3. 13.

Services that cost nothing, what they are I. 8. 4.

Servants; The Duty of Servants II. 4. 2, 3.

Servitude, what it is, and how many Sorts of it I. 12. 8.

Shipwreck; several Cases that happen then, decided I. 5. 27, 28.

Silence; when Innocent, and when not I. 10. 4.

Simony; what I. 14. 3.

Single Life; in what Cases justifiable II. 2. 3.

Sins; what not punishable in Human Courts II. 13. 11.

Slave; The Owner must make good the Damage done by his Slave, and how I. 6. 11. The Condition and Duty of Slaves II. 4. 4, &c.

Sloth, a very vicious Temper, and contrary to the Laws of Nature I. 8. 2.

Sociability, one of the general Principles of the Law of Nature I. 3. 13.

Society; The Nature and Rules of that Contract whereby Society is formed I. 15. 12.

Society Civil; The Inducements that made Men form themselves into Civil Societies II. 5. What is the internal Constitution of such a Society II. 6.

Sodomy, contrary to the Law of Nature II. 2. 2.

Soldiers, their Duty II. 18. 12. II. 13. 2.

Sovereign, His Duty II. 11. What Power he has over the Goods of his Subjects II. 15.

Sovereignity, of what Parts it consists II. 7. Its Character and Qualifications II. 9. The different Manner of holding it II. 9. 7.

Soul; God not the Soul of the Universe I. 4. 3. Wherein consists the Care that every Man ought to have of his Soul I. 5. 2.

Speech; what Rules to be observ'd in the Use of it I. 12.

State; What is meant by an Adventitious State I. 6. 1.

State; (See *Society Civil*) What it is II. 6. 10. States united, what and how II. 8. 13.

State of Nature; What are its Rights, and what Inconveniences it is subject to II. 1.

Subjects, their Duties II. 18.

Succession; to those who dye intestate, what is the Reason and Manner of it I. 12. 10, 11. Of the Succession to Crowns II. 10. 6 &c.

Supererogation; How false and dangerous the Opinion of Works of Supererogation is I. 5. 3.

Superstition; All Superstition ought to be ever banish'd I. 5. 3.

Sureties; what are their Duties I. 15. 14.

T

TAXES, why laid, and how to be rais'd II. 11. 10.

Temper, See *Natural Inclinations.*

Temperance, wherein it consists I. 2. 13.

Testament, or last Will. See *Will.*

Theology; The Difference there is between Moral Theology, and the Law of Nature *Preface* §4, &c.

Thief; We ought not to restore to a Thief what he hath stollen and deposited in our Hands I. 13. 2.

Things; In what respect different Things may be look'd on to be the same I. 15. 11. What fungible Things are I. 15. 11.

Treaty; Publick Treaties their Nature II. 17.

Trove; Treasure-Trove what, and to whom it belongs I. 12. 6. I. 13. 5.

Tyranny, what is understood by it II. 8. 11.

V

VENGEANCE. See *Revenge.*

Veracity or *Verity,* wherein it consists I. 10. 7.

Understanding; what it is I. 1. 3. It usually is rightly inform'd in Matters of Morality I. 1. 4. What Use Men ought to make of this Faculty I. 5. 3.

Usury; Lending Money at Usury, not in it self contrary to the Law of Nature I. 15. 11.

W

WAGERS, what they are I. 15. 13.

War, the Rights of it II. 16.

Will, Last Will, what it means I. 12. 13.

Will; (Faculty of the Soul) what it is, and the several Acts of it I. 1. 9. What Use Men ought to make of this Faculty I. 5. 4. How an Union of the Wills of a Multitude may be brought about II. 6. 5.

Witnesses, their Duty II. 1. 11.

Woman; on what Account she may be said to have some Authority over her Husband II. 2. 4.

Words; what Rules are to be observ'd in the Use of them I. 10.

Z

ZEAL; A Zeal without Knowledge, such as furiously animates Men against those of a different Persuasion in Religion, how blameable and criminal I. 5. 3.

TWO DISCOURSES AND A COMMENTARY
BY JEAN BARBEYRAC

NOTE ON THE TRANSLATION

The eighteenth-century dissemination of Pufendorf's Latin works owed not a little to the French translations, notes, and commentaries of Jean Barbeyrac. These had some impact, for instance, on the English editors of the 1716/35 edition of *The Whole Duty of Man*. Publicist and apologist that he was, Barbeyrac nonetheless had a mind of his own on certain key issues in the intellectual debate generated by postscholastic Protestant natural law. The three writings here, translated into English for the first time—the celebrated defense of Pufendorf against Leibniz in the *Judgment of an Anonymous Writer,* together with the *Discourse on What Is Permitted by the Laws* and the *Discourse on the Benefits Conferred by the Laws*—contribute both to Barbeyrac's status as Pufendorf's publicist and to his own standing as a natural law thinker. These three writings, which appeared as appendices in the fourth edition of Barbeyrac's translation of the *De officio, Les Devoirs de l'Homme et du Citoien,* published in Amsterdam in 1718, are thus reunited in the present volume with Pufendorf's text.

The reader will note that the *Judgment of an Anonymous Writer* constitutes a triangular exchange among Leibniz (the "Anonymous Writer"), Pufendorf ("our author"), and Barbeyrac (in his own first-person voice). In fact, Leibniz's words have already been made available in English, in Patrick Riley's 1972 translation from the original Latin.[1] However, the continuous uninterrupted prose of that translation was not at all the form in which Barbeyrac's readers encountered the ex-

---

1. G. W. Leibniz, *Political Writings,* P. Riley trans. and ed. (Cambridge, 1972), pp. 64–75. Riley translates the title as "Opinion on the Principles of Pufendorf."

change. As Barbeyrac informed them at the start of his translation of the German philosopher's attack, he had broken Leibniz's prose into twenty paragraphs, to each of which he then provided an appropriate response (some directly contradicting Leibniz, some conceding ground, some revising Pufendorf). Whereas Barbeyrac indicated Leibniz's words by use of quotation marks, we have thought it more convenient to print them in italics. Also, we have translated Leibniz's critique as it was presented in Barbeyrac's French, to capture the integrity of the latter's triangulation of positions in this early modern debate on natural law.

The *Discourse on What Is Permitted by the Laws* and the *Discourse on the Benefits Conferred by the Laws* were originally delivered in French by Barbeyrac in his official capacity as Rector of the Lausanne Academy, in 1715 and 1716, respectively. Unusually for academic orations, each was published (and republished) in the year of its delivery before being included in the 1718 edition of *Les Devoirs*.[2] It might seem to contradict the very point of his translation of the Latin of Pufendorf (and of Leibniz) into French for a spreading Protestant Francophone readership, but, as the reader will see below, Barbeyrac loaded the *Discourses* and the *Judgment* with Latin quotations, especially in the notes. His purpose was both practical and symbolic: to provide the Latin original as a means for readers to check the accuracy of his rendering (of both classical sources and of Leibniz), and to display the towering humanistic erudition of a natural law scholar whose library would grow to contain ten thousand volumes. In fact, for the most part, the Latin texts cited in Barbeyrac's notes have their translation or paraphrase in the body of his text (which is here translated into English). However, in the fewer instances in which lengthy and interesting Latin notes do not have this English accompaniment, we have included an English translation.[3]

---

2. *Discours sur la Permission des Loix* (Fabri et Barillot, Genève, 1715); republished by Pierre de Coup, Amsterdam, 1715. *Discours sur le Bénéfice des Loix* (Fabri et Barillot, Genève, 1716); republished by Pierre de Coup, Amsterdam, 1716.

3. In the following translation of the *Judgment* and the *Discourses,* the page numbers given in square brackets refer to Barbeyrac's text as printed in the 1735 edition of *Les devoirs de l'homme et du citoien.* The numbered footnotes are Barbeyrac's.

The Judgment of an Anonymous Writer on the Original of This Abridgment

With reflections of the translator, intended to clarify certain of the author's principles

[379] There fell into my hands, a year or so ago, a Latin letter in which an anonymous writer[1] gives his opinion on this abridgment, *De Officio Hominis et Civis.* The letter, which appeared in print in 1709, forms part of an academic program in which Justus Christoph Böhmer, a professor at Helmstadt,[2] gave notice of twelve public disputations on the system of natural law that our author, Samuel Pufendorf, publishes in this short book. Anonymous, who is described as an "Illustrious Man," doubtless had reasons for not revealing his identity. He feared, perhaps, that he would be suspected of wanting to denounce, as if out of [380] personal envy, a work that has enjoyed such general esteem. Perhaps for this same reason he preferred to publish his thoughts only within the context of an academic program, in other words in a printed form that has rather a limited dissemination. Or perhaps he never even thought that such a use would be made of the letter that the Helmstadt professor

---

1. That is to say, the late Mr Leibniz. See the postface to the fourth edition of my translation.

2. Böhmer was then Professor of Politics and Rhetoric. In 1710 he became Professor of Theology, while retaining his other two chairs. Subsequently, in 1723, he was made Abbot of Loccum, succeeding his uncle Gerhardt Walter van den Muelen. He was neither the brother, nor the relative of the famous Mr Böhmer, Professor at Halle, as I had conjectured he might be.

has released without seeking permission.[3] Whatever the case, since his name has now been published, I trust there will be no offence to its author's modesty if I give it a yet wider dissemination,[4] not just by another reprint but by translating the work into one of the best known of modern languages. I shall not seek to draw aside the curtain behind which the anonymous writer is hidden, but leave each reader free to conjecture.

I shall do no more than record how, in reading his letter, I discerned the marks of a penetrating mind, one that was far from allowing itself to be swayed by the judgment of other men. I congratulated myself on the happy chance which had brought such a [381] tract to me, from such a distance, a tract of which not only had I heard no mention, even when I was living much nearer to the place where it appeared, but

3. This was pure conjecture on my part, given my intention to appear to know nothing of the identity of the writer, although I knew it perfectly well. Leibniz had himself sent this piece, by the post, to one of my friends in the neighbourhood of Lausanne, knowing that it would be communicated to me. Therefore I could scarcely imagine that it had been published without his permission. If Mr Böhmer had paid attention to what I subsequently stated, in my Postface, when, the situation having changed with the death of Mr Leibniz, I believed I could reveal the name of the anonymous writer, the author of this *Opinion* here translated with my commentary, he would soon have recognised that I had not seriously suspected him of taking the liberty of printing the work without the author's consent. This was his complaint to me in a gracious letter that he did the honour of writing to me in November 1719, when sending me a second edition of his *Academic Programs*. In the letter he informed me that, in response to a request, Mr Leibniz had written and conveyed his *Opinion* to the late Mr Gerard Molan, Abbot of Loccum and Director of the Churches of the Electorate of Brunswick, Mr Böhmer's own uncle. The piece had been sent on 22 April 1706, with full permission to have it printed under the title *Epistola Viri Excellentissimi ad Amicum, qua monita quaedam ad principia Pufendorfiani Operis De Officio Hominis & Civis continentur.* But it was three years before Mr Böhmer had occasion to act on the permission. Given this declaration on my part, I hope that Mr Böhmer will not find it displeasing if I do not erase with a "perhaps" what I said here concerning him. To do so would require me to change my plan to leave—for good reasons—the text of my reflections precisely as it was composed.

4. I did not know then what I later learned on arriving at Groningen, that the late Mr Alexandre Arnold Pagenstecher had already had Mr Leibniz's letter printed in 1712, and revealed the author's identity, having himself found the name indicated in a Flemish journal, the *Neuer Bücher-Saal.* He published it at the end of Van Velsen's edition of Pufendorf's *De Officio Hominis et Civis,* an edition of which I had not heard.

which must still be as rare as it is little known. Since I already knew that I would shortly have to deliver to the printer the abridgment, *Les Devoirs de l'Homme et du Citoien,* I resolved to adorn this new edition of my translation with the anonymous writer's *Judgment* of the original, attaching to it my comments. This could contribute, it seemed to me, to a greater awareness that, if the work he criticizes is not without fault, since few are, it is all things considered nonetheless a good work.

I will confess once more the pleasure I had in discovering that I had anticipated the anonymous writer in respect of certain matters concerning which I had already written that I too was not entirely pleased with my author's thinking. This led me to hope that it would not be taken amiss were I to defend him on other matters. If I so succeed, I take no great pride in it. Nor [382] do I in any way set myself alongside this "Illustrious Man" who, it appears, is a great genius. If, as he tells us, he had not read for a considerable time the work he is examining, and if it was doubtless just as long since he had read my author's other works, it should come as no surprise that he had not understood my author's principles as well as I, who have committed such labor to winning understanding for them. I shall therefore translate the letter in question, not in a continuous form but by interposing my reflections, to the extent that I shall have occasion. However, there will be no confusion. The separate elements of this little piece, that I shall number for the convenience of references and quotations, will be clearly distinguished by [italics], thanks to which it will be easy to recombine these elements should one wish to read the entire letter without interruption. I shall attempt to express the anonymous writer's thoughts with the utmost exactitude; and I shall record in the margin, or in footnotes, the exact terms of his original, whenever I fear I might not have caught the sense, or for some other reason. Here follows the preamble.

I. You ask me, Monsieur,[5] *on behalf of a friend of yours, for my judgment on the treatise,* Les Devoirs de l'Homme et du Citoien, *written by*

---

5. The person to whom the letter is written—he too is not named—is addressed here as "most eminent man," *vir summe.* It is Mr Abbot Molan, or Molanus. See the note to p. 380.

Samuel Pufendorf, a man whose merit made him famous in his lifetime.[6]
*I have glanced [383] at this work, it being long since I had consulted it, and
I found considerable defects in its principles. However, since most of the
thoughts developed in the work have scarcely any link with the principles,
not being logically derived from the principles as from their causes but
rather being borrowed from elsewhere, from a variety of good authors, nothing prevents this little book from containing numerous good things, or from
serving as a compendium of natural law for such persons as are content with
a superficial knowledge, as is the case with most of the public, and who do
not aspire to a deeper understanding.*

It would surely be a grave fault, or rather a fault that would render
the work in question inappropriate to its author's purpose, if it was
nothing but a kind of rhapsody, *scopae dissolutae, arena sine calce,* as it
seems to be represented here. But I leave it to the public to judge
whether, for all the faults one may find in the system of natural law out-
lined here and now known throughout most of Europe, one does not
in general discern in it both fairly sound principles and a fairly clear link
between the fundamentals of each particular topic and these principles.
I admit that the whole is not arranged in the manner of the geometers,
with Issues, Definitions, Axioms, Corollaries, etc., but their dry
method is in no way necessary in every field of knowledge, and less so
in those fields concerning manners than in any other. To bring to bear
a geometric mind is enough, that is to say a precise mind,[7] and this does
not always depend on [384] a deep study of the abstract sciences: an
orderly mind, precise and sharp, attentive to following the plan that has
been adopted without admitting any major principle that is either false
or doubtful or drawing a wrong consequence that cannot be traced
back, from principle to principle, to the most general. I hope to demonstrate clearly, in examining what our anonymous writer says below
against the principles expounded by my author, that, all in all, these

---

6. "*Suo quondam merito celeberrimi.*" He is yet more renowned since his death
than he was in his lifetime.

7. See the fine and judicious *Reflexions sur l'Utilité des Mathématiques* of Mr de
Crousaz.

principles are indeed well-grounded. And as for the consequences, let us take what chapter we will, and I dare say that we shall quickly be convinced—if we read him carefully—by our author's breadth of reasoning on some truth that follows, directly or indirectly, from the general principles informing the work as a whole. It would be easy to show this by a full analysis: but that would go beyond the scope of my reflections, and be superfluous, given the book itself, where those who read the work can undertake the analysis for themselves.

II. My wish, nevertheless, would be for a stronger and more solid work in which one could find rich and illuminating definitions; in which the conclusions would follow logically [veluti filo] from correct principles; in which the grounds of all actions and exceptions in accord with nature were set down in order; and in which, finally, nothing would be neglected of what is required by those beginning their studies of natural law in order to furnish themselves with what may have been omitted, and to determine according to rules and principles [determinata quaedam via] the questions that are posed. For this is [385] what we expect of a complete and well-ordered system.

For myself, I would wish that Anonymous was himself willing to give us a work such as he conceives a good system of natural law to be. He is without doubt more capable than anyone of fulfilling the program that he has proposed. My only fear, with regard to the "actions and exceptions in accord with nature" of which he appears to insinuate there are many, is that he may be confusing the subtleties of the civil law of the Romans with the simplicity of the natural law. We must take care lest we repeat here what happens when someone, offended by a few irregularities in a building that is otherwise solid and well-conceived, rather than seeking to remedy as best they can the inconsiderable faults, chooses instead to demolish the whole edifice and draw up a new plan, which in various ways could turn out to be far more defective.

III. One might have anticipated something like the sensitive judgment and immense erudition of the incomparable Grotius, or the profound genius of Hobbes, if only the former had not been sidetracked by the many concerns that prevented him doing what he could have done on this topic, or if the latter had not proposed bad principles which he then followed all too closely. Felden [Jean de Felde, in Latin, Feldenus] too could have given us something better and more complete than what is commonly taught, had he chosen more fully to apply his mind and knowledge.

I am not sufficiently acquainted with the last of these authors to judge whether he deserves the praise accorded to him; [386] nor do I know whether what he published on Grotius could lead us to attribute to him the capacity for something like the work at issue.[8] As for Grotius, it must be recognized that he is the first to have systematized a science that, prior to him, was nothing but confusion and, more often than not, impenetrable darkness. With the result that it was scarcely possible this great man should have done more, above all in the times in which he lived. It can thus be said that his excellent work, *Droit de la Guerre et de la Paix,* provided a wealth of starting points sufficient to guide all who have subsequently worked, or who will do so in the future, to produce something more exact and complete.

IV. It would also be most useful to introduce into a system of natural law the parallel laws in the civil law [parallela juris civilis &c.] as recognized

---

8. *Stricturae in Grotium, etc.* This work, and its author, are not held in great esteem by judicious scholars even in his own nation. See *L'Histoire du Droit Nat.* by Mr Buddeus, §.27, at the head of the *Selecta Jur. Nat. & Gent.* et la *Bibliotheca Juris* de Mr Struvius, p. 347, 5th Edit. The latter speaks of Felden (or de Felde) on the occasion of a book that he published in 1664 at Frankfurt and Leipzig, under the title *Elementa Juris Universi, & in Specie Publici Justinianei.* I have since seen this work, and as a result am more than ever convinced that there is no reason to expect from such a mind all that Mr Leibniz promised himself regarding what is required. I wrote further on this in my Preface on Grotius (p. ix), and I do not retract what I said there. What is more, Mr Leibniz's defender, having never apparently heard of Feldenus, thought to work a miracle in changing this name to that of Seldenus, as if there was a printing error or some inadvertency in the original text. However, the name of Feldenus appears also in the second edition that Mr Böhmer published in 1716. Basically, no-one who knows the works of the English scholar will ever imagine that Mr Leibniz could have judged him likely to provide a system of natural law, according to the concept and plan that he believed this should follow. His good opinion of Feldenus was based, it appears, on the *Elementa Juris Universi,* to which he refers in his *Nova Methodus docendae discendaeque Jurisprud.,* printed in 1668 at Frankfurt, p. 39.

among men, above all the civil law of the Romans, and of the divine law *also. In this way, theologians and jurisconsults could more easily make use* *of natural law; whereas, due to the manner in which natural law is taught,* *it consists more in theory than in practice [magis sermonibus celebratur,* *quam negotiis adhibetur], and finds little application in the business of life.*

[387] Grotius, in the book of which we have just spoken, and Pufendorf, in his great work *De Jure Naturae et Gentium,* frequently drew the comparison that Anonymous finds so useful. But I fail to see that it is so necessary in a system such as that in question, which must be designed for the needs of beginners and, as a result, should contain only the elements of the science. The admixture he proposes might rather be harmful, to the extent that it confused the picture, there being few civil laws that do not add something to natural law or otherwise change it. When one learned of natural law only those elements that appeared, piecemeal, in the civil law of the jurisconsults' books, the ideas that one formed whether of natural law or civil law were anything but accurate. The truth of the matter is that before undertaking a comparative study, one must first gain a solid knowledge of natural law alone, only then proceeding to a comparison with the civil law, through study of the laws particular to each country. In this way there is no fear of confusion: it is simply a case of recalling and applying principles that one has already learned. This is the reason behind our author's project of constructing a kind of *Index* on the books of Roman law, to distinguish that which belongs to natural law [388] from that which belongs to positive law. And we can only wish death had not prevented him from executing this project, as well as certain others, of which he speaks in the Preface to the second edition of his major work. If the jurisconsults and theologians make little use of natural law in deciding the particular cases with which the affairs of life confront them, this is scarcely because in studying natural law they did not compare it with the civil law of all peoples on earth. Rather, truth be told, it is because most of them never studied natural law or, if they did, they studied it wrongly.

V. However, since we still lack a work presenting what a good system of nat- *ural law ought to be, as I have just said, and since Pufendorf's abridgment is, amongst us, the best known instance of the genre, in my view it is right to give readers and listeners some warnings, particularly with regard to the principles most liable to abuse. The most important thing, in this respect, is that the author seems to have correctly established neither the end and the object of natural law, nor its efficient cause.*

Here revealing himself as German, Anonymous could have added that it is not only in Germany that the work which he finds so defective is considered one of the best or even the very best of its genre. Elsewhere, it is regarded [389] similarly, including among nations that are somewhat too liable to discount what comes from abroad, especially from certain countries. I shall not speak of the manner in which the French translation was received: but I can confirm that prior to this fourth edition, there was a fourth edition of the English translation,[9] which was in fact a fifth, since from what I learn this little work was included in its entirety in an abridgment of the *De Jure Naturae et Gentium* that has just appeared.[10]

VI. The author states explicitly that the "end of the science of natural law lies within the limits of this life" [Preface, §.6 of the French Translation; §.8 according to the division of the last editions of the original]. And since he clearly saw the possible objection that the immortality of the soul can be demonstrated by natural reason and that, regarding law and justice, the consequences of this pertain to the science of law as understood in the light of natural reason, the author answers at this same point: "Indeed, man sighs impatiently for immortality, and cannot envisage without horror the destruction of his being, and as a consequence even most of the pagans believed that the soul survives its separation from the body, and that the good are rewarded and the wicked punished; but it is only the word of God which can enlighten us on this, and give us the assurance that produces a faith that is whole and all-embracing." That is what the author says. But, even sup-

9. By Mr Andrew Took[e], Professor of Geometry at Gresham College, printed at London in 1716. The translator added my notes, but he had seen only my first edition.

10. By Mr Spavan who, from what is said, also used my notes on both of Pufendorf's works. This abridgment appeared at London, in 1716, in two octavo volumes.

posing true what is in fact false, namely that natural understanding does not furnish a perfect demonstration of the soul's immortality, it would always satisfy a wise man that the proofs derived from reason are at least weighty, and serve to give good people great hope for another life better than this one, and to inspire in the wicked a just fear of dire punishment to come. For when it is a matter of a great evil, one should take steps to guard against it, even though one has small reason to fear it, but especially when one is most likely to be exposed to it. Nor must one disregard reason supported by the consensus of almost all peoples on this matter, or reason that reflects the natural desire for immortality. But a strong argument, recognized by all, not to mention other more subtle arguments, is furnished by sheer knowledge of God, a principle that our author correctly accepts and establishes as one of the foundations of natural law. For it could not be doubted that the supreme ruler of the universe, most wise and most powerful, has resolved to reward the good and punish the wicked, and that He will execute His plan in the life to come, since in this life as we manifestly observe He leaves most crimes unpunished and most [391] good actions unrewarded. Thus here and now to neglect consideration of the next life, inseparably linked as it is to divine providence, and to rest content with a lower degree of natural law valid even for an atheist [inferiore quodam juris nat. gradu, qui etiam apud atheum valere possit], (I have treated this question elsewhere),[11] *would be to deprive this legal science of its finest part and, at the same time, to destroy many of this life's duties. Indeed, why would one expose oneself to loss of property, of honor or even of life itself on behalf of those who are dear to us, or on behalf of country, or state, or to uphold law and justice, when one could be at ease, and live among honors and wealth, at the expense of others' prosperity [eversis aliorum rebus]? For would it not be the height of folly to prefer real and solid goods to the simple desire to immortalize one's*

11. So our anonymous writer has published something else, as it appears also from what he says at the end of his letter. But I am no clairvoyant. This is what I said, speaking as if I did not know the author of this piece. Now I can indicate the work to which he refers. It is the Preface to the *Codex Juris Gentium Diplomaticus*, pp. 7, 8. See also his *Jugement sur les Oeuvres de Mylord Shaftsbury*, published after his death, by Mr Des Maizeaux, in the *Recueil de diverses Pièces sur la Philosophie, la Religion Naturelle, etc.*, Vol. II, p. 282.

name after death, that is, to be spoken of in a time from which one no longer draws any advantage? The science of natural law, explained according to Christian principles (as Praschius has done),[12] *or even according to the principles of the true philosophers, is too sublime and too perfect to measure everything against the advantages of this present life. What is more, unless one is born with such a disposition or brought up in such a way that one takes great pleasure in virtue and finds great distress in vice, [392] which is not everyone's good fortune, nothing will be able to prevent one from acting most criminally when, by crime, one can acquire great wealth with impunity. Should "one hope to go undiscovered, one will profane the most sacred things."*[13] *But no one will escape divine retribution, which extends beyond this life to the life to come. And this is a sound reason to make men understand that it is in their interest to practice in full the obligations that the law imposes on them.*[14]

I had already observed in the first edition of my translations both of the major work, *De Jure Naturae et Gentium* [Book II, chap. iii, §.21, note 6 of 1st Edit., note 7 of 2nd and 3rd Edit.] and of its abridgment *De Officio Hominis et Civis* [note 1, §.6 of Preface], that all consideration of the life to come must not be excluded from natural law. In order to show this, I adopted the same argument that Anonymous uses, following others. Our author has never denied the principle on which this argument rests: far from it, he recognizes it himself, in that part of his major work where, concerning the choice of advantageous things [*De Jure Naturae et Gentium* Book I. chap. iii. §.7],[15] he cites a passage from Arnobius [In my translation these passages were transposed to note 5] and refers to Pascal's fine chapter on the issue.

I do not examine here whether the proofs that human reason alone

---

12. In a dissertation of Jo. Ludovici Praschii, entitled *Designatio Juris Naturalis secundum disciplinam Christianorum,* which appeared in 1689.

13. *Sit spes fallendi, miscebis sacra profanis.* It is a line of Horace, Book I, Epist. xvi, 54.

14. *Eaque firma ratio est, quâ homines omnem Juris obligationem in factum traduci debere intelligant, si sibi ipsis consulere velint.*

15. See my comment in this volume, Book I, chap. I, §.11, note 3.

offers of the immortality of the soul, and of the rewards and punishments of another [393] life, have demonstrative force, as Anonymous
submits. Nor do I examine whether the contrary might not appear with
the instance of the wisest heathens, who could only speak of this important truth without full knowledge, even though they had discovered
the very reason which is asserted here, and which is indeed the strongest
of all.[16] It suffices for me to observe that Anonymous proceeds to argue
in such a manner as to reveal that he lacks accurate and consistent ideas
as to the nature and force particular to duty. Whereas our author's slight
omission can be excused on the grounds that he was led to it by his
noble conception of the impressions surely made by the mere sight of
law on the heart of any reasonable person. Anonymous evidently confuses duty and the effects or the motivations that observing obligation
produce; that is, he confuses the immanent force of duty and the impact that it has on men's spirit, given the make-up of the majority. Absent consideration of reward and punishment in the life to come, so he
claims, one would have no reason not only to "expose oneself to loss of
property, honor or even life itself on behalf of those who are dear to us,
or on behalf of country, or state, or to uphold law and justice," but one
could even "be at one's ease, and live among honors and riches, at the
expense of others' prosperity," or by doing whatever harm one can to
others so as to destroy their business and bring them to despair. For that
is what [394] is entailed by the expression in the original, *eversis aliorum
rebus,* far stronger than that of my translation. Without the prospect of
a happy immortality after this life, so he supposes, one's practical conduct could measure up to one's duty only through desire for an illusory
immortality. According to our author's principles, one is obliged not
only not to harm others, in order to procure some benefit to oneself,
but also sometimes to sacrifice one's property, one's honors and even
one's life, regardless of the prospect of rewards and punishments in the

16. See a passage from Plato that I cited in my Preface to *Droit de la Nature et des
Gens,* §.21, p. lxxxvi of the second edition.

life to come,[17] and for the simple reason that these are duties imposed on us by the wise author of natural law, by the sovereign leader of the universe. Which of these two moral codes, I beg you, is the purer, the more noble? Which most conforms to the ideas of the heathen wise, who distinguished so well between the virtuous and the useful? But how can we reconcile Anonymous's argument with his statement that there is a "degree of natural law valid even for an atheist"? Or with what he further maintains below, in section 15, namely that "there would still be a natural obligation even were one to allow that there is no God"? If ever there was a palpable contradiction, this is it. For, once you postulate that there can be some obligation, properly so-called, some indispensable necessity to act or not to act in a certain manner, independently not only of the life to come but also of the existence of God, then all duties—excepting those directly concerning God Himself—are in place, since, as Anonymous recognizes (section 13), they all have a real foundation "in the very nature of things." See my comment on section 15.

So in seeking to pick our author up on a simple omission, Anonymous has put himself into difficult straits. There are clearly two different questions: *Why is one obliged to do or not to do certain things?* And: *What is the motive best able to drive men to practice what they recognize as their duty?* As to the latter question, we easily recognize that the motive of *utility*—above all, the punishments and rewards of the life to come—is what determines the greatest number of people. From this we see how greatly men needed a clear and certain revelation of the state of the life to come. A revelation, nonetheless, whose goal is not to bring men to virtue or to turn them from vice solely on consideration of their interest, but rather to lead them in this way little by little to fulfil their duty for a nobler motive: to find in the practice of virtue this profound pleasure, of which Anonymous speaks, the pleasure that is produced not by the prospect of rewards or less still by the

---

17. See what our author says in *Droit de la Nature et des Gens*, Book II, chap. iii, §.19, where he maintains that *it has not yet been proven, that every good action must necessarily be followed by some external reward.*

prospect of punishments in the life to come, but by long and deep reflection on the sheer beauty of virtue. For there are wicked persons who are struck by the fear of ills and the hope of good to come, but who for all that remain insensible to the pleasure of the practice of virtue, or to the horror of vice. They desire [396] eternal happiness, yet remain far from loving that which alone can lead them there, and which for its own sake merits our love.

Considering utility alone, we would still have good reason to commit ourselves to virtue, and to flee from vice, regardless of the rewards and punishments in the life to come. Of itself, virtue is certainly more fitted than vice to render us happy in this world. And in the normal course of things, there is far more evidence that we gain a solid advantage from living a good life, rather than letting ourselves lapse into disorder, as our author judiciously remarked in his major work [Book II, chap. iii, §.21], where I included a very fine passage from Isocrates on this topic [note 4]. The question has been discussed very fully by various authors.

VII. Nor, therefore, must we admit what the author insinuates, namely that the internal actions of the soul, which lack external manifestation, lie beyond the jurisdiction of the science of natural law. Having cut short its end, he now evidently seeks to restrict its object too narrowly. For after stating, at the end of paragraph 8, that "the maxims of natural law apply only to the human tribunal, which does not reach beyond the limits of this life," he then adds at the start of the following paragraph that "the human tribunal deals only with man's external actions, and that it cannot penetrate internal actions save insofar as they manifest themselves in some effect or some external sign." Hence he does not trouble himself with them. Whatever lies beyond, the author relates to "moral theology, the principle of which is [397] revelation" (§.4) [§.1 of the translation], and which is the discipline that "forms the Christian man" (§.8) [§.6]. Here he adds that "regarding certain things the maxims of natural law are wrongly applied to the divine tribunal, the rules of which lie principally within the jurisdiction of theology." This is why, he says in the following paragraph, "for moral theology it is not sufficient to regulate man's conduct to conform to external pro-

priety, " (as if this was the whole concern of those who teach moral philosophy or natural law!), "but it seeks above all else to regulate the heart, such
that the heart's every movement conforms exactly to the will of God. Moral
theology condemns in particular those actions which on the outside appear
correct and beautiful but which flow from a bad principle or an impure
conscience." It therefore pertains to theologians alone, according to our
author, to treat this whole matter. Yet we see that not only Christian
philosophers, but also the ancient pagans, made this the subject of their
precepts, such that even pagan philosophy is in this regard more wise, more
severe and more sublime than the philosophy of our author. I am astonished
that despite the great enlightenment of our century this celebrated man
could have uttered things as absurd as they are paradoxical [non minus
paraloga, quam paradoxa].*

But softly, please. *Parcius ista viris tamen objicienda memento,* etc.
When it is a question of a person whose merit is undeniable, we
should—it seems to me—before accusing him of advancing absurdities
be sure to have examined thoroughly whether there is not a way to
give a positive turn to his thoughts. I am myself astonished that [398]
Anonymous, in transcribing so many passages, failed to take note of
something essential which lies between two of those he quotes and
which would have forced him to step back from his astonishment and
to moderate his zeal. In paragraph 9 (paragraph 7 in my translation)
it is explicitly stated that "natural law is concerned *in large measure* to
form men's external actions."[18] What is more, in one of the passages
that Anonymous actually cites, does not our author say that the rules
of the divine tribunal, whose jurisdiction is over internal actions, "are
principally the concern of moral theology"?[19] According to our author,
then, there is some other science, a natural science, which does not

18. *Jus quoque Naturale MAGNAM PARTEM circa formandas hominis actiones ex-
teriores versetur.* In his 1728 edition of *De Offic. Homin. & Civ.,* Mr Otto here declared himself opposed to Mr Leibniz and his defender.

19. See what the author says in his *Specimen controversiarum &c,* chap. iv, §.19, to
which I refer below regarding section XI.

neglect these rules governing internal actions. Note should also have been taken of what our author says in his major work (Book I, chap. viii, §.2) and in this present abridgment (chap. ii, §§.11 and 12). It should have been recalled that he treats the issue of conscience and its different kinds (Book I, chap. i, §.5 et seq.). But this only serves further to show decisively just how unfounded is Anonymous's censure. Only the author of an action can know and judge for sure whether that action is morally good internally, as well as externally. On this no other person ever has anything but signs to go on, and these are notoriously equivocal. Now one learns natural law in order to judge the actions of others, as well as one's own. In consequence, the application of the rules of natural law [399] most often has to be limited to the external act.

As is clear from the very passages that Anonymous cites, our author's wish is to speak of this application to actions whose principle we can penetrate only through some effect or some external sign. His wish is to speak of those things that the human tribunal can know. Moreover, is it not true that the greatest number of natural laws turn on what men have a right to require one of another? Now this right does not extend beyond the external act. Once one has done in this regard all that one was required to do, whether the internal act was as vicious as you please, nobody can ask any more of us, nor, finally, must they do so, even though the internal principle of the action by which one has acquitted oneself of what was required had something about it that the divine tribunal and our own conscience would condemn. The author does not exclude from the ambit of natural law that judgment which each can and must exercise over their own actions, to assure oneself that they are good and innocent in all respects. Rather, he simply generalizes this judgment as the application of the rules of natural law to particular cases, in consideration of the morality of this or that action on some person's part.

VIII. The Platonists, the Stoics and even the poets taught that the gods must be imitated, that one must offer to them "a heart shot through with sentiments of justice and [400] honesty."[20] *Nor was it to a philosopher, but to a jurisconsult of the civil laws that Cicero attributes the idea of resting content with externalities, when he says that the laws concern themselves only with what is palpable, whereas philosophers consider rather what only the light of an acute reason can uncover. Will Christians now allow the philosophy that was so holy and noble in the hands of the pagans to degenerate to such an extent? Certain ancient authors complained that Aristotle was too lax [de laxitate Aristotelis]: but he lifted himself far higher than our author, and the schools correctly followed him in this. For Aristotle's philosophy embraces all virtues in the idea of universal justice. We are surely obliged, not only for our own sake but also on behalf of society, and above all with regard to the society we have with God through the natural law written in our hearts, to fill our spirits with true knowledge, and to direct our wills always toward that which is right and good.*

These reflections are all as ill-directed as they are commonplace, and they remain inseparable from an invective based entirely on the false assumption of which I have just spoken. Has Anonymous forgotten that, in the Chapter "On duty to oneself," our author seeks above all to have us see that natural law [401] wants each of us to work at forming his mind and his heart by filling the former with true and useful knowledge, and by ruling the inclinations of the latter? The passage that we are offered from Cicero is not taken here in its proper sense.[21] For Cicero it is a question neither of purely internal acts nor of external actions considered as being or not being the effect of a good internal disposition, but simply of certain injustices or certain more sophisticated frauds unpunished by the civil law, despite being outwardly manifest, as well as other cruder ones. This is clear from all the prior and subsequent arguments and examples. Immediately before the formu-

---

20. *Compositum jus fasque animi, sanctosque recessus, / Mentis, et incoctum generoso pectus honesto, Haec cedo, ut admoveam templis, et farre litabo.* Persius, *Satirae* II, 73, et seq.

21. See the treatise *De Officiis: Sed aliter Leges, aliter Philosophi, tollunt astutias Leges, quatenus manu tenere possunt; Philosophi, quatenus rationi & intelligentia.* Book III, chap. xvii.

lation in question, the Roman orator had just spoken of those who do not reveal in good faith to a buyer the faults they know to exist in the thing they are selling.

IX. The author recognizes that oaths have great force in natural law; yet I do not see what place they can have in this science, if natural law does not concern that which is internal.

This remark appears to have been added subsequent to the composition of the letter as a whole, and is therefore badly placed, interrupting the flow of the argument, as anyone can see. Anonymous continues to assume, mistakenly, that according to our author consideration of acts internal to the soul in no way falls within the ambit of natural law. Yet, surely, do not oaths [402] essentially embrace an exterior as well as an internal act? The force of the exterior act, I admit, derives from the disposition of the one who swears the oath. But, aside from the fact that this disposition, by very virtue of being internal, remains hidden from other men who can only presume as to its nature, is one not obliged to keep an oath that has been sworn as to something neither illicit nor invalid, even though one did not intend to swear? And would it not be very bad form to swear to an illicit subject, even though one only mouthed the oath?

X. This is why those responsible for directing the education or instruction of others are obliged, by natural law, to give them the taste for sound precepts and to orient them so as to acquire a habit of virtue which, like a second nature, will guide their wills toward the good. This is the best method of effective teaching, for, as Aristotle rightly observed, manners are stronger than laws.[22] *Although difficult, it may happen that hope or fear make a sufficient impression to prevent evil thoughts leading to another's harm, but these motives alone will never lead people to doing good. Thus*

22. Our author himself cites a passage from this philosopher, to this effect. Other references have been added in the notes on *Droit de la Nature et des Gens,* Book VII, ch. ix, §.4.

an ill-disposed man will sin not least by failing to do what he should do.
So it is dangerous, or at best [403] unrealistic, for our author to imagine
a corrupt heart, the external actions of which are entirely innocent.[23]

This is called singing the same song, *eadem oberrare chorda.* One has
only to look at what our author says in this abridgment (Book II, chap.
iii, §.2 and chap. xi, §.4), not to mention his major work, where he
expands considerably on this topic. Then one will be amazed to find
so many wasted words in so slight a piece as is this letter by Anonymous.

XI. I admit that some scholars—and they deserve our admiration for this—
have rectified this harsh and reprehensible opinion [sententiam duriorem
& reprehensionibus obnoxiam &c.], although in other respects they follow
our author's doctrine. Thus they have attributed to moral philosophy or to
natural theology that which they exclude, as he does, from the sphere of
natural law, namely the consideration of internal actions. But it cannot
be denied that law and obligations, sins committed against God and good
deeds in His sight alone, by their nature involve internal actions.[24] *Where,*
I ask you, should we treat of these things, which are unquestionably elements
of law and natural justice, if not in the science of natural law? Unless one
wishes to imagine another universal jurisprudence that embraces the rules
of natural law both in relation to men and in relation to God, though this
is manifestly vain and redundant.

[404] There is nothing more arbitrary than the division of the sciences. Provided that everything belonging in those sciences which have
some common relationship finds a place in one or another of them,
and provided that in treating a particular science whose boundaries
have been specified nothing essential has been omitted from the scope
as prescribed, no one can ask more. Now here is our author's own

---

23. *Ut adeo etiam parum tuta aut facilis sit hypothesis, animi intus pravi, foris in-*
noxii.

24. *Sed quum in internis quoque jus & obligationem, peccataque in Deum, & rectas*
actiones, natura constitui, nemo negare possit &c.

response, one that he gave long ago. From this it will be clear that, in what Anonymous calls a "rectification" of Pufendorf's opinion, the latter's partisans have simply followed his ideas: "Whosoever has read my book *De Jure Naturae et Gentium* with a fair mind," he says in *Specimen controversarium* (chap. v, §.25), "and not with an intent to quibble or to defame me, will easily recognize that the principal task I set myself was to explain the mutual duties men have to one another and the law that exists among them. On this matter, it is clear, no more fitting principle could be found than sociability. And therefore, in this work, there is no chapter on natural religion, which belongs to the natural science that concerns divinity, a science that some attach to the first philosophy, others to natural theology, since it is the part of the natural sciences that concerns divinity. Later, however, when I had to offer for the young an abridgment of *De Jure Naturae et Gentium,* I borrowed from natural theology or, if you will, from first philosophy, a chapter on natural religion for inclusion in this short work." Given such a declaration, which was not made yesterday, our author should be well protected against the arrows of a less than temperate critique. [405]

XII. In the science of law, moreover, if the wish is to give a complete idea of human justice, this must be derived from divine justice, as from its source. The idea of the just, like that of the true and the good, pertains unquestionably to God, and more to Him than to men, since He is the measure of all that is just, true and good [tamquam mensuram ceterorum &c.]. Divine justice and human justice have common rules, which can doubtless be reduced to a system [communesque regulae utique in scientiam cadunt &c.]; and these rules must be taught in universal jurisprudence, the precepts of which also pertain to natural theology. Thus we could not approve those who wrongly restrict the scope of natural law, even though this error is not dangerous as long as one transfers to another area of philosophy consideration of internal probity, and does not treat the latter as belonging solely to divinely revealed knowledge.

Divine justice and human justice indeed have something in common, and never stand in opposition one to the other. But there is nonetheless so great a difference between them, in respect both of their origin and also of their reach, that one cannot say—to put it precisely— that divine justice is the source and measure of human justice. God is by His nature just; He can neither act, nor wish to act, other than justly. It is in Him a happy impossibility, and a glorious necessity, that comes purely from His infinite perfection. Men, by contrast, are far from being naturally just. Justice is a quality that they have to acquire, and this [406] obligation is imposed on them by some external principle, that is to say, by the will of God Himself, and not by His justice, as we shall see shortly. It is human justice that is recognized, rather than divine justice, as I have said, echoing our author, in *Droit de la Nature et des Gens* (Book II, chap. iii, §.5, note 5). Concerning the question of reach, the sheer excellence of God's nature entails that there are certain acts of human justice which absolutely could not relate to Him, a point that our author also makes in his polemical works at the places to which I refer in my note as cited. Anonymous, who should have read and refuted all this, will be obliged according to what he recognizes at the end of this paragraph at least to find our author not guilty of the charge he laid against him, namely of advancing a "dangerous error." The passage I have cited in relation to the previous paragraph makes it clear that our author in no way excluded the "consideration of internal probity" from the philosophical sciences.

XIII. So much for the end and the object of natural law. Let us now demonstrate that the author has failed to establish the efficient cause of this law. He looks for this, not in the very nature of things or in the maxims of right reason that conform to it and emanate from the divine understanding, but—this is surprising and would appear contradictory—in the will of a superior. He defines duty (in Book I, chapter i, §.1) as a "human action conforming exactly to the laws that impose the obligation." He then defines the law (Book I, chapter ii, §.2) as "a will of a superior by [407] which he imposes on those who depend on him the obligation to act in the manner that he prescribes to them." This being granted, no one will freely do what he must, or rather, there will be no duty when there is no superior to compel its exercise. Nor will there be any duty for those who have no superior. And since, according to the author, the idea of duty and the idea of acts prescribed by justice are coterminous, his natural jurisprudence being wholly contained within his system of duties, it follows that all law is the prescription of a superior. These are paradoxes proposed and sustained by Hobbes in particular, who seemed to destroy the possibility of any obligatory justice in the state of nature (as he terms it), that is, among those who have no superior. Yet is it not an act committed against justice when a sovereign behaves as a tyrant toward his subjects, robbing them, abusing them, making them suffer torment and even death, for no reason other than his passions or his whim, or when for no good reason he declares war on another power?

What Anonymous here terms, in scholastic style, the "efficient cause" of natural law is nothing other than the reason why one is obliged to conform to the maxims of the natural law. Our author recognizes (and we must not fail to say this) that these maxims, considered in themselves, are grounded in the very nature of things, such that God could prescribe nothing to the contrary without contradicting Himself. [408] (See *Droit de la Nature et des Gens,* Book I, chap. ii, §§.5 and 6, and what I have cited from his other works in chap I, §.4, note 4.) But, he maintains, it is not consideration of the nature of things that properly and directly imposes the necessity of acting in one particular manner rather than another. It is here that Anonymous believes he is criticizing our author most tellingly. However, if the reflections we shall offer on what he says above are carefully considered, I hope there will be agreement that he is perhaps nowhere more ill-founded than here.

First, let me observe that the whole paragraph is beside the point since, as Anonymous himself recognizes (section XV), according to our author all men, no matter what their state, have a superior in common, namely God. Why create monsters for oneself, just in order to fight them? Why draw an odious parallel with Hobbes's principles, which are so diametrically opposed to those of our author?

XIV. Similarly, persuaded by our author, certain scholars deny the possibility of any voluntary law of nations, on this ground among others, that peoples as such cannot establish a law on the basis of reciprocal pacts, there being no superior to validate the obligation. Too much is proved by such reasoning, since, were it valid, it would follow that men cannot establish a superior by their pacts (which in fact is something they can do, as even Hobbes allows).

Those who reject, correctly, the voluntary law of nations that Anonymous along with the [409] run of scholastic jurisconsults accepts, do not base their argument on the fact that nations, having no superior in common, cannot make a valid reciprocal pact. Rather, they say, as is the case, these pacts are not laws properly speaking, since they are made between equals, whereas every law is imposed by a superior. They maintain, moreover, (and no one has proved or will prove the contrary) that there is no general pact among all peoples with respect to purely voluntary things over which this supposed law of nations should have jurisdiction. The whole extent of obligation that there can possibly be with respect to the matters brought before it, and it is indeed truly voluntary (for some of the articles attributed to the law of nations are found to be based in natural law and thus are not contingent on the agreement of peoples) [see *Droit de la Nature et des Gens,* Book II, chap. iii, §.23], the whole extent of obligation, I say, that there can be with respect to truly voluntary things derives, to my mind, from the fact that custom having established these things little by little among the majority of peoples, without there being any general agreement between them, one is and can be assumed to want to conform to them, as long as in any such matter, one gives no clear sign that one does not wish to follow the custom, as anyone is free to do. This remark, whose application will be seen in my notes on Grotius, serves to dispel even the most specious claims of the partisans of a voluntary law of nations.

XV. It appears possible, in truth, to redress somewhat the dangerous consequences of this doctrine by considering God as the superior of all [410] men, and this our author does from time to time. On this basis, someone will say that the doctrine in question only appears bad, since it is self-correcting and provides its own remedy, there being no state in which men are independent of every superior, though in an abstract system one can hypothesize such a condition. All men are by nature under God's empire; thus they can, through their pacts, establish a master for themselves; and, likewise, by their reciprocal agreement peoples can establish a law common among themselves, there being a God who gives these pacts all necessary power. The whole truth is that God is by nature superior to all. Yet this notion, that all law derives from the will of a superior, remains shocking and no less fallacious, no matter what is done to moderate it. For without repeating here what Grotius judiciously observed,[25] namely that there would still be a natural obligation even were one to allow—as one cannot—that there is no God or that one momentarily denied His existence, since the concern of each for his survival and advantage [propria conservationis commoditatisque cura, &c.] would undeniably involve a considerable concern for others (as Hobbes half notes, and as becomes clear in the example of a group of bandits who, while sworn enemies of others, are obliged to observe among themselves [411] certain obligations; although, as I said above, a law derived from this alone would be far from perfect); to put all this aside, I insist, we need to recognize that God is praised because He is just, and thus there is justice in God, or rather a supreme justice, no matter that He recognizes no superior, and that by propensity of His excellent nature [sponte naturae excellentis] He acts always as He must, such that none can with reason object. And the rule of His actions, like the very nature of justice, depends not on a free decision of His will, but rather on the eternal truths which are the objects of the divine mind and which are established, so to speak, by His divine essence. As a result, the theologians are right who have criticized our author for having maintained the contrary, since he appears to have failed to recognize the harmful consequences of his doctrine. For justice will not be an essential attribute of God, if He created law and justice by an act of His own free will [arbitrio suo]. Justice follows certain rules of equality and proportion, rules which are founded in the immutable nature of things and in the ideas of the divine mind no less than are the principles of arithmetic and geometry. Thus one can no

---

25. *De Jure Belli ac Pacis*, Prolegom., §.11.

more argue that justice or goodness depend on the divine will than that truth depends on it likewise. This would be an astonishing paradox, one that escaped Descartes; as if the reason why a triangle has three sides, or why two contradictory propositions are incompatible, or, finally, why God Himself [412] exists, was that God had willed it so! A remarkable example, which shows that great men can make great errors. From this it would also follow that God can without injustice condemn the innocent, since, given this supposition, He could by His will render such a thing just. Those who have happened to advance such propositions have failed to distinguish between justice and independence. By virtue of His supreme power over all things, God is independent; for this reason He can be neither constrained nor punished, nor can He be required to account for His conduct; but, by virtue of His justice, He acts in such a way that every wise being can only approve His conduct, in such a way that—the highest point of perfection— He is Himself content.

Anonymous begins very weakly here, representing as the effect of a favorable judgment an apparent softening of view, whereby he insinuates that our author, out-of-step with himself, now foresaw the danger of certain consequences. One would think it was almost only by chance, and certainly not planned, that our author speaks of God as the supreme sovereign of all men [*quod etiam subinde fit ab Auctore &c.*]. Yet isn't this precisely a principle that provides the great foundation of his whole system?[26] It angers me to say this but, finally, nothing is truer, and it would be useless to hide what I am obliged to point out: Anonymous has undertaken to criticize our author [413] without sufficiently understanding his principles, and this explains why he does not really grasp the question as it now stands.

Our author does not claim that all we call law or justice derives from will, still less from the free will of a superior. He speaks of law and justice as these apply to dependent subjects; he seeks the rule of human

---

26. See chap. iii of this Abridgment, §§.10, 11.

actions. He has said again and again that God is supremely just;[27] that
He follows inviolably the rules of justice that conform to His infinite
perfections, such that He neither wills nor could will to act otherwise.
Likewise, because of His independence, no one has the right to require
Him to act in such and such a manner, nor to call Him to account for
His conduct. Regarding men, our author has also recognized that,
though they are subjects in the empire of the Creator, it is not God's
free will that makes law and justice; and that God could not, without
shattering His perfections and contradicting Himself, prescribe for men
rules other than the rules of justice, which are founded in their nature.
But, this withal, he maintains that the proper and direct reason why
men are obliged to follow the rules of justice, and which imposes on
them the moral necessity to conform to those rules, is the will of God
who, as their sovereign lord, has complete right to curb their natural
liberty, as He judges fit.

In this way we dispose of the "dangerous consequences" that Anonymous, over-eager to second the prejudices and passions of certain [414]
scholastic theologians who attacked our author during his lifetime,
wants to draw from an innocent opinion, concerning which we had
sufficiently rebuffed sinister interpretations. So the question reduces to
this: whether it is the will of God itself, or some other thing, that
constitutes the near and immediate ground of that indispensable necessity whereby men are to do that which God surely wants them to
do?

Anonymous is inconsistent in his principles: he says too much, or
he does not say enough. He grounds the obligation to observe natural
law in the "very nature of things, and in the maxims of right reason
that conform to it" (section XIII), maxims which consist in "certain
rules of equality and proportion" (section XV). Indeed, he posits that
"there would still be a natural obligation even were one to allow that
there is no God." However, his view requires that "a law derived from

---

27. See *Droit de la Nature et des Gens,* Book II, chap. i, §.3, and chap. iii, §§.5,
20; and in *Eris Scandica,* Apolog., §§.7, 8; *Specimen controver.,* chap. iv, §§.3 et seq.,
and chap. V, tot., etc.

this alone would be far from perfect" and limited to what "the concern of each for his survival and advantage" demands. Now these "rules of equality and proportion, these maxims of reason conforming to the nature of things," surely occur in all duties, no matter what? Anonymous makes and can make no exceptions. He must therefore recognize that, with the exception of those duties that directly concern God, all others will retain their full force, even were it granted that there was no divinity. For when all is said and done, the nature of things remains the same, and while the writer speaks of "the ideas of the divine mind," it is not in these ideas that we contemplate the nature of things and the relations deriving from them, just as it is not in a rarified metaphysics that we [415] must seek sound principles of natural law and morality. But here too, Anonymous (as he already did above, in section VI) patently confuses the honest with the useful, something which is also evident in the example he proposes of a "group of bandits." For is it a principle of honesty that sees these rogues divide up the booty in equal shares? Does anyone believe that, occasion permitting, they would conscientiously not make off with more, or that we should grant them this scruple, as if it was a duty they had fulfilled?

There is thus no middle point: either obligation to the rules of justice among men is absolutely independent of the divinity, and grounded solely in the very nature of things, like the "principles of arithmetic and geometry"; or it is no way grounded in the nature of things. Now, of itself, the nature of things could not impose an obligation upon us, properly speaking. That there is such and such a relation of equality or proportion, of propriety or impropriety, in the nature of things, of itself commits us only to recognizing that relation. Something more is required in order to constrain our liberty of action, in order to command us to govern our conduct in a certain manner. Nor can reason, considered in itself and independently of the Creator who granted it to us, absolutely compel us to follow these ideas, although endorsed by them, as founded in the nature of things. For:

1. The passions counter these abstract and speculative ideas with ideas that are sensuous and palpable. In many actions where there is some relation of impropriety, the passions reveal to us [416] a much

more vital relation, a sense of pleasure that comes with these actions at the point where we commit to them. If the intelligence of our mind diverts us from actions of this sort, the inclination of our heart draws us all the more strongly on. Why then would we follow the former rather than the latter, if there is no external principle, no superior being that compels us? In this supposition, is not the inclination of the heart as natural as the ideas of the mind? Reason, you will say, clearly shows us that by observing rules of propriety founded in the nature of things we shall be acting in a way more fitting to our interests than if we allow ourselves to be led by our passions. But, without speaking of what the passions could say to counter this advantage, it is not a question here of utility, it is a question of duty and obligation. I agree, as I have already indicated, that if we weigh the matter as we should, we shall convince ourselves that, everything considered, our interest requires that we follow what reason dictates. Yet is not each of us free to re-nounce our advantage, as long as nothing prevents us from doing so, as long as there is no other person with an interest in our doing nothing contrary to their interests, and who has a right to require that those interests be met? Thus in not conforming to the ideas of propriety, founded on the nature of things, one would merely be acting impru-dently, and imprudence is not here opposed to a duty, properly speak-ing, because we are still asking whether duty as such exists.

2. But what must be addressed above all, [417] and what is enough to destroy the thought I am fighting, is the fact that our reason, con-sidered aside from any dependence upon the Creator from whom we receive it, is finally nothing other than ourselves. Now no one can impose on himself an unavoidable necessity to act or not to act in such or such a manner. For if necessity is truly to apply, there must be absolutely no possibility of it being suspended at the wish of him who is subjected to it. Otherwise it reduces to nothing. If, then, he upon whom necessity is imposed is the same as he who imposes it, he will be able to avoid it each and every time he chooses; in other words, there will be no true obligation, just as when a debtor comes into the property and rights of his creditor, there is no longer a debt. In a word, as Seneca long ago put it, no one owes something to oneself, strictly

speaking. The verb "to owe" can only apply between two different persons: *Nemo sibi debet . . . hoc verbum* debere *non habet nisi inter duos locum* (*De Benefic.*, Book V, chap. viii).

I conclude, then, that even the maxims of reason impose no obligation, no matter how conformable they are to the nature of things, until this same reason has revealed to us the Author of the existence and the nature of all things. The question now is to see from where obligation therefore derives, whether from the will of God, or from some other thing that is in Him.

It seems to me that here there is little ground for hesitation. For from the moment that one has [418] a just idea of God, one cannot but recognize His right to set whatever limits He pleases to the faculties He has granted us. Nor could one prevent oneself thinking that He surely wishes men to follow the light of their reason, as that which is best in them, and which alone can lead them to the destiny of their nature. Moreover, in His will is found all that is required as the ground of obligation, since it is the will of the master of all men, a will always in harmony with the every perfection of the divine nature. Why then go in search of some principle other than this, which lies within reach of everyone, and which follows so naturally from the relation between Creator and creature?

Take whatever other attribute of the Divinity you please, detach it from His will, and you will not find a more solid foundation for obligation than in the very nature of things. If, to do the impossible, one could conceive in the manner of the Epicureans a God quite unconcerned with whether or not men acted in a manner that accorded with the nature of things and with their own nature, the vision of such a Divinity, even granted all its infinite perfections, would at the most constitute only an example. And the example alone cannot impose an absolute necessity to imitate it. Or again, if you do not suppose that God wishes men, and all intelligent creatures, to observe among themselves the rules of justice, what then becomes of justice? Towards whom will justice be exercised? What use will be made of it? Will it be holy and just, if it [419] is indifferent to Him whether or not men observe the rules of justice, or if He does not absolutely oblige them to do so?

To say that He obliges them, although they were already obliged before He willed them, would be to say that this will is here reduced to a sort of accessory which, at the most, serves only to strengthen the obligation. It would be to diminish the reach of His supreme authority, to reduce it to directing things indifferent in themselves. It would be to attribute to the will of God, in respect of the rules of justice, no greater force than that of a prince, a father, a master or any other superior here below, who wishes his subordinates to be good people. Finally, is there anything more basic in Holy Scripture than to express the practice of duty, of attachment to virtue, by "doing the will of God"? If sometimes God proposes His example to be followed, it is to show that He asks of men nothing that he does not do Himself, insofar as His supreme perfections require or allow it [Matt. V, 48; Luke VI, 36], and that He is not a cruel master [Matt. XXV, 24].

XVI. What we said before has great utility for the practice of true piety. For it is not enough that we submit to God as one would obey a tyrant; nor should we simply fear Him because of His greatness, but also love Him for His goodness. These are sound maxims of right reason, as well as precepts of Scripture. Universal jurisprudence and its sound principles lead to this same point, confirming the wisdom of sound theology and guiding us to true [420] virtue. It is not the case that those who act well, not from hope or fear of a superior but purely from the inclination of their own heart, fail to act justly. To the contrary, these are they who act most justly of all, since in a certain manner they imitate divine justice. For when one does good for the love of God or one's neighbor, one finds pleasure in the act itself (such being the nature of love); one needs no other stimulant, nor the command of a superior. Of such a person it is said that "the law is not made for the just" [I Timothy, I, 9]. To this extent it is contrary to reason to say that law alone, or constraint alone, constitutes justice. Yet it must be admitted that those who have not advanced to this point of perfection respond to the demands of duty only through hope or fear, since it is above all in the prospect of divine retribution that one finds a complete and ineluctable necessity, backed by the requisite force, for all men to observe the rules of justice and equity.[28]

28. *Non nisi spe metuque obligari, & in divina maxima vindictae exspectatione,*

These reflections, some of which miss the present point, in no way contradict our author's principles. Although one grounds the obligation (properly so-called) to practice the rules of justice in the will of God, who, as our sovereign lord, imposes this unavoidable necessity upon us, it in no way follows that one must obey God only [421] as one obeys a tyrant, or from a pure motive of fear. Frankly, Anonymous is too liberal in drawing odious consequences from those principles that have the misfortune to displease him. Whoever has a true idea of God knows that He is good, as well as great, and that His will necessarily conforms with His perfections; wise and holy, He can will nothing that is not just and which, moreover, is not for our good. It follows, then, that even when God wishes us to do things indifferent in themselves, one must obey Him as one obeys a good father, not as one obeys a tyrant. To conform to this wholly good and sacred will, on which we recognize that we depend, is to act according to duty; this is what imposes moral necessity on all men, regardless of any other consideration. Hope or fear are only motives to encourage us to practice duty, to overcome the resistance we may find within us, and to sustain us in the midst of strong temptations.

It does not advance matters to pose the question of which is acting more justly, whether it is the man who commits himself to his duty from motives of hope or fear, or the man who practices duty from the inclination of his heart. This happy inclination, to be worthy of praise, must surely have to be informed and, in this respect, produced by a precise idea both of duty itself and of God, in whom one can reasonably [422] distinguish the relation of Creator and master of humankind from His will that men observe the rules of justice, in keeping with their nature.

In order to say something substantial against our author's principles, it would require asking which of the two is the more just, whether it is the man who commits himself to virtue because he believes that the holy will of God imposes this obligation on him, or the man who,

---

quam nec morte effugere detur, necessitatem plenam, & in omnes valituram, servandi juris & aequi, posse inveniri.

without knowing or thinking that he depends on God, and that God wishes him to follow the maxims of virtue, would observe these as simple rules of propriety, founded in the nature of things, or, if you will, in the "eternal truths which are the objects of the divine mind"? It is for Anonymous to answer the question.

I shall comment *à propos* of what he says concerning the impulse to good conduct, that in God it is truly a great perfection not to be able to act otherwise than in keeping with His nature; when it comes to men, however, essentially imperfect as they are and subject to a certain law, it is good fortune rather than merit to have whether by birth or education the happy disposition that makes us commit ourselves easily to duty.[29] In this way, it is the man who, encountering great obstacles, whether in his temperament or in the bad habits he has been allowed to acquire since childhood, works to overcome them and in the end succeeds, is without contradiction more just and praiseworthy than another, for whom being a man of virtue has cost almost nothing.

What I have just said wholly cancels the advantage that Anonymous claims for his own doctrine, at the expense of our author's, in respect of the "practice of true piety." We, on the contrary, in arguing against him, can claim a very real advantage that lies manifestly with us. It is that we equally avoid the two vicious extremes to which men have been drawn on this question: one is the false thinking of the philosophers and theologians, who have maintained that justice depends on an entirely free divine will whereby God could, were He so to wish, render the unjust just; the other is the opinion of those who, conceiving justice to be independent of the will of God, and founding it purely in the nature of things, have also depicted virtue as independent of religion, and atheism as a doctrine that retains morality and natural law in all their force. Monsieur Bayle, as we know, in pleading for atheists, has made great efforts to show that "they can believe themselves obliged

---

29. *Itaque ego illum feliciorem dixerim, qui nihil negotii secum habuit: hunc quidem de se melius meruisse, qui malignitatem naturae suae vicit, & ad sapientam se non perduxit, sed extraxit.* Seneca, *Epistolae* LII. And see preceding.

to conform to the ideas of reason as a rule of the moral good, as distinct from the useful" (*Continuation des Pensées sur la Comète*, art. clii).

XVII. From what we have said, it will be clear how important it is for the young, and even for the state, to establish better principles of legal science than those proposed by the author. He is also wrong when he says (Book I, chapter ii, §.4) that "if a man recognizes no superior, no one has the right to impose on him the necessity to act in a certain [424] manner." As if the very nature of things and the concern for our own happiness and security did not require certain things of us! Reason too prescribes many things, in respect of which we have obligations, if we are to act in accordance with the highest principle of our nature and avoid evil,[30] or if we are not to deprive ourselves of some good. All these maxims of reason pertain to justice, given that they involve our relations with others, and others' interest in our observing these maxims.[31] I am aware that certain authors take the word "duty" [officium] in a broader sense to refer to any act of virtue, without excluding those acts which do not involve another person or in which the interests of others do not figure; and in this sense one may say that strength and temperance have a place in our duty, and that our duty extends, for example, to caring for our own health, since one is right to blame those who neglect it. Yet I do not reject our author's way of using the word "duty," restricting it to what the law requires [ad eaquae a jure desiderantur].

Having thwarted the attempt to draw false consequences from my author's principles, and having shown that these are, instead, the soundest of principles, I may—so it seems to me—regard the conclusion of Anonymous as null and void. On the contrary, I declare that, without detriment either to the state or to youth, [425] this abridgment, *Les Devoirs de l'Homme et du Citoien*, may be placed in hands of all who wish to study natural law. If it is not free from all shortcomings,

---

30. *Et multa nobis imperat ipsa ratio, ut naturae melioris ductum sequamur, ne nobis vel malum accersamus, etc.*

31. *Hoc rationis praeceptum omne quum simul alios spectat, quorum id refert, ad Justitiam pertinet.*

it nonetheless poses no dangers. Its principles are in general excellent, and it would be easy for me to show that one may correct that which is not wholly exact by changing a handful of lines here and there. Let us be fairer, and more reserved, when it comes to criticizing the works of others because of a few faults that we detect in them. Whoever undertakes to write for the public has an interest in this.

But I am weary with having to repeat that Anonymous still confuses propriety with obligation, and interest with duty. Let us see if the comment on the different usage of the Latin word *officium* has led to some great discovery, as we are promised in the following paragraph.

XVIII. But in justification of this usage, I have a reason that is unknown to our author, namely that in the whole society of men under the government of God [in generali societate sub rectore Deo &c.], every virtue, as we have already said more than once, is contained within the duties of universal justice. Thus it is not only external actions, but also all our sentiments [sed etiam omnes adfectus nostri &c.], that are directed by the infallible rule of the law. A sound philosophy of law considers not only peace between men, but also friendship with God, possession of which promises us [426] enduring happiness. We are not born for ourselves alone; for others have some claim on us, while God's claim on us is total. [Sed partem nostri alii sibi vindicant, Deus totum.]

What Anonymous proffers here as a thought original to himself, and consequently unknown to our author, is nothing but an idea of the ancient Stoic philosophers.[32] And our author was so far from not knowing this idea, that he speaks of it explicitly as an idea that he does not reject, but rather treats as *popular:* "If it was fitting," he says, "to employ popular ideas, one could say that this world is like a great state, of which God is the sovereign."[33] So it is with the doctrine of Anonymous,

32. *Duas Respublicas animo complectamur: alteram magnam, et vere publicam, quâ Dii atque Homines continentur; in quâ non ad hunc angulam respicimus, aut ad illum, sed terminos civitatis nostrae cum sole metimur: alteram, cui nos adscripsit conditio nascendi.* Seneca, *De otio Sapientis,* chap. xxxi.

33. *Si popularia ad rem quid facerent, dici quoque posset, hunc Mundum magnam esse civitatem, cujus supremus Rector Deus est. Specimen Controvers.* chap. iv, §.7.

as with those of many other moderns who, seeking to say something new, have done little more than change the language, with the result that they end up coming back essentially to our author's doctrine. Indeed, this "universal justice" in "the whole society of men," under the empire of God, what is it other than the laws that God prescribes to men as their master? Consequently, natural law draws all its force from the authority and the will of this supreme legislator. As for the regulation of our internal "sentiments" and the need to gain for oneself the "friendship with God," it suffices to refer back to what was said above, on sections VI–XI and XVI.

XIX. Perceptive though he was, the author [427] fell into a contradiction for which I do not see how he could easily be excused. For he bases all legal obligation on the will of a superior, as appears from the passages I have cited. Yet, shortly afterwards, he then says that a superior must have not only power sufficient to oblige us to obey him, but also just cause for claiming a certain power over us (Book I, chapter ii, part 5). Therefore the justice of the cause precedes the establishment of the superior. If to discover the source of the law a superior must be identified, and if, on the other hand, the authority of the superior must be founded in causes drawn from the law, then we have fallen into the most blatant circularity ever. For from where will one learn if the reasons are just, if there is as yet no superior from whom, it is supposed, the law can emanate? We could well be surprised that an acute mind could so manifestly contradict itself, if we did not know that it comes easily to those who love paradoxes to forget their own opinion when ordinary sense prevails. It is appropriate to record the author's exact words, so that no one will think we are imputing something to him: "He who imposes obligation, and who imprints this sentiment into a man's heart, is properly a superior, that is to say, a being who not only has sufficient power to inflict some ill on those who contravene, but who also has good reasons [428] for claiming to constrain, as he sees fit, the liberty of those who depend on him. When these two things are brought together in the person of someone, he no sooner makes his will known than in the mind of a reasonable creature there arises a feeling of fear, accompanied by a sense of respect. . . . Whoever cites no reason other than the power he holds in compelling me to do his will, may well get me in this way to prefer to obey him for a time, rather than expose myself to a greater harm that my resistance would incur. But when that fear is removed, nothing will prevent me from following my own wishes, rather than his. Conversely, if he has good reasons for requiring my compliance, but lacks the power necessary to make me suffer some ill should I refuse to obey him with good grace, I can then disregard his authority with impunity, unless some other, more powerful than him, is willing to support his authority and take revenge on my disregard." Now the reasons for which one may rightly require me to submit my will to theirs are "that he has afforded me some considerable benefit, that he is manifestly well-disposed toward me and better able to serve my interests than I can myself, and that he presently wishes to take responsibility for my conduct; and finally, that I have willingly submitted to his direction." These are the author's words. But if we examine this well, we easily see both that he is not consistent with himself, and that he fails to resolve the difficulty. If force without reasons does not suffice, nor reasons without force, why is that—I ask you—when force ceases, and [429] reasons alone remain, I do not regain the liberty and the rights I was said to have before, when there were reasons but as yet no force? For according to the author, "when that fear is removed, nothing will prevent me from following my own wishes, rather than his." This would apply even if reasons existed. Or if reasons alone had sufficient power to compel obedience, why did they not have it before fear was provoked? What virtue does fear add to reasons, other than the effect of fear itself, if in the absence of reasons, fear cannot claim to impose obedience of its own accord?[34] *Or can such a passion, though short lived, impress a permanent trace on our unwilling spirit? Suppose that a man, owing obedience to another solely by virtue of reasons that this other has to require obedience from him, ends by being constrained by the power that the other possesses, yet he remains committed to the resolution to obey the other only insofar as he is constrained to do so. I do not see why, because he was once so*

---

34. *Et quam, quaeso, vim rationibus ultra se ipsum metus dabit, quam sine rationibus non praestat sibi?*

constrained, he should remain perpetually in submission to the other. Suppose a sick Christian is taken prisoner by a Turkish doctor whose remedies the invalid had long known to be effective. With the remedies now imposed coercively, would the prisoner, if he has [430] a chance to escape, be obliged to follow the regime more faithfully than before he was made prisoner? We have to say one of two things: either reasons establish obligation prior to force, or they no longer impose obligation once force is removed.

The vicious circle imputed to our author disappears, I have no doubt, in the sight of those who have read what I said above regarding section XV. Every superior, below God, bears an authority founded on reasons, the justice of which derives from some law of nature, being related to the rules of that justice whose obligation truly emanates from the will of a superior, or from the will of the king of kings and the lord of lords. But this supreme being's right of command is founded in reasons whose justice is immanent, such that they do not need to draw their force from elsewhere. Before knowing God, or when taking no account of His existence, we perceive nothing so great as to merit the homage of our submission of our will, nothing so just as to be a rule that we believe we cannot dispense with. Our liberty of action, that noble faculty at the root of our nature, cannot find in the nature of things anything with sufficient force to constrain that liberty: the relations of propriety, order, beauty, honesty, relations to which justice reduces, remain so many speculative notions until we understand that He who is the author of the nature of things and of the reason that reveals them to us, approvingly, wants [431] us to conform our external and internal acts to these relations. At this point duty begins: the will of the supremely perfect being is the rule of our will, and, beyond doubt, He who made us in all that we are can require that we do not do all that we might wish to do. Once we have recognized in His will the ground of obligation, we then find in His goodness and His Strength the greatest practical motives to encourage us and to enable us to fulfill our duty. I leave it to the reader to judge whether this doctrine contains anything that is not dependable and consistent.

As to what our author says concerning force linked to reasons, note should have been taken of the words "with impunity" that appear in the passages cited, because this is the key to his thinking. If the superior, he writes, "has good reasons for requiring my compliance, but lacks the force necessary to make me suffer some ill should I refuse to obey him with good grace, I can then with impunity disregard his authority, unless, etc." He does not say: "I can then with reason disregard his authority." He does not claim that duty ceases at this point, and that "just reasons" here lose their force; he speaks of the impression that these reasons could then have on the disposition that characterizes most men. This is enough to discredit all the arguments that Anonymous advances on this matter.

I nonetheless admit that our author's thinking is not sufficiently clear at this point, since he should have drawn a sharper distinction between that which correctly gives the superior the *right* to command and, on the other hand, that which enables him to *command effectively*. I indicated this in a short note, [432] the first note on the paragraph in question. I am not one to be dazzled by authority, or to find justifications for someone at any price; as will be clear from the longer note that follows in the same place, I picked out other shortcomings that Anonymous either did not notice or for which he excused our author. But all these little faults do not mean he has not shown the right way or that his doctrine, overall, is not well founded. Though I may, it seems, have developed some points a little better than did our author and rectified some details, I am concerned not to claim the glory that is due to him, and not to attribute to him my own thoughts, for which I remain in his debt.

I will offer just one further remark, with respect to the example that Anonymous proposes of the Christian invalid who falls under the power of a Turkish doctor. Just as it is not as an invalid that this prisoner is a prisoner, so it is not as a doctor that the doctor has command over the other's body. The relations are different. Thus I do not see what is the point of comparing the remedies of this doctor, as doctor (or, rather, the content of these remedies, for one can scarcely suppose, as we would have to, that he composed these remedies before the invalid was taken prisoner, but only that the invalid knew beforehand the utility of the things prescribed), what is the point—I ask—of comparing these remedies as to whether they were made before or after the invalid's captivity? Both before and after, in prescribing [433] things beneficial for the sick man's health, the doctor always acts as a doctor, not as a master. Or if he wishes to use force to oblige the invalid to take the remedy, he no longer acts as doctor. But whether the doctor orders the remedy as doctor or as master, the obligation to follow the remedy comes from elsewhere, or from that natural law whereby each works to conserve the life that God has granted, and consequently adopts to this end all legitimate means, no matter who brought them to his knowledge. What Anonymous has to say about the "chance to escape," like the example as a whole, is irrelevant. So let us come to the conclusion.

XX. Enough has been said to show that the author lacks secure principles on which to found the true reasons of law, because he preferred to contrive, as he saw fit, principles that are unsustainable [quoniam principia pro arbitrio ipse effinxit, quae sibi sufficere non possunt]. For the rest, I have treated elsewhere both the foundations common to every sort of law, without neglecting the law which derives from equity [etiam quod ex aequo & bono tantum descendit], and the proper foundations of strict law, which is also the law that establishes a superior. To summarize in brief all that I have said, this is what must be generally thought: the end of natural law is the good of those who observe it; the object of this law is everything that others would wish us to do and which is within our power; and the efficient cause is the light of eternal reason that God has kindled in our spirit.[35] In my opinion, these [434] principles, so clear and simple, seemed too obvious to certain subtle minds who, because of this, have turned the principles into paradoxes, the novelty of which flattered them,[36] and prevented them from seeing either the imperfection of the paradoxes or the fruitfulness of the principles. And so, Monsieur, this is what I believed I should write to you,

---

35. *Finem Juris Naturalis esse bonum servantium: Objectum, quidquid aliorum interest & in nostra est potestate: Causam denique efficientem in nobis esse Rationis aeterna lumen divinitus in mentibus accensum.*

36. *Viris quibusdam acutis nimis obvia visa esse, atque inde paradoxotera quaedam excogitata, quae novitatis specie blandirentur &c.*

to prove that the work of Mr Pufendorf, though not to be despised, none-theless requires many corrections as to its principles. For the present, I do not have time to go into particulars.

The reader will draw for me the opposite conclusion, one that follows from what I have said. Suffice it for me to add a word on the principles that Anonymous wishes to substitute for those of our author.

For my part, I admit that I find only great vagueness here. What Anonymous proffers as the "efficient cause" of natural law and with which we should begin is the general principle of all the natural sciences. For is there any of the true natural sciences that does not emanate from this "light of eternal reason that God has kindled in our spirit"? The object (or, to speak more precisely, the matter of natural law, for the object is more correctly those who must observe this law), the object as Anonymous establishes it, given his preference for remaining at the level of generality, is reduced to the principle of sociability; for I cannot think that Anonymous, in the words *quidquid aliorum interest,* seeks [435] to include God himself, and thus to imply, or give us reason to believe, that it is the concern of God that we should pay Him our homage, or that He who is sufficient to Himself has need of His creatures and can find some utility in what they do. Finally, the end of natural law—which Anonymous would have lie in "the good of those who observe it"—offers us nothing that is not common to the practical sciences, all of which propose a certain good, a certain advantage. It remains to be seen which good is particular to natural law. Are these really the "rich and illuminating definitions" for which we have been waiting?

At Lausanne, this 1st of October, 1716.

Discourse on What Is Permitted by the Laws

*In which it is shown that what is permitted by the
laws is not always just and moral*

Magnificent and most honored Lord Bailiff, most honored Lords of the
Council of this City, learned and respected members of the Academy,
my most honored colleagues, listeners of no matter what rank, sex and
age.

The subject I have chosen will be for many a great paradox, both in
itself and coming from me. It is usual to set the probity and the duties
of a good citizen squarely within the frame of what the [438] laws of the
land require.[1] It is an equally common assumption to imagine that
knowledge and observation of the laws must constitute the entire scope,
indeed the *non plus ultra,* of the studies of a jurisconsult, a man of law,
an advocate and, in general, all who are involved in work that has some
relation to the laws. But the great masters of the art, the wise inventors
of the most famous and the most widely received laws, in other words
the jurisconsults of Ancient Rome, were of a different mind. They professed a substantial philosophy that embraced the whole extent of justice and equity; they proposed to turn men into good persons, not only
through fear of punishment but also through love of virtue, which car-

---

1. *Vir bonus est quis? Qui consulta Patrum, qui Leges Juraque servat Sed videt hunc
omnis domus & vicinia tota Introrsus turpem, speciosum pelle decora.* Horace, Book I,
Epist. xvi, line 40 et seq.

ries its own reward;[2] they drew a careful distinction between the rules of law, that determine the findings of the judge (see Monsieur Noodt, *Julius Paulus,* chap. x), and the precepts of right, that determine the conduct of a good man. As their maxim, they proposed: "Not everything that the laws permit is just and moral."[3]

It is this same maxim that I want to set down and develop. If, on an occasion such as this, one can discuss matters more appealing to those whose only wish is for amusement, there is [439] scarcely any matter that could be more useful for everyone. After all, why should discourses of this sort not be designed in such a way that each person can take from them something amusing and something that can be put to profitable use? So let us try to convince those who either do not know, or who do not pay adequate heed to the fact, that, setting aside even the imperatives of Christianity, for something to be judged innocent, it is not enough that it is permitted or authorized by the laws. There are two different ideas here, each of which opens up a vast field for our considerations: the idea of a tacit permission, and the idea of an explicit entitlement. Sometimes the laws pass in silence over certain bad actions that they consequently permit; and sometimes the laws positively authorize performance of such actions. Today, we shall limit ourselves to the first of these two headings.

The question reduces to knowing whether the civil laws are the sole rule of citizens' conduct. For if they are not, if there is another rule, prior and higher, it is clear that something is in no way rendered innocent by the mere fact that the laws of the land do not forbid it, either directly or indirectly, either expressly or by implication.

Now, as to there being another rule, prior to and thus the very measure of all civil laws, [440] this is what the wisest and most enlightened

---

2. *Jus est ars boni & aequi. Cujus merito quis nos Sacerdotes adpollet. Justitiam namque colimus, & boni & aequi notitiam profitemur: aequum ab iniquo separantes, licitum ab illicito discernentes: bonos non solum metu poenarum, verum etiam praemiorum quoque exhortatione efficere cupientes: veram, nisi fallor, Philosophiam, non simulatam adsectantes.* Digest Book I, title I, *De Justitia & Jure,* Leg. I, §.i.

3. *Non omne, quod licet, honestum est, Digest,* Book L, title 17, *De diversis Regulis Juris,* Leg. CXLIV, princ.

persons among the civilized peoples have always agreed.[4] There have always been ideas—more or less distinct, more or less far-reaching, more or less accurate—of a law founded in men's very nature, taught by reason, and fitting the true interests both of human society in general and of each state in particular, a perpetual and irrevocable law that is the same in Rome, in Athens, in every country and in every century, a law from which no one can have dispensation, a law that no authority has the right to abolish or amend, in whole or in part.[5]

Therefore all legislators have claimed to establish nothing that is con-

4. Cicero made the point well: *Constituendi vero Juris ab illa summa Lege capiamus exordium, quae saeculis omnibus ante nata est, quàm scripta Lex ulla, aut quàm omnino Civitas constituta.* [In determining the truth of justice, let us start with that supreme law that was born centuries before any law was written, or before any state was established.] *De Legibus,* Book I, chap. vi. *Nec, quia nusquam erat scriptum, ut contra omnes hostium copias in ponte unus adsisteret, a tergoque pontem interscindi juberet, idcirco minus Coclitem illum rem gessisse tantam, fortitudinis lege atque imperio, putabimus: nec si, regnante Tarquinio, nulla erat Romae scripta Lex de Stupris, idcirco non contra illam Legem sempiternam Sextus Tarquinius vim Lucretiae, Tricipitini Filiae adtulit: erat enim Ratio, profecta a rerum natura, & ad rectè faciendum impellens, & a delicto avocans: qua non tum denique incipit Lex esse, quum scripta est, sed tum, quum orta est.* [That nowhere was it written that one man should stand at the bridge against all the forces of the enemy and command that the bridge should be torn down behind him, does not mean we should not believe that Horatio did this great deed according to the law and the command of courage. Nor that, because there was in the reign of Tarquinius no Roman written law of rape, the violence used by Sextus Tarquinius against Lucretia, Tricipitinius' daughter, was not against the eternal law. In fact reason existed, derived from true nature, directing people towards doing good and calling them away from crime, and did not become a law only when set in writing, but when it first originated.] *Idem, ibid.* Book II, chap. iv.

5. This is the description that Cicero offers, in a passage of the *Republic* that one of the Church Fathers has conserved for us: *Est quidem vera Lex, recta Ratio, natura congruens, diffusa in omnes, constans, sempiterna, quae vocet ad officium jubendo, vetando a fraude deterreat: quae tamen neque Probos frustra jubet, aut vetat, nec Improbos jubendo, aut vetando, movet. Huic Legi nec obrogari fas est, neque derogari ex hac aliquid licet, neque tota abrogare potest. Nec vero, aut per Senatum, aut per Populum, solvi hac Lege possumus. Neque est quaerendus explanator aut interpres ejus alius: nec erit alia Lex Romae, alia Athenis, alia nunc, alia posthac, sed & omnes gentes & omni tempore una Lex & sempiterna, & immortalis, continebit: unusque erit communi quasi Magister & Imperator omnium Deus ille, Legis hujus inventor, disceptator, lator, &c.* Lactantius, Book VI, chap. viii.

trary to this law.[6] Never has a sovereign, no matter how unreasonable, dared to attribute openly to himself the power to make laws purely according to his whim, with no regard to the natural principles of just and unjust, at least to the extent that these were known to peoples. Where they wished to establish laws themselves, peoples have often sought and followed the counsel of philosophers, these being men they believed most versed [441] in the study of the maxims of reason that are to be taken as the ground of every civil law. [See Mr Perizonius, on Elien., *Var. Hist.,* Book II, chap. 42, note 6.] And legislators, to enhance reception of laws they proposed or wished to establish, have sometimes pretended that they brought the laws down from heaven, a device they imagined all the more effective because they knew that, in some respects, God is regarded as the power of the rules of justice. [See what one has said on Pufendorf's *Droit de la Nature et des Gens,* Book II, chap. iv, §.3, note 4.]

Given all that, it was indeed difficult to avoid some unjust laws slipping in among the many that were just. From the records of Antiquity, it seems that the first laws had their origin largely in custom, which all too often is a very poor master.[7] What enters the laws in this way usually does so with little analysis or reflection. Ignorance, prejudice, passions, instances, authority, caprice have all clearly played a bigger part than reason. Custom is the opinion and the decision of a blind multitude, rather than of the wise.

---

6. On this ground, the same author I have just cited maintains that an unjust law is not a true law: *Ex quo intelligi par est, eos qui perniciosa & injusta Populis jussa descripserint, quum contra fecerint, quam polliciti professique sint, quidvis potius tulisse, quam Leges: ut perspicuum esse possit, in ipso nomine Legis interpretando inesse vim & sententiam Justi & Juris legendi.* [From which this is to be understood, that those who instituted laws harmful and unjust towards the people, by doing what was contrary to what they promised and proclaimed, brought forth anything but laws; thus it must be clear that the very term "law" carries the sense of choosing that which is just and right.] Cicero, *De Legibus,* Book II, chap. v. See what Plutarch said on the subject of Stratocles, in his *Life of Demetrius,* pp. 899, 900, Vol. 1, Ed. Wechil (Vol. V, p. 30, Edit Londin, 1729).

7. Hence in Hebrew and in Greek, the same words that signify "law" and "justice" can sometimes also stand for "custom." See Mr Le Clerc on I Samuel, chap. viii, verse 2.

When later it came to the making of explicit laws, published in standard written forms and thus rendered fixed and unalterable, the established usages [442] that had for so long had the force of law could not but be retained for the most part,[8] only taking on a new form that gave them weight and durability.[9] As for the other laws of which notice was taken, whether their establishment derived from the will of the people, the will of the state aristocracy, or the will of a single man, no matter what the precautions, the ideas of justice and equity were not always or adequately known for people to have been able to keep to them everywhere and in everything, nor were people sufficiently committed to these ideas to consult them and to follow them exactly. The philosophers themselves were not always such good advisers in this matter, as the following example shows. [See Elien., *Var. Hist.,* Book II, chap. 42, and Diogen. Laert., Book III, §.23.] The Arcadians begged Plato to come and teach them the laws that he judged necessary for a new city they wished to establish, at the persuasion of their allies, the Thebans. Flushed with this honor they did him, the famous Athenian prepared to set out. However, he quickly changed his mind when, through an interview with the Arcadian representatives, he realized that this people was in no mood to allow introduction of the community of wealth and women that the philosopher regarded as a rare secret of government, one that he established in his imaginary republic, in the absence of a real state that was willing to introduce it. If the great Aristotle had been called to a place on a similar commission, he would not have been concerned with proposing such community, [443] having rejected the idea in his writings. But he would nonetheless have advised something just as bad: I mean that no child born with some bodily defect would be raised or that pregnancies to women having already given birth to a cer-

---

8. See Plato, *De Legibus,* Book III, p. 681, Vol. II, Edit. H. Steph.

9. There is a short discourse of Dion. Chrysostom (*Orat.* LXXXI), in which this orator shows how men subject themselves more easily to customs than to laws, and how difficult it is to abolish the former and to establish the latter, given this prejudice.

tain number of children would be aborted. This is one of Aristotle's political maxims. [See *Politics,* Book VII, chap. xvi.]

Yet no matter how the laws were introduced and no matter what the intellectual capacities of those who played the major part in their establishment, it is a certainty that in various times and various places there were laws that were unjust. Among the Egyptians, a people once so celebrated for their wisdom, it fell to daughters alone to support their father and mother, if need arose, sons being spared this duty. [See Herodotus, Book II, chap. xxxv.] A law of the Persians imposed the identical fate, for certain capital crimes, on those who had committed the crime and on those who had no part in it: the innocent children and all the relations of a guilty father [see Herodotus, Book III, chaps. 118, 119. Amm. Marsellini, Book XXIII, chap. vi, p. 416, Ed. Vales. Gron.]. This was the practice too, not only among the Carthaginians [see Justinian, Book XXI, chap. iv, no. 8] and the Macedonians [see Q. Curt., Book VI, chap. xi, no. 20, and Book VIII, ch. vi, no. 28], but remains so still today, among some peoples of Asia [for example in Japan: see Varen, *Descript. Jap.,* chap. xviii; Ferdin. Pinto, chap. 55]. In Taprobane, the island in the great Indian ocean, there was a law against living beyond a certain age, at which point it was necessary—with a light heart—to lie upon a poisonous herb which brought a gentle death [Diod. Sic, Book II, chap. 57. Today this is the island of Ceylon]. At Sardinapolis, in Lydia, when a father became aged, his children themselves had to slaughter him [Elien., Book IV, chap. I]. The pitiless severity of an [444] Athenian legislator, who had decreed the death penalty for the least offence as for the most enormous crimes, caused it to be said, with good reason, that his laws were written in blood [Dracon. See Aristotle, *Politics,* Book II, chap. xii; Plutarch, *Solon,* p. 87; Aulus Gellius, Book XI, chap. xviii]. Established among the same people, ostracism threatened with exile the most honest persons of that state, for no reason other than their merit. The Spartans permitted theft as an exercise of skill [Aulus Gellius, as above; Xenophon, *De Rep. Laced.,* chap. ii, §.7 et seq. Ed. Oxon.; *De exped. Cyri.* Book IV, ch. vi, §.11, &c.], and adultery in order to produce healthy children [Xenophon, *De Rep. Laced.,* chap. I, §.7; Plutarch, in *Lycurg.,* p. 49, Vol. I, Ed. Wech]. Roman law, beyond the obvious inclusion of persons liable for punishment for various sorts of crimes [see Pufendorf, *Droit de la Nature et des Gens,* Book VIII, chap. iii, §.25], condemns to the maximum penalty every slave who happened to be under the same roof as their master at the time when the latter was assassinated, even though there exists no proof that they were accomplices to the murder [see Tacitus, *Annal.,* Book XIV, chap. 42; *Digest,* Book XXIX, title 5, *De Senatus-consulte Silanien.* &c.]. If, wherever it was able to reach, Christianity finally saw such laws abolished, this did not prevent other laws, no less bad, from being introduced in respect of other things. Look at the Theodosian and Justinian Codes and there you will find numerous laws, thoroughly inhumane and utterly unjust, against people whose only crime consisted in not sharing the opinion of the more powerful party in respect of speculative matters. Did paganism produce anything more tyrannical and more abominable than those tribunals of the Inquisition which, to the shame of religion and of humanity itself, handed over to the secular authorities innocent people condemned by rogues, whilst granting full indulgence [445] for every sort of crime before the judges of this order, with the authority of the laws of various countries? In light of this, it comes as no surprise that in a Christian state [Poland], where this religion is dominant, the political law-makers judged it appropriate to permit cut-price homicide: in Poland a gentleman who has killed a peasant pays just ten *écus.*

That, I think, is more than enough of what is needed to indicate the extent to which civil laws are liable directly to contradict the clearest laws of nature. And to indicate, in consequence, how very insecure it is to consider civil laws as infallible interpreters of the laws of nature, or as embodying all that is required to provide a model of conduct. In truth, one must not lightly tax with injustice the laws established in the country where one lives; indeed, it is the case that, where doubt arises, the presumption must be in their favor.[10] But meanwhile one must be

---

10. It is on this basis that one can apply to individuals what Quintilian said of judges, namely that they must not always dissect to an ultimate degree the justice of the laws, these having been established in order to specify the range of judgments on many things about which there was no agreement as to what was just: *Interim hoc*

alert, one must always be open as far as is possible to the ideas of justice and equity, ideas of which we each carry the seeds within us. For in the end, the instant that the most genuine laws of the most legitimate sovereign conflict in any way whatsoever with these immutable laws written in our heart, there is no question of seeking a balance, because it is absolutely necessary, cost what it may, to disobey the former in order not to do damage to the latter. Men's submission [446] to civil government does not extend, and never could extend even when they wished it, to the point where a human legislator is set higher than God, the author of nature, the creator and supreme legislator of men. As for things indifferent, it is entirely reasonable if, beyond the mountain or the river, something is considered just, while as a result of the contrary wills of the legislators of two different states, on this side it is considered unjust. But when it is a question of that which is clearly commanded or forbidden by the universal law of humankind, all the laws in the world can no more render just what is unjust than they can render healthy what is toxic for our bodies.[11] Thus in relation to such things, the conduct of the good man is everywhere the same. He never believes himself bound to obey manifestly unjust laws, and even less does he be-

---

dico, Judices, Perniciosissimam esse Civitati hanc Legum interpretationem. Nam si apud Judicium hoc semper quari de Legibus oportet, quid in his justum, quid aequum, quid conveniens sit Civitatis supervacuum fuit scribi omnino Leges. Et credo fuisse tempore aliquando, quae solam & nudam Justitia haberent aestimationem. Sed quoniam hac ingeniis in diversum trahebatur, nec umquam satis constitui poterat, quid oporteret; certa forma, ad quam viveremus, instituta est. Declam., CCLXIV.

11. *Quod si Populorum jussis, si Principum decretis, si sententiis Judicum, Jura constituerentur; Jus esset, latrocinari; jus, adulterare, jus testamenta falsa supponere; si haec suffragiis aut scitis multitudinis probarentur. Quod si tanta potestas est stultorum sententiis atque jussis, ut eorum suffragiis rerum natura vertatur: cur non sanciunt, ut quae mala perniciosaque sunt, habeantur pro bonis ac salutaribus? aut cur, quam jus ex iniuria Lex facere possit, bonum eadem non facere possit ex malo.* [If the laws were established by decree of the people, by the order of princes or by the decisions of judges, it would then be lawful to commit robbery, lawful to commit adultery, lawful to fake wills, if this was approved by the popular vote or plebiscite. Because if the views and judgments of fools have such power that they can turn nature upside down by their decree, why do they not confirm that those things which are bad and harmful are to be considered good and healthy for us? Or why, since law is able to make injustice just, can it not make good from evil?] Cicero, *De Legibus*, Book I, chap. xvi.

lieve himself authorized to exploit the most explicit permission in the world when it conflicts with moral good.

It is even clearer that the silence of the laws is not, of itself, a warrant for the innocence of actions concerning which the laws say nothing, actions that are not embraced within their valid scope. The examples here are infinite in number: travelers' reports, ancient and modern, are little more than a tissue of things, as vicious as they are excessive, that can be observed openly practiced [447] and adopted as custom among one people or another. Let us do no more than cite two or three instances capable of shaking the best secured mind from a false and erroneous idea of its duties. Were not the greatest impurities, the most infamous sins against nature, formerly so much to the liking of the Greeks and Romans that even the wise men gave in to them without any shame? [See Grotius on Romans I, 27.] Did not Roman women quite publicly abort their pregnancies, until a rescript of Severius and Antonius forbade them so to do, under pain of banishment for a given time [*Digest,* Book XLVII, title xi: *de extraord. crim.* Leg. IV; see Mr Noodt's *Julius Paulus,* chap. xi]? Throughout the Roman Empire, as well as among the majority of the Greeks, that is, among the most enlightened and civil of peoples, could not a father and mother expose or kill their own children with impunity—I am horrified at the thought—if they did not wish to raise them?[12] And was not this barbaric custom preserved—who would believe it?—under Constantine the Great and some of his successors? [See generally on this, Mr Noodt's *Julius Paulus,* where the whole matter is fully considered.] Among the Christians of past centuries, was not the rage for duels so extreme that the laws required to suppress it are counted as the most hard-won and celebrated achievement of certain states?

[448] Notwithstanding this, let us not condemn the civil laws more

---

12. This still happens in China, in Japan, and perhaps in various other countries of the Orient. There is even talk of a law, observed for more than a century in Matamba, according to which fathers and mothers were obliged, under pain of severe sanctions, to expose or kill the male children that were born to them. See the extract from an Italian voyage, in the *Bibliothèque Universelle,* Vol. IX, pp. 418 et seq. One can also consult the *Analecta Sacra* of J. H. Ursinus, Book I, chap. ix.

than they deserve. It is not always the fault of these laws if they do not forbid unjust or dishonest things. Doubtless they must rectify vice up to a certain point; but beyond that, it is absolutely outside their jurisdiction. Since they are, as it were, secondary laws, their sphere too is correspondingly restricted.[13] Once proven, this principle will serve not only to undermine in their entirety the foundations of the illusion which we are challenging, but also, if we pursue the consequences, to dissipate false ideas on other important points.

Let us therefore briefly consider the nature and the end of the civil laws. What does a human legislator as such propose? What must he propose? Is it to bring men to practice the full range of all their duties? Surely not. There are some duties of a kind that their very nature requires that they be left entirely free, like those of beneficence, which is no longer beneficence, from the moment when for some purposes coercion is involved. Should the human legislator act solely to prevent a man committing some irregular and morally bad action? In vain would a mortal man set his mind on this. It is simply beyond human nature. As long as there are men there will be vices; and these vices will always create internal agitations, some external effects of which [449] may well be stifled by the fear of some great ill, but not all of them could be, not even most of them. I will go further and maintain that the end of the civil laws, in themselves, is not to render truly virtuous those on whom the laws are imposed. [See the Discourse of Mr Noodt on *Liberté de Conscience,* p. 159 and following p. 194, p. 215 of the third edition, Vol. 1 of his *Recueil de Discours,* published in 1731.] For that, the laws would

---

13. *Sed nobis ita complectanda in hac disputatione tota causa universi Juris est, ac Legum, ut hoc, Civile quod dicimus, in parvum quemdam & angustum locum concludatur Natura.* [But it is for us in this argument to address the whole issue of universal law, such that what we call "civil law" is contained within a small and narrow part of nature.] Cicero, *De Legibus,* Book I, chap. v. Mr Davies, in his 1727 edition, omits the final word *Natura,* because, he says, it disturbs the meaning. But by his admission this word is in most manuscripts and it makes, in my opinion, perfect sense. Cicero means to say that the civil law constitutes a very limited part of this universal jurisprudence which, he then explains, is founded in nature itself, as he declares immediately afterwards. The word *Natura,* which opens the following sentence, has eclipsed *Natura* in the rare manuscripts in which this final word of the cited sentence is missing.

have to be able to regulate men's interior; but since they cannot reach this, they have no business in meddling with what happens there; this is the preserve of the infinite scrutineer of hearts. As for the external signs, it would be very difficult, not to say impossible, to isolate what is bad in an infinity of equivocal actions, where vice often masks itself with the appearances of virtue. Nor are the means available to the laws such that, through a principle of virtue, they can achieve compliance with what they require as most just and moral. The laws do not take the path of the heart; they do not work to persuade, nor do they reason; rather, they command, they forbid, they intimidate, they threaten: he who does such and such a thing will be punished in such and such a manner. This is their language, this is their sole and common rationale: it all comes down to fear of the coercive power with which ministers and those who execute the laws are armed.

Now, note this well, whatever partakes of force is of itself incapable of winning over the mind and, it follows, of softening the heart. Force does not enlighten, it shocks. It [450] may assist in holding a man to his duty, but force does not incline him to practice his duty willingly, and as a duty. When one is constrained only by fear, one is all the more ready for a bold evasion the instant that fear ceases or a way is glimpsed of avoiding the effect of the threats. Coercion even serves to inflame desire the more. And this is why those who seek to persuade have to take care to do nothing that might encourage the suspicion that their aim is to coerce. Men like to act freely for themselves; and they enjoy a sense of doing so when they heed only those reasons they find convincing. The great secret of persuasion consists in appearing to be oneself persuaded without meanwhile displaying any great wish to persuade others. This zeal to possess others' spirits passes for an attempt on their freedom; the overly zealous doctor is considered one who seeks to take control or who is unsure that his own reasoning is sound. In a word, to the extent one has recourse or appears to have recourse to coercion, so to that same extent impressions that reach the heart will be rejected. The slightest air of authority renders almost useless whatever an orator, sacred or profane, might say. If force sometimes contributes to forming good people, it is only insofar as it disposes them to turn away from certain largely involuntary aberrations, and to return to one's self, to reflect, examine, and discipline oneself, in this way allowing that which alone is capable of forming virtuous sentiments to act. But this happens very rarely, and only when one is already favorably disposed to virtue. For in those whose heart and mind are astray, in them fear produces only forced actions that are nothing but external.

[451] Such is the ordinary effect of the civil laws, which speak only by threatening. Mosaic law itself, for all its divinity, no matter what the beautiful precepts that come with it, obtained from the Jews a purely servile obedience that remained unreliable, corresponding only to the impact of fear [see Romans VIII, 15]. Thus no matter how virtuous a legislator is or should be, the proper and natural end of his laws is not to raise men to virtue. So then what is it? Here is the answer. For the civil laws, the end is to prevent citizens from doing each other some considerable harm, whether in their persons or in their property; and with this aim, to curb the external actions of vice which tend towards such wrong, to the extent that society's peace demands and permits. Now, to achieve this, repression of the grossest excesses and the most palpable injustices is sufficient. Indeed, sometimes prudence requires that these are suffered in order to avoid more onerous risks. Those whose ill-doing harms only themselves are sufficiently punished by their own actions; no one has an interest in having them punished further by the public authorities. As to injustices, if these cause victims minor harm, or if they are so subtle and hidden that it is difficult to determine their authors, or if they are so common that most people could accuse each other of committing these harms, the law suits they entailed would be beyond count, and would occasion an interminable debate that exhausted the most constant patience. What is more, the impact of the inquiries would generate greater disturbances than would connivance or toleration. There are even times and places in which one would be openly jeopardizing the authority of the laws and the magistrates if [452] an untimely attack was made on some enormous iniquity that was backed by all the forces of custom. In general, it is in light of the circumstances that a legislator takes steps to proscribe more or fewer bad actions, and to punish them with more or less severity.

However, no matter what limits the legislator sets to vice when he proscribes vicious things, it is not specifically as immoral that he proscribes and punishes them, but as harmful to the public or to individuals. And, conversely, when he prescribes things that may be linked to some virtue, it is not specifically as so many acts of virtue, but as so many necessary means to achieving the ends of civil government; it is not as praiseworthy things, but as useful things. Therefore he does not concern himself with the principle or motivation by which one obeys his laws. Whether one believes them to be just or unjust; whether one observes them consciously or unconsciously; whether one regards them as a duty or as an impediment, provided that one does externally what the law demands, the legislator has what he wants: the effect that his laws can produce has been produced, and society is no less calm than if obedience had derived from a sense of virtue. It is only indirectly, and as it were in another persona, that the legislator can and must work toward the true interests of virtue, by furnishing the citizens with solid instruction and such other means as are appropriate to achieving that which he could not himself achieve, even with all the force at his disposal.[14] For the rest, the office of legislator and [453] the office of moralist are always quite distinct; the latter complements the former, and the legislator leaves a vast field of action to the moralist. The legislator, as legislator, permits many things which he condemns in others and which he severely forbids to himself as a man and, more strongly still, as a Christian. Legal permission does not always presuppose that the legislator finds what he permits to be just and moral: often it is a mere *permission of impunity* and not a *permission of approval.* Or rather, legal permission must always be viewed on this basis, no matter what the legislator's ideas about the nature of the things that are not forbidden.

It has even been necessary, in order to prevent abuse of the legislative power, for the authority of legislators not to be extended to the point of forbidding, under pain of sanction, all that they might judge to be contrary to some moral virtue. For, not all being sufficiently enlightened,

---

14. See my *Traité de la Morale des Pères,* published in 1728, chap. xii, §.53.

under such a pretext they could easily punish entirely innocent things. There are only too many examples of this. Suspicious-minded princes have sometimes made something a crime on the basis of a dream that had upset them. [See Tacitus, *Annales,* XI, 4; *Amm. Marcellin,* XV, 3.] There was a time when people of distracted mind were burned, like sorcerers, and for this purpose one saw nothing but pyres burning everywhere. In certain places marionettists came close to being mistaken for magicians, and were punished accordingly. On the basis of the false ideas that uninformed ecclesiastics had given him on the subject of interest on money loans, a Christian emperor (Basil the Macedonian), not content with reducing interest to an equitable rate, forbade it altogether as an [454] illegal contract, both in its nature and in the light of the rules of the Gospel. Thanks to this vain scruple and this ill-informed piety, he ruined commerce and reduced a multitude of people to wretchedness, with the result that his son and successor, Leon known as the Philosopher—and more of a philosopher in this respect than his father—was forced to constantly raise the defenses and to permit interest, as previously, on a modest scale [see Leon's *Novelle,* LXXXIII]. But do we not still see today, in various places, supremely unjust and inhumane laws which, under the fine pretext of advancing the glory of God and repressing vice, directly persecute virtue? Though they are doing no more than fulfil the essential obligation, as is only natural for each individual, to follow the light of one's conscience, people are being punished, and punished cruelly, because others wish to believe them guilty either of wilful and rectifiable errors, or of a malicious and unbending stubbornness.

This last example would suffice to demonstrate the importance of establishing that the laws must not punish something simply because it is morally bad and, following from this, that impunity does not here win out over innocence. Such impunity, therefore, does not prevent certain things of a vicious nature from sometimes being known to be vicious, in the very countries where they are nonetheless permitted. Civil laws leave to the forces of ill-reputation the task of punishing that which deserves punishment, if [455] in the general opinion of citizens the thing is considered morally bad,[15] while the judgment of the wise at least conserves its rights. Under the Roman laws, a mere false oath, which causes harm only to the person who swore it, remains unpunished [see Cujas, *Obl.*, II, 19];[16] nevertheless, there has at all times been outrage at whosoever rendered himself guilty, no matter in what way, of a crime such as this that directly impugned the divinity.[17] Ingratitude, a vice as shameful as it is common, was punished only among a few ancient peoples [see on Pufendorf, *Droit de la Nature et des Gens,* Book III, chap. iii, §.17, note 3]: but, as Seneca tells us, it is condemned by all.[18] The trades of courtesan, gaming-house keeper and others such are nothing less than honest in the actual places where they are publicly exercised. It was allowed to the ancient philosophers to utter lofty censures on the *mores* of the times, even when, without great risk, they could not have raised their voice against the idolatry and superstitions of the vulgar.

The civil laws and the laws of virtue thus form as it were two distinct jurisdictions, which may well converge up to a certain point, but beyond this point virtue alone remains, and commands absolutely. Or rather virtue is always the supreme mistress. No human ordinance can in any way exempt anyone whomsoever from the natural empire that virtue holds over men: whatever virtue calls for is always indispensable, [456] whether or not the civil laws lend it their authority; whatever virtue forbids is always illicit, whether or not it is permitted by the civil laws, the wisest and most perfect of which necessarily leave to each per-

15. On this one may also see Bernardi Henrici Reinoldi, *Var. ad Jus Civile fere pertinent.,* chap. xv.

16. As occasionally occurs also in the most corrupt of times. See the *Continuation des Pensées sur la Comète,* by the late Mr Bayle, pp. 636 et seq., Article CXXX.

17. It is in this light that Cicero establishes as one of his proposed laws, in Plato's manner: *Perjurii poena divina, exitium: humana, dedecus, De Legibus,* Book II, chap. ix.

18. *Hoc frequentissimum crimen* [ingrati animi] *nusquam punitur, ubique improbatur. Neque absolvimus illud: sed, quum difficilis essa incerta res aestimatio, tantum odio damnavimus, & inter ea reliquimus, quae ad Judices Deos mittimus. De Benefic.,* Book III, chap. vi.

son's freedom and conscience no small number of vicious and immoral things. Of this I offer another and final proof, but a proof that is irrefutable. When He gave laws, God Himself as temporal legislator allowed such things. The law of Moses certainly punished false oaths [see Leviticus V, 1 and VI, 3], but not vain and foolhardy oaths [see Matthew V, 33 et seq.]. Among the Jews there was no action in respect of insults [*Ibid.,* verse 22]: that nation's rough and gross temperament made abstinence from crude speech and from outbursts of uncontrolled anger too difficult. Likewise it was to accommodate the untamed savagery of a husband, that the law permitted him to divorce his wives as often and whenever he wanted, for no other reason than his aversion and his own good pleasure [Deuteronomy XXIV, 1; Matthew XIX, 8]. There were places designed to receive and shelter those men whose misfortune it was to have killed someone accidentally and without intent; but if the involuntary homicide, having been declared such by the judges, happened to stray outside the limits of the asylum, whether by imprudence or by chance, and if once outside he was killed by the closest relative or the heir of the deceased, the latter was not held to be guilty of murder. Such was the privilege granted to the vindictive spirit of the blood avenger [Numbers XXXV, 27]. Nevertheless, all this was later clearly forbidden by Him who was the true end of the law, by Jesus Christ the perfect doctor, the infallible preacher of virtue [Romans X, 4]; and even had the Jews [457] taken note of it, they would also have found the condemnation of things of this sort within the precepts of their own law, precepts that are in essence the same as those of nature and of the Gospel.

I have thus proved quite decisively, so it seems to me, that mere permission or impunity under the laws does not always authorize before the tribunal of conscience and reason that which the laws permit. And what would it be, if I were now to go into the detail of the many things that, though permitted almost everywhere, are clearly contrary to the essential duties of man in general, or of a good citizen, or of the different statuses of life? But to do that would require a complete account of the manners of our times, and the limits of the present discourse allow scarcely enough space to give a few samples.

There have been laws against idleness, among the Egyptians, the Athenians, the Spartans and the Lucanians. [See Ménage, on Diog. Laerce., Book I, §.55; and Mr Perizonius, on Elien., *Var. Hist.*, II, 5; IV, 1.] There everyone was obliged to declare to the magistrate his means of livelihood and his occupation; and those who found themselves without a profession were punished, to the extent that in Egypt and at Athens, under the rules of Dracon, it was a matter of paying with one's life. But today, if one excepts Persia, where it is said this ancient regulation has been kept in force [J. Cartwright, in J. de Laet., *Descript. Pers.*, p. 260], I know of no country in which one may not be idle with impunity, and in which one believes one cannot be idle without fear, once one has the wealth to do so, or is satisfied with what one has. In certain countries, it is true, one is more subject to regulation than in others, but everywhere there is a multitude of people who even [458] boast that they pride themselves on spending their days calmly doing nothing but drinking, eating and amusing themselves. Yet is there anything more unworthy of man, naturally endowed with so many faculties of body and mind, than to waste them in feeble indolence? Is there anything more insulting to the generosity of the Creator and Supreme Master, from whom men received these talents, some in greater number and strength, others less, but all wonderful and useful of their kind; all fitting to give us a high idea of His power, His goodness and His wisdom; all fruitful in productions that tend of themselves to render human life happier and more comfortable? Is there anything more contrary to the duty of man, and *a fortiori* to the duty of the citizen who, as such, beyond the general obligation to be good for something in this world, still has a concrete commitment to make himself as useful as he can to the civil society of which he is a member? If there was not a great number of people, reduced by their condition to the necessity of working assiduously, and some small number who do so for the love of work and out of duty, what would become of the others, who wish to shirk it? Where would they find what they need to provide for their pleasures, or even for the necessities of life? Most of them believe they are not obliged to work, because they have no need to do so, that is to say, because they would be in a position to choose the occupation which most pleased them, and to which they would be most suited, and which they would therefore exercise with more success than so many others who are not masters of their time, and who cannot employ their time as they would wish [459].

What a mental reversal, to seek to justify idleness precisely in terms that make the obligation to busy oneself even stronger! The freedom allowed by the laws on this account does not provide any more valid an excuse. If they do not prescribe anybody's style of life, if even in the shadow of their protection one can live idly, the laws do not for all that relieve nor can they ever relieve anyone, no matter whom, from a duty imposed by nature, or rather by the author of nature, by the great protector of society. The laws do no more than lay on the conscience and the honor of each individual the responsibility for busying oneself in the most fitting and advantageous manner. The impunity the laws grant is no more capable of disculpating those who embrace no useful and honest profession or occupation than of justifying those who with impunity seek exercise or employments for which they neither are nor wish to become competent. The latter case is, perhaps, more common than the former; but neither is excusable. While more harm comes from involving oneself in that which one does not understand, with the result that one does damage to the public and to many individuals, more than enough harm follows from involving oneself in nothing, and living a wholly inactive life.

But I am mistaken. No, idle ones, yours is not a wholly inactive life: try as you might, you could never bear the crushing burden of total idleness. Nature, which has granted you so many talents, talents that you seek to neglect, has refused you this one that you often sigh for. And please to God that you may always be as motionless as statues; or that you may do nothing but drink, [460] eat and sleep like swine; or that you may only seek to end your boredom like that emperor who spent hours in his room, catching flies [Domitian, see Suetonius on his life, chap. 3]. But you have too much time left, when you would be a burden to yourselves if, in the absence of any honest or useful occupation, your passions did not provide you with a thousand shameful and damaging amusements. Debauchery, malign gossip, gaming, criminal plotting and other such things, these are your stock in trade, for in the end you have one. But these are also a deadly source of quarrels, disorder, public and private ills, which combine to earn you the titles of scourges and plagues of the state, and no-goods and useless deadweights of the earth.

Is it possible that one can lead such a life, and still believe that one is a moral person, and be so regarded by many people who do not have a more reasonable idea of true probity and authentic honor? Yet such is, shall I say, the glory or the shame of virtue, that everybody approves it, praises it, admires it in general, yet nevertheless the respect that is its due is most times given to vain phantoms, or rather to the opposite of virtue, to its mortal enemy, to vice itself. In the commerce of life, how many instances of bad conduct do we not see, how many falsehoods, sometimes even gross, which walk as it were with head held high, and whose authors, under cover of the fact that the laws take no notice, even pride themselves on evading public censure? You are someone's friend, or at least you pretend to be. As long as there is no [461] conflict of interest, all is well; yet when a conflict arises, not only will you not make it your duty and pleasure to give way, whether right is on your side or not, but, not content to claim honestly the rights you believe are yours, you will have recourse to a thousand secret manoeuvres, a thousand tricks, to outdo your friend; you will try to darken his reputation, cost what it may, and sometimes spare no effort in defaming him. You are not going to lie in wait for travelers on the highway, in order to rob them, you are not directly taking someone else's property, that is true; but you seek out hidden ways to get it, to draw it towards you. Sometimes you take advantage of someone's penury, of the sad state of his affairs, of his negligence or his ignorance, in order to get at a very low price things that he could have sold elsewhere for much more. Sometimes you provoke a thousand disagreements, a thousand difficulties, a thousand problems, a thousand complications for some poor Naboth, to force him, willing or unwilling, to strip himself of his father's inheritance. Sometimes you conceal the faults, well known to you and of which you are often yourself the author, in something that you wish to dispose of at a better price than you should. A creditor, in return for a good service that he has provided, finds himself reduced either to suffering or to losing part of his money, when an urgent need forces him to seek repayment. A workman is deprived of benefit of his wages by the delays by which you keep him waiting and purchase his labor.

It would take too long just to note all the deviousness and injustices of this sort which, favored by impunity under the laws, are practiced daily by innumerable [462] so-called moral men, sometimes even by those who claim to be devout. What a shame for them that they were not born in some country where legal permission extended further still! Ah! They would have known how to exploit that situation! But let us not be surprised that they make such ill use of the freedom that the laws allow them. Let us not be surprised that they explain this to the gross disadvantage of virtue's inviolable rights. They no longer respect the sacred authority of the clearest, the most explicit, the most just laws, when the negligence of those who should ensure respect for the laws makes impunity almost as certain as it is with regard to those actions on which the legislator in fact maintains a complete silence. It is futile for the laws to forbid pulling of strings and bribery: these are the only ways for many good people to improve their situation. A thousand means are found to elude these and many other laws. Pulling of strings, in particular, is so common in every country that those with rectitude and a sufficient competence are reduced to seeking out friends and patrons to compensate for their not having on display a merit which alone should speak for them, but which on its own is usually quite ineffective. Such is the life of these good people, in coarse grain, that it would still be a great deal for them, and for the public, if the civil laws, imperfect though they are, were the constant rule of their conduct.

So here "it is long since we lost the true names of things,"[19] to express myself in the words of an Ancient, who himself gave the lie to his speech [463] by his actions, but from whom the force of truth drew some fine moralizing, whether in the mouths of others or uttered by his

---

19. *Jam pridem equidem nos vera rerum vocabula amisimus: quia bona aliena largiri, liberalitas; malarum rerum audacia, fortitudo vocatur.* Sallust, *Catilin.*, chap. lv.

own lips. So and so is a good man; such and such a thing is permitted; equivocal words if ever there were, poorly understood and misapplied most of the time! A palpable example of the usefulness of that neglected art of distinguishing the different ideas attaching to the one term! A sad proof of the fatal consequences that sometimes flow from neglecting grammar! Yes, by dint of saying and hearing others say "This is permitted, who is going to stop me?," we unconsciously get used to confusing impunity with innocence; we almost cease distinguishing these two kinds of permission, so often diametrically opposed one to the other. All my preceding reflections aim to lay bare this unfortunate ambiguity, and, it seems to me, they leave no doubt about it. But let me be permitted to add one word more, to underscore the ambiguity, and for this purpose to address some of those people who seem to recognize it the least, or to abuse it the most.

Where shall I begin? To whom shall I speak? So many different characters crowd into my mind that I have difficulty choosing. Let us take whatever by chance comes first. Whoever you may be that I omit to mention, or that I shall pass over, learn from what I say to others the true sense of a word, a word on which it is no less important for you to have some accurate ideas.

What strikes me immediately is that man of vanity, he who is also seeking always to have himself noticed; in him I see his like. Men of ambition, you are thus *permitted* to consider nothing as above your reach, to seek out [464] with the utmost zeal the most frivolous marks of distinction, to deploy every sort of trick to achieve your ends. Misers, you are *permitted* to make your money your idol, to enrich yourselves by deceptions and frauds that are too subtle to be discovered or punished by the laws. Hedonists, you are *permitted* to live like little lords, to sacrifice everything to your appetites as far as you can do so, without fear of public stigma. Men of influence, credit and authority, you are *permitted* to misdirect your patronage, to listen only to reasons of interest, kinship or recommendation. Men of justice, you are *permitted* to judge according to fortuity, or to base your judgments on any reason whatsoever other than those of law and equity. Men of the sword, you are *permitted* to sell your services and your life to the highest bidder, without even thinking to examine the justice of the cause. Men of commerce, you are *permitted* to subtly falsify your merchandise, to make it appear what it is not by presenting it in a false light, to exploit the naivety and ignorance of the buyer. Barkeepers, gaming-house keepers, publicans, you are *permitted* to offer youth every occasion and means for debauchery. Artisans, workmen, you are *permitted* to promise to several clients what you wish to provide to none, to offer bad work for good, to apply yourself negligently to the task. Husbands, you are *permitted* to behave toward your wives like real brutes and petty tyrants. Wives, you are *permitted* to try the patience of your husbands to breaking point. Masters, you are *permitted* to mistreat your servants for no reason, [465] feeding them poorly and paying them poorly. Servants, you are *permitted* to take no care for the interests of your masters, and to serve them only so far as they can see you. Fathers, you are *permitted* to give your children only bad lessons and the worst of examples, to think at most of amassing wealth for them, without troubling yourself to make them truly virtuous and capable of the employments that you plan for them. Children, you are *permitted* not to respond to the rare diligence of a father who overlooks nothing and who spares no effort for the sake of making you worthy members of human and civil society. People of no matter what age, rank or sex, you are *permitted* to do a thousand similar things. But the same applies to you as it did under an ordinance of the Spartan magistrates regarding the outrages committed in their country by some young foreigners: Clazomenians are permitted to be without shame [Elien., *Var. Hist.,* Book II, chap. xv].

It is for each of us to see whether he wishes still to profit from so disgraceful a privilege. I leave it to the legislators to examine whether they could not, without undue complications, define more sharply the limits of what their laws permit, or at least arrange indirect yet appropriate means to make more citizens willing to renounce voluntarily the right that most believe they have under this poorly understood permission. Nor do I wish here to draw on the help of religion; I shall not put before your eyes this plea by an apostle: "that whatsoever things are true, whatsoever things are honest, whatsoever things are just, whatsoever things are pure, [466] whatsoever things are lovely, whatsoever things are of good report, if there be any virtue, and if there be any praise, think on these things" [Philip. IV, 8]. By which he gives us to understand that we must not be satisfied simply with doing nothing that is against the laws. Indeed no, I do not call you to the school of Jesus Christ, I call you to the school of your own reason. I do not cite you before the tribunal of Him who will judge the living and the dead in the last instance, I cite you before the natural tribunal of your consciences. We must be human, before being Christian; and whoever does not listen to the voice of nature will no more listen to the voice of the law or that of the Gospel. Pride yourselves only on having ideas and sentiments as reasonable as those of the wise of antiquity, I ask no more. This is what they said, and on which you will reflect at your leisure: "Is it not an insufficient thing, to conduct oneself well only to the extent that the laws require it? How much further does the rule of our duties extend, than that of the law? How many duties flow from natural affection, humanity, liberality, justice, good faith, on which the civil laws are silent?" These are Seneca's words.[20]

Young men, (for it is concerning you that I must finish, since you are the occasion of this my discourse), are you too *permitted* to neglect those duties that are yours, and to abandon yourselves to dissolute behavior? Ah! if your parents, [467] if those who are most concerned with directing your conduct, are sadly willing to grant you such a fatal freedom, may it not please God should you find any support in us on this matter. May it not please God should we neglect any of our responsibility for stopping the heat of youth from overcoming you, and for forming in you early those good dispositions that will give you immunity from the pernicious lures of the bad things that the laws, or your parents, may permit. But it is not possible constantly to oversee your

---

20. *Ut hoc ita sit, quam angusta innocentia est, ad Legem bonum esse? quanto latius Officiorum patet, quam Juris regula? quam multa Pietas, Humanitas, Justitia, Liberalitas, Fides, exigunt, quae omnia extra publicas tabulas sunt?* Seneca, *De Ira*, Book II, chap. xxvii. Mr Schulting has made a commentary on this passage of Seneca, in a speech pronounced on leaving the rectorate at the University of Leyden, and which was soon printed, in 1730, under the title *Sermo Academicus Sollennis De angusta innocentia Hominis ad Legem boni.*

every action; and you know only too well how to hide them from the most intense vigilance. Beware of yourself, each time you are tempted to do something without your superiors' knowledge or approval; you are not yet at a stage to be able to govern yourself, and you must question your desires. You prefer by far the trivial to the substantial, the pleasant to the useful; and if the ideas of the good touch you just a little, when they are put to you in a certain way, they still have infinitely less power over you than the ideas of your passions. Keep in mind, therefore, that nothing you do when you follow your inclinations alone is *permitted* to you. Take care not to imitate the bad examples of older people, and pride yourself on actually being smarter than those who would always be by comparison less smart than you, were you to act like them. Follow the precepts of your superiors, who are wise and committed [468] to your well-being (you will easily know who they are), and do nothing that might displease them. Love them in your turn; fear them too; take heed of the effects of their justified indignation. We have to take you as best we can; and at a time when reason is still weak, it is often necessary to bring in some appropriate constraint to overcome the obstacles that would end by making you unreceptive to reasonable sentiments. If nothing can be obtained from you by kindness, you will nonetheless be made to obey by fear, such that we shall have nothing with which to reproach ourselves.

But this is not the time for punishment or censure; this is the day for praise, the day for rewards. We give them with the greatest pleasure in the world, even to those who have barely merited them. May this encourage them, and encourage others, to give us day by day ever greater proofs of their commitment to study, and to all their duties generally!

Discourse on the Benefits
Conferred by the Laws

*In which it is shown that a good man
should not always take advantage of the benefits
conferred on him by the laws*

Magnificent and most honored Lord Bailiff, most honored Lords of the Council of this City, learned and respected members of the Academy, my most honored colleagues, listeners of no matter what rank, sex and age.

If to have commenced is to have done half the work, as an antique saying puts it,[1] to have done half is to have finished. Yet [472] in taking up today the topic half of which I treated a year ago on a similar occasion, I fear that I face no fewer obstacles to overcome, no fewer—and perhaps more—prejudices to confront, than if I was still at the starting point. I am like one who easily agrees to a principle based on reasons to which he sees no objection, then at other times just as easily contradicts himself when he recognizes certain consequences arising from his agreement that he had not noticed. One should abandon the clearly contradictory maxims to which one adhered without knowing why, but which in practice one has become used to following with a certain pleasure. One then looks for what is needed in order to question or, rather, entirely to reject certain awkward truths, which have emerged to dispel our easy error. If anyone followed what I previously said, I would like

---

1. As attributed by Lucian to Hesiod, in *Hermotim.,* Vol. I, p. 506, Amsterdam Edit. Plato goes further, saying that to have begun is to have done more than half, *De Legibus,* Book VI, vol. ii, p. 753, Edit. H. Steph. See Erasmus, *Adages,* for the proverb: *Principium, dimidium totius.*

to think that some will have been almost persuaded that mere legal permission—the mere silence of the laws—which is finally nothing but an impunity, does not prevent many things permitted by the laws from being truly bad and dishonest. But when you hear me roundly condemn the exercise of certain positive privileges granted by the laws, privileges of which virtually no one hesitates to take advantage, I do not know whether you will at once decide this is a folly, no matter how clear its links to what you recognized were sound principles, [473] and then rebel, without more ado, against arguments which you had found striking.

Whatever the case, it will not deter me from following my plan, or from taking my ideas as far as they will go. Men's fickleness, whims and prejudices must not prevent us from following our argument through, nor from proposing some important truths when there is the opportunity. We would deem that we had done all too little, were we to leave things standing as they were in our previous discourse. To do so would be to content oneself with having attacked only the most obvious prejudices, leaving the more subtle ones undisturbed, that is, those which are the most difficult to dispel. Thus today, in completing my functions as Rector for this solemn occasion, let us—if it is possible—finally disabuse those who, under the shelter of human laws, believe themselves authorized to ride roughshod over the laws of God and of nature. Let us show, for this purpose, *that in good conscience one cannot always take advantage of benefits conferred by the most explicit civil laws.*

There are some totally unjust laws from which, it follows, only injustices can flow. There are laws, in themselves quite just and created for sound reasons, but that confer benefits from which the interested parties sometimes cannot profit without injustice. There are laws the benefits of which we can always enjoy without doing harm to anyone; yet what strict justice then allows, some other virtue in certain cases forbids. Such will be the order and structure of this discourse.

I

[474] I repeat, first, that there can be, that there have in fact been, and that there are still some totally unjust laws. Such laws, in consequence, always lack the virtue of rendering just and equitable the enjoyment of the benefits they confer. It was long believed that among the ancient Romans a law of the Twelve Tables, that is, one of those famous laws developed with such care and circumspection, expressly permitted the creditors of an insolvent debtor to kill and dismember him, each taking a part of the debtor's body.[2] This is a clear example of a law as cruel as it is absurd, one that is contrary even to the interests of those whom the legislator intended to favor. However, some years ago, a famous Dutch jurisconsult [Mr de Bynkershoek, *Observ. Jur. Civil*, Book I, chap. I] restored the honor of the *Decemvirs* of Ancient Rome. With critical advantage over the wise men of Roman Antiquity themselves, for whom the archaic terms of the Twelve Tables could not but remain obscure, even though the Latin of those times was their native tongue, he demonstrated to us in an entirely plausible manner that in the law in question, the legislator had sought to permit not the killing of the debtor, but his sale at auction, [475] such that the creditors could share the price of his freedom amongst themselves. Nevertheless, it remains that distinguished scholars, philosophers no less than jurisconsults—whether a Quintilian [*Instit. Orat.*, Book III, chap. vi, p. 261] or a Cecilius, whether a Favorin [see Aulus Gellius, *Noct. Att.*, Book XX, chap. i], an Aulus Gellius or a Tertullian [*Apologet.*, chap. iv]—found nothing

---

2. These are the terms of the law, as Aulus Gellius recorded them: *TERTIIS. (inquit) NUNDINIS.PARTIS.SECANTO.SI.PLUS.MINUS.VE.SECUERUNT.SE. FRAUDE.ESTO, Noct. Artic.*, Book XX, chap. i. In his Preface on Vol. 3 of the *Thesaurus Juris*, p. 24, Mr Otto sacrifices the humanity and the good sense of the *Decemvirs* who composed the Twelve Tables to the elevated idea he has of some authors of much later centuries. He could not bring himself to believe that the latter had misunderstood the terms of this law, even though Aulus Gellius recognizes, in the same place, that there were in the Twelve Tables many things the sense of which had long been lost. It is not even the sole instance of ancient authors who, for all their skill, went astray in explaining words in their own language. One has only to see one of the letters of the celebrated Tanneouy Le Fèvre, Book I, Epist. iv.

strange in the supposition of civil laws created in such a style as to afford inhuman privileges, contrary to the most evident laws of nature, as Quintilian gives us to believe.[3] And this was not the only instance that they had noticed.

Here is another example, well attested, even if it went unnoted until recently, and which, if not of the same kind, nonetheless has something very harsh about it.[4] Among these same Romans, up until the time of Praetor Cajus Aquilius Gallus, in other words for more than three centuries following the establishment of the laws of the Twelve Tables, one had to take every care not to use—even in jest—the consecrated terms of *stipulations* or formal promises. Suppose one father had said to another, in conversation or at a festival, when nothing was further from the issue than discussion of serious business: "Do you want to marry your daughter with my son?," if the other person had responded, by [476] way of joking and banter: "I so wish," then the former had only to take him at his actual word. The party for his son was found. It was futile for the girl's father to claim that he had neither intended nor given reason to believe that he had any such marriage in view; it was futile for him to prove that the words by which he had supposedly committed himself meant nothing more, in the circumstances in which they were uttered, than if he'd spoken them in his sleep. No joking was tolerated, and the judge would without further trial find against him. It was obligatory to go through with what an impertinent plaintiff wanted, one who under the pretext of an apparent agreement, extorted an imaginary promise as unjustly and with all the violence of a highway robber. Such was, for some centuries, the superstitious attachment of the Roman courts to the letter of the law and its formulas, and this despite a manifest intention to allow these words a usage quite other than that which they had at law. Even when the Praetor, of whom I spoke, had recog-

---

3. *Sunt enim quaedam non laudabilia naturae. Sed Jure concessa: ut in XII. Tabulis, debitoris corpus inter creditores dividi licuit, quam legem mos publicus repudiavit. Instit. Orat.,* Book III, chap. vi, p. 173. Edit. Obrecht.

4. It is Mr Noodt who discovered this. See his *Julius Paulus,* chap. xi, *in fin.,* and his treatise *De forma emendandi Doli mali,* chap. vi.

nized the injustice and the need for a remedy, he dared not act directly; he contented himself with avoiding the plea by allowing an exemption from fraud for the party whom the other was bold enough to summons to fulfil a promise that had not in fact been made.

Since then, on other matters, we still find laws no less contrary to equity. Judge for [477] yourselves, whether the following law does not deserve to be described in this way. A man purchases some wine that he must measure and collect within a certain limit of time. This he fails to do within the time. The seller, who wishes to use the barrels, can then, according to Roman law, pour the wine away; nothing more is asked of him than that he warns the purchaser. The jurisconsult Ulpian, whose opinion was authority on this matter, openly admits that it would be better not to go to this extreme; that there would be other courses of action more fitting in order not to deprive one of the two persons of the use of his goods, and at the same time conserve the other's goods; that the barrel owner could hire other barrels, at the expense of the person who owns the wine, or sell the wine for his own account as profitably as possible.[5] Nonetheless, Ulpian dispenses with all this, and grants the owner of the barrels complete freedom to empty them, without regard for the loss of the wine, and without concerning himself as to whether the one to whom the wine belongs has encountered obstacles that prevented him from coming to collect it.

Let us leave the Romans there, and pass on to other peoples. Here we shall see, beyond doubt, some no less palpable examples of laws that scarcely conform to justice and equity, the maxims of which these peoples, all things considered, have not cared to consult. First to be pre-

---

5. *Licet autem venditori vel effundere vinum, si diem ad metiendum praestituit, nec intra diem admensum est. Effundere autem non statim poterit, prius quam testando denunciet emtori, ut aut tollat vinum, aut sciat futurum ut vinum effunderetur. Si tamen, quum posset effundere, non effundit, laudandus est potius, . . . commodius est autem, conduci vasa, nec reddi vinum, nisi, quanti conduxerit, ab emtore reddatur, aut vendi vinum bona fide, id est quantum sine ipsius incommodo fieri potest, operam dare, ut quam minimo detrimento sit ea res emtori.* Digest, Book XVIII, De peric. & commod. rei. vend. Leg. I, §.3. See the dissertation of Mr Brenckman, de Eurematicis &c, chap. xii, §.16, n. 14.

sented is that supremely barbarian law or custom [478] concerning the goods of those who have been shipwrecked. Imagine two vessels driven by a furious storm and about to go down. The men on one of these vessels, to avoid drowning, discharge the cargo as quickly as possible, jettisoning their most valuable goods into the sea. The others do not have even this chance, their vessel suddenly being smashed on a reef. However, the storm abates, and the former's vessel arrives at safe harbor, without further ill than the loss of cargo; the others, whose vessel has perished, manage to survive by swimming, or in a skiff. By a fortunate chance, the effects of both are washed up on the shore. They lay claim to these, justifying their right. There is no room for doubt that what has come ashore is truly what they had on board their vessels. But the ruler of that coast, more cruel than the winds and the waves, seizes or allows certain people to seize this sad collection that the ocean seemed to have delivered to him only so he might have the pleasure of restoring it to the rightful owners. In the circumstance where humanity should be moved to console these wretched men, indeed to aid them with one's own goods, instead they are stripped of what was left of their [479] own. [See what I have said on Pufendorf, Book IV, chap. xiii, §.4, note 2, third Edition.] If we do not distinguish here between the subject or citizen and the foreigner, what has become of the bond of the civil pact that called for protection and special assistance? What if we indulge in robbing foreigners, by withholding that which the ocean had restored to them? Is not this a relic of the savagery of those ancient times when all those who were not fellow citizens believed they were right to treat one another as enemies; when it was no affront to ask unknown travelers: "Are you bandits, sirs? Are you pirates?," and no dishonor for them to reply: "Indeed we are"?[6] Perhaps you imagine that this was an established custom only among pagans and infidels. [See Grotius, *Droit de la Guerre et de la Paix*, Book II, chap. vii, §.1, note 3; and Selden, *Mar. Claus*, Book I, chap. xxxv, *in fin.*] But no, it is under Christianity that

---

6. This is what Thucydides teaches us, taking his proof from the ancient poets. See Homer, *Odyss.* Book II, verse 71 et seq., Book IX, verse 252 et seq., and *Hymn. in Apoll.*, verse 452.

we see it most generally adopted.[7] And whilst the Siamese have a law explicitly forbidding it [see in Moteri's *Dictionary*, under "Siam," the article "Manners and customs of the Siamese"], there are as yet few Christian states in which consideration has been given to limit the rights of the State Treasury over things that have escaped shipwreck, such that those who have lost their goods have time enough to come and reclaim them.[8] What is more, we learn of certain places along the Baltic Sea, where Protestant preachers pray [480] to God in his temple that He may please bless the right of shipwreck, as they call it.[9] What strange prayers, no matter how one views them, and scarcely worthy of a minister of this holy doctrine, which breathes only justice and charity!

Do you want another similar example? It is easy to provide one. A man has been robbed. The thief is arrested, together with the stolen goods. It is known from whom he stole them; he admits everything. The owner asks for return of the goods. But, instead of returning them to him, the Treasury or the judges seize the goods. This custom, still practiced in some places, was explicitly authorized under a law of the Saxons [*Specul. Saxon.*, Book II, artic. 25 and 31]. And, even though it was modified by allowing the owner of the stolen goods a year and a

---

7. Bodin, in his treatise *De la République*, speaks of this *droit de Bris*, or of *Warech* (a word from the German), as of something whose usage was, in his time, "common to all those carrying goods by sea." And on this he records a response of the Supreme Commander Anne de Montmerency to the Ambassador of the Emperor, Book I, chap. x, p. 247, French Edit., Genev. 1608 (pp. 267, 268 of the Latin Edit., Francf. 1622). Some German authors say that this custom was observed also with respect to shipwrecks occurring on the Rhine, and other rivers. See Hertius, dissert. *De Superiorit. Territor,* §.56, Vol. I, Comm. & Opusc., and Nicol. Henelius, *Otii Vratislav.* chap. xxxvii.

8. In Holland, one year and six months are allowed. Even when this time has elapsed, the original owners can still easily repurchase their goods at a low price. See Vinnius, on the *Institutes,* Book II, title I, §.47; and on the practices in other nations, Loccenius, *De Jure Maritimo,* Book I, chap. vii, §.10.

9. Mr Thomasius speaks of this as if it was well known and proven, in his dissertation *De Statu Imperii potestate legislatoria &c,* §.42; and another German professor names the island of Nordstrand, in the Duchy of Schleswig, as one of the places where this practice has been recorded. See Mr Weber, in a note on Pufendorf, *De Offic. Hom. & Civ.,* Book I, chap. v, §.3, where it appears the author himself had this practice in view.

day to come and reclaim them, the Emperor Charles-Quint was right to abolish this law [*Ordin. Crim.,* arts. 207, 218], together with that other law of which we spoke. The injustice of it is no less evident [see Pufendorf, Book III, chap. i, §.2, with note 3]; and though some color could be found to disguise it, nothing is more contrary to good policy than such a usage. Of itself, it tends to unsettle certainty [481] of possession with respect to all movable property, and virtually assures impunity to rogues. For, in the end, who would pursue a thief from whom he has small hope of snatching back his goods, save with help from the public forces, when—in the event that the thief is caught—all the owner can expect is the distress of seeing his recovered goods pass irretrievably into the hands of another, who has no more right to them?

Shall I add, to broaden the range of examples, that there have been countries where the princes and great lords had acquired over their vassals the right—was it infamous or grotesque?—to take the place of the newly-married husband on the wedding night? This was once established in Scotland by an explicit law, one that was abolished only after a long space of time;[10] and even then, they changed the privilege into a kind of tribute,[11] which is still in existence, like a perpetual monument to the ancient usage, of which proofs are found elsewhere, even among the canonicate.[12]

---

10. It was Evenus III who made this law, as recorded by Buchanan: *Ut rex ante nuptias Sponsarum Nobilium, Nobiles Plebejarum praelibarent pudicitiam: ut Plebejarum uxores cum Nobilitate communes essent, Hist. Scot.,* Book IV, fol. 37, Edit. Edimburg. 1582.

11. Milcolumb III (or Malcolm), at the request of his wife, Queen Marguerite, allowed new husbands to buy back the wedding night, by paying their lord half-a-marc of silver: *Uxoris etiam precibus dedisse fertur, ut primam novae nuptae noctem, quae Proceribus per gradus quosdam, lege Regis Eugenii* (it is the same name as Evenus) *debebatur, sponsus dimidiata argenti marca redimere posset: quam pensionem adhuc Marchetas mulierum vocant.,* Buchanan, Book VII, fol. 74. Polydor. Virgil, *Hist. Angl.,* Book X, p. 223, edit. Lugd. Bat. 1649. Hector Boethius, *Hist. Scot.* This tribute is still called "marchet" or "maidenrents." See the *Laws of Scotland,* Edit. Edimburg., 1609, Book IV, chap. xxxi, with notes, and the *Glossary* of Du Cange, under the word "marcheta," where he reports other similar examples.

12. The canons of Lyon, and, before them the counts: see Choppin, *Ad Leg. And.,*

We shall also note that in England (so difficult is it even under the best ordered governments to rescind bad laws once they are established) [482], a husband who in the sight and knowledge of all, has been away from his home for several years, provided that he has not been outside the realm or the island as a whole, is obliged by the laws to recognize as his own a child born to his wife during this long absence. [See Eduard Chamberlayn, *Notit. Angl.*, Part I, chap. xvi; and Meteren, *Hist. des Pais-Bas*; in the description of the *Laws and Police of England*, Book III, fol. 271, of the French Translation.] This undeniably favors, on the basis of groundless presumptions, the unfaithful mother and the actual father, to the prejudice of the husband who has suffered a savage outrage at their hands. It does legitimate children a visible wrong by allowing the bastard child to compete with them for the succession.

If these examples do not suffice, I do not know what more is needed to persuade you that laws or received customs sometimes accord rights and privileges that are always unjust. All those found to be of such a nature (and perhaps more than we might expect will be uncovered, if everyone examines the laws and customs of his own country), all those which appear such, no matter how well authorized by human tribunals, are surely the result of a shameful indulgence, exploitation of which could be approved neither before God, nor before men who have sound ideas of justice and equity.[13] This much is self-evident; and what I said in the previous discourse excuses me from pausing here to prove it.

Book I, *De Jurisd. Andegav.*, chap. xxxi, no. 2; Camil. Boreli, *Conf.* I, no. 150. This right was called *jus luxanda coxae,* right of thighage, also known by another more expressive name. See Nicol. Henelius, *Otii Vrastislav.*, chap. xlvii, p. 401.

13. Quintilian, the father or grandfather of the rhetorician, introduces a husband who, having killed his wife caught *in flagrante delicto,* as was formerly permitted among several nations, comes to reproach himself; Quintilian draws out from this the maxim that what the laws permit does not always set the conscience at rest: *Mori volo, quia uxorem meam occidi, qualemcumque. Licuit, scio: Sed non semper ad animam pertinent jura. Occidere adulteros lex permittit: ego mihi sit irascor, tamquam nefas fecerim. Declamat.* CCCXXXV, p. 691, Ed. Burm.

II

But there is more. It can happen, and often does, that laws directly [483] or indirectly conferring certain benefits contain nothing unjust in themselves, and yet to enjoy those benefits would be unjust. This proposition, which at first sight seems contradictory, will become crystal clear once we have drawn attention to the principles on which it rests.

Not everything that is just is susceptible, by its nature, of being prescribed by the civil laws, as we have sufficiently established in the preceding discourse. But even regarding what lies within the ambit of the civil laws, things cannot always be regulated in the manner most conforming to the immutable laws of justice that apply to everything and everywhere. A law has no point if it is not implemented; but far beyond this, such an unimplemented law is then harmful, because it provides grounds for disregarding the legislator's authority even with respect to other laws. Now, if we wished to take this to the last detail, if it was necessary to recognize the very least injustices and to eliminate them by public authority, it would be very difficult, not to say impossible, ever to complete the task. Moreover, it is very important to reduce the number of law suits as far as we can; their multiplication remains a real problem, more so than the freedom that allows the rules of justice to be observed only up to a certain point. Danger also follows from allowing the slightest exception to certain laws, and above all from granting those judges having authority to pursue cases in their own right the power to allow exceptions. Rather, these laws must be let stand [484] in all their force, even when particular circumstances might place the present case beyond the sphere intended by the legislator. The diversity of characters and manners, times, places and other circumstances, requires laws sometimes to accord their authority to certain just things, and sometimes to withhold it. Every legislator generally proposes, or should propose, like Solon the famous Athenian,[14] to make laws that are not necessarily the best laws in themselves, but the best that the citizens, or the subjects, are capable of receiving. And no matter how wise the lawmak-

14. Plutarch, in *Vit. Solon,* Vol. I, p. 86, C. Ed. Wech.

ing, it is always true to say, with the Roman orator, that the laws redress injustices in one way, but the philosophers correct them in another. The laws restrict themselves to that which is crude and palpable, as it were; the philosophers (and each person must be his own philosopher, as each can be) dissect everything, to the very limits of an attentive and penetrating reason.[15] It is thus the duty of each person to make good the unavoidable imperfection of the most excellent laws, the authors of which could not, even had they wished to, exempt whomsoever it might be from observing that part of justice and equity which they were constrained to leave outside their jurisdiction. For the rest, they force no one to take advantage either of the impunity the laws allow [485] or of the benefits they confer in this respect; they do not prevent you renouncing these.[16] And there are many cases where men have publicly renounced their impunity or benefits, although the public interest and the end of the laws do not allow such acts of renunciation to be cited in the regular course of justice. In short, the civil laws are themselves most often just, but they do not embrace all that is just. If they sometimes refuse their protection to those who suffer injustices, if indeed they seem to accord a certain right to those who commit injustices, this is without prejudice to what each person must do willingly, in compliance with the inviolable rules of virtue, and independently of the authority of human legislators.

Examples are not lacking that let us appreciate the truth of what I have just said, and by means of which one will easily judge like cases that will present themselves in relation to other matters.

If there is some duty that the law of nature prescribes without fail or exception to all men, it is undeniably the duty to keep one's word, to do exactly that which one has knowingly and freely agreed upon with

---

15. *Sed aliter Leges, aliter Philosophi tollunt astusias: Leges, quatenus manu tenere possunt; Philosophi, quatenus ratione & intelligentia.* Cicero, *De Offic.,* Book III, chap. xvii. The poet Persius says that it is not for a Praetor, or a judge, to prefer precise rules of conduct: *Non Praetoris erat stultis dare tenuia rerum / Officia, atque usum rapidae permittere vita., Sat.* V, vers. 93, 94.

16. This is what Pliny the Younger gives us to understand, in a passage of Letter xvi of Book II, which will be cited toward the end of this discourse.

another, and without there being anything in the matter itself that could annul the agreement. Nonetheless, it has not been judged appropriate always to enforce the word that has been given, and there have been sound reasons for proceeding in this way. It would be bad policy, I admit, to allow no action at law for any sort of [486] promise or contract, as has been the practice in certain countries.[17] Given how most men are made, this would have the immediate effect of banishing confidence and commerce from the world. If you entirely remove constraint, there will be few people with whom one wishes, or is safely able, to enter into an agreement other than one that is executed immediately by both parties. But in order to prevent surprises and the remorse of an agreement too casually entered into, one may very well recognize promises and conventions as being valid only when they are made in a certain manner or bear on certain things. It is then for each person to take appropriate precautions; and if one runs the risk of sometimes being deceived, one now at least has a means of knowing those who are capable of deception, and those in whom one must no longer trust. This is the touchstone of a sincere probity. Thus, under Roman law, when it was not a question of contracts having a specific name and whose obligatory nature was fully authorized at law, if you say to someone: "I give you this so that you give me that," the agreement is sound and valid.[18] [See *Digest.,* Book II, title xiv, *De Pactis,* Leg. VII, §§.1, 2 et seq. Leg. XLV, & Book XIX, title iv, *De Permutat. rerum,* Leg. I, §.2.] But if one says: "I shall give you this so that you give me that," it is not sound and valid, whether [487] such a promise is written or spoken. However, if in the form of a question one said: "Will you give me this, and I shall give you

---

17. See Grotius, *Droit de la Guerre et de la Paix,* Book II, chap. xviii, §.10; and Pufendorf, *Droit de la Nature et des Gens,* Book V, chap. ii, §.3, note 1.

18. Such that whoever gave his word in this way had, with regard to such contracts, the freedom to withdraw his word, before the other party had fully executed his part, even when the latter had committed no fault, and was ready to perform the agreement; an evident inequality, contrary to the end of agreements and natural equity. See what I said on Grotius, *Droit de la Guerre et de la Paix,* Book II, chap. xii, §.1, note 8. It is also to be observed that a simple agreement (*pactum nudum*) remained null and without force, even when it had been sworn.

that?,," and if the other party, being present, had answered: "Yes," then there is a promise that has full force. In good faith, are we to think that formerly (for this futile subtlety no longer holds today, even in countries where the Roman law is followed), are we to think that formerly a good man found himself obliged or exempt from keeping his word, depending on whether he had adopted, in giving his word, this or that turn of phrase which, finally, carried the same sense as when one was in fact talking and acting seriously? Such was indeed the view of the sages: Seneca is quite clear on this.[19] And is it not apparent that they moved past the pure formalities of the *stipulations,* and that they renounced the right to exploit a formal error, from the moment when one party counted on the word of the other, and the latter showed that he could count on that word without need for further surety? It is simply that, then, they wished not to be subject to any sort of constraint, but rather to account for any breach of faith only before the invisible tribunal that each had in his heart. Therefore the Roman jurisconsults themselves recognize that, in such a case and [488] others similar, natural obligation retains its full force.[20] And, apart from various exceptions which, in those times, involved nullification of agreements on grounds of some formal error,[21] agreements of this sort achieved their effect indirectly, according to the Praetorian law, on all occasions when one had undertaken to demand nothing of that which was due, no matter what the

19. This philosopher places the breach of an agreement on the same level as the indiscretion of those who reveal the confidences that a friend has shared with them; and he gives these as examples of things which are dishonest, even though permitted under the laws: *Sed lex, inquit, non permittendo exigere, vetuit. Multa legem non habent, nec actionem, ad quae consuetudo vitae humanae, lege omni valentior, dat aditum. Nulla lex jubet amicorum secreta non eloqui, nulla lex fidem, etiam inimico, praestare. Quae lex ad id praestandum nos, quod alicui promisimus, adligat? Querat tamen cum eo, qui arcanum sermonem non continuerit, & fidem datam, nec servatam, indignabor. De Benefic.,* Book V, chap. xxi.

20. *Puta, quadam earum [usurarum] ex stipulatione, quadam ex pacto naturaliter debebantur, Digest,* Book XLVI, Title iii, *De Solution. & liberationibus,* Leg. V, §.2. *Is natura debet, quem jure Gentium dare oportet, cujus fidem sequenti sumus,* Book L, Title xvii, *Diversis Reg. Juris,* Leg. LXXIV, §.1.

21. See, on all these matters, the fine treatise of Mr Noodt, *De Pactis & Transactionib.,* chap. x, et seq.

reason; because at that time the promise tended to relieve an obligation, which could have given rise to a law suit. This is clear proof that the purpose of these laws, which declared other agreements null and void on the grounds of a formal error, was not to break the sacred bond of the given word, but simply to regulate things in a way that was believed to be best for public utility. The proof is also that the Emperors Diocletian and Maximian fixed the damages incurred when one was relieved in a contract at a level above half the fair price [*Cod.*, Book IV, title xliv, *De rescindend. vendit.*, Leg. II].

The privileges of minors, in relation to the nullity of agreements contracted without the approval of their guardians, are also undeniably very wisely delimited, and it would not have been appropriate for the judges to introduce exceptions. But does not good faith require exceptions? Do we not sometimes see young people who, though not yet at the age of majority fixed by the laws, are no less prudent and competent than many adult persons, and no less so than they themselves will ever be? May they not [489] engage with persons who do not believe them to be still dependent, in their dealings, on another's will, or who have no reason so to believe? But once they are known to be minors, if no fraud has been used toward them, nor any artifice, and even if they have acted entirely freely and in full knowledge, even if one has dealt with them solely for their pleasure, have they not manifestly renounced their benefit under the laws, by the very fact of seeking to enter a serious agreement while fully aware of their own legal status? Would it not be a signal act of deceit on their part to take advantage of the fact that they had been treated as competent to reason, and had been taken at their word? Have the laws, in order to prevent minors from being deceived, in fact helped them to be deceivers, and given them the means to profit at others' expense, by granting them full restitution or by providing no form of action against them at law?

The same may be said concerning the agreements contracted by women, without the authorization of husbands or some male relation. This sex, that in various ways we so underestimate in relation to ourselves, is sometimes more intelligent and circumspect in business than those from whom we wish women to take counsel. And the particular virtue, that we have as it were assigned to the sex as its share, requires that women take every care to flee from whatever has the scent of infidelity.

In all this, I do not make exception for certain agreements in which there can be, and often is, [490] something immoral and illicit, but where this is only incidental to the agreement. Thus in gaming, for instance, where the laws allow the misfortunate gambler to demand return of his losses.[22] Society sees it as a gross injustice, as it has always been seen, and rightly so, that a man who has played willingly and lost fairly should have recourse to the courts to recover his money or refuse to pay up, on the grounds that he cannot be compelled to do so.

The severity of the laws of the Ancient Greeks and Romans against insolvent debtors was perhaps necessary [see Saumaise, *de Modo Usurarum,* chap. xvii, xviii], but I am not sure that in recent times we have not relaxed matters too far. Yet it was up to the creditors alone to be less severe; and I will be told that they sometimes needed to make exceptions that the legislator had not judged it appropriate to make. There is certainly a clear difference between a debtor in bad faith and a negligent or imprudent debtor; between a man who has made himself incapable of paying by his bad conduct and a man who is reduced to this incapacity as the result of a misfortune that renders him deserving of sympathy. When one lends to another, especially with interest, one takes or should take account of the possibility that a thousand unfortunate accidents can happen that make it impossible for the debtor to repay the debt. All that can be required of him is that he does not expose himself to such accidents. Is it therefore just, [491] when it is in no way his fault, to clap him in irons, to make him one's slave, either in perpetuity or (which often comes to the same thing) until he has paid? If the laws permitted it, even in this case, it is not—as Seneca aptly put it—that the legislators had been insufficiently bright to see that one cannot treat as identical, without grave injustice, those who have squandered their

22. See my *Traité du Jeu,* Book III, chap. ix; and what I said in defense of my principles in the *Journal des Savans,* August 1712, Paris Edit. (October 1712, Amsterdam Edit.), and in December 1713, Paris Edit. (February and March, Holland Edit.).

fortune in debauchery or gaming, and those who, as the result of a fire, a theft or some other accident, have at the same time lost both their creditor's goods and their own.[23] Rather, to teach men to be true in their commerce, it was thought better that a small number of people should run the risk of being excluded from offering a legitimate excuse, than that everyone should be able to find some specious pretext to avoid guilt.

But let us turn to examples of another kind. The law of prescription provides one that we should not omit. This law, no matter how odious it appears, no matter that it has been taxed with blatant and perpetual injustice by overly rigid casuists, nonetheless has as its fundamental goal—if one takes the trouble to see it—that of securing property in goods, a goal that clearly requires both that a possessor in good faith should, as such, enjoy the full rights of the true owner, and also that he should himself ultimately become the owner.[24] [492] Nor do I wish to treat as unjust the Roman laws which at one moment authorized prescription without evidence of good faith, but at another time required good faith only at the outset of possession. [See a dissertation of Mr Thomasius, *De perpetuitate debit. Pecuniar.*, §.32 et seq.] In view of the difficulty that would very often lie in proving that a man knew the property he was acquiring or possessed belonged to someone else, the legislator is quite justified in judging it appropriate not to take this circumstance into account, so as to obviate some vastly tangled law suits. Yet, whether or not the civil laws presume good faith on the part of the possessor, good faith is nevertheless necessary according to natural law, which always requires it, from the outset of possession up to the time when possession becomes ownership. The legislators neither would nor

---

23. *Quid tu tam imprudentes judicas majores nostros fuisse, ut non intelligerent, iniquissimum esse, eodem loro haberi eum, qui pecuniam, quam a creditore acceperat, libidine aut alea absumsit, & eum qui incendio, aut latrocinio, aut aliquo casu tristiore, aliena cum suis perdidit? Nullam excusationem receperunt, ut homines scirent, fidem utique praestandam. Satius enim erat a paucis etiam justam excusationem non accipi, quam ab omnibus aliquam tentari. De Benefic.*, Book VII, chap. xvi.

24. See what I said concerning this matter, on Pufendorf, *Droit de la Nature et des Gens*, Book IV, chap. xii, §.8, note 3.

could accord a true right either to retain a property known to belong to someone else, or to appropriate that property to oneself, even if you believed it to be yours, until a considerable time had elapsed, so that the former owner himself, with good grace, could renounce all his claims. If the laws uphold a possessor in bad faith, after expiry of the term of the prescription, they can no more render him the true owner in the sight of the tribunal of reason and conscience than they can so render a man who knows full well that he failed to deliver the sum against which another gave him a promissory note, on which score the latter is nonetheless obliged to make repayment, once the time has lapsed beyond which one loses the legal capacity to prove that the original sum was never accounted for. [See *Instit.*, Book III, title xxii, *De litterarum obligat.*]

This last case is notable, and merits a separate article. But here is something that [493] is just as striking. Before the Emperor Zeno, who ruled in the East at the end of the fifth century, if in certain cases one had demanded more than was owing, that is, not only if the sum owing was less than what was now demanded, but even if one had sought repayment at another time or place, then no matter how small the difference, under Roman law one lost one's case, on that ground alone.[25] [See *Instit.*, Book IV, title vi, *De actionibus,* §§.33, 34.] If one had demanded less, and if later one had realized that much more was owing, though the judges doubtless saw this too, they would not adjudge the creditor entitled to anything more than he had first asked. It is undeniably right to stop a false debt from being boldly substituted for a true debt; and every person must take care not to claim repayment greater than he can legitimately require. Yet is it right, for instance, that a man who is recognized as being legitimately owed nine hundred and ninety nine *écus* should entirely lose them, because he asked for one thousand? Is there ground for presuming that he was willing to risk the entire sum, and so large a sum at that, just to gain one *écu*? Is it not easy to make a mistake, when the additional amount is so slight? How does the debtor dare to

25. In what were termed *Stricti. juris,* or rigorous law. See the treatise of Mr Noodt, *De Jurisdict. & Imperio,* Book I, chap. xiii.

appropriate another's property, by sheltering behind an accident that would not have befallen the creditor, if the debtor had given satisfaction with good grace, as he was [494] supposed to do? If, because of this accident, the courts did not condemn the debtor to pay, it was because their powers were constrained by the laws, which, in order to avoid certain improprieties, imposed on the judges a scrupulous precision, neither the force nor the aim of which were finally to extinguish the debt. Proof of this is that the creditor, having had his request rejected, did not easily obtain a full restitution from the higher tribunal; if, notwithstanding this, he could cite strong reasons to show that his mistake was one of ignorance and that he had committed no fault, he was relieved just as if he had been a minor.[26] But supposing that the surplus of the true debt had been considerable, and that there was ground for presuming bad faith on the part of the plaintiff, was it not compensated by an equal presumption that he could at least raise with no less justification? Was the debtor, who had allowed himself to be cited in the original action, without offering what he truly owed, himself acting in good faith, and had he good grace on which to pride himself, to the detriment of the creditor? The same can be said of an excess demand that advanced the due date or altered the due place.

For those who demanded less than was owed to them, there was no indication that they intended to acquit the debtor of the amount that they had not included in their demand for repayment. A donation cannot be presumed, and must not [495] be presumed, in the absence of clear indications. And when one is in the mood to dispense liberalities, it would not be towards a person who wished to extort from you even greater liberalities by his refusal to pay the balance of that debt, part of which you had been willing for him to discount. Nor, moreover, in the present instance could the plaintiff be suspected of some evil design that

---

26. *Si quis agens, in intentione sua plus complexus fuerit, quam ad eum pertineat: caussâ cadebat, id est, rem amittebat, nec facile in integrum a Praetore restituebatur, nisi minor erat viginti quinque annis. . . . Sane si tam magna caussa justi erroris interveniebat, ut etiam constantissimus quisque labi posset; etiam majori viginti quinque annis succurrebatur . . . Plus autem quatuor modis petitur; re, tempore, loco, caussa. Institut.,* Book IV, Title vi, §.33.

would make him deserving of the slightest punishment. If at the very outset he did not state his claims in their full extent, what harm can that be to the debtor? It was for the latter to signal himself the mistake; he would have done so, had he taken care to render to each his own. And on his part it is a huge diversion, and a further injustice, to compel the creditor to commence another law suit.

But this is not the sole example of injustices committed in favor of laws that regulate the process of judgments. At all times and in all countries, there has been much abuse of the advantages that can be derived from formalities generally. These formalities, I admit, have their use and, sometimes, their necessity. They are required in greater or lesser number, depending on the times, the places and the issues: as few as possible, that is always the best. But it is certain that, in many places, by dint of multiplying formalities, the accessory has been made the principal, giving rise to many more problems, some of them considerable, than those to which one sought a remedy. This is a vast field for creating diversionary tricks.[27] Here you have a good means of muddling [496] the clearest cases, and of causing the most just of causes to lose; of dragging out trials; of imposing on one another ruinous expenses, from which only the judge and the lawyers benefit, and which often mean that in winning one's case one is winner of nothing. But let us leave to those whose task it is the responsibility of preventing what was established for the sake of order from degenerating into the occasion for disorder. It is enough to have brought it to your consideration that individuals are profoundly deluded in imagining that the observance or the omission of formalities of the bar, whatever they may be, can ever create a valid right to retain that which one owes, or to appropriate to oneself that which otherwise would legitimately have belonged to another. It is not the legal formalities and the procedures, nor even the judge's sentence, which make a thing belong to someone or come into their possession; it already belongs to him or has already been acquired

---

27. Pliny the Younger says that practitioners, such as himself, learn many tricks at the bar, even though they do not approve of them: *Mos enim, qui in Foro verisque litibus terimur, multum malitia, quamvis nolimus, addiscimus.* Book II, Epist. iii.

by him. The judge neither seeks nor is able to do other than to recognize that person's right, and to put or keep him in possession of that which was refused him, or about which he was challenged.[28] He who is forced to plead in order to have or to hold his property, could not lose it through the sole lack of some incidental thing, established with a view to enabling each more easily to obtain his own, but which, by accident, now impedes instead of serving this end. [497] The effect that the laws have tied to the omission of formalities does not fundamentally make the cause of the one better, nor that of the other worse; and it is not even the intention of the legislator, nor of the judges, to have things regarded in this way. It is no more than a matter of certain preliminaries that were deemed important enough for a case not to proceed further if these preliminaries had not been duly met, and to impose a sanction on whoever had not complied, in some respect or other, by not commencing discussion of the main issue. But since, supposing it well founded, an existing right is simply being recognized, it is recognized in full. If there is any fault on his part, the first and most considerable fault—or rather the only fault that here justifies the parties' going to law—is wholly that of the other pleader. It was the latter's duty to warn of the problem, and not to seek to profit from it. Given its inflexibility, the law depended on him, regarding what the legal officers could not themselves do, restricted as they are by the generality of the rules. The law waited for him to come to their aid, as he was required to do. If he had sound reasons to allege, he was to renounce this privilege, which was a separate matter. In short, all the incidentals, all the factors external to the case, everything that does not bear on the essence of the cause, detract so little from the right of the man who has right on his side that he is [498] not truly deprived of right even by a final negative

---

28. Here one can apply what the jurisconsult Ulpian says regarding a right of servitude that he judges inappropriate: *Sive perperam [pronuntiatum est, non debet ei Servitus cedi] quia per sententiam non debet servitus constitui, sed, quae est, declarari. Dig.* Book VIII, title viii, *Si Servitus vindicetur,* Leg. VIII, §.4. The Roman jurisconsults also recognized that a genuine debtor, although absolved by the judge's verdict, still remained a debtor *naturaliter.* See Grotius, *Droit de la Guerre et de la Paix,* Book III, chap. ii, §.5, note 2.

verdict on the principal question.[29] It would be in vain should all the courts of the world condemn a man who is not wrong; their error, no matter what its source, could not alter the nature of things. Evil always remains evil; injustice, unjust. If the victorious pleader has in bad faith denied the debt, or even if, no matter how blinded he might have been by self-regard and self-interest, he was sufficiently aware to suspect and, however slightly, to recognize the injustice of his cause, he remains the debtor, and even more so than before. Doubly guilty, doubly responsible, both for the stubborn refusal to restore what belongs to another, and for all the damages and costs of the law suit. His debt only grows from one day to the next.

Sometimes, too, one loses one's initial case, solely because the actions on which it rests lack certain formalities, which have no relation to the right of the parties and which are established for quite another purpose than to order and assist the course of justice. A sovereign, for example, has need of revenue from taxation. To achieve this simply and imperceptibly, he has a certain imprint made on paper that, as a result, commands quite a high price. He then orders that all contracts should henceforth be written on such paper, failing which they will not be recognized at law. Let us suppose that a man, in making a loan, did not think of this, and makes do with a note written on ordinary paper. Do you believe that, as a result, he has anything less than the full rights of a creditor because in this way he lacks an adequate guarantee of [499] the debt? Will you dare, unfaithful debtor, to deny what you have written; will you violate your word, detain another's goods, under the pretext that the judges do not constrain you to pay, in order to sanction a neglect of which you are at least as guilty as the man to whose detriment

---

29. "It is true, they say, this sum is owed to him, and right is on his side; but I shall lie in wait for him with this little formality; if he forgets it, he will never recover, and in consequence he loses his money, or else is incontestably deprived of his right; so now he will forget this formality. That is what I call a practitioner's conscience. A fine maxim for the courtroom, useful to the public, imbued with reason, wisdom and equity, it will be precisely the contrary of the maxim that said that form overrides content." La Bruyère, *Caractères, ou Moeurs de ce Siècle*, ch. *De quelques usages*, pp. 216, 217, Vol. II, Edit. Amst., 1731.

you now seek to enrich yourself? The legislator rightly supposed that there would be low and knavish spirits who would have no scruple in turning this kind of punishment to their own advantage; and it is for fear of having to deal with such people that the legislator hoped to render others circumspect and meticulous in paying the tribute. But for all that, the legislator did not want the debt to be confiscated for your gain, and when it was a case of true confiscation, you would have no right to seek it for yourself.

Here we have some cases, of nearly every sort, in which a manifest injustice arises from enjoying the benefits conferred by a law that in itself is just. The paradox dissolves, and the duty of individuals is easily reconciled with the will of the legislator.

III

This is not yet all. Here is something that will make what I have just established seem less strange. *One must sometimes willingly renounce enjoyment of a benefit that is not only conferred by a just law, but also whose enjoyment is always just.*

If men are men, if they act as reasonable creatures, if they wish to conform to what their nature demands, if they are of a mind to show themselves worthy members of that universal society of which God is the author and protector, it is absolutely necessary that they be religious observers of justice, but not of justice alone. There are other virtues which, while free from [500] all constraint, nonetheless carry a clear and imperative obligation. Conversely, this obligation is all the stronger for being free of coercion, since the man who imposes it thereby relies more on one's willingness to fulfil the obligation. Yes, humanity, compassion, charity, beneficence, liberality, generosity, patience, gentleness, love of peace, these are not empty names, nor are they indifferent things; they are not even new commandments contained in the Gospel. Rather, they are sentiments which all reasonable persons in all times have counted among their duties; they are dispositions that one cannot but admire and praise in others, even in an enemy, though one may not feel them in one's own heart nor wish to make the effort to install them there.

Human laws, far from exempting us from such virtues, furnish a thousand occasions for their practice. Let us indicate some of these.

A merchant and man of virtue finds himself reduced by misfortune of circumstances to an incapacity to meet a payment whose term has fallen due. If the creditor forces him, there is no way he can avoid bankruptcy; so here we have a ruined man. If he is given time, there is reason to hope that he will put his affairs to rights. This creditor is rich; he can, without inconvenience to himself, manage without this sum which, compared to what he has at his disposal, is inconsiderable. Were he to lose it, will he be so hard-hearted as to ruin a man whom he can save?

Another wealthy man has had possession for the period required by the law of prescription [501] of a property that he acquired by legitimate title, without ever having the slightest suspicion that it belonged to someone other than the man from whom he obtained it in this way. So his right is established beyond any doubt. The former owner, who has since reappeared, has no claim; and, strictly speaking, nothing is owed to him. The same laws of justice that had given him a right in the property in question to the exclusion of all other claims have transferred this right to the present possessor in good faith by virtue of his length of possession. But notwithstanding this, this new master will not be at ease until he restores the right to the other man who lost it through no fault of his own, and who will benefit greatly from its restitution. If ever there was a time to be generous, this is it. And given that it is generosity towards one who is in dire straits, compassion and charity are now allied with generosity.

A legitimate heir is deprived of an inheritance by a will in which defects are found, by virtue of which he could have it annulled if he wished, something he could indeed do without giving anyone grounds for appeal. No matter how sure he is that this defective document nonetheless expresses the testator's true and unforced wish, it is not this wish that, of itself, should here be his rule of conduct. The formalities and other conditions without which a will is regarded as null and void were not established only to prevent frauds and trickery; another aim, perhaps the principal one, is to set limits to how one can dispose of one's estate after death, so that the expectations of those that the laws recognize for the succession are not easily thwarted. The testator could dispose of his estate to their detriment only by an [502] act that conforms to the law, the heirs having done nothing to indicate their renouncing the right to have the will declared invalid. In this way, when they ask for the will to be annulled, no injustice is involved, whether toward the living or toward the dead. But let us suppose that the inheritance is a trifle for the legitimate heir, and that in allowing it to pass to the person specified in the will, he enables the latter to live in comfort, he affords the man and his family a means of serving society far more fully than they could otherwise have done. Will he envy so many human creatures, like him made in the image of the supreme benefactor, refusing them an advantage that he can so easily procure for them, an advantage that he should procure for them by acting in a more direct way than providence might do? If the circumstances do not involve the specified heir, a legatee can find himself in this situation: the legacy will have been made to him on just grounds, say for important services that he rendered to the deceased. So, again, let the will then be annulled, but let the legacy stand, and let justice cede its rights in favor of humanity.

To this point I have supposed persons worthy of the good that is done them when one relinquishes one's legal right. But there are also cases in which one is called to make this sacrifice even in favor of unworthy subjects.

A person has caused you harm by their gross and inexcusable imprudence. Nothing is more just than to seek reparation, and the imprudence makes this entirely legitimate. But were you to pursue such reparation, or demand it to the full, the man who has to meet the cost would, in so doing, be reduced to the utmost wretchedness; whereas, in [503] acquitting him in whole, or in part, you would be inconvenienced only a little or not at all. Oh man, so often liable to need the understanding of your fellows, on this occasion show some understanding yourself; excuse the fault, forget it, if this is possible; but at least, since it is up to you alone, do not pursue its ruinous consequences for another man. Respect in the other man the fragility of your own nature, and do not fail to exercise gentleness and charity, since these acts will shine all the more and be the more deserving.

You have been maliciously slandered, you have been insulted. Will your first move be to seek satisfaction through the magistrate, satisfaction which often you may not need? If your reputation is sound, if you have nothing with which to reproach yourself, the offender's barbs will fall back on him alone. The best means of revenge, if revenge were permitted, is scorn. It will at least spare you anxiety and disturbance of mind on account of a harm that in fact is imaginary, when it entails no real damage.

I wish there was something more than mere words that the wind carries away in an instant. Let me suppose that someone has stolen from you, or withheld from you, or demanded from you, contrary to all right and reason, something which most legitimately and most incontestably belongs to you. Ah! best let it go, as far as you can without too much trouble, without some irritating inconvenience; give it up, sacrifice something, rather than calling someone before the courts, or letting yourself be called. It is as true for a law suit as it is for war: it is always an [504] evil; necessity alone can justify those who expose themselves to it. When I think of the ease with which so many people go to court, often for trifles, I do not know what it is about them that amazes me most, whether a lack of concern for their duty, or a lack of care for their true interests. What is one who pleads in court? Let us imagine him in the best possible light; let us leave aside the bad faith, the devious mentality, the oblique paths, the tricks, the duplicities deployed to influence or corrupt the judges. Let us, instead, suppose a man who believes his case to be well-founded, as indeed it is, who wishes to uphold or pursue his right but only by legitimate means. So what is a plaintiff considered from this point of view? He is a man who can scarcely be of peaceful mind: the rival party's bad procedure irritates him; the more he has right on his side, the more he conceives a bitterness toward the other party, toward all who take the other's side, toward all who have some link, some relation with him. This is a man who has abandoned his business, his most productive and most pleasant occupations, in order to suffer so much distress, so much fatigue, so many rebuffs, so much deviousness, so many disappointments, such great expenses; and all this without knowing how long the case will continue, or whether he will win his case, no matter how just it is, nor whether he will finally obtain damages which, when all is added up, never equal what it has cost him. And if he wins, then he now faces a deadly and constant source of hatreds, animosities and enmities that sometimes persist between families from generation to generation, and from which is born an infinity of evils. A Latin poet put it well: [505] "Is it possible that a person, who has first lost his case, could be so lacking in sense, so great an enemy to himself, as to want to spend twenty years in litigation?"[30] Let us say rather: is it possible that one would want to go to court when there is even the slightest chance of avoiding it, by compromising or by giving something up when one is not compelled to proceed by the state of one's affairs, or by some other pressing and necessary reason?

At this point I seem to hear someone protesting at the upshot of my entire discourse: "If this is so, we should close the law courts and demolish the tribunals of justice; no more judges, no more assessors, no more lawyers, no more *procureurs,* no more clerks, no more ushers, no more of those whose only occupation is to exploit the freedom people still believe is theirs to enjoy their legal benefits, and to exploit people's haste to have recourse to law." The objection appears strong: but the one thing I find annoying here is that this objection is not strongly enough embraced by those very people who silently agree, and so we cannot flatter ourselves that the prospect it envisages could in fact ever arise. Yes, please God that men may grow wise enough to render redundant all those professions, employments and institutions that are based only on men's follies! Please God that we may see the birth of a golden age in which, each one of us taking care to give offence to none, but on the contrary being eager to do good to whosoever needs it, we may be disposed to forgive the faults of others, to behave toward everyone in the same [506] manner that we would wish others to behave towards us, and to embrace and search out every possible means to avoid disputes, or to resolve them amicably in the shortest possible time! But be reassured, you who are alarmed by the very thought of so happy a

---

30. *Ah! miser & demens, viginti litigat annis / Quisquam, cui vinci, Gargiliane, licet?,* Martial, Book VII, *Epigr.* lxiv, I, 5.

revolution that you would regard as fatal for your own fortune. There will always be only too many quarrelsome and devious persons, who reduce the most pacific of men to the necessity of using, despite themselves, the instruments of justice. Egoism, interest, human passions are your good guarantee for your revenues. Only allow that the rare few who take their duty and their tranquillity to heart may avoid, insofar as they find it possible, having any dealings with you. May they be permitted to renounce their advantages.

Christianity prescribes this moderation in terms so strong that they have occasioned overstatement [Matth. V, 39, 40]. "Resist not evil, but whosoever shall smite thee on thy right cheek, turn to him the other also. And if any man will sue thee at the law, and take away thy coat, let him have thy cloak also." The least one can understand by this, and all that a sound and judicious criticism finds here, is this: that one must not [507] always take advantage of the law of an eye for an eye, a tooth for a tooth; and that, rather than proceeding to court to seek reparation for some trivial insult or to avoid losing some small possession, one must expose oneself to a further insult or to a new loss.

But here the pagans themselves, guided only by the light of reason, thought and acted in a manner that leaves many Christians covered in confusion. Among the pagans this was a common saying: "that right pursued too rigidly is a great impediment and a supreme injustice."[31] Cicero offers the following rule: "that, in many cases, one must give up one's right; abstain from litigation, to the extent that one can do so without inconvenience, and perhaps somewhat further still."[32] Pliny the Younger missed no occasion to desist from enjoying benefits the law granted to him. We see him at one time making the donations or other charges imposed on him by a codicil that the laws of those times

---

31. *Verum illud, Chreme, Dicunt, jus summum saepe est malititia,* Terent., *Heaut.,* Act IV, sc. v, verses 47, 48. *Ex quo illud, summum ius, summa iniuria, factum est jam tritum sermone proverbium.,* Cicero, *De Offic.,* Book I, chap. x. See on this the interpreters.

32. *Convenit autem . . . aequum & facilem [esse]; multa multis de jure suo cedentum; a litibus vero, quantum liceat, & nescio an paulo plus etiam, quam liceat, abhorrentem. De Offic.,* Book II, chap. xviii.

deemed null and void on the ground that it had not been confirmed in the subsequent will;[33] at another time, we see him granting freedom and a legacy to a slave, who had no claim to either, because of the defective manner in which the testator had expressed himself;[34] [508] at yet another time we see him relinquishing to his country [the city of Como], instituted as inheritor conjointly with himself, his portion of the inheritance, and a considerable portion, that he could have kept to himself as entirely within his right;[35] finally we see him allowing even his slaves to make a form of will, and then executing their dispositions with the utmost punctiliousness.[36]

Let us conclude (for it is time to finish, and we can do so), let us conclude with Aristotle that "it is not exactly the same thing, to be a good citizen and to be a good man."[37] The latter title has a far greater reach than the former. One may do nothing that is against the laws, one may act only in accordance with the laws and, notwithstanding this, still fall short in an infinity of things that true probity demands.

33. This is what Pliny says to a friend who warned him of the nullity of the codicil: *Tu quidem, pro cetera tua diligentia, admones me, Codicillos Aciliani, qui me ex parte instituit heredem, pro non scriptis habendos, quia non sint confirmati testamento. Quod jus ne mihi quidem ignotem est, quum sit iis etiam notum, qui nihil aliud sciunt: sed ego propriam quamdam legem mihi dixi, ut defunctorum voluntates, etiamsi jure deficerent, quali perfectas tuerer? . . . Nihil est, quod obstet illi meae legi, cui publicae leges non repugnant.* Book II, Epist. xvi, num. 1, 2, 4, Edit. Cellar.

34. *Scribis, mihi Sabinam, quae nos reliquis heredes, Modestum servum suum nusquam liberum esse jussisse; eidem tamen sic adscripsisse legatum: Modesto, quem liberum esse Jussi. Quaeris, quid sentiam. Contuli cum prudentibus. Convenit inter omnes, nec libertatem deberi, quia non sit data; nec legatum, quia servo suo dederit. Sed mihi manifestus error videtur. . . . Neque enim minus apud nos honestas, quam apud alios necessitas valet. Moretur ergo in libertate, sinentibus nobis, fruator legato quasi omnia diligentissime caverit. Cavit enim, quae heredes bene elegit.* Book IV, Epist. x.

35. *Nec heredem institui, nec praecipere posse Rempublicam, constat. Saturnius autem, qui nos reliquit heredes, quadrantem Reipublica nostra, deinde pro quadrante praeceptionem quadringentorum millium dedit. . . . Mihi autem defuncti voluntas (verior quam in partem Jurisconsulti, quod sum dicturus, accipiunt) antiquior jure est, utique in eo quod ad communem patriam voluit parvenire.* Book V, Epist. vii, num. 1, 2.

36. *Alterum [solatium] quum permitto servis quoque quasi testamenta facere, eaque, ut legitima, custodio, Mandant, rogantque, quod visum, pareo ocius: Suis dividunt, donant; relinquunt dumtaxat intra domum.* Book VIII, Epist. xvi, num. 2.

37. *Ethic. ad Nicomach.,* Book V, chap. v, p. 61. Vol. I, Ed. Paris.

But how to find some link here with the solemnity of the present occasion? How to draw from what we have said what is needed to address a small exhortation to these young people? I glimpse something that will not be too far off our topic.

My children, we prescribe rules for your studies, we teach you lessons, we set you tasks: you have to be assiduous in your exercises, to listen attentively to your masters, to try to retain what they teach you, to do exactly what they command. But that is not enough. If you have it in your heart to acquire all [509] the knowledge that is useful and necessary to you, you have also to work for yourselves, and make time for that in the leisure that you are allowed. Although, at your age, you have a great need to be pushed and guided almost constantly, you can nonetheless take some small steps on your own, should you wish to. And there are some among you, who must be ready to move ahead a little, beyond the master's gaze. No matter what care is given you, however well you employ the time needed to work in a manner that will please your masters, there will often be more than enough time left for you to relax. And it is very dangerous lest you then become attached to things that are bad and harmful in themselves, or that will turn you against work from which but little is gained, unless you love it. If you study only to complete the set tasks, if you do not early accustom yourself to taking your pleasure in your work, you will never reach the point of exercising with honor the employments at which you aim. As you grow older, sources of distraction will multiply, and temptations will be stronger and more numerous; yet it is then that you will have greater need, from one day to the next, to study under your own discipline, with commitment and eagerness. So we can do no more than [510] point the way. It will then be up to you to walk, to take care not to stop and not to wander. The best teachers in the world will then be able to do no more than introduce you to the sciences, give you some openings, and show the method to adopt. All this amounts to little, if one does not use it to go further by oneself, if one rests content with the basic elements, and with a mediocre routine which has cost you next to no effort but which you follow shamefacedly, to the great detriment of society, whose interests you could and should have furthered. If the rewards that we shall now distribute, according to custom, to those of you who have achieved some distinction, led to no improvement, they would not have been put to good use, and this would be nothing but an empty childish ceremony. May God grant that we have no reason to regret the time we commit to it! May you surpass our hopes, and indeed our wishes, if it is possible!

INDEX

Note: Page numbers followed by *n.* and a number indicate material in footnotes.

abilities, misapplication of, 80

Abimelech, ignorance of, 31

abortion, in Roman law, 315

absolutism: German, ix; Pufendorf's, xvii, 198 n. 38, 229 n. 65

actions, 27–28; allowable, 47–48; approbation of, 41; good and evil, 32–35, 48, 49–50; imputability of, 36–42; instigation to, 41; involuntary, 35–36; under law of morality, 48; object of, 48 n; regulation of, 42; repetition of, 34; voluntary, 35; will in, 27, 31–33

actions, external, 279, 282, 283, 284, 317; justice and, 302; under natural law, 280

actions, internal, 282, 283, 317; justice and, 302; in law, 284; of mind, 229; and moral theology, 280; and natural law, 284; in obligation, 284; of soul, 279

adultery, 23, 177, 339; in antiquity, 312

agency: in civil society, 195–96; as instituted office, 196 n. 36

agents, intention of, 48 n

aggressors: civil magistrates as, 88 n. 29; pardon of, 85; prevention of, 87; punishment of, 100; self-defense against, 82–83, 85–87; self-defense by, 90–91

agnation, 214

agreements: *versus* contracts, 145; simple, 342 n. 18. *See also* consent; contracts

allegiance, inalienable, 238. *See also* subjects; superiors

Allestree, Richard, xvi

alliances, 202; in civil society, 200–201; between civil sovereigns, 245–47; divided, 245; with inferiors, 246. *See also* leagues

alms, 153

ambassadors, duties of, 250

ambition, 327

anarchy, 206

anger, regulation of, 78

animals: dominion over, 37; natural liberty of, 99

Anonymous Writer. *See* Leibniz, Gottfried Wilhelm

antiquity: adultery in, 312; customs of, 315; laws against idleness in, 323

Apelles, 26

appetites, 54, 55; subjection to judgment, 74

Aquilius Gallus, Caius, 334–35

aristocracy, 197, 203; disadvantages of, 204; imperfections of, 205, 206; and monarchy, 207

Aristotle: conception of man, xii, 187 n. 20; conception of state,

Aristotle (*continued*)
   190 n. 28, 202 n. 40; on customs,
   283; on goodness, 358; laxity of,
   282; *Nichomachean Ethics,* 50 n;
   political maxims of, 311–12
arrogance, 54, 75
arts, cultivation of, 78
Asia: infanticide in, 315 n. 12; laws of,
   312
astrology, judicial, 71
atheism, 61, 69, 71, 297–98; and natural law, 297
auctions, 151
authority: civil, 221, 225–32; and human responsibility, 37; of legislators, 319–20; parental, 179, 182–83;
   versus persuasion, 317; political,
   44 n. 5, 45 n. 6; sovereign, 208; of
   superiors, 44 n. 5, 45, 300, 303

Barbeyrac, Jean: career of, xiv; on
   civil and theological domains,
   48 n; on compulsion, 39 n; on
   conscience, 29 n, 224 n; as critic of
   Leibniz, 265–66; on discourse,
   119 n. 40; engagement with Pufendorf, x, xv, xvii, 10 n. 13, 170 n. 8;
   erudition of, 266; on goodness,
   50 n; on human understanding,
   28 n; on legislative power, 17 n. 4;
   on natural law, xv, 20 n, 59 n, 276,
   280–81, 283, 287, 288, 291–92,
   300, 302, 304; on permission,
   164 n. 1; on positive law, 51 n,
   199 n; on property, 128 n; on punishment, 227 n; on Roman law,
   273; on self-defense, 88 n. 29; on
   sociability, 59 n; on sovereignty,
   198 n. 38, 199 n; on state of nature,
   167 n. 2, 172 n. 9, 170 n. 8; on subjection, 45 n. 6; on Tooke, 274 n.
   9; Tooke's use of, xvii; use of

Weber, 69 n. 19; view of civil government, 169 n. 7; view of civil obligation, 40 n; view of civil society,
   129 n. 43; view of common rights,
   101 n. 36; view of superiors, 44 n.
   4; on will, 35 n. Works: *Discourse
   on the Benefits Conferred by the
   Laws,* xiv, 265, 266; *Discourse on
   What Is Permitted by the Laws,* xiv,
   49 n, 265, 266; *Judgment of an
   Anonymous Writer,* xiv, 44 n. 4,
   64 n. 15, 265–66. See also *Les Devoirs de L'Homme et du Citoyen*
barter, 143–44, 145; in contracts, 149
Basil the Macedonian (emperor),
   320
Bayle, Pierre: *Thoughts about Comets,*
   62 n, 321 n. 16
benefactors, 104–5
beneficence, 107; duty of, 50 n
benefits, 106; renunciation of,
   352–53; thanks for, 107
benevolence, under equality, 102
bequests, 136
Berlin, Protestant refugees in, xiv
Bijnkershoek, Cornelis van, 333
blasphemy, 22
Bodin, Jean, 337 n. 7
body, care of, 80
Böhmer, Justus Christoph, 267–68,
   272 n. 8; *Academic Programs,*
   268 n. 3
boundaries, removal of, 137
bravery, ostentatious, 81
bribery, 326
brides, right of lords over, 338
brotherly love, 107
Buchanan, George, 338 n. 10
Budaeus. *See* Budé, Guillaume
Budé, Guillaume, 89 n, 272 n. 8
buying: conditions in, 150; *per aversionem,* 150–51

caciques, 25

Cadmus, myth of, 168 n. 5

Calvinists, xiii; view of conscience, 28 n

Carthage, laws of, 312

Catholic Church, and civil state, xii

cattle, damages to, 99

causes: subordination to one another, 60–61; unalterable consequences of, 71

chance, contracts involving, 154–55

charges (contracts), 146, 147–49

charity, duty of, 50 n

Charles V (Holy Roman emperor), 338

chastity, 175; defense of, 89; of wives, 176

children: duties of, 179–84; education of, 183; illegitimate, 213, 339; inheritance by, 134; parental power over, 180–82; punishment of, 181; rearing of, 174, 179–84; reason of, 181; responsibility of, 40; servitude of, 183; of slaves, 186–87. *See also* youth

choice, in human action, 28

church, and state, xi, xii, 216 n, 220 n. 58, 229 n. 65

Cicero, 282–83; on forbearance, 357; on good and evil, 314 n. 11; on natural law, 308 n. 4; on perjury, 321 n. 17; on universal jurisprudence, 316 n. 13; on unjust laws, 309 n. 6, 314 n. 11

citizens, 197; duties of, 224 n, 307. *See also* subjects

civil ethics: and natural law, 20 n; Pufendorf on, 50 n, 59 n

civil government: authority over subjects, 225–32; consent of subjects in, 210; constitution of, 192–98; defects in, 204; elections in, 211; ends of, 319; forms of, 197, 203–7; human agreements under, 129 n. 43; injuries in, 217; legitimacy of, 203 n. 42, 208–9; mandatory duty to, 225; military preparedness of, 220; obedience to, 209; officers of, 218; parts of, 198–202, 221; punishment by, 217, 226–27; qualifications of, 208–14; reputation under, 234; role of religion in, 68, 216 n; ruling body of, 197; *versus* sovereignty, 202 n. 59; special laws for, 221–25; *versus* state, 202 n. 59, 203 n. 41; submission to, 314; supreme authority in, 208; unaccountable, 208; unity in, 220. *See also* sovereignty; state

civil law, 16; actions under, 223; circumstance in, 318; citizens' conduct under, 308; coercive effect of, 318; forms of, 224; good faith in, 346; and law of God, 224; and laws of virtue, 319–22; legislative power in, 17; maxims of, 17; morality under, 320–21; and natural law, 17, 18, 48 n, 222, 272–73, 313; nature of, 316; omissions from, 341; origin of, 221; positive, 222 n. 61; privileges under, 334; prosecution of, 223; punishment under, 222; purpose of, 316, 318; submission to, 314; virtue under, 316, 318. *See also* law; Roman law

civil society: agency in, 195–96; agreement concerning, 193; alliances in, 200–201; allowable actions in, 48; collective will in, 194, 196, 197, 223 n. 62; common name for, 196; constitution of, 195; controversies in, 200; covenants under, 195; defense of property in, 90; divine law and, 199 n;

civil society (*continued*)
foundation of, 192, 197; idleness
in, 323–24; inclination toward,
187; influence in, 326; limits on,
129 n. 43; under natural law, 72;
natural liberty in, 199; obedience
to laws under, 48 n; obligation to
subjects, 219; officers of, 201; perpetual, 193; philosophy of, xi;
power in, 45; power of war in,
200–201; public doctrines of, 202;
public good of, 215; punishment
in, 199–200; role of moral theology in, 21; ruling body of, 197; security in, 187–95, 199, 215–16; self-
defense in, 84; separation of
theological domain from, 48 n;
single persons in, 176; sovereignty
in, 196; submission of will in, 199;
united forces of, 194; vices in,
325–26; will of God toward, 198.
See also communities; society; state
of man, civil
civil sovereigns, 223; allegiance to,
238; alliances between, 245–47; as
conquerors, 211; delegation by,
218; diminution of power, 246;
duty of, 214–20; duty of subjects
to, 224–25, 248; education of, 215;
enemies of, 240 n. 71; friends of,
215; legislation by, 309; legitimacy
of, xii, 314; maintenance of,
237–38; power of taxation, 201,
237; power of war, 200–201, 287;
power over property, 236–38; Protestant, xii; reputations among,
235-36; right of coinage, 144 n. 46;
right of extraordinary dominion,
237; right to make alliances,
200–201; right to prescribe laws,
236; use of natural law, 57 n. 12;
use of public revenues, 237–38;

virtues of, 215 n. 53; will of, 199.
See also sovereignty
civil state: Catholic Church and, xii;
controversies in, 173–74; duties to,
187; individual rights in, 193 n. 30;
in natural law, xii; natural rights
in, xvii–xviii; Pufendorf's conception of, 170 n. 8; religion in, xviii,
216 n; religious legitimacy of, xii.
See also state of man, civil
civil war, 240; religious, xiii, xviii
civis, Pufendorf's use of, 45 n. 7,
189 n. 22, 218 n. 55, 220 n. 57
civitas: Hobbes's use of, xvii, 16 n. 2;
Pufendorf's use of, ix, xvii, 87 n,
144 n. 46, 180 nn. 14–15, 182 n. 16,
187 n. 19, 190 n. 27, 200 n. 59,
203 n. 41, 214 n. 52; Tooke's translations of, 16 n. 2, 17 n. 2, 87 n. 28;
translations of, xvi–xvii, 16 n. 2.
See also state
classics, role in civil philosophy, xi
clergy, duties of, 249
coercion: to commit evil, 39–40; fear
of, 317
cognation, 214
coinage, 144–45
commerce, prices in, 140
commissions (contracts), 146
common law, English, 46 n. 7, 221 n
communis juris. See right, common
communities: under common law,
129 n. 43; constitution of, 187–92;
crimes by, 232; internal bonds of,
67; nature of, 214; necessity of,
192; parental rights in, 180; primitive, 187 n. 19; resolutions of, 123;
revenue of, 237–38; security under,
190–91. *See also* civil society; state
compassion, duty of, 50 n
compulsion: Barbeyrac on, 39 n; and
human responsibility, 39

conditions: in contracts, 158; impossible, 118–19; in oaths, 126; possible, 118

confederacies, 207; superior and inferior, 245–46

conjecture: from absurdity, 163; limited, 163; natural reason in, 163; in speech, 162–63

conquest, 211, 243

consanguinity. *See* kinship

conscience: Calvinist conception of, 28 n; doubting, 29–30; effectiveness of, 191–92; effect of religion on, 69; grounded on probability, 29; informed, 29; in obedience to sovereigns, 224 n; and political authority, xv; Pufendorf's conception of, 29 n; role in civil duties, 29 n; and social peace, xvii–xviii

consent: capacity for, 112; silence as, 111; during youth, 112–13

constitutions: of communities, 187–92; imperfections of, 205–6; irregular, 206–7; unsound, 204

contracts, 108–19; *versus* agreements, 145; altered cases in, 158; barter in, 149; broken, 114, 117; on chance, 154–55; chargeable, 146, 147–49; commissions in, 146; compensation in, 156; conditions in, 111, 158; conflicts in, 165; conjecture in, 160; consent to, 111; creditors in, 155–56; damages in, 148; debtors in, 155–56; deposits in, 147–48; dissolution of, 156–59; division of property in, 153–54; effect of oaths on, 126; equality in, 148–49; errors in, 113–14, 343–44; falseness in, 158; following death, 159; formalities in, 351; form of, 342; fulfillment of, 156–57; gratuitous, 146; guileful, 114–15; illicit agreements in, 117, 345; inequality in, 149; insurance in, 154–55; intermediate, 108; interpretation of, 159–65; invalid, 114; loans in, 146, 152–53; made through fear, 115–16; matrimonial, 175–78, 180; mediatory, 119; by minors, 344; mutual breaking off of, 158; mutual consent in, 116; necessity of, 109; nullification of, 343–44; obligations under, 111, 156–59; partnership in, 153–54; permutations in, 149; pledges in, 155–56; popular terms in, 160; prices in, 150; priority in, 118; *versus* promises, 110; promises in, 342–43; property in, 145–56; release from, 113–14, 158; reparations under, 149; role in sociability, 109; under Roman law, 342–43; suspicious, 115; tacit, 111; terms of art in, 160; time limits in, 158; trusts in, 147–48; unlawful, 117, 345; value in, 145–56; veracity in, 109–10; by women, 344–45. *See also* agreements; promises

controversies: in civil state, 173–74; settlement of, 239; in state of nature, 173–74

courtesy: duties under, 110; neglect of, 107; thanks for, 106

covenants. *See* contracts

covetousness, 23

creditors: assignment of debts by, 159; in contracts, 155–56; extensions to, 156; restitution for, 348; rights of, 333, 345–46, 351, 353

crimes, 96, 100; by communities, 232; effect on others, 232; greatness of, 230–31; mitigating circumstances in, 230–31; pardon of, 230; quality of, 227; and reputation, 234; by servants, 185

Crousaz, Jean-Pierre de: *Reflexions sur l'utilité des mathematiques,* 270 n. 6

customs: abolition of, 311 n. 9; of antiquity, 315; Aristotle on, 283; role in will, 34; support of iniquity, 318

damages, 311 n. 9; accounting of, 96; to cattle, 99; by chance, 98; in contracts, 148; done by many, 97; to expectations, 97; under natural equity, 99; by negligence, 98; pardon for, 99; to property, 147; reparation of, 96–97; revenge for, 99–100; unintentional, 99; by vassals, 99

Davies, Mr., 316 n. 13

debauchery, 328

debtors: assignment to creditors, 159; bad faith by, 351–52; in contracts, 155–56; extension of time to, 156; killing of, 333; payment by, 156; right of creditors over, 333; in Roman law, 345

debts: gambling, 345–46; lawsuits over, 348–51; repayment of, 347–52; under Roman law, 333, 347; Seneca on, 345

deceit: in discourse, 120, 121; in natural law, 119–20; in oaths, 126. *See also* lies

De jure naturae et gentium. See *Law of Nature and Nations* (Pufendorf)

democracy, 203; disadvantages of, 204; equality under, 206; imperfections of, 205

De officio hominis et civis. See *Les Devoirs de L'Homme et du Citoyen* (Barbeyrac); *The Whole Duty of Man* (Pufendorf)

deposits (contracts), 147–48

Descartes, René, xi, 290

desire: for pleasures, 76–77; of property, 76; regulation of, 75–77; and will, 42

destiny, 71

Les Devoirs de L'Homme et du Citoyen (Barbeyrac), 276, 298–99; in editions of 1716/35, 17 n. 4, 59 n, 265, 269; footnotes of, x, 10 n. 12. *See also* Barbeyrac, Jean; *The Whole Duty of Man* (Pufendorf)

dignity, natural, 102, 235

Dio Chrysostom, 311 n. 9

Diocletian (emperor), 344

discourse: circumstances in, 161; counterfeit, 121; deceit in, 120; duties in, 119–23; interpretation of, 159–65, 161; obligations concerning, 120–21; oral, 120; plainness in, 120–21, 122; verity in, 122; written, 120. *See also* speech

dissent, political, 223 n. 62

divine law: and civil law, 224; and civil society, 199 n; Leibniz on, 273; natural and positive, 52

divine providence: aid to man, 75; and natural law, xvii, 56–57

divine revelation: in moral theology, 19; *versus* natural reason, xii

divorce, 177, 322

dominion: over animals, 37; property exempt from, 141; sovereigns' right of, 237

Domitian (emperor), 324

donations, reciprocal, 149

droit du seigneur, 338

drunkenness, 80; consent during, 112; effect on will, 35

duels, 88; illegal, 315

duties: absolute, 95, 108, 119; as act of virtue, 298; adventitious, 108 n. 38; of ambassadors, 250; in care of the soul, 71–73; of children, 179–84;

Christian, 16; of citizens, 307; civil, x, 16, 29 n, 187; of clergy, 249; conditional, 95, 108, 119; conflicts in, 165; courteous, 110; definition of, 27; in discourse, 119–23; done through fear, 295, 296; to do no wrong, 95; of envoys, 250; to God, 291; under human institutions, 94, 96; ignorance of, 38; imperfect, 50 n; and interest, 299; Leibniz on, 277, 278; and love of self, 70 n; in making contracts, 108–19; of marriage, 174–79; of masters, 184–87; of military officers, 249, 250; moral, 316; under natural law, 59–60, 324, 341–42; in natural state of man, 166 n. 1; neglect of, 329; toward neighbors, 50 n, 104; opportunity for, 38–39; of parents, 179–84; perfect, 50 n; and pleasures, 77; of privy counselors, 248–49; of public readers, 249; Pufendorf's division of, 95 n. 32; reciprocal, 94–100; regarding property, 128–39; relating to pacts, 95 n. 32; of restitution, 116; resulting from self-knowledge, 73–75; of revenue collectors, 250; role of conscience in, 29 n; to self, 60; of servants, 184–87; social, 98; of subjects, 51 n, 247–50; of superiors, 51 n; to superiors, 286–87; in taking oaths, 123–27; transitory, 246; of war, 242; under will of God, 295; toward wronged persons, 41–42. See also obligations

Edict of Nantes, xiii–xiv
Egypt, laws of, 312
elections, 211
enemies: secularized conception of, 240 n. 71; in state of nature, 172

engagements. See agreements; contracts; promises
entitlement, explicit, 308
envoys, duties of, 250
envy, 54; regulation of, 78
Epicurism, 71
equality: benevolence and, 102; in contracts, 148–49; in government, 206; justice and, 102–3; natural, 100–104; Pufendorf's conception of, 101 n. 35; as remedy against contempt, 104; as remedy against pride, 103
equity: in emergent cases, 163–64; under law, 47–48; laws contrary to, 335; natural, 99, 169; right of prescription in, 135; under Roman law, 307
error: in constitutions, 206–7; in contracts, 113–14, 343–44; versus injustice, 51 n; vincible and invincible, 30
estates: disposal of, 353–54; inheritance of, 135–36
esteem, intensive, 75
Evenus III (king of Scotland), 338 n. 10
evil, coerced, 39–40. See also good and evil
exchange, 143–44, 145

factions, in government, 220
false witness. See perjury
fate, Stoic concept of, 71, 73 n. 22
fathers: authority of, 183; rights of, 180. See also husbands; patriarchy
Favorinus of Arles, 333 n. 2
fear: of coercion, 317; duty done through, 295, 296; of God, 59, 65, 67 n. 18, 296; in making contracts, 115–16; in making promises, 115; oaths taken under, 126; obedience through, 330; regulation of, 78

Felde, Jean de, 272
forbearance, Christian, 357
foreigners, assistance to, 336
forgiveness, 356
forum humanum. See judicature, civil
fraud, under Roman law, 335
friendship: mutual, 107; of sovereigns, 215; in state of nature, 172
fugitives, obligations to, 241
fungibles, 152, 156

games, contracts involving, 154
Gellius, Aulus, 333
generosity, 103, 107
gifts, 136; by presumptive owners, 139
glory, desire for, 75
gluttony, 80
God: acts of devotion toward, 72; attributes of, 63–64; as author of law of nature, 57; covenant with man, 19; as creator of the world, 61–62; deistic treatments of, 62 n; divine essence of, 289; duties toward, 59, 60–69, 169, 292; enforcement of natural law, 57 n. 12; existence of, 60–61; external worship of, 64, 65–66; fear of, 59, 65, 67 n. 18, 296; friendship with, 299; glorification of, 22; government of, 62; honor of, 65, 66, 73; infiniteness of, 63, 64; injunction of social life, 58; just nature of, 286; knowledge of, 275; love of, 70 n; oaths in name of, 65, 124; obedience to, 65–66, 302; as object of good actions, 49 n; as object of knowledge, 64 n. 15; obligations toward, 60; perfection of, 62–64, 286, 295, 297; as prime mover, 60–62; providence of, xvii, 56–57, 65; reverence for, 65; as source of

justice, 309; as sovereign, 299; submission to, 302; as superior of all, 288–89; supreme authority of, 295, 300; supreme power of, 289–90; as temporal legislator, 322; will of, 198, 290, 291, 294–95, 300, 302
gods, pagan, 281–82
gold, price of, 144
Golden Rule, 24
good and evil: Cicero on, 314 n. 11; in human action, 32–35
good deeds: coerced, 317–18; cost to benefactors, 106; gratitude for, 106; mutual, 104–7; recipients of, 106; thanks for, 107; willingness for, 105
goodwill, thanks for, 107
government. *See* civil government
governors, military, 240
governors, supreme. *See* civil sovereigns
gratitude, 106–7; duty of, 50 n
Grotius, Hugo, xii–xiii; *Law of War and Peace,* 9, 108 n, 272, 273, 342 n. 18; Leibniz on, 271; on obligation, 289; Pufendorf's knowledge of, xi; on sociability, 55 n. 10
guile, in making contracts, 114–15

habit, role in will, 34
hatred, regulation of, 78
hazard. *See* chance
hedonism, 327
heirs, 134; under defective wills, 353–54; of intestate estates, 133; to kingdoms, 212–14; naming of, 136
hiring, 151–52, 153
Hobbes, Thomas: on *civitas,* xvii, 16 n. 2; on equality, 101 n. 35; on justice, 287; Leibniz on, 271; on natural law, xiii; Pufendorf's

knowledge of, xi; on state of nature, 171 n. 9; on superiors, 287, 288

Holland, stolen property in, 337 n. 8

homicide, involuntary, 322

honor: capacity to receive, 235; desire for, 75; loss of, 90 n; right to, 103

hope, regulation of, 78

hospitality, duty of, 50 n

hostages, 244

Huguenots, xiii, xiv

human nature, pravity of, 46, 85, 96, 192

humility, 103

husbands: murder of wives, 339 n. 13; role in marriage, 176. *See also* fathers; patriarchy

idleness, 53, 105; in civil society, 323–24; justification of, 324; laws against, 323; regulation of, 219

idolatry, 22

ignorance: in commission of crime, 230; concomitant, 30–31; of duties, 38; efficacious, 30–31; and human responsibility, 38; voluntary and involuntary, 31

immigrants, 197

immortality, 19 n, 20, 274–75, 276, 277; belief in, 278

imprudence, 293

impunity: innocence and, 327; under law, 322, 326

incest, 178

inequality, in contracts, 149

infanticide, 315

inferiors, alliances with, 246

ingratitude, Seneca on, 321

inheritance: consanguinity in, 133–34; of estates, 135–36

injustice, 51; under laws, 309, 312, 314, 320, 332, 335–39; victims of, 318

innocence, and impunity, 327

Inquisition, Spanish, 313

institutions, duties under, 94, 96

insurance, in contracts, 154–55

intemperance, bodily, 80

intention: conjecture on, 163; emergent cases of, 163–64; in obligations, 159

interest, and duty, 299

interregnums, 211

intestates: heirs of, 133; succession by, 213

Jena, Pufendorf at, xi

Jesus Christ, on vengeance, 322

jewels, 142

joy, regulation of, 77

judges: corruption of, 218; Quintilian on, 313 n. 10

judgment, human: in natural law, 20

judicature, civil, 29

jurisprudence, universal, 285, 295, 316 n. 13

jus protimeseos, 150

justice: as attribute of actions, 49; as attribute of God, 289–90; commutative, 51; distributive, 50–51, 249; division of, 50–51; and equality, 102–3; and external acts, 302; Hobbes on, 287; human and divine, 285–86; and independence, 290; and internal acts, 302; moral rights under, 51 n; obligation to, 296; and observation of formalities in, 350; particular, 50; as positive law, 51 n; reasons for, 302; as relative virtue, 49, 50 n; under Roman law, 49 n. 8, 307; sale of, 141; universal, 50, 51 n, 282, 300; and will, 290

justice, divine, 284, 291, 294; and human justice, 285–86; imitation of, 295

Justinian, codes of, 49 n. 8, 313

Kathēkon, 27 n

killing: of debtors, 333; of thieves, 90 n

kindness: cheerfulness in, 106; and obligation, 107; societal, 106

kingdoms: hereditary, 213; right of holding, 210. *See also* monarchy; sovereignty

kinship: in inheritance, 133–34; marriage within, 178; in state of man, 169

knowledge: as attribute of God, 63; in human action, 28; and human responsibility, 38

labor, hiring of, 151–52, 153

Law of Nature and Nations (Pufendorf), xi–xii, xiv, 9, 286; Barbeyrac's translation of, xiv, 276; sovereign state in, xiii; Weber's borrowings from, 8 n. 5

laws: of antiquity, 312; of Asia, 312; beneficial, 47; benefits conferred by, 331–60; against bribery, 326; Carthaginian, 312; for civil government, 221–25; communities under, 129 n. 43; compliance with, 47; conflicts in, 165; contrary to equity, 335; definition of, 43; dispensation from, 47; Draconian, 312, 323; durability of, 311; Egyptian, 312; equity under, 47–48; exceptions to, 163–65; execution of, 217; foundations of, 304, 311; against idleness, 323; against immorality, 320; imperfect, 340–41; impunity under, 322, 326; injustice under, 335–39; internal actions in, 284; interpretation of, 161–62; Mosaic, 318, 322; of nations, 287–88; nautical, 94; number of, 216; obedience to, 319; origin in custom, 309;

perfect, 46–48; permission under, 164 n. 1, 308, 319, 322, 326; plainness of, 216; practicality of, 340; of prescription, 346; privileges granted by, 332; promulgation of, 46; of property, 346–48; reasons for, 161–62, 304; renunciation of benefits under, 341; requirements of, 307; Saxon, 337; science of, 285; of shipwreck, 336–37; silence of, 315, 332; source of, 304, 311; Spartan, 312; standardization of, 311; sumptuary, 219; Thomistic conception of, 43 n. 2; transcendent, xiii; true meaning of, 45–46; true reasons for, 304; unimplemented, 340; universality of, 163, 314. *See also* civil law; positive law; Roman law

laws, unjust, 309, 312, 314, 320; benefits under, 332; enjoyment of, 340

lawsuits, 340; cost of, 355–57; formalities of, 349–50; oaths in, 127; over debt, 348–51; tricks in, 349; trivial, 355

lawyers: Roman, 307–8, 333; tactics of, 349 n. 27; use of natural law, 273

leagues, 207, 220; in civil society, 200, 201; equal, 245, 246; personal, 246–47; real, 246–47; unequal, 245–46. *See also* alliances

leasing, 151

Le Fèvre, Tanneguy, 333 n. 2

legislators: advice of philosophers to, 309, 311; authority of, 319–20; positive laws under, 52; proscription of vice by, 319; reasons for, 45–46; support of virtue, 319; will of, 162, 164. *See also* civil sovereigns

Leibniz, Gottfried Wilhelm: attack

on Pufendorf, xiv, 44 n. 4, 64 n.
15; Barbeyrac on, 265–66; death
of, 268 n. 3; on divine justice, 285;
on divine law, 273; on divine punishment, 277–78; on duty, 277,
278; on moral theology, 279–80;
on natural law, 271; on obligation,
277; "Opinions on the Principles of
Pufendorf," 265 n. 1, 267–68; political rationalism of, xv; preface to
Codex Juris Gentium Diplomaticus,
275 n. 11; on Roman law, 271, 273
Leipzig, Pufendorf at, xi
Leon the Philosopher (emperor), 320
lex commissoria, 150, 156
liberality, duty of, 50 n
liberty: in war, 242; of will, 42. *See
also* natural liberty
lies, innocent, 122–23. *See also* deceit
life rent, 210
litigation. *See* lawsuits
loans (contracts), 146, 152–53; conditions for, 146–47
logic, 79
lotteries, 154
Louis XIV (king of France), xiii
love, regulation of, 77–78
Lucian, 331 n. 1
lust, human, 54, 80

magistrates, civil: aggression by, 88 n.
29. *See also* civil sovereigns
maidrents, 338 n. 11
Malcolm III (king of Scotland),
338 n. 11
malice, under natural law, 190–92
man: accountability of, 36–42; adventitious state of, 94, 95 n. 32,
166, 174; Aristotelian conception
of, xii, 187 n. 20; autonomy of, 81;
benefits of religion to, 67; capacity
for harm, 55; Christian duties of,

16; civic duties of, 16; disruption
of society, 189–91; duty toward
God, 59, 60–69; duty toward self,
69–94; fall of, 23, 24, 26; God's
covenant with, 19; good conduct
of, 314–15; ingratitude of, 107–8;
just and unjust, 49; mutual duties
of, 104–7; mutual esteem among,
100; natural equality of, 100–104;
natural inclinations of, 33–34; under natural law, 21–22; natural
state of, 166–74; obligation to self,
69–70; as political animal, 187 n.
20, 188, 189; proclivity for mischief, 54–56, 57; reciprocal duties
among, 289; security against one
another, 190–91; self-estimation of,
100; self-love of, 69–70; single life
of, 175; sociability of, 16; understanding of natural law, 57 n. 13;
universal law of, 314. *See also* state
of man
Marguerite (consort of Malcolm III),
338 n. 11
market value, 143
marriage: ceremony of, 178; contracts
in, 175–76, 177, 178, 180; duties of,
174–79; between kindred, 178;
moral impediments to, 177; in
natural law, 183; obligation to, 175,
177; parental authority in, 182–83;
paternal authority in, 179; procreation in, 174, 176; propensity for,
174; role of husbands in, 176; role
of wives in, 176, 179
Martial, 356
masters, duties of, 184–87
Maximian (emperor), 344
meaning: in contracts, 159–65; interpretation of, 161
Megabyzus, 26
metals, precious, 144

metaphysics, Pufendorf's view of, 64 n. 15

military officers, duties of, 250

mind: cultivation of, 79–80; effeminacy of, 80; internal acts of, 229

ministers of state, 218; agreements by, 247

minors, contracts by, 344. *See also* youth

mischief: apprehension caused by, 88; human proclivity for, 54–56, 57

misfortune, *versus* injustice, 51

mistrust, in contracts, 115

Molan, Gerard. *See* Muelen, Gerhard Walter van den

monarchy, 197, 203; absolute, 209; acquisition of, 210–14; advantages of, 204; aristocrats under, 207; by conquest, 211; imperfections of, 204–5; interregnums in, 211; limited, 208 n, 209; succession in, 212–14. *See also* civil government; kingdoms; sovereignty

money, value of, 144. *See also* coinage

monogamy, 177

Montmorency, Anne de, 337 n. 7

morality: bonds of, 43; under civil law, 320–21. *See also* religious morality

moral theology, 15, 17; divine revelation in, 19; formation of the mind by, 20–21; internal actions and, 280; Leibniz on, 279–80; and natural law, 18; purpose of, 19; role in civil society, 21

mortgages, 156

mothers, rights of, 180

Muelen, Gerhard Walter van den, 267 n. 2, 268 n. 3, 269 n. 5

nations: conquest of, 243; free, 197; laws of, 287–88; secular legitimacy of, xiii; Tooke's treatment of,

218 nn. 55–56, 220 n. 57. *See also* civil government; civil society; communities

natural law, 15, 52–60, 309; age of consent under, 112–13; Aquinas on, xii; and atheism, 297; Barbeyrac on, xv, 20 n, 59 n, 276, 280–81, 283, 287, 288, 291–92, 300, 302, 304; cause of, 286, 305; ceremonies under, 178; Cicero on, 308 n. 4; and civil ethics, 20 n; and civil law, 17, 18, 48 n, 222, 272–73, 313; civil society under, 72; civil state in, xii; consequences of, 56; deceit in, 119–20; definition of, 56; divine authorship of, 57; divine enforcement of, 57 n. 12; and divine providence, xvii, 56–57; duties under, 59–60, 324, 341–42; effectiveness of, 191–92; equality under, 101, 102; external actions under, 280; before the fall, 24; foundation of, 291; Hobbes on, xiii; human judgment in, 20; and internal action, 284; knowledge of, 58; knowledge of God in, 275; as law of God, 66; and law of nations, 288; lawyers' use of, 273; Leibniz's view of, 271; limits to, 16; love of neighbor under, 24, 25; malice under, 190–92; man under, 21–22; marriage in, 183; maxims of, 17; and moral law, xii; and moral theology, 18; necessity of, 52; oaths under, 173, 283; obscurity in, 223; obviousness of, 52; peace treaties under, 245; and positive law, 52, 199 n, 222 n. 61, 227 n, 273; procreation under, 174–75; Protestant, 265; Pufendorf on, xi–xii, xiii, 191 n. 29, 222 n. 61, 270; punishment under, 227 n; purpose of, 19,

274, 304; Quintilian on, 334; rank among sciences, 26; and religion, 59–60; reputation in, 233; revenge under, 100; right reason in, 17, 18, 286; self-defense under, 84; self-preservation under, 53, 57, 81–82; of sociability, 171 n. 9, 222 n. 61; society under, 25, 59–60; and the soul, 279; sovereigns' use of, 57 n. 12; speech in, 121; in state of nature, 171 n. 9; teaching of, 283; Tooke on, 7; and will of God, 198, 300. *See also* state of man, natural

natural liberty, 169–70; abandonment of, 190; of animals, 99; in civil society, 199; constraints on, 302; contrariety in, 193; loss of, 188; punishment under, 227; reputation under, 235; self-defense under, 83; self-preservation under, 170; uncertainty under, 172; violence in, 241

natural reason: conjecture by, 163; *versus* divine revelation, xii

natural religion, 59 n, 60–69, 285; benefits to mankind, 67; benefits to society, 67–69; benefits to subjects, 68; effect on conscience, 69; practical, 60; role in government, 68; salvation and, 66–69; theoretical, 60. *See also* religion

natural rights: in civil state, xvii–xviii; Lockean, xv. *See also* rights

nature: dignity of man under, 102; as original cause, 61. *See also* state of man, natural

nature of things: foundation of obligation in, 294; natural law in, 291–92; propriety in, 293

necessities, value of, 140, 141

negligence, 328; reparations for, 98; in social duties, 98

neighbors: benevolence toward, 102; duties to, 50 n, 104; love of, 24, 25; property of, 137; self-defense against, 85; services to, 132–33; in state of nature, 172

Neuer Bucher-Saal (journal), 268 n. 4

Noodt, Gerard: *De forma emendandi doli mali,* 334 n. 4; *De pactis & transactionibus,* 343 n. 21; *Julius Paulus,* 308, 315

oaths: binding, 125; conditions in, 126; consequences of, 123; deceit in, 126; divided, 127; duties of, 123–27; effect on contracts, 126; false, 321; foolhardy, 322; form of, 124, 127; interpretation of, 126–27; in lawsuits, 127; made under fear, 126; mental reservations in, 125; in name of God, 65, 124; in natural law, 173, 283; obligations under, 125–26; promissory, 127; purpose of, 124; sense of, 127; validity of, 125

obedience: to civil government, 209; through fear, 330; to God, 65–66; to laws, 48 n, 319; motivation for, 319; to sovereigns, 224 n; toward superiors, 300

obligations, 43–45; Barbeyrac on, 40 n, 276, 278; in care of the soul, 70–73; civil, 40 n; coerced, 302; common, 94; conflicts in, 165; to defend friends, 242; definition of, 43; in discourse, 120–21; foundation in nature of things, 294; free will in, 159; to fugitives, 241; to God, 60; Grotius on, 289; human capacity for, 43–44; imposed by virtue, 352–53; intention under, 159; internal action in, 284; to justice, 296; kindness and, 107;

obligations (*continued*)
  under law, 276; Leibniz on, 277; to
  marry, 175, 177; moral, 43; natural,
  291; under oaths, 125–26; perfect,
  96, 110; power of, 47; property
  and, 299; reason and, 293–94, 298;
  for restitution, 96; separation of
  power from, 44 n. 4; to superiors,
  43–45; among thieves, 289, 292;
  uncoerced, 352; understanding
  and, 43; of virtue, 296; will and,
  43; to will of God, 302. *See also*
  contracts; duties; promises
occupations, shameful, 324–25
offices, friendly, 27 n
officium, 27 n, 299. *See also* duties
opportunity, in human responsibility,
  38–39
ostentation, 54
Otto, Mr., 280 n; *Thesaurus juris,*
  333 n. 2
overtures, by ministers of state,
  247
Ovid, myth of Cadmus, 168 n. 5
owners, presumptive, 138–39. *See also*
  property

pacts, *versus* contracts, 145
paganism, 313; forbearance under, 357
Pagenstecher, Alexandre Arnold,
  268 n. 4
parents: consent to marriage, 182–83;
  duties of, 179–84; rights of, 180
parliament, in limited monarchy,
  209
parlimentarianism, English, ix
parricides, 25
partnership, in contracts, 153–54
Pascal, Blaise, 276
passions, 54, 292–93, 324; effect of
  will on, 34–35; exorbitant, 80; subject to reason, 77–78

patriarchy, 168–69, 170, 171; foundations of, 179–80; limits to power
  of, 182; in marriage, 179
patrimonies, 237–38
patriots, 188, 189
payment: of debts, 156, 347–52; of
  loans, 152–53; in *specie,* 152, 156
peace, 299; and conscience, xvii;
  government's maintenance of,
  220; perfect, 244; treaties of, 244,
  254
Peace of Westphalia, xi, 240 n. 71
peasants, murder of, 313
penalties. *See* punishment
perjury, 23, 124; under Roman law,
  321
permission: ambiguity in, 327; under
  law, 164 n. 1, 308, 319, 322, 326;
  tacit, 308; for vices, 327–28
persecution, religious, xiii
persuasion, 317
Phaedrus, 18–19
philosophers: advice to legislators,
  309, 311; ancient, 281–82; on injustice, 341
piety, 72, 295, 297; filial, 183
Plato, 277 n. 16
Platonism, 281; Leibniz's, xv
Plautus, 39 n
pleasures, innocent and criminal,
  76–77
Pliny the Younger, 341 n. 16, 349 n.
  27; and benefits of law, 357–58
polytheism, 22
positive law, 51 n, 91, 178 n. 12, 199 n;
  and natural law, 52, 222 n. 61,
  227 n, 273. *See also* laws
possession: good faith in, 346–47;
  profits from, 138–39. *See also*
  property
poverty, 23
power: in civil society, 45; coercive,

317; of consent, 112; and human responsibility, 37, 39; legislative, 17; and obligation, 44 n. 4, 47; paternal, 179–81; of superiors, 44–45, 301

Prasch, Johann Ludwig, 276 n. 12

precepts, affirmative and negative, 164–65

preemption, right of, 150

premier seisin, 131–32

prescription: laws of, 346; right of, 135

prices: common, 140; in contracts, 150; determination of, 141–42, 143; eminent, 140, 143–44; legal, 142–43; mistaken, 149; vulgar, 143

pride, 54; vice of, 103

princes. *See* civil sovereigns; monarchy

Prince's Schools, xi

private associations, 220, 232 n. 68

privy counselors, duties of, 248–49

procreation, 174–75; in marriage, 174, 176

promises: concerning third parties, 118; conditional, 118–19; in contracts, 342–43; *versus* contracts, 110; effect of oaths on, 126; fear in, 115; impossible, 116–17, 118; mistaken, 113; obligations under, 111; observation of, 109–10; perfect, 111; in Roman law, 334–35; Seneca on, 343; unlawful, 117. *See also* agreements; contracts

property: accessional advantages in, 132; common, 129–30, 131; in contracts, 145–56; damage to, 147; defense of, 90; demand for, 141 n; derivative acquisition of, 130, 133, 135; desire for, 76; destruction of, 93–94; division of, 129, 153–54; duties regarding, 128–39; exchange of, 143–44, 145; forcible possession of, 136–37, 243; gifts, 136; hiring of, 151–52; improvement of, 130, 132; inherited, 133–34; introduction into society, 128–29; laws of, 346–48; lending of, 152–53; letting of, 151–52; lost, 139, 353; of neighbors, 137; and obligation, 299; original acquisition of, 130, 131–32; power of governors over, 236–38; price of, 140–44; private, 129; Pufendorf's conception of, 128 n; purchase of, 150–51; restitution of, 137–38; in Roman law, 135, 346; sale of, 150–51; scarcity of, 142, 143, 144; services from, 132–33; slaves, 186; standards for, 140; stolen, 337–38, 355; taken in war, 243; value of, 140–41

Protestants: in Berlin, xiv; Calvinists, xiii, 28 n; Huguenots, xiii, xiv; sovereigns, xii

public good: laws for, 216; as supreme law, 215; taxation for, 218–19. *See also* security, in civil society

public readers, duties of, 249

Pufendorf, Samuel: absolutism of, xvii, 198 n. 38, 229 n. 65; on Aristotelian man, 187 n. 20; biography of, x n. 4; career of, xi–xii, 7; on care of the self, 69 n. 19; civil ethics of, 50 n, 59 n; on civil law, 222 n. 61; as disciple of Hobbes, xiii n. 10; dissemination of works of, 265; division of duties, 95 n. 32; early life of, x–xi; education of, xi; on fear of God, 67 n. 18; on natural law, xi–xii, xiii, 191 n. 29, 222 n. 61, 270; on natural rights, 129 n; polemical defenses by, 10; political vocabulary of, ix, 9, 45 n. 7;

Pufendorf, Samuel (*continued*)
reception of, xv; secularization of
political philosophy, 190 n. 28; on
sovereigns, 154 n. 52, 209 n. 48; on
sovereignty, 129 n, 195 n. 33, 196 n.
37, 198 n. 38, 202 n. 40, 203 n. 42,
208 n, 229 n. 65; *Specimen controversarium*, 285; on state of man,
166 n. 1, 167 n. 2; on state of nature, 167 n. 2; statism of, 46 n. 7,
129 n. 43, 214 n. 52; use of *civis*,
45 n. 7, 189 n. 22, 218 n. 55, 220 n.
57; use of *civitas*, ix, xvii, 87 n,
144 n. 46, 180 nn. 14–15, 182 n. 16,
187 n. 19, 190 n. 27, 200 n. 59,
203 n. 41, 214 n. 52; use of *respublica*, 203 n. 41; use of Roman law,
49 n. 8; view of civil obligation,
40 n; view of civil state, 170 n. 8,
194 n. 32; view of conscience, 29 n,
67 n. 18; view of duty, 27 n, 286;
view of equality, 101 n. 35; view of
human society, 67 n. 18; view of
law, 43 n. 2, 46 n. 7; view of metaphysics, 64 n. 15; view of natural
religion, 59 n; view of positive
laws, 178 n. 12; view of property,
128 n; view of punishment, 226 n.
63, 227 n, 229 n. 65; view of sociability, 55 n. 10, 98 n. 34; view of
superiors, 44 n. 4; view of understanding, 28 n. See also *Law of
Nature and Nations; The Whole
Duty of Man*
punishment, 46–47; advantages of,
191–92; of aggressors, 100; benefit
of, 227; capital, 226, 228; of children, 181; under civil government,
217, 226–27; under civil law, 222;
in civil society, 199–200; of debtors, 333; divine, 19–20, 21, 68,
277–78, 279; exemption from,
229–30; fear of, 307; for good of
offended party, 228; for good of
offender, 228; human, 20; kinds
of, 231; for mental disorders,
229–30; for minute lapses, 229;
under natural law, 227 n; under
natural liberty, 227; and person of
the offender, 231; Pufendorf's conception of, 226 n. 63, 227 n, 229 n.
65; purpose of, 228; as retribution,
227 n; under Roman law, 312–13;
of servants, 185–86; of sins, 229; of
slaves, 313; of sorcery, 320

Quintilian, 333; on judges, 313 n. 10;
on natural law, 334
Quintilian (grandfather of the rhe-
tor), 339 n. 13

rainment, necessity of, 54
rapine, 137
rationalism: Leibniz's, xv; Lutheran,
71 n. 21
reason: in childhood, 181; eternal,
304, 305; in giving consent, 112;
grounded in self, 293; impairment
of, 40–41; and knowledge of natural law, 58; in natural law, 17, 18,
274, 286; and obligation, 293–94,
298; in state of nature, 170; subjection of passions to, 77–78. *See
also* right reason
refugees, protection of, 241
Reinoldi, Bernardi Henrici, 321 n. 15
religion: and natural law, 59–60; and
public good, 216. *See also* natural
religion
religious morality: and civil duties, x;
in civil state, xviii, 226 n. 63; human actions under, 48
remembrancers, value of, 142
reparations, 96–97; for accidents, 98,

99; for broken contracts, 114; under contracts, 149; for damage of cattle, 99; liability for, 97–98; necessity for, 97; for negligence, 98
repayment, of loans, 152–53
reputation, 232–36; accumulative, 233, 235–36; care of, 75; under civil government, 234; and condition of life, 234; definition of, 232; diminished, 233; lost, 233, 234; under natural liberty, 235; among princes, 235–36; preservation of, 233; simple, 233–34; slurs on, 104
resolution, mental, 80
respect, right to, 103
responsibility, 36–42; of children, 40; compulsion and, 39–40; ignorance and, 38; impaired reason and, 40–41; limitations of, 37–38; opportunity in, 38–39; power in, 37, 39; role of authority in, 37; during sleep, 41
respublica, Pufendorf's use of, 203 n. 41
restitution: duty of, 116; partial, 138; by presumptive owners, 138–39; of property, 137–39
retribution: divine, 276, 295; punishment as, 227 n
revelation. *See* divine revelation
revenge, 53; for damages, 99–100; desire for, 78; Jesus Christ on, 322; under natural law, 100
reverence, 44
rewards, external, 278 n. 17
right reason: duties under, 74–75; maxims of, 291, 292, 294, 295, 298; in natural law, 17, 18, 274, 286. *See also* reason
rights: to be honored, 235; in civil state, xvii–xviii, 193 n. 30; common, 101, 102; to equality, 101,

102; imperfect, 50 n, 110, 121; natural, xv, xvii–xviii; parental, 180; perfect, 50 n, 121, 236; of preemption, 150; relinquished, 352–54
Riley, Patrick, 265
rivalry, in state of nature, 172
Roman law, 46 n. 7, 49 n. 8; abortion in, 315; Barbeyrac on, 273; contracts under, 342–43; debt in, 333, 345, 347; equity in, 307; fraud under, 335; justice under, 307; Leibniz on, 271, 273; perjury under, 321; Praetorian, 343; promises in, 334–35; of property, 135, 346; punishment under, 312–13; stipulations in, 334, 343. *See also* laws

safety. *See* security
salvation: and natural religion, 66–69; and public security, 216 n
Sarah (wife of Abimelech), 31
Saxons, laws of, 337
sciences: curious, 79; distinctions among, 19–21, 284; education in, 359; harmony among, 17–18, 21; natural, 305; principles of, 19; purpose of, 19; rank of natural law among, 26; useful, 79; vain, 79–80. *See also* civil law; moral theology; natural law
security: in civil society, 187–95, 199, 215–16; collective, 192–95; against malice, 191; as object of government, 226 n. 63
self-defense, 82–83; by aggressors, 90–91; allowable, 84–86; without civil authority, 83 n. 24; in civil society, 84; justifiable, 83–84; against maiming, 89; through maiming, 91; management of, 88; in mistaken cases, 88; moderation in, 83;

self-defense (*continued*)
under natural law, 84, 86; against
neighbors, 85
self-knowledge: duties resulting
from, 73–75; strength in, 74
self-preservation, 55; in cases of necessity, 91–93; in cases of want, 93;
damage to others through, 92; destruction of property for, 93–94;
under natural law, 53, 57, 81–82;
under natural liberty, 170; sacrifice
of others in, 92
self-sacrifice, 81; for common
good, 92
selling, 150–51
Seneca, 293–94; on debt, 345; on ingratitude, 321; on promises, 343;
on virtue, 329
senses, as attribute of God, 63
sermo. See discourse
servants: duties of, 184–87; punishment of, 185–86; wages of, 185
services: personal, 132–33; real, 132
servitude: temporary *versus* perpetual, 185; voluntary, 185
shipwreck, laws of, 336–37
silence, 120; as consent, 111; of laws,
315, 332
Silverthorne, Michael, 119 n. 40,
166 n. 1
simony, 141
sins: indulgence of, 72; punishment
of, 229
slander, 355
slaves: alienable, 186; captive, 185,
186; offspring of, 186–87; punishment of, 313; wills made by, 358
sleep, human responsibility during, 41
sociability, 16, 284; Aristotelian conception of, 55 n. 10; Barbeyrac on,
59 n; and care of the soul, 71; discourse in, 119; equality in, 101;

laws derived from, xiii; natural law
of, 171 n. 9, 222 n. 61; Pufendorf's
conception of, 55 n. 10, 98 n. 34;
role of contracts in, 109; subordination of natural religion to,
59 n
social peace, and conscience, xvii
society: abandonment of natural liberty for, 190; benefits of religion
to, 67–69; constraint of desires in,
95; good of mind in, 82; introduction of property into, 128–29; love
of, 70 n; man's disruption of,
189–91; multiconfessional, xi, xv;
mutual benefits in, 105; under natural law, 25, 56, 59–60; necessity
of, 53; primitive, 188; state of man
in, 167–68. *See also* civil society
soldiers, duties of, 250
solitude, 53
Solon, 25
sorcery, punishment of, 320
sorrow, regulation of, 77
soul: care of, 70–73; immortality of,
19 n, 20 n, 274–75, 277; internal
actions of, 279; world, 62
sovereignty: absolute *versus* limited,
208 n; Barbeyrac on, 198 n. 38,
199 n; in civil society, 196; diminution of, 246; *versus* government,
202 n. 59; legitimacy of, 203 n. 42;
limits of, 196 n. 37; Pufendorf on,
129 n, 195 n. 33, 196 n. 37, 198 n. 38,
202 n. 40, 203 n. 42, 208 n, 229 n.
65; Tooke on, 198 n. 38. *See also*
civil sovereignty
Sparta: laws of, 312; vice in, 328
Spavan, John, 274 n. 10
speech: conjecture in, 162–63; favorable construction of, 162; figurative, 121–22; indifferent construction of, 162; interpretation of, 160;

invidious construction of, 162; in natural law, 121; uniform significa-tion of, 120; various significations in, 162. *See also* discourse

state: Aristotelian conception of, 190 n. 28, 202 n. 40; and church, xi, xii, 216 n, 220 n. 58, 229 n. 65; constitution of, 192–98; deconfes-sionalized, xi, xv; desacralized, 226 n. 63; *versus* government, 202 n. 59, 203 n. 41; Hobbes on, 16 n. 2; limits of, 196 n. 37; mixed, 202 n. 40; as "moral person," 196 n. 36; religiously unified, xv; reprisals by, 241–42; secrets of, 123; sound and unsound, 204; suprem-acy of, 194 n. 32. *See also* civil gov-ernment; civil society; communi-ties; nations

state of man: adventitious, 94, 95 n. 32, 166, 174; kindred in, 169; pa-ternal authority in, 168–69; servile, 184–85; in society, 167–68

state of man, civil, 187; controversies in, 173–74; *versus* natural state of, 167, 168. *See also* communities; civil society

state of man, natural: *versus* civil state of, 167, 168; controversies in, 173–74; duties to God under, 169; enemies in, 172; equality in, 227 n; friendship in, 172; Hobbes on, 171 n. 9; inconveniences of, 170; obligations in, 168; Pufendorf on, 167 n. 2; reason in, 170; relation to God, 167; rivalry in, 172; self-defense in, 84, 86; uncertainty of, 171–72; violence in, 173

state of nature. *See* state of man, nat-ural

statism, Pufendorf's, 46 n. 7, 129 n. 43, 214 n. 52

status. See state

stipulations, in Roman law, 334, 343

Stoicism, 281, 299; concept of fate, 71, 73 n. 22; Pufendorf's view of, 62 n

Suárez, Francisco, xii

subjection, political: consent to, 45 n. 6; reasons for, 45

subjects: benefits of religion to, 68; civil authority over, 225–32; civil laws governing, 221; conquered, 243, 250; consent of, 210; contro-versies between, 200, 201; duties of, 51 n, 247–50; duties to civil government, 225; duties to one another, 248; duties to sovereign, 224–25, 248; good, 188, 189; honor among, 236; loss of natural liberty, 188; military service by, 225; obli-gation of sovereigns to, 219; pun-ishment of, 189; specific duties of, 247; vulnerability of, 45 n. 6; wel-fare of, 215. *See also* citizens; supe-riors

succession: disputed, 214; in inheri-tance, 133–34, 339; in monarchies, 212–14; through parent, 214; pop-ular will in, 212–13; restrictions on, 213

summum imperium: Pufendorf's use of, ix, xvii, 214 n. 52; translations of, xvi–xvii. *See also* sovereignty

supererogation, 72

superiors: authority of, 44 n. 5, 45, 300, 303; duties of, 51 n; duty to, 286–87; effective command by, 303; as example for youth, 330; fear of, 301; free will of, 290; Hobbes on, 287, 288; intention of, 159; obedience toward, 300; obli-gation to, 43–45; power of, 44–45, 301; right to command, 303;

superiors (*continued*)
    submission to, 301; will of, 286.
    See also civil sovereigns; subjects

Taprobane, laws of, 312
taxation: fairness of, 218–19; sover-
    eigns' power of, 201, 237
temperament, role in will, 33–34
temptation, to crime, 230
Ten Commandments, 22–23
Tertullian, 333
theft, 23, 137–38
Theodosian Code, 313
theologia moralis. See moral theology
thieves: killing of, 90 n; obligations
    among, 289, 292
Thirty Years' War, x, 240 n. 71
Thomas Aquinas, Saint, on natural
    law, xii
Thomasius, Christian, 337 n. 9
time, in determination of price, 143
toleration, religious, xv, 229 n. 65
Tooke, Andrew, ix–x, 274 n. 9; on
    civil law, 221 n; on civil state,
    194 n. 32; on legal ceremonies,
    178 n. 12; lexical choices of, xvi–
    xvii, 9; marginal notes of, 33 n; on
    natural law, 7; on patriotism,
    188 n. 22, 189 n. 25; and Pufen-
    dorf's political vocabulary, 16 n. 2;
    on salvation, 66 n. 16; on sover-
    eignty, 198 n. 38; on state of man,
    166 n. 1; treatment of common-
    wealth, 247 n. 76; treatment of
    community, 180 n. 15, 187 n. 19,
    232 n. 68; treatment of govern-
    ment, 203 n. 41; treatment of ig-
    norance, 30 n. 1; treatment of na-
    tions, 218 nn. 55–56, 220 n. 57;
    treatment of sovereigns, 154 n. 52;
    use of Barbeyrac, xvii; and Whig-
    gism, xvi, xvii, 214, 218–19 n. 56

travelers, kindness to, 106
treasure trove, 131–32
treaties, 239; peace, 244, 245; of
    truce, 244
truces, 243–44; tacit, 244
trusts (contracts), 147–48
truth, moral, 122. *See also* veracity
Twelve Tables, law of, 333
tyranny, 206, 227 n

Ulpian: on debtors, 350 n. 28; on eq-
    uity, 335
understanding: as attribute of God,
    63; in giving consent, 112; in hu-
    man action, 27, 28–30; and obli-
    gation, 43; Pufendorf's conception
    of, 28 n
unions, 207
usufructuaries, 210
usury, 153, 320

vainglory, 75
value: common, 140–41; in contracts,
    145–56; market, 143; of money,
    144; of necessities, 140, 141; senti-
    mental, 142
vanity, 327
vassals, damages by, 99
veracity: in contracts, 109–10; in dis-
    course, 122; logical, 122; in prom-
    ises, 110, 111
vices, 80; and civil law, 316; in civil
    society, 325–26; covert, 325; men-
    tal, 229–30; permission for,
    327–28; pride, 103; Spartan, 328
vinculum juris, 43 n. 3
violence, 189; under natural liberty,
    241; in state of nature, 173
virtue: and civil law, 316, 318; of civil
    sovereigns, 215 n. 53; commitment
    to, 279; duty as act of, 298; inde-
    pendent of religion, 297; inviol-

able rights of, 326; laws of, 319–22; legislators' support of, 319; love of, 307; obligations imposed by, 296, 352–53; Seneca on, 329

wagers, in contracts, 154–55

wages, 151; of servants, 185

want, human, 54, 55; extreme, 93; limitations to, 76

war, 54, 238–44; civil, xiii, xviii, 240; in civil society, 200–201; deceit in, 239; in defense of others, 241, 242; defensive, 239; liberty in, 242; necessity of, 238; offensive, 239; power of, 200–201, 240; preparedness of, 220; property loss in, 136; for protection of refugees, 241; reasons for, 239; solemn, 240; spoils of, 243; truces in, 243–44; unjust, 225, 239

wealth, desire for, 76

Weber, Immanuel, 8 n. 3, 9 n. 8; Barbeyrac's use of, 69 n. 19; on common rights, 101 n. 36; use of *Law of Nature and Nations,* 8 n. 5

Weigel, Erhard, xi

West Indies, laws of, 25

Whigs: London audience of, xvi; politics of, 218–19 n. 56; sensibilities of, 9 n. 6; and sovereignty, xvii

The Whole Duty of Man (Pufendorf): arrangement of, 270; Barbeyrac's appendices to, xiv, 265; Barbeyrac's revisions to, 10 n. 13; conclusions of, 271; first edition of, 7; purpose of, 15; reception of, x, xv; references to *Law of Nature and Nations,* 9; sovereign state in, xiii; translations of, ix–x, 8, 274; Van Velsen's edition of, xiv, 265. See also *Les Devoirs de L'Homme et du Citoyen* (Barbeyrac)

—editions of 1716/35, 8 nn. 3–4, 265; additions by editors of, 69 n. 19; footnotes in, 9 n. 12; modifications to Tooke, xv, xvi; self-defense in, 88 n. 29; separation of civil and theological in, 48 n; state of man in, 167 n. 2; treatment of ignorance, 30 n

will: as attribute of God, 63; in civil society, 199; collective, 194, 196, 197, 223 n. 62; effect of intoxication on, 35; effect of passions on, 34–35; end and means in, 32; factors affecting, 32–35; of God, 290, 291, 294–95, 300, 302; in human action, 27, 31–33; justice and, 290; of legislators, 162, 164; liberty of, 42; and obligation, 43; political, 223 n. 62; restrictions on, 42, 44; role in natural inclination, 33–34; role of custom in, 34; spontaneous, 32; subjection to judgment, 74; of superiors, 286; unforced, 31–32

wills: inheritance under, 135–36; invalid, 353–54; of slaves, 358. *See also* intestates

wives: illegitimate children of, 339; murder of, 339 n. 13; role in marriage, 176, 179

women: contracts by, 344–45; defense of, 89; exclusion from succession, 214

world soul, 62

youth: conduct of, 329–30, 359–60; consent during, 112–13; contracts by, 344; example of superiors for, 330. *See also* children

Zeno (emperor), 347

This book is set in Adobe Garamond, a modern adaptation by Robert Slimbach of the typeface originally cut around 1540 by the French typographer and printer Claude Garamond. The Garamond face, with its small lowercase height and restrained contrast between thick and thin strokes, is a classic "old-style" face and has long been one of the most influential and widely used typefaces.

Printed on paper that is acid free and meets the requirements of the American National Standard for Permanence of Paper for Printed Library Materials, z39.48-1992. ♾

Book design by Louise OFarrell,
Gainesville, Florida
Typography by Impressions Book and Journal Services, Inc.,
Madison, Wisconsin
Printed and bound by Sheridan Books, Inc.,
Chelsea, Michigan